THE WORKERS' PARTY AND DEMOCRATIZATION IN BRAZIL

D0816226

THE WORKERS' PARTY AND

DEMOCRATIZATION IN BRAZIL

MARGARET E. KECK

YALE UNIVERSITY PRESS

NEW HAVEN AND LONDON

Copyright © 1992 by Yale University.
All rights reserved.
This book may not be reproduced, in whole
or in part, including illustrations, in any form
(beyond that copying permitted by Sections
107 and 108 of the U.S. Copyright Law and
except by reviewers for the public press),
without written permission from
the publishers.

Portions of this book appeared previously in
the following publications:
Politics and Society 15:1 (1986–87):67–95,
used with the permission of the publisher;
*Democratizing Brazil: Problems of Transition
and Consolidation,* ed. Alfred Stepan, Copyright
© 1989 by Oxford University Press, Inc.,
reprinted by permission.

Designed by Sonia L. Scanlon.
Set in Bembo type by
the Composing Room of Michigan, Inc.
Printed in the United States of America by
BookCrafters, Inc., Chelsea, Michigan.

Library of Congress Cataloging-in-Publication Data

Keck, Margaret E.
    The Workers' Party and democratization in
    Brazil / Margaret E. Keck.
        p.   cm.
    Includes bibliographical references and index.
    ISBN 0-300-05074-7 (alk. paper)
        1. Partido dos Trabalhadores (Brazil)—
    History.   2. Brazil—Politics and
    government—1964–1985.   I. Title.
    JL2498.T7K43   1992
    324.281'07—dc20   91-28446
                                                        CIP

The paper in this book meets the guidelines
for permanence and durability of the
Committee on Production Guidelines for
Book Longevity of the Council on Library
Resources.

10 9 8 7 6 5 4 3 2 1

For Larry

CONTENTS

TABLES

PREFACE

Ten years ago, when I began this study of the Workers' party in Brazil, I frequently had to respond to puzzled queries from Brazilian and foreign social scientists about why I thought this party worth studying. Certainly there were good reasons for believing, in the early 1980s, that the Partido dos Trabalhadores (PT) would be a short-lived phenomenon; its difference from other Brazilian parties, its lack of fit with the predominant characteristics of the Brazilian transition to democracy, and the serious difficulties it confronted in its first years of existence seemed likely to overwhelm the best efforts of its leaders and supporters. Like the PT itself, this study was grounded in a bet—a bet that even in the context of powerful forces of continuity, a space existed in the Brazilian political landscape for innovation. In spite of compelling evidence to the contrary, the party continued to promote a different vision of politics "as if it were possible." In 1991, two years after the PT's candidate came close to winning the presidency of the Republic in the first direct presidential elections in almost three decades, a study of the party no longer needs justification. Nonetheless, many of the issues that its creation helped to place on the agenda—both for the party itself and for the democratization process in Brazil—remain unresolved.

The core of this study focuses on the formative years of the party from the late 1970s through the first years of the 1980s. The most extensive field research took place in 1982 and 1983; since then, I have made almost yearly trips to Brazil and have continued to follow the party's evolution. Although I include some developments of the late 1980s, my focus is on the challenges presented to the party in its formative period, particularly in the Greater São Paulo area, and with special attention to the party's interaction with the labor movement. This focus has both advantages and disadvantages. While it provides a good standpoint from which to assess some of the general dynamics of the PT's early development, it is by no means the only standpoint, and there are many more stories of the origins of the PT than I was able to tell here. Much more work is needed on the party's relationship with the Catholic church and the social movements with links to the church; more also needs to be written on the relationship of the party to the variety of leftist organizations that chose to work within the PT. We especially lack studies of the party's growth outside of São Paulo, particularly during the second half of the 1980s when the party's appeal became increasingly national in scope. Its influence in rural constituencies, in rural unions and in the landless movement, grew enormously in those years and was not treated in my research. The PT's appeal to middle sectors, noted in Rodrigues's recent study, is something I can only discuss hypothetically; this too cries out for further work. As the party prepares to reassess its first decade of development in its November 1991 Congress, it is to be hoped that a new generation of analysts will begin to respond to these questions.

This book would not have been possible without the support of teachers, colleagues, and friends in the United States and Brazil, and of PT leaders and members who helped me in Brazil. At Columbia University, Douglas Chalmers and Alfred Stepan provided support and criticism for the dissertation on which this study is based, as did the ongoing study group of graduate students in Latin American Politics there. Columbia University's Institute for Latin American and Iberian Studies financed a portion of the fieldwork. At the Helen Kellogg Institute for International Studies at the University of Notre Dame, where I spent 1985–86 as a fellow, Guillermo O'Donnell and Scott Mainwaring were particularly encouraging; Mainwaring commented exhaustively on several drafts of this manuscript. I am grateful to all my colleagues at Centro de Estudos de Cultura Contemporânea in Brazil, and especially to Francisco Weffort, whose support and critical perspective have been invaluable from the beginning. Luís Inácio Lula da Silva, Francisco Weffort, and Eduardo Suplicy opened doors for me in the PT. Weffort, Maria Helena Moreira Alves, and Francisco Salles gave me access to valuable documentation in their personal collections. Cristina Saliba helped me work through mountains of press clippings in 1982 and in recent years has provided me with a home away from home in São Paulo. I also benefited from summer research and travel grants from the Yale Center for International and Area Studies and from the invaluable logistical and moral support of Ann Carter Drier, administrative assistant of Yale's International Relations Program. John Covell at Yale University Press has been an encouraging and patient editor, and Elizabeth Casey did a fine job of editing the manuscript. For their comments or other contributions to this work I would also like to thank Regis de Castro Andrade, Lucia Avelar, Maria Vitória Benevides, Peter Brooks, David Cameron, Marc Chernick, Emilia Viotti da Costa, Roque Aparecido da Silva, Evelina Dagnino, William Foltz,

Daniel Friedheim, Miriam Golden, Luiz Eduardo González, Frances Hagopian, Daniel James, Marc Kesselman, Herbert Klein, Carol Martin, Rachel Meneguello, José Alvaro Moisés, Edson Nunes, Leigh Payne, Paulo Sergio Pinheiro, Maria Tereza Sadek, Kathryn Sikkink, Maria de Carmo Campello de Souza, Kurt von Mettenheim, Carol Wise, and an anonymous reader from Yale University Press. Finally, I will always remember the discussions I have had over the years about the PT and democracy in Latin America with Charlie Gillespie, who died a few weeks before this manuscript was completed. His life enriched his friends as well as the study of Latin American politics. Although all these people helped to make this study possible, any errors or faults of interpretation are of course my own.

This book is dedicated to my husband, Larry Wright, who has been a part of this project from first to last and has managed not only to survive it but to remain interested.

ABBREVIATIONS

ABC: The ABC (or ABCD) region refers to the industrial suburbs of São Paulo where the bulk of large automobile and metalworking plants are located. It includes Santo André, São Bernardo do Campo, and São Caetano, and usually Diadema as well. Broad definitions include the municipalities of Mauá, Ribeirão Pires, and Rio Grande da Serra.

APML: Ação Popular Marxista Leninista, Marxist Leninist Popular Action.

ARENA: Aliança de Renovação Nacional, Alliance for National Renewal. Pro-regime party during military rule, established after Institutional Act no. 2 (1965) abolished preexisting political parties.

CEB: Communidade Eclesial de Base, Ecclesial Base Community.

CEBRAP: Centro Brasileiro de Análise e Planejamento, Brazilian Center for Analysis and Planning.

CEDEC: Centro de Estudos de Cultura Contemporânea, Center for the Study of Contemporary Culture.

CGT: Confederação Geral dos Trabalhadores, General Workers' Confederation, formed in 1986. This acronym was also used by the Comando Geral dos Trabalhadores, General Workers' Command, from 1961–64; the Central Geral dos Trabalhadores, General Workers' Central, resulted from a split in the CGT (confederação) in the late 1980s.

CLT: Consolidação das Leis do Trabalho, Consolidated Labor Laws. Dating from 1943 under Getúlio Vargas, the labor code has been modified over the years but remains the cornerstone of Brazilian corporatism.

CONCLAT: The acronym CONCLAT has been used on three different occasions, which can lead to a certain amount of confusion. The National Conference of the Working Class (Conferência Nacional da Classe Trabalhadora, CONCLAT) was held in August 1981 in Praia Grande, São Paulo. The National Congress of the Working Class (Congresso Nacional da Classe Trabalhadora, CONCLAT) was held in São Bernardo in August 1983 and founded the United Central Workers' Organization (Central Unica dos Trabalhadores, CUT). The third CONCLAT, or National Coordination of the Working Class (Coordenação Nacional da Classe Trabalhadora) was founded by a meeting in Praia Grande, SP, in November 1983, by unions which supported a different kind of trade union strategy from that of the CUT.

CONTAG: Confederação Nacional dos Trabalhadores na Agricultura, National Confederation of Agricultural Workers.

CUT: Central Unica dos Trabalhadores, a central union organization created in 1983 by the *autêntico* current of the labor movement. Its president has been Jair Meneguelli, former president of the Metalworkers' Union of São Bernardo do Campo and Diadema, since the beginning.

DIEESE: Departamento Intersindical de Estatística e Estudos Sócio-Econômicos, Interunion Department of Statistical and Socio-Economic Studies. Formed in 1955, DIEESE is a unitary research organization with support from a broad range of unions. It is primarily known for its data on cost of living and purchasing power of the minimum wage; it also keeps extensive data on strikes and engages in a range of union educational activities.

DOI-CODI: Destacamento de Operações e Informações–Centro de Operações de Defesa Interna, Department of Operations and Intelligence–Operational Center for Internal Defense, the army secret police headquarters in São Paulo during much of the military regime.

FGTS: Fundo de Garantia do Tempo de Serviço, Time in Service Guarantee Fund, instituted in 1966, removed job security guarantees for workers with more than ten years' employment in the same firm and changed the method of financing compensation paid to workers dismissed "without just cause," making dismissal less costly for employers. Workers receive monies from the fund when dismissed without just cause; they may also draw upon it in specified other instances—when buying a house, for example, or in case of serious illness.

FO: Fração Operária, Workers' Faction.

IDESP: Instituto de Estudos Sociais e Políticos, Institute for Social and Political Studies (São Paulo).

Libelu: Liberdade e Luta, Liberty and Struggle.

MDB: Movimento Democrático Brasileiro, Brazilian Democratic Movement. Legal opposition party under the military regime, formed after all existing parties were abolished under Institutional Act no. 2 in 1965.

MEP: Movimento pela Emancipação do Proletariado, Movement for the Emancipation of the Proletariat.

MR-8: Movimento Revolucionário 8 de Outubro, 8th of October Revolutionary Movement.

PCB: Partido Comunista Brasileiro, Brazilian Communist party.

PCBR: Partido Comunista Brasileiro Revolucionário, Revolutionary Brazilian Communist party.

PC do B: Partido Comunista do Brasil, Communist party of Brazil.

PDS: Partido Democrático Social, Democratic Social party. Successor party to ARENA.

PDT: Partido Democrático Trabalhista, Democratic Labor party.

PFL: Partido da Frente Liberal, Liberal Front party.

PMDB: Partido do Movimento Democrático Brasileiro, Party of the Brazilian Democratic Movement. Successor party to the MDB, it was the predominant party in the early stages of the democratic transition.

PP: Partido Popular, Popular party.

PRC: Partido Revolucionário Comunista, Revolutionary Communist party.

PSB: Partido Socialista Brasileiro, Brazilian Socialist party.

PSD: Partido Social Democrático, Social Democratic party (1945–65).

PSDB: Partido Social Democrático Brasileiro, Brazilian Social Democratic party.

PTB: Partido Trabalhista Brasileira, Brazilian Labor party. The party has had two incarnations. The first, and most important, was as a party formed in 1945 on the basis of the Varguista labor unions and social security bureaucracy; a center-left party, the PTB was one of the three most important parties in the 1945–64 party system. The PTB formed in 1980 is a center-right party that has little to do with its predecessor.

PV: Partido Verde, Green party.

UDN: União Democrática Nacional, National Democratic Union (1945–65).

THE WORKERS' PARTY AND DEMOCRATIZATION IN BRAZIL

INTRODUCTION

Brazil's transition to democracy began in 1973 with military president Ernestro Geisel's decision to initiate a gradual liberalization of the regime and ended in 1989 with the first direct presidential elections in three decades. The length of the transition was notable, as were the military's attempt to maintain control throughout much of the process and the unwillingness of key democratic political forces to precipitate a decisive rupture with the authoritarian regime. For scholars attempting to understand transition from authoritarian rule, the Brazilian experience initially represented a model to be emulated, providing as it did an opportunity for contending forces to negotiate a series of bargains or pacts that could guarantee the continuity of democratization.[1] Later assessments were less optimistic, as the pact-making process proved so elastic and permeable as to undermine its credibility. By 1988, scholars like Guillermo O'Donnell had come to doubt the conventional wisdom that Brazil's relative economic prosperity and less repressive authoritarian experience would produce an easier transition. "Because the authoritarian regime in Brazil had greater relative success, both economic and political, than those in other Latin countries, actors left over from that period have retained significant power and influence in the current Brazilian government," O'Donnell argued. "As a result of their continued presence, Brazil is particularly vulnerable to the 'slow death' style of regression."[2]

Studies of the Brazilian transition have produced a somewhat schizophrenic view of the past several decades of the country's history. Scholars examining political institutions and the state have rightly emphasized the essential continuity of patterns of policy making and political interaction, the persistence of clientelist and patrimonial relations, the prevalence of informal elite deals over institutional bargains, and the maintenance of military prerogatives.[3] At the same time, many Brazilian and foreign scholars have discussed at length changes in Brazilian civil society—the emergence of a wide range of social movements raising socioeconomic demands and questioning elitist notions of politics; a reading of this kind of work can lead to the impression that change, rather than continuity, has been the dominant characteristic of the Brazilian transition. Real historical actors also differed in their assessments of the political opportunities available during the transition—indeed, the very definition of what was possible became an arena of political struggle. For many political elites, the emergence of new forms of collective action in the 1970s illustrated the need for an end to military rule and represented a wave of support for democratic transition. Yet, these movements comprised new actors whose demand for a place on the political stage went well beyond the demand for an end to military rule. There has been very little work on the interaction between these two processes: one a highly conservative process in which traditional forms of elite dominance have been maintained and even reinforced, and one in which new forms of political and social organization have arisen to challenge the status quo.

Part of the difficulty in putting together the two visions of contemporary Brazil reflects a lack of interaction during the transition between the state and elite-led political parties on the one hand and new forms of societal organization on the other. The two visions reflect, in a very real sense, two Brazils: one where personal interactions among elites are the stuff of politics and another where increasingly representative membership organizations demand more institutionalized relationships. Their lack of interaction was graphically illustrated when the Sarney government attempted to negotiate a social pact with unions by granting a privileged position in talks to labor leaders most likely to support government proposals rather than to those who represented the most powerful new labor organizations. The government's failure to recognize that pact making requires dealing with the most representative institutions rather than with the most docile ones doomed the talks from the beginning.[4] This example, however, leads us to a second reason for disjunction between the two accounts of the transition.

Understandably, most scholarship on democratization has emphasized process and dynamics rather than structures and institutions. The emphasis on process grew out of an attempt to understand and map the diversity of paths to democratization, and this focus places justifiable stress on the essential uncertainty of regime transition. Nonetheless, even within early theorizing about regime transition in Latin America, the idea that negotiating pacts could play an important role implicitly raised questions about the nature of the parties to such pacts. During the course of a transition to democracy, one might expect that negotiations among a restricted group of elites might gradually give way to negotiations among representative institutions.

A focus on institution building highlights important aspects of the democratic transition in Brazil that a process model misses. In particular, it directs our attention to the mediation—or lack thereof—between the kinds of societal developments evident in the formation of social movements and the revitalization of the labor movement and the public sphere of political debate and decision making. Even more than its length, the most remarkable element in the Brazilian transition to democracy was the degree to which nominally representative political institutions—especially political parties—remained highly permeable, elitist, and personalistic.

This is a study of an anomaly. Unlike other political parties created the 1980s, the Workers' party (Partido dos Trabalhadores, PT) had a solid base in labor and social movements, took seriously the question of representation (both in internal organization and with regard to electoral constituencies), and couched its appeal in programmatic terms. The Workers' party and the central union organization with which it is organically (though not institutionally or juridically) linked, the Central Unica dos Trabalhadores (CUT), are the most coherent and institutionalized new political actors to emerge during the Brazilian transition.

The PT grew out of the conjunction between massive labor upsurge in the late 1970s and a period of debate on the left about what kind of political party (or parties) should be constructed in the transition to democracy. The party's agenda included both substantive and procedural challenges to the status quo. As a socialist party, it proposed sweeping changes in the orientation of social and economic policy to benefit the less privileged. As a participatory and democratic party, it proposed a new conception of politics, in which previously excluded sectors of the population would be empowered to speak for themselves. From the beginning, supporters and detractors alike recognized the PT as a novel experience in Brazilian political history. The left of the legal political spectrum in Brazil had traditionally been occupied by elite-led populist parties or, during its brief period of legality in the mid-1940s, by the Communist party.[5] Never before had a party emerged from below, with a strong working class base and a substantial proportion of its leadership drawn from the labor movement.

The PT's very existence seemed to imply the breakdown of entrenched patterns of elite dominance of the political system. Nonetheless, throughout most of the 1980s, it appeared to be largely marginal to the political process. This marginality was only partially due to the party's inexperience and to the weakness of the left. It was also due to the nature of the transition itself and to the ability of elite politicians (both those initially allied with the military and those in the opposition) to maintain a high level of discretionary control over the political process in the name of conciliation and flexibility. As the indirectly elected civilian government of José Sarney drew to an end, pervasive corruption, governmental incompetence, and deep economic crisis had eroded the legitimacy of these elites. In the 1989 direct presidential elections voters favored those least associated with the transitional regime.

The resulting confrontation between Fernando Collor de Melo and Workers' party leader Luís Inácio Lula da Silva starkly posed the distinction between the two Brazils noted above, or, as some postelection commentators put it, between unorganized and organized Brazil. Of all the candidates participating in the first round of the elections, Collor and Lula were the ones with the least and the most defined positions, respectively. While Collor's victory demonstrated that elitist patterns of politics in Brazil still predominated, the narrow margin of his victory indicated the degree of polarization that existed. For a former metalworker, trade unionist, and founder of the Workers' party to come within six percentage points of winning the first direct presidential election in three decades, something, in fact, had changed in Brazil. The Workers' party was both a reflection and a cause of that change.

What follows is an interpretive study of the origins and the formative years of the Workers' party and of those aspects of the transition to democracy that both constrained and sustained it. Because it was so different from other Brazilian parties, the PT's political trajectory provides us with an interesting optic from which to view institutional change during the transition. Because the PT survived, however anomalous it may initially have appeared, it highlights changes in Brazilian society that were not sufficiently taken into account by transitional elites. At the time the bulk of the research for this study was being conducted, survival was by no means inevitable. How, then, can we account for the party's development?

This study argues that to understand the formative years of the Workers' party we need to take into account both contextual and organizational elements. The transitional context provided both opportunities and constraints for the party at different moments. In the early stages of the transition, there was an enormous sense of possibility, a widespread belief that great changes were possible, which helped to break down cultural barriers to popular participation in politics and facilitated the creation of the party. Later, as most opposition politicians adopted an increasingly conservative view of the possibilities for change, the sense of limitless options faded, and the PT was widely viewed as utopian, or, because of its identification with class politics, as rigid and sectarian. From 1982 through the mid-1980s, the PT's difficulty in finding a place within the institutional political arena fomented a series of dilemmas and crises that almost destroyed the party. Finally, widespread disillusionment with the length of the transition and especially the disastrous performance of the Sarney administration helped to propel the PT into the position of a real alternative.

The stress on the context in which the PT was formed is consistent with approaches to collective action that see mobilization as a response to expanding political opportunities.[6] More than most scholars writing within this perspective, however, I see political opportunity as subject to interpretation by the actors involved and political space as constructed in struggles over the interpretation of what is possible. Political opportunities are not always recognized and, even when visible, are not always seized. Contextual elements alone cannot explain why the Workers' party survived, or why it was able finally to become an important vehicle for expression of discontent with the regime. Nonetheless, they help us to understand why the passage from movement building to institution building in the Brazilian case was not a linear process, signaling the winding down of a cycle of mobilization, but rather a more circular and mutually reinforcing process that involved an attempt to redefine the boundaries of the political.

The approach I have taken in this work falls within the family of political science writing currently categorized as historical-institutional. It seeks to address, in a concrete historical setting, an unexpected act of political creation, rendering problematic elements both of the context in which the party emerged and the new historical actor created. Rogers Smith argues that political science would do well to take as its central unit of analysis "not classes or groups or systems or instrumentally rational choices, but rather, as Skocpol and the new institutionalists suggest, the more general 'structure-agent' problem itself, the interaction of (possibly) influential structural contexts and the (possibly) meaningful actions of political agents."[7] Focusing on the complex interaction between the structural context in which the Workers' party was formed—a context in which socioeconomic factors combined with the specifically political variables and the web of meanings associated with the transition to democracy—and the set of decisions and conflicts involved in the formation of the party itself, I hope to shed new light on both. At the same time, such an interactive approach may avoid some of the perils either of a reductionist determinism or of a voluntaristic idealism, and help to illuminate both the limits of political volition and the choices that may be available in interpreting political constraints.

From the very beginning, the party faced a number of serious organizational and political dilemmas whose resolution was far from assured. What were the trade-offs involved in becoming a legal party within the limits established by the military regime? How could the party simultaneously help to promote autonomous organization of the working class (broadly conceived) and represent workers and the poor at the political level? Were elected officials from the party responsible to the party membership or to a broader constituency? How could the party best insure internal democracy and widespread participation? How would it deal with internal factions? How would it resolve the electoral dilemma, that is, the competing demands of remaining closely identified with a working class base and developing a sufficiently broad appeal to win elections?[8] Would alliances with other parties dilute its programmatic message? All these problems were posed in very concrete form, often simultaneously, during the party's first decade. The way in which the party addressed these questions profoundly shaped its early evolution and positioned it to reap the benefits of its early marginalization. Examining this formative process is therefore crucial. My perspective here concurs with Panebianco's, when he sets out "to reaffirm a fundamental intuition of classical sociology, in particular Weberian, concerning the importance of the founding moment of institutions":

> The way in which the cards are dealt out and the outcomes of the different rounds played out in the formative phase of an organization, continue in many ways to condition the life of the organization even decades afterwards. The organization will certainly undergo modifications and even profound changes in interacting throughout its entire life cycle with the continually changing environment. However, the crucial political choices made by its founding fathers, the first struggles for organizational control, and the way in which the organization was formed, will leave an indelible mark.[9]

Besides its interaction with the political environment of the transition, a crucial element in the Workers' party's formative experience (what Panebianco would call its "genetic model") was the relationship between the party and the labor movement. Labor was not the only constituent of the party's initial base—the organized left, Catholic activists, progressive politicians, intellectuals, and representatives of other social movements played and continue to play key parts in various aspects of party organization. Nonetheless, the PT's initial legitimacy and its ability to survive in spite of an adverse political conjuncture has a great deal to do with its links with an increasingly autonomous and powerful movement of Brazilian unions for substantive change.

The combative labor movement that first manifested itself in the massive strike waves in 1978–79 sent a powerful signal to Brazilian elites that workers were determined to take their fate into their own hands. Beginning in the industrial suburbs of São Paulo, the heart of the automobile industry, strikes spread to other industrial and service sectors all over Brazil. New leaders emerged, the most prominent of whom was the charismatic Luís Inácio da Silva in São Bernardo do Campo, known universally as Lula, who would become the first president of the PT.[10] For many of those advocating the formation of a new political party with a popular base, a process discussed in chapter 3, the appearance of new and authentic labor leaders changed the focus of the dialogue. From then on, the participation of these unionists was crucial to the formation of a party that claimed to represent workers.

While this relationship was thus vital to the Workers' party's formation and early development, it was not a simple one. The PT was not an "externally sponsored"[11] party in the same sense as the Labour party in Britain was; trade unionists played a central role in the party's creation, but it was not created by unions qua organizations. Changes in Brazilian labor organization during the late 1970s and the 1980s did not produce a single national organization, nor did they lead to a consensual approach to political action. These changes will be discussed at some length in chapter 8. Nonetheless, while the PT was not sponsored by the unions, it was, at particular moments in its development, legitimated by its relationship with them, and this relationship played a key role in the constitution of a dominant coalition within the party. The PT was never simply the political arm of a sector of the labor movement. Still, defining the kind of relationship that the party as an institution should have with labor, especially with the central union organization CUT, was one of the more difficult challenges it faced during the period studied.

The Workers' Party in Comparative Perspective

One of the most appealing aspects of the emergence of the Partido dos Trabalhadores in Brazil in 1979–80 for European and North American researchers, myself included, was its seeming resemblance to labor-based socialist parties in Europe at the turn of the century. Many initial reports on the formation of the party compared it with the British Labour party. The idea was that with the growth in size and militancy of the Brazilian industrial working class (and some sectors of service workers as well), the emergence of the working class as a *political* force was a natural next step in the process. By implication, the political space that such a party should occupy was organically given, lacking only an occupant.

Sociological approaches to political parties and political development largely reinforce this sense. Lipset and Rokkan's discussion of the salient cleavages in the formation of party systems[12] could lead us to interpret the emergence of the Workers' party as the assertion of class as a relevant cleavage in Brazilian politics—and would instruct us to look at the relationship between the development of class politics and other salient cleavages in the political system. Both Marxists and liberal developmentalists have often assumed that once a working class reaches a certain level of development—in terms of its size and organizational sophistication—it is likely to be considered and treated as politically relevant. While this does not mean that class is *always* a politically salient variable in countries with a developed working class, the power of the prediction is such that the absence of class as a significant factor becomes something that must be explained.[13] The renewed attention to class as a politically significant variable in Western Europe after the labor unrest of the late 1960s and early 1970s only reinforces our expectations by implying that while the political relevance of class may not always be apparent, it is nonetheless there as a potential.[14]

Brazil has never had a mass membership party that corresponded to the European socialist, social democratic, or labor party tradition, and the levels of urbanization, industrialization, and working-class organization would lead us to expect that one might emerge were such a correlation to be automatically made. The assumption of correspondence (which is effectively the assumption of class salience in political organization and voting behavior in societies that have reached a certain level of industrialization and urbanization and universal suffrage) has in fact been subjected to a great deal of theoretical critique. From Lipset and Rokkan's argument that class is only one of a number of cleavages that have been historically relevant in party formation to Downs's rational behavior hypotheses to Sartori's attack on sociological reductionism in dealing with politics, the point has been made that there is no direct translation from class distinctions in a given socioeconomic context to a particular kind of party and/or voting behavior.[15] The distinction between a descriptive use of the concept of class in the relations of production and the idea of class formation, what Marxists used to call simply the difference between class-in-itself and class-for-itself, has itself been discussed as a political process in the work of Adam Przeworski.[16]

In examining the existence of this apparent historical correspondence in the case of the European social democratic parties, Alessandro Pizzorno argued that it was not the socioeconomic processes themselves that gave rise to mass parties but rather the political conjuncture that they produced in the political systems of these countries. The *crisis* created by the emergence of urban masses and the extension of suffrage, not the rate of employment in industry or the increase in the size of cities, provided the context and opportunity for their formation. These conditions were by definition destined not to last.[17] The ability of such parties to perform an integrative function, that is, to gain allegiance of the working class for democratic institutions, may also have been linked to the kinds of contextual conditions outlined by Robert Dahl: the prior existence of a parliamentary system supported by a large and allegiant middle class with experienced and allegiant elite leadership; the peaceful extension of political participation via suffrage, allowing for the development of working-class leadership with the right to participate in the political system and enter the government; entrepreneurs willing and able to provide better socioeconomic conditions for workers; and the ability of the government to undertake structural reforms without alienating other social strata.[18] While the crisis over democratization in Brazil may in fact be similar in its impact to the one that Pizzorno argued existed in Europe at the turn of the century, Dahl's conditions are unfulfilled in Brazil.

To point out these problems is not to claim that the PT's project was impossible and unrealistic. It is only to emphasize that the kinds of conditions under which mass parties emerged and grew in the European context are unlikely to pertain here. While some insights developed in that context will provide a basis for formulating questions about dynamics and dilemmas in the development of the Workers' party, we cannot import the models in their entirety. In the development of Latin American party systems, or models of political participation, only Chile corresponds reasonably well to the European literature; unlike most other Latin American countries, Chile did have a relatively well developed legislature prior to the development of strong bureaucratic state structures, and some of Dahl's conditions seem to pertain better in the Chilean case. It may well be that, as Cardoso argues, the combination of circumstances presented by the transition process and the dynamics between the existence of a centralized and bureaucratized state and the emergence of new forms of participation will produce a different configuration of parties in Brazil.[19]

Thus there are serious reasons for doubting that Brazil's political parties will follow the developmental trajectory of the early industrializers. Nonetheless, analysts of Brazil continue to note the need for a political mechanism to mitigate the country's extreme levels of social and economic inequality. The achievement of a modicum of "social citizenship" under capitalism has virtually always occurred in the presence of a significant left party (or parties) allied in some way to a labor movement. The appearance of a party like the PT, which differs in significant ways from parties on the left in Brazil's past, in conjunction with significant changes in the organization and capacity of the labor movement, inevitably raised the question of whether the Workers' party could be a vehicle for these kinds of changes.

Historically, politically relevant cleavages in Brazil have not been primarily sociological; rather, they have been political and relational cleavages, or, more specifically, cleavages based on access to and attitudes toward holders of state power (what Brazilians usually call *a situação*, the situation). Thus the 1945–64 multiparty system was organized largely around the figure and legacy of Getúlio Vargas, and the 1965–80 two-party system was organized around support for or opposition to the military government.[20] While both class and region figure as important variables in analyzing voting behavior, they have never been adequate predictors. Instead, sociological cleavages must be understood *in relation* to the primary political-relational divisions. Appeals based on issues of substantive justice—what O'Donnell calls *lo popular*—have concealed a class dimension under a broad populist message.[21]

Nor have politically relevant cleavages in Brazil been primarily ideological. The centrality of the state in Brazilian political life organizes an opposition between ins and outs rather than among organizations with alternative programmatic visions.[22] Douglas Chalmers hypothesizes that in the Latin American sociopolitical context, parties without clear sociological and ideological identifications may in fact be functional.[23] This argument seems to break down, however, in the face of highly polarizing issues, particularly redistributive conflicts that polarize along class lines and challenge the ability of the vertical hierarchies to contain them. A typical case in Brazil in the early 1960s was the agrarian reform question; another was Goulart's call for basic reforms, which included not only agrarian reform but also incorporation of new groups (illiterates) into the political system, and the possible legalization of the Communist party. The emergence of these issues, particularly in the context of increasing social agitation in both rural and urban areas, polarized Congress into two opposing blocs (each of which was formed by factions of most parties), and ended the possibility of compromise based on shifting alliances.

As long as the "social question" was dealt with mainly outside the competitive political system, this kind of fluid party configuration could work, albeit conflictively. The Brazilian Congress was not a mere rubber stamp, in spite of its relatively poor record in terms of legislative initiative. It was particularly important for its ability to provoke governmental crises. Nonetheless, the weakness of Brazilian political parties has been reinforced by the relative insulation of major social policy decisions from the process of competitive politics, a legacy of Vargas's centralized state.[24] Changes that took place under the military, both in labor relations and in social security policy, retained the state's centrality but eliminated much of the paternalistic dimension of its administration of social issues. This delinking had an important impact on the politicization of social issues during the transition to democracy. With the increased powers granted to the legislature in the 1988 constitution, this politicization is likely to grow.

In a fluid polity like Brazil's, it is difficult to find the appropriate level of analysis for discussing political institutions. Most scholars agree that it is problematic to talk about political parties in the context of a party "system" in Brazil; indeed, in the preface to the Brazilian version of his *Parties and Party Systems,* Giovanni Sartori denies the appropriateness of his model for analyzing Brazilian party systems because of their lack of structural consolidation. Sartori argues that the appropriate unit of analysis in the case of Latin American countries (with the exception of Mexico and Chile) is the individual political party.[25]

Nonetheless, political parties do not develop in isolation. They develop in relation to the challenges and dilemmas arising in the struggle for political control over the shape of a society. If they become institutionalized, it seems likely that, as Panebianco and others have argued, they develop an increasing interest in their own organizational survival, and the incentives that motivate loyalty to the organization become less concerned with collective identity and more concerned with selective benefits.[26] These insights regarding the pattern of party institutionalization presume, however, a level of institutionalization of a political system and of political behavior that is historically lacking in Brazil and has been slow to develop during the transition to democracy.[27]

On the face of it, the prospects for a party like the PT to become consolidated appeared dim. Political space on the left is not organically given, but constructed. In an institutional environment like Brazil's, where political parties have historically defined themselves more in relation to the state than to each other, location of parties along a left-right spectrum has always been a precarious enterprise. The institutional arenas within which a party like the PT—even linked with an increasingly organized labor movement—could promote meaningful changes were so weakly institutionalized (in the Huntingtonian sense of the word)[28] that they often serve to disorganize, rather than organize, political life in Brazil.

There are other differences as well. In most of the European countries that developed strong labor, socialist, and social democratic parties, the manufacturing sector alone represented over 20 percent of the economically active population (EAP) by the early twentieth century. If we combine manufacturing, mining, construction, and transportation, this proportion is even more dramatic.[29] In Brazil, these sectors represented 15.24 percent of the EAP in 1872, and they had only reached 19.65 percent by 1960. The change over the next two decades was enormous by comparison: between 1960 and 1980 employment in these sectors tripled in absolute terms, and went up to 29.07 percent of EAP.

If the only factor to be taken into account were size, one could argue that the sector of the working population that had historically participated in or supported the formation of socialist or labor parties had only attained a necessary "critical mass" in Brazil after the period of rapid industrial growth in the late 1960s and early 1970s having attained such a critical mass, the formation of such a party was to be expected and correspondingly similar results could ensue.

Nonetheless, there are significant problems with this formulation, which make it unlikely that the PT's development will follow, almost a century later, quite the same path as that of European socialist, social

Table 1.1 Employment in Manufacturing, Mining, Construction, and Transport

Country	Year	Total Employed	Percentage of EAP
Belgium	1880	1,001,500	37.3
	1910	1,767,800	51.1
	1961	1,815,500	51.7
	1978	1,596,391	39.1
France	1886	4,590,000	27.6
	1906	6,884,000	33.2
	1962	8,316,700	42.2
	1975	7,858,500	36.0
Germany*	1882	6,690,300	37.9
	1907	12,012,200	44.8
	1961	16,655,100	64.6
	1978	9,531,000	35.3
Great Britain	1881	7,039,000	55.3
	1911	10,996,000	60.0
	1961	12,720,400	53.0
	1977	11,004,000	41.9
Italy	1881	4,558,700	27.2
	1911	4,912,300	29.9
	1964	9,061,000	45.0
	1978	8,565,000	39.4
Sweden	1880	173,200	9.5
	1910	676,500	30.8
	1960	1,669,400	51.5
	1975	1,380,599	35.8
Brazil	1872	810,500	15.2
	1920	1,443,000	15.1
	1950	2,928,300	17.1
	1960	4,453,000	19.7
	1980	12,572,706	29.1

Source: Data through the 1960s from T. Deldycke, H. Gelders, J.-M. Limbor, *La Population Active et sa Structure* (Brussels: Université Libre de Bruxelles, 1968). European data for the 1970s from the International Labour Office, *Yearbook of Labour Statistics 1979* (Geneva: International Labour Organization, 1979). For Brazil, 1980 data from the Instituto Brasileiro de Geografia e Estatística, *Censo Demográfico do Brasil: Mão de Obra, 1980.*
*For 1882 and 1907, data for unified Germany; 1961 and 1978 Federal Republic of Germany.

democratic, or labor parties. The difference lies in the moment in "world time" at which the party emerged. The older parties based in labor movements went through their formative periods at a time when both the absolute and the relative size of the industrial working class were expanding and would continue to do so for some time. The notion that "we shall be all" seemed a reasonable one. Working-class communities and socialist organizations coalesced to form a distinctive cultural base whose only serious competition, at the ideological level, was the Catholic Church, as witnessed by the growth of strong working-class Christian Democratic or Social Christian currents in such countries as Italy and Belgium.

The formation of a mass party at this juncture in world history also brings to mind various factors that have been analyzed to explain the decline of mass parties in the European context. The centrality of state bureaucracies in decision making undermines the role of parties in providing access to government; the growing role of the mass media as a source of political information undermines its educational and informational role; the welfare state has replaced the social worker role that some parties once played; an increase in leisure time and a wealth of voluntary associations compete with the party as a social network and as a focus of membership participation; and in some cases state financing has replaced membership financing in importance to these parties.[30] At the very least, the first two of these factors are as salient in Brazil as in the countries for which the decline of the mass party is posited,[31] and the first one perhaps even more so. The sociohistorical processes associated with the rise of working-class mass parties, that is, industrialization and the extension of suffrage (to all literate adults—illiterates were still excluded) took place in Brazil under the auspices of a centralized state, with a very limited parliamentary role in the determination of policy. Under late twentieth-century conditions, the possibility of constituting a "ghetto party" is not an available option.[32]

Working-class parties adopted electoral strategies, initially, because they believed that the process of industrialization would lead irrevocably to a situation in which workers were an absolute majority of the population. Thus universal suffrage, an early goal of European working-class parties, would, in parliamentary democracies, sooner or later bring these parties to power. In fact, workers never became a numerical majority in these countries, a situation which forced these parties to make a choice between maintaining their class "purity" and broadening their appeal to other classes at the risk of lessening the salience of class as an organizing principle of political behavior.[33]

As the data in table 1.1 show, by the time the Workers' party was formed in Brazil, the size of the industrial working class in most of the world was actually shrinking. In Brazil from the 1960s to the 1980s it had expanded at an extraordinarily rapid rate, as industrialization moved into expanded production of consumer durables and capital goods. Current tendencies in Brazilian industry suggest, however, that the rate of expansion of the industrial working class can be expected to slow down as more capital-intensive technologies are applied. In spite of relatively cheap labor costs in Brazil, auto companies, for example, are already far advanced in introducing robotics to replace human labor in their Brazilian plants. If this occurs, the PT can expect to see its social base among industrial workers stabilize or even shrink, placing it in a defensive position almost from the outset, a situation which its European counterparts faced much later in their histories.

In ideological terms, the competition for the "hearts and minds" of Brazilian workers was much more powerful and sophisticated than it was for European labor parties in formation. The widespread diffusion of radio and television as instruments of cultural homogenization militated against the kind of working-class identity that European socialists sought to build in the late nineteenth and early twentieth centuries.

The PT has also had to contend with a whole complex of new social questions that have challenged the boundaries of the traditional left social agenda in Brazil at a time when, in the case of the PT, that agenda is barely formed. While the party initially defined its primary base as the industrial working class, from the beginning it included members of other groups. Some of these became an increasingly important part of the labor movement itself in the 1980s, with the sharp rise in "middle sector" unionism. Others included a variety of organizations ranging from "old" social movements focusing on material demands to "new" ones concerned with qualitative questions—ecology, rights of women, racial minorities, homosexuals. These groups gravitated toward the PT in its capacity as an alternative political proposal promoting democratic participation and discussion of forms of direct democracy. The mix within the PT between "old" and "new" types of movements[34] has been uneasy, leading one observer to comment early on that instead of movements becoming a "transmission belt" to the PT the opposite was occurring: the PT was on the receiving end for a laundry list of concerns of a variety of groups, which were not organically integrated into any coherent form of party practice. The glue that held all these elements together, to the extent that anything did, was their common condition of exclusion from the political agenda in Brazil. This was a precarious commonality. The orientation of labor activists in the party was toward traditional concerns of labor and socialist parties, predicated on economic and industrial growth. These were primarily quantitative concerns, though the notion of an active citizenship provided a qualitative component. For the primarily middle class activists of most of the "new social movements," the qualitative issues were the most important ones; for some—the ecologists, for example—the quantitative orientation was even counterproductive. Nonetheless, the persistence of egregious inequality in Brazil might well convince these "postmaterialists" that their desire to live in an egalitarian and participatory society requires that political action pass through a stage in which the two must be combined. Discussing the rise of postmaterialist values in Europe, Inglehart notes a gravitation toward the left precisely because of the egalitarian dimension of the desire for a qualitatively different society.[35]

European socialist and social-democratic parties have also increasingly faced challenges from new social movements in the last decade. Once again, however, they have done so at a stage much later in their histories, and long after most had consciously made the decision to accept the trade-offs implied by seeking allies in other classes. The attempt to integrate new qualitative demands into socialist agendas took place in the context of an effort to expand the base of these parties at a time when workers' movements, while on the defensive, had to a large extent won themselves a place in the political system. It was not a case of an alliance of the excluded in the Brazilian sense.

We must be cautious in drawing upon the history of European socialist and social democratic parties for insight into the early development of the PT. Indeed, in many ways Brazil's political system bears a stronger resemblance to the United States—on which its first constitution was patterned and where a strong socialist party did not arise—than it does to the European examples. Nonetheless, the above discussion remains pertinent for two reasons. First, in attempting to define what it means to be a socialist party in a country like Brazil, the PT has been constrained to define itself in relation to historical socialist currents. This has not been an easy process, particularly insofar as the rise of the PT has coincided with a worldwide crisis of the left. At times the party has opted out of the debate, insisting on the singularity of the Brazilian experience; at other times, on the contrary, it seems rather to have transposed the last century of conflicts within European socialism to Brazilian soil. Resolution of the ideological struggle within the PT over the meaning of socialism therefore requires coming to terms with the party's specificity in time *and* space, both with what it means to be later, and with what it means to be different.

The comparative discussion is also pertinent because the differences discussed above raise important questions about the party's emergence and survival in the concrete setting in which it arose, and they counter a view of the PT as merely a "late developing" socialist party that can be explained by its having arisen in a "late developing" country. Despite the fact that there is no sign that most Brazilian political institutions are becoming more representative, more coherent, or more autonomous (more institutionalized, in fact), both the Workers' party and parts of the labor movement have done increasingly well on all of Huntington's measures of institutionalization, though not all to the same degree. The party was an anomaly when it was created largely because it seemed to respond to a different set of dynamics than those which dominated the early stages of the Brazilian transition to civilian rule; it continues to be an anomoly because it continues to obey a different logic and confront different dilemmas than do other political parties in Brazil.[36] To be an anomoly does not necessarily denote irrelevancy. Precisely because it was an anomoly, the PT could serve as a vehicle for the expression of widespread dissatisfaction with the status quo, as it did in the elections in the late 1980s. But the ability to serve as a vehicle for protest is not the same as the ability to promote the implementation of substantive social change. The formative period of the party, the subject of this study, is now over. Whether the PT manages to use its new legitimacy as a vehicle for mass protest to become a fully institutionalized mass party, and whether in so doing it can transform the political environment in Brazil, remain open questions.

Organization of the Study

The chapters that follow attempt to integrate contextual and organizational elements in understanding the formation of a party that was in many ways a novel experiment in Brazil. Throughout most of the party's formative period, it was often more notable for its failures than for its successes; as the transition drew to a close, the focus of many observers shifted from assessments of success or failure to a recognition of what it had attempted.

Chapter 2 provides an overview of the Brazilian transition to democracy and its institutional and historical contexts. Chapter 3 discusses the development of social and political organization within the democratic opposition during the 1970s, and the development of what initially appeared to be a consensual discourse in the debate about democracy on the left. This was a fragile consensus, whose unity was based on a common opposition to the authoritarian regime more than on a common vision of the role of the very different kinds of organizations and movements involved in a democratic one. Chapter 4 moves from the logic of consensus to a logic of difference, looking more specifically at the development of a combative labor movement and the debates and events leading to the founding of the Workers' party. Chapter 5 examines the party's attempt to give institutional form to its claim to be a mass democratic and participatory party, within the constraints of state regulation of party and electoral systems.

Chapter 6 looks at the evolution of the party's approach to elections. It pays particular attention to the PT's first electoral experience in 1982, where the results were significantly worse than the party had expected, and which led to a major reassessment both of the internal balance of forces and of the relative strength of the party's social base. While the decision of many PT activists to focus after 1982 on organizational activities within trade union or social movements rather than on party organization seemed at the time to be a retreat from politics, the growing strength of the labor movement in particular indirectly reinforced the party's image; this relationship is discussed in chapter 7. The growth of the party's influence in the labor movement and other social movements helped to make it the recipient of an important protest vote in 1985, 1988, and 1989 and contributed to its steady growth in the legislative elections of 1986 and 1990. The PT faced serious difficulties in dealing with those few institutional positions they had won in 1982, and the widespread "return to the base" attitude did not initially put a premium on resolving them. The political dilemmas involving the relationship between the party organization and elected representatives are discussed in chapter 8.

In the first half of the 1980s, when most of the research for this book was conducted, it often appeared that the difficulties in resolving internal and environmental challenges would destroy the party. Had the political conjuncture remained one in which the Partido do Movimento Democrático Brasileiro (PMDB), the predominant party in that period, could claim credit for a successful transition to democracy, they might well have done so. But the wide gap between expectations and performance, particularly during the Sarney government, and the PMDB's increasing institutional amorphousness, undermined that claim. When the PT's fragile public presence was reinforced by electoral gains in 1985 and 1986, the incentive to take more seriously both the need for greater internal institutionalization and the need to formulate political strategy grew as well. As the party matured, its ability to capitalize on the political resources it had been developing was enhanced. Its difference, initially the reason for its weakness, had become a source of strength.

In spite of the PT's explosive emergence as a key national actor in the 1988 and 1989 elections, its future remains an open question. Although the party can claim to reflect and represent significant developments in Brazilian society, it is still, to some extent, speaking into a void. While prevented by its very project from fully adapting to its political environment, it has not succeeded in changing it. Ten years after it began, the PT remains an anomaly. Nonetheless, its survival and growth bear witness to the fact that Brazil is changing, from below as well as from above.

THE BRAZILIAN

TRANSITION TO

DEMOCRACY

During the 1980s, the demise of Latin American military regimes stimulated a number of theoretical and empirical studies on transition from authoritarian rule.[1] Current studies of transition to democracy occupy an interesting place in the more general study of patterns of change. The use of the term *transition* in this sense is itself somewhat problematic: there is a tension between the day-to-day use of the word (as in, for example, the formation of a transition team to handle the details of transfer of power between one government and another) and its place in social theory, where we have been wont to speak of transition between one mode of social organization—or social formation—and another (as in the transition from feudalism to capitalism or the transition to socialism). The word has not generally been employed in social theory to describe a change from one kind of political regime to another. In fact, to speak of "transition to authoritarianism" sounds distinctly odd, yet the justifiable emphasis placed by those writing about democratization on the reversability of the process implies that it should be possible to use the term in this manner.

To point out the contradictory elements in the notion of transition is not in any sense to deny its appropriateness—just the opposite, in fact. The term takes from social theory its sense of fundamental transformation and from common usage the idea of a change in personnel, and it is precisely this kind of tension that characterizes the political processes which are being called "transitions to democracy." The ambiguity lies in the tension between the sense of enormous possibility on the one hand and of very powerful constraints on the other.[2]

Unlike the studies of regime breakdown, which were undertaken in *reaction* to the events that provoked them, much of the new work on democratization began well before the reinstitution of democratic regimes in these countries. Those writing about transition to democracy in the 1980s had no illusions that economic development would bring an 'inevitable' movement toward political democracy, as was commonly believed two decades ago; instead they sought observable tendencies in that direction which could be reinforced. The study of democratization, then, was both a reflection and an integral part of the process being examined.

Indeed, the focus of this research often followed the dynamics of the process. As the arena of political contestation shifted, so did the center of analytical attention. During the 1970's in Brazil the search for a counterweight to authoritarian state power encouraged opposition intellectuals to seek out and study potential sources of resistance within civil society—grass-roots church organizations, neighborhood movements, and labor unions; their studies increased the visibility of these movements.[3] With the approach of political party reform in 1978–79, attention shifted from societal organization to political institutions. Intellectual debates about the nature and possibilities of the transition to democracy were thus closely tied to political debates about opportunity and strategy. Both returned to a core question in democratic theory—the relationship between citizenship and social justice. It is no accident that so many Brazilian social scientists writing in the 1970s cited the work of T. H. Marshall.[4]

Many of those writing on redemocratization in Latin America stressed the need to separate procedural and substantive issues relevant to the process. The logic of making such a separation seemed inescapable. Transitional regimes faced staggering foreign debts, pressure to implement International Monetary Fund (IMF) stabilization programs or their equivalent, low domestic growth rates, and often astronomical rates of inflation. At the same time they had to deal with social unrest over income inequality, which had often been exacerbated during the authoritarian period. In Brazil, for example, the percentage of income going to the top decile of the economically active population went up 8.1 percent between 1960 and 1980, while the proportion going to the bottom 50 percent declined by 3.2 percent.[5] Illustrative of the level of income inequality is the fact that income levels are discussed as multiples of the minimum wage, whose value ranges between $35 and $50 per month in U.S. dollar terms. The 1980 census showed 31.41 percent of the economically active population earning salaries less than or equal to the minimum wage, 27.97 percent earning 1–2 minimum wages, 11.68 percent earning 2–3 minimum wages, 10.11 between 3 and 5 minimum wages, 6.66 between 5 and 10 minimum wages, and 4.32 percent earning 10 minimum wages or more.[6] There was little likelihood of an early solution to these problems. Consolidation of new democratic regimes therefore seemed to require a specifically *political* basis of support, in democratic procedures and institutions, without recourse to the substantive dimension historically contained in populist or developmentalist programs. In other words, it would involve the separation of what O'Donnell once called the dimensions of *citizenship* and *lo popular* involved in state legitimacy.[7]

The distinction between procedural and substantive questions has a certain analytical neatness, but it corresponds less and less to the expectations that real historical actors have about democratic political systems. From Joseph Schumpeter's minimalist definition of the democratic method as "that institutional arrangement for arriving at political decisions in which individuals acquire the power to decide by means of a competitive struggle for the people's vote" to Robert Dahl's definition of polyarchy as requiring that citizens have the opportunity to formulate preferences, signify their preferences, and have their preferences be weighted equally, emphasis has been placed on the input side of the system.[8] Concern with the output side fell into the realm of political economy. Obviously there were links; Schumpeter's project was precisely to discover those links, to determine whether it was possible to maintain a democratic method in a socialist system.[9] Dahl was certainly aware of the constraints placed on citizens' ability to participate by socioeconomic factors. Much of the work on political development in the third world in the 1960s and 1970s was concerned with these questions. The difficulty was to understand the *relationship* between input and output, ends and means, effective citizenship and effective governmental performance, for the legitimacy and stability of a democratic political system. This is a problem not only for those studying new democracies in the third world but also for those focusing on democratic politics in advanced capitalist countries. Issues presumed to be resolved with the rise of the welfare state have returned with a vengeance. Recent attention to distributive justice[10] and to the relationship between the input and output sides of democratic politics[11] represent attempts to redefine these relationships. The extent to which democratic legitimacy and stability rest on the *performance* of democratic governments as well as (and perhaps more than) on the maintenance of democratic procedures is a subject of ongoing debate.[12] This debate has recently gained a new dimension with the breakdown of Communist regimes in Eastern Europe. In the Eastern European cases, many commentators have stressed the need for economic liberalization as a precondition for political democracy; nonetheless, proponents of democracy are likely to find it difficult to ignore distributive issues.

Thus the central theoretical problem in the study of democratic transition in Latin America is a familiar one: what would make it possible to consolidate a political system based on generally accepted rules of political competition and citizenship rights, in countries characterized by glaring social inequality; and as a corollary, can (or should) democratic governments in these countries be expected to address the question of social democracy at the same time that they are faced with the installation of a functioning political democracy?

The inauguration of a process of regime transition is likely to open up a broad-ranging debate about the parameters and goals of the process. This debate about democracy is important for several reasons. First, it involves a reassessment of inherited terms of discourse, in which concepts such as power, politics, freedom, and democracy—what some theorists call "essentially contested concepts"—are subject to conceptual revision.[13] While not a sufficient condition of political change, a part of the process of political change is this conceptual debate, whereby "events once considered mere facts come to be seen as the outcomes of a political process and thereby as properly subject to political debate and the play of pressure."[14] In a transitional period this debate has a visibility and an urgency that are not apparent during periods in which the institutional embodiments of "power" and "democracy" exercise a more predictable control over the degree to which they are contested.

Second, the debate about democracy becomes an arena for struggles over the rules of the game and over who will be recognized as legitimate participants in the political process. The more the various participants in the debate accept the legitimacy of a multiplicity of definitions of what is possible and create institutions (or use existing institutions) to mediate the inevitable conflicts that result, the more likely is a democratic outcome. If, on the other hand, powerful participants insist on the need for a single definition of what is possible, usually couched as "common sense" or "realism," they are less likely to be concerned about developing institutions capable of mediating among differing definitions or goals, and democratic outcomes are less likely.

The Transition in Brazil: An Overview

What does it mean to democratize Brazil? The winding down of military rule produced a plethora of conflicting expectations and hopes among Brazilians, to say nothing of social scientists attempting to understand processes of regime change and other foreign observers who saw the spread of democratic ideas as a happy replacement for the contagion of authoritarianism in the previous decades. During the late 1970s, when democratization was a hope on the horizon, the distinctions between (or potential for conflict between) these expectations were still subsumed under a broad movement of popular sentiment in favor of a return to civilian rule. As the transition process wore on, however, differences over the kinds of changes contemplated moved from the periphery toward the center of political debate.

In the course of Brazil's transition, which began with a relaxation of some of the strictures that the military had placed on civil rights and continued through the inauguration of a civilian government and the writing of a new constitution, a number of different kinds of political actors took part in the ongoing debate and struggle over the country's future. In the early stages, new social actors joined with the opposition political party to pressure the military for further concessions. In this period, neighborhood movements, professional associations, and a resurgent trade union movement took on an increasingly political appearance, producing (or adding to) a ferment that some authors have called the explosion of civil society. Civil society became the primary arena of political interaction. In later stages, as the arena of political struggle shifted to state institutions, the relevant political actors shifted as well—to political party organizations, together with bureaucratic apparatuses and those with the ability to influence them. Social movements did not disappear; indeed, during the 1980s some of them, particularly urban squatter movements and the rural landless movement, were much larger and more militant than their counterparts during the early phases of the transition. The difference lies in the fact that during the late 1970s such movements were interpreted as part of the broader fabric of a democratic opposition, while in the 1980s it was their contestatory role and their capacity for disruption that appeared paramount.

The Brazilian transition process was noteworthy for its length and for the moderation and caution displayed by the dominant forces of political opposition to the authoritarian regime. As time went on, these characteristics reinforced several particularly ambiguous aspects of the transition process, and the political indeterminacy that initially appeared as a space for creativity came to represent simply an avoidance of decisive action. First, the Brazilian transition lacked clearly defined temporal and substantive limits. Second, the liberalization project involved a very narrow range of political actors, and it was carried out within constraints that made the maintenance of consensus among those promoting democratization appear more important than decisive action. Finally, the military was not discredited when it left power and maintained a significant degree of internal unity; it thus retained, or was seen as retaining, a substantial capacity to intervene in the political process.

The Brazilian military regime had a number of exceptional characteristics that many observers hoped would facilitate the transition process. First, it was less repressive than its Southern Cone counterparts.[15] Brazil had a lower incidence of disappearances and deaths at the hands of the military than did Argentina or Chile, for example, despite mechanisms for arbitrary rule. Institutional Act no. 5, decreed at the end of 1968, and the National Security Law of 1969, denied such basic rights as habeas corpus and gave the regime broad powers to arrest and imprison citizens for a long list of vaguely defined offenses to the nation.[16] Second, throughout most of the military regime, Brazil retained many of the trappings of constitutional rule. These included a functioning legislature (albeit with very limited prerogatives), regular elections for legislative and some municipal offices, and a two-party system (however artificial). The military attempted to maintain control over these institutions through a variety of decree laws and institutional acts and through changes in electoral rules designed to favor the party that supported the military (Aliança de Renovação Nacional, later Partido Democrático Social). The fact that the military did not attempt to come up with an alternative legitimacy formula or implant alternative institutional arrangements led Juan Linz to his famous characterization of Brazil as an "authoritarian situation" rather than an authoritarian regime.[17]

The liberalization begun by President Geisel in 1974 gradually restored many of the civil and political rights that had been suspended over the preceding decade, allowing for the growth of a vocal and increasingly broad-based movement for the restoration of democracy that included political elites, professional associations, a newly militant sector of the labor movement, and a range of social movements associated with the Catholic church. Nonetheless, the military retained a great deal of control over the process, intending to hold onto executive power at least until 1991. A party reform in 1979 abolished the two-party system that had been artificially created by the military in 1966. The Aliança de Renovação Nacional (ARENA), the pro-regime party, and the Movimento Democrático Brasileiro (MDB), the officially sanctioned opposition party, were abolished and six new parties were created, of which five survived. The Partido Democrático Social (PDS) was formed as a successor party to ARENA; the Partido do Movimento Democrático Brasileiro (PMDB), Partido Democrático Trabalhista (PDT), and the Partido dos Trabalhadores (PT) were formed out of the opposition to the military regime; and the Partido Trabalhista Brasileiro (PTB) fell somewhere in between. The PMDB was initially by far the largest of the opposition parties.

Elections for state governors were held in 1982 for the first time in seventeen years, along with elections for the federal Chamber of Deputies, one-third of the Senate, state legislatures, and mayors and municipal councils of most municipalities. Unable to decide on an acceptable military candidate for the 1984 indirect presidential elections, President Figueiredo (1979–85) abdicated control over the choice of his successor. The split in the government party (PDS) that resulted from the selection of former São Paulo governor Paulo Maluf as its candidate led to the victory of the opposition coalition slate of Tancredo Neves and José Sarney in the indirect presidential election. PDS dissidents formed a new party, the Partido da Frente Liberal (PFL), which joined with the PMDB in a "Democratic Alliance" to support Neves. A conservative opposition leader, Tancredo Neves had been elected PMDB governor of Minas Gerais in 1982. Sarney, who split with the PDS over the nomination of Maluf, had previously been its president. Thus with the sudden death of Tancredo Neves before his inauguration, the former president of the party that had supported the military regime through two decades of authoritarian rule became the chief executive of the "New Republic," charged with leading the transition to democracy. This ambiguity came to be reflected within the PMDB as well; a substantial portion of PMDB deputies elected in 1986 were former members of the government party. The Congress elected in 1986 was charged with writing a new constitution, promulgated in 1988, and direct presidential elections were finally held at the end of 1989.

The length of the transition was initially the product of the military's determination to maintain control over the process. Political leaders of the democratic opposition, however, contributed to its indeterminacy by their caution in successive steps of negotiated change. A full decade after liberalization of the regime began, many opposition politicians, including Tancredo Neves, gave only contingent support to the mass movement for direct presidential elections that mobilized literally millions of Brazilians in state capitals and smaller cities in 1984. After the defeat of a PMDB-sponsored constitutional amendment calling for direct elections, the possibility of an opposition victory that was presented by a split in the government party—even in a less than fully democratic contest—seemed preferable to PMDB leaders to the far riskier course of confronting the military by continuing to mobilize the population. Even after Sarney had been inaugurated, while the possibility of fixing an early date for direct elections of a new president was often debated, not much was done about it in fact, and the decision was left to the Constituent Assembly elected in 1986. Thus, for the first two years of the New Republic, basic rules of the game, such as the length of the presidential term, remained indeterminate.

This indeterminacy was characteristic of the Brazilian transition. It is especially notable when we compare it with the Spanish case, often cited as another example of gradual regime change. There are in fact a number of similarities. In both cases, prior to the foundational moment of a new regime there was a long period of erosion of the social base of authoritarianism. Key economic actors, for example, became convinced in both cases that the maintenance of a dictatorship was not only no longer necessary but was even detrimental to healthy capitalist development. In both cases intellectuals played an increasingly oppositional role, and in both a convergence developed between political leaders within the regime seeking reform and moderate opposition leaders willing to collaborate in a process of gradual liberalization. In both cases political leaders of the authoritarian regime played the dominant role in the early stages of the transition; liberalization took place in stages, and there was a marked effort on the part of traditional elites to control the degree of opening.[18]

However, important differences between the two grew striking as the Brazilian transition progressed. While there was not a clear political rupture between the old and new regimes in the Spanish case there was an important symbolic rupture—the death of Franco. Although there was substantial continuity in both policy and personnel in the immediate pre- and post-Franco period, his death provided a reference point toward which political actors could both prospectively and retrospectively orient strategies and behavior. There was no comparable dividing line in Brazil. Furthermore, the importance of the international context in the Spanish case has no counterpart for Brazil. The desire to be part of Europe functioned on economic, cultural, and political levels as a powerful incentive for rapid establishment of democratic institutions. For Spanish industrialists, the advantages of participating in the European Economic Community (EEC) far outweighed any advantages offered by continuation of a dictatorship; and participation in the EEC was blocked by a political system that no longer offered any real benefits.[19] During the 1970s, many Brazilian industrialists concluded that the maintenance of the military regime was not necessary to their well-being, and might even be an impediment. But however visible these industrialists may have been within the Brazilian opposition, the change in the business community's attitudes was neither as widespread nor as unambiguous as it was in Spain. There was no clear *positive* incentive for democratization in Brazil equivalent to the desire in Spain for incorporation into the EEC.

These two factors—the symbolic importance of Franco's death and the pull toward democratization exerted by external factors—in turn influenced the dynamics of the process itself. In Spain, there were good reasons for elites to want to implement the transition process as quickly as possible after Franco's death, though still proceeding with some caution. In Brazil, elites were more divided, and domination of the process by the military rather than by civilians meant that institutional aspects of the transition had to be negotiated with (and by) a powerful bureaucratic institution which, though divided, was not going to be an integral part of running democratic political institutions in the same way that civilian elites in Spain potentially were. While military attitudes in Spain were an important component of the political environment, the military were normally commentators rather than protagonists. The Brazilian military's desire to return to the barracks was both ambivalent and conditional; the desire of Spanish elites to join Europe was much less so.

The extension of civil rights and institutional change in Spain began with Franco's death, although at a societal level it had started earlier, as rights not legally guaranteed began to be exercised de facto. Occasional harshly repressive measures punctuated a period of several years before

Franco's death during which union organization grew, clandestine publications circulated, and antiregime sentiment was fashionable. When Franco died in November 1975 most civil rights were restored and reformist leaders entered the cabinet. As in Brazil, there was a period characterized by ambiguity and lack of a clear project, but it lasted for less than a year. In 1976 and 1977 Suarez granted amnesty to political prisoners, legalized the Communist party, and convinced the Cortes to dissolve itself. The elections held in June 1977 (the first free legislative elections in 43 years) gave around three-quarters of the vote to the centrist UCD and the moderate socialist PSOE. In October a pact was signed in which the Communist and Socialist parties promised to moderate economic demands during the economic crisis, and by 1978 a new democratic constitution had been written and was overwhelmingly passed by a national referendum. The entire process had taken three years.

The differences in timing and sequence between this and the Brazilian case are striking. When the first Spanish elections were held, only two years after the transition began, the Communist party was legal, and reformists were already in the government. The stakes were clear; the winner would form a government. In Brazil, the lengthy uncertainty over when the first direct presidential elections would be held, and the fact that the stakes in the 1982 elections were still defined by the presence of the military in power, gave a different kind of meaning to those elections. The creation of new political parties and the popular election of state governors for the first time since 1965 were clearly important; these factors contributed to the sense that these were "foundational" elections. Nonetheless, centralization of resources and decision making in the hands of the federal executive and a technocratic bureaucracy limited the power of both governors and legislators; this meant that the expectations generated by the enthusiasm and the discourse of change surrounding the 1982 elections were higher than the ability of elected "opposition" candidates to respond to them. In Spain there may have been disillusionment with the performance of democratic government, but it was an elected government. In Brazil, there was ample possibility for disillusionment with the transition to set in prior to the establishment of fully democratic institutions, especially a president elected by popular vote. The varying periodizations of the Brazilian transition reflect ambiguity about the progress toward democracy: some began to speak of "democratic" politics in Brazil begin-

ning in 1982; others claimed that the transition ended with the inauguration of a civilian government in 1985; still others waited until the
presidential elections of 1989.

Ambiguity has been a defining characteristic of the Brazilian transition; it reflects not only the way the military left power but also endur-
ing aspects of the Brazilian political system. The reference point for
transition from authoritarianism is not only the immediate predecessor
of the new regime but also the institutional history of the country. The
degree to which we are talking about *re*democratization matters. It is no
accident that upon restoration of competitive politics in Argentina,
Uruguay, and even Peru, the political parties relevant for the transition
were those relevant before the authoritarian period.[20] In Chile, the
influence of the pre-1973 political parties continued to structure the
opposition to Pinochet; the "Campaign for the No" in the 1988
plebiscite and the victorious coalition in the 1989 presidential elections
resulted from negotiations among those parties.[21]

Unlike its counterparts in Argentina, Uruguay, Peru, and Chile, the
Brazilian military regime maintained a functioning legislature (albeit
stripped of some of its powers) and a party system throughout most of
its tenure in power. It was not the same party system; preexisting
political parties were abolished in 1965 and two new parties were created from the top down—one which supported the government
(ARENA) and one which was to act as a loyal opposition (MDB). In
spite of their artificiality, these parties did compete in regular elections
between 1966 and 1978, and their lifetime was not significantly shorter
than that of their predecessors. The ARENA/MDB system was in
place from 1966 to 1979; the party system instituted at the end of the
Estado Novo, centered around the PSD/PTB/UDN, lasted only seven
years more (1945–65).[22] Between 1945 and 1964 the party system was
highly polarized around the figure and legacy of Getúlio Vargas; the
party system in place between 1965 and 1979 was polarized around the
issue of military rule. While the MDB was always potentially a disloyal
opposition under the authoritarian regime, its behavior throughout
most of its history was similar to what Linz has called a semiopposition;
its inability to take a more principled stand against the regime was due
to the efficiency of selective repression of its leaders, the government's
firm control over the electoral rules and patronage, and the weakness of
potentially countervailing forces in society.[23] Between 1945 and 1964
the UDN could knock at the barracks door; for the MDB, there was no
such option. The MDB became an effective electoral opposition only

when the Geisel government liberalized the electoral rules in 1974, and as a result of its unexpectedly successful electoral performance, it adopted an increasingly vocal position of principled opposition to the military regime itself.[24]

The formation of new political parties was a key part of the strategy of controlled regime transition adopted by the military, just as it had been for the regime transition from Vargas's Estado Novo in 1945. Both the military and the Vargas governments initiated preemptive reform from within and attempted to use the benefits of incumbency to privilege their political heirs. Central to the political reforms instituted in 1945 was the establishment of a date for elections (for president and a constituent congress) and provision for the formation of political parties. The 1945 electoral law provided for electoral courts, compulsory vote for all literate adults, a secret ballot, a majority principle for election of the president, state governors, and senators, and proportional representation with an electoral quotient system for the federal Chamber of Deputies and state assemblies. The party law was explicitly intended to consolidate parties and make elections a vehicle for transition to a new regime. While the 1932 party law had allowed for single-state parties and candidacies without party sponsorship, the 1945 law required that parties be organized nationally and that candidates obtain party sponsorship; the 1945 law also outlawed parties with an "anti-democratic" orientation and provided for block registration of voters on the basis of lists prepared by government officials.[25]

The 1945 party legislation rewarded incumbency. The PSD, organized by state elites who served as Vargas's appointees in state governments, was in the best position to benefit; to a lesser extent, the PTB profited from access to the corporatist unions and the resources of labor and social welfare bureaucracies to constitute its initial base. The União Democrática Nacional (UDN) was organized on the basis of a rather broad political spectrum of opposition to the Vargas dictatorship. Unable to benefit from access to patronage machines and held together by what it was against, the initially broad UDN front splintered quickly, and the party remained highly fractionalized throughout its history. It was involved in constant struggles over whether to ally with the PSD against threats to class interests (particularly proposals for agrarian reform) or to adopt an intransigent position of opposition to all of Vargas's heirs. Although UDN members participated in most cabinets of PSD presidents and during the Dutra presidency formally collaborated in making up a congressional majority, the party's inability to win presidential elections made it particularly susceptible to the temptation to call for military intervention.[26]

In both the 1945 transition and the one which began in the 1970s, authoritarian incumbents were determined to retain a great deal of control over the process. In both cases party and electoral legislation favored regime supporters. Nonetheless, in 1945 the institutional boundaries of the process were clearly delineated from the beginning: the "foundational" elections of the new regime involved direct popular election of a new president and of a Congress that would act as a Constituent Assembly. Gubernatorial elections were to come later; this postponement insured that Vargas appointees still controlled state political machines at the time of the formation of parties and the first elections. In the 1980s the order of the process was reversed. The first elections under the new party law were gubernatorial, legislative, and municipal, producing the possibility that opposition candidates might win control over state patronage machines, which could affect future contests. Opposition victories in 1982 undoubtedly helped to weaken the military's ability to maintain control over the presidential succession. Nonetheless, those elections were not intended as the foundational elections for a new regime, although they contained foundational elements (for example, direct election of state governors for the first time since 1965). A Constituent Assembly would not be elected until 1986, and the first direct presidential elections would not take place until the end of 1989.

The social bases of political parties during the two transitions also differed, particularly with regard to organized popular sectors. Unlike the Vargas regime, where corporatist legislation had been perceived as an extension of the social and organizational rights of workers and the poor, application of corporatist legislation under the military was perceived as exclusionary and repressive, and changes in the labor relations system reinforced its coercive aspects and eliminated most of the positive benefits that labor had derived from its relationship to the state. During the 1970s, alongside the demand for restoration of civil and political rights, opposition discourse protested the exacerbation of inequality under the authoritarian regime and won a growing portion of votes from poor areas, particularly from the industrial working class.

The allegiance of the working class to Vargas in 1945 meant that workers did not become part of the movement in opposition to the regime. In fact, prior to the 1945 elections, unions joined with the Communist party in calling for Vargas to remain in the presidency during the Constituent Assembly; Vargas's susceptibility to this appeal was one factor in the military ultimatum forcing him to resign. Labor support for the PTB was organized through the state labor and social welfare bureaucracies and the unions; while workers were elected on the Brazilian Communist party (PCB) ticket to the Constituent Assembly, and to a lesser extent by the PTB (whose labor candidates were more likely to be lawyers than workers), they were not particularly effective in the Constituent Assembly itself. It may be that organizing the labor vote through corporatist state institutions prevented strong political articulation of labor interests during most of the 1945–64 period. The Dutra government's repression of labor militancy and outlawing of the Communist party in early 1947 certainly reinforced that tendency,[27] as did the fact that major social policy decisions were made in the federal bureaucracy rather than in Congress.[28]

In the transition that began in the mid-1970s, the most combative and well-organized sectors of the working class were resolutely opposed to military rule, and new labor leaders were calling for unions to become more autonomous from the state. Proposing greater autonomy from the state, however, called for a thorough reassessment of the strategies and instruments of labor action—including consideration of the need for and the possibility of influencing the political shape of Brazil's future. For some, the formation of the Workers' party was intended to play that role. Others expected that the PMDB, as a successor party to the broad opposition front built during the 1970s, would continue to constitute a major pole of attraction for those seeking social change. In 1945, corporate interests were aggregated from above into distinct political organizations whose role was to mediate social struggles through state institutions; in the transition that began in the 1970s, the question of how to link "social" and "procedural" aspects of the democratization process was much more conflictual.

The indeterminacy of the Brazilian process had a significant impact on the strategies of opposition forces. The prolonged period of uncertainty over the timing of the military's exit from power reinforced the claim of the largest opposition party, the PMDB, that the issue was one of military regime versus democratic opposition (embodied by the PMDB). While PMDB discourse continued to call for change, the party adopted a conservative approach when it came to actual confrontation with the regime. The presumption, reinforced by the party's gains in successive elections from 1974 on, was that in the natural course of things the PMDB would come to power.

This presumption was not unreasonable. Throughout the early phases of the transition, the PMDB was able to draw upon the reservoir of legitimacy it had built since 1974 in order to retain its position as the hegemonic opposition force, and its essentially bipolar view of the available alternatives was the reigning common sense. While it participated in the massive 1984 campaign for direct presidential elections, PMDB leaders also engaged in negotiations behind the scenes to win the military regime's acceptance of a possible victory of conservative PMDB leader Tancredo Neves in indirect elections; when the constitutional amendment proposed to implement direct elections failed to win the necessary two-thirds majority, the party was ready to accept the verdict.

Within this definition of the situation, the very existence of the Workers' party was illegitimate—the PT was a spoiler, which, by dividing the opposition, played into the hands of the military regime. The prevailing "common sense" dictated that a transition to democracy would come about through a series of delicate negotiations among elites, that only very limited change was possible, and that the maintenance of a broad consensus within the opposition was paramount. There were thus several struggles going on at the same time: one was between the military and the various components of the democratic opposition over the timetable and the breadth of the political opening; and one, within the opposition, was over the legitimacy of conflicting views of the transition and of a desired future.

The existence of a prevailing common sense among political elites—a belief in limited possibilities and the need for consensus—had important institutional ramifications. For most opposition leaders, the avoidance of conflict seems to have been much more important than the construction of mechanisms to deal with it. The "end" of the transition was implicitly defined as the arrival of the opposition in power. Because the military regime had continued to hold elections for most offices and had not abolished the legislature and judiciary, democracy did not have to imply an institutional rupture with the previous regime. Once direct elections were restored for all offices, the end of the transition would have been reached. For some, the indirect election of a civilian opposition leader, with the presumption that the next presidential elections would be direct, was already sufficient grounds to claim that Brazil was a democracy.

This is quite a weak conception of democracy—one that certainly fits with a minimalist definition of democratic regimes but that leaves out many of the interactive dimensions of democratic politics. To call for subsumption of differences under a universalistic interpretation of reality, of what is possible, eliminates a key element of democratic practice, which calls upon a logic of difference. José Nun has argued that the possibility of *comparison,* rather than subsumption, is what creates democratic deliberation. Comparison is essentially a political problem; democratic politics does derive from justice and freedom but rather *makes them possible.* Genuine democratic politics requires that we abandon the idea of a single rationality; the main task is to create *political institutions* that make possible the communication and confrontation of different discourses and facilitate "authentic transactions" based on a logic of differences.[29]

For most opposition political elites, the Brazilian transition was about building a democratic regime rather than about building the institutional conditions for a democratic politics. Once the regime transition was accomplished, there would be time to talk about differences. The assertion of such differences during the transition itself was not only premature but actually detrimental to democratization. This separation between the process of regime transition and a process of building democratic politics was particularly pronounced in the Brazilian case; even in Spain, the most-often-cited comparative example of a gradual transition to democracy, political elites expected the two processes to occur simultaneously.

The Workers' party challenged the prevailing common sense and insisted that the construction of a political institution able to represent a different view of what democracy should mean in Brazil was a necessary component in the democratization process. For the founders of the PT, the most important development in the 1970s was not the growth in strength of opposition to the regime as measured by successive MDB electoral triumphs (though these were deemed important), but rather the emergence of a wide variety of social movements demanding substantive change and claiming a political voice of their own. The transition, therefore, had to provide an arena within which these new societal actors could participate; the recognition of differences was not the end of the process but the beginning.

The democratic transitions of the 1980s have drawn scholarly attention to the role of parties in Latin America. While scholars have recognized that Latin American parties have not by and large been as central to political life as their counterparts in Western Europe and the United States, there remains an intuition that consolidating democratic regimes presumes the existence of parties that are able to process conflicts,[30] articulate coherent political choices,[31] and produce consent.[32] As Scott Mainwaring points out, scholars are increasingly asking not why parties in Latin America fail to live up to first-world models but rather what role they do play, how they relate to the state and to other political and social actors, and how differences in party strategies and roles among countries help us to understand processes and outcomes of regime change.[33] Of crucial importance for the latter is the historical configuration of parties in relation to the state and other actors, what happened to parties under the military regimes, and the role they play in defining the rules—and stakes—in the transition process. Interestingly enough, in most of the Southern Cone countries undergoing transition to democracy, the configuration of parties at the end of military regimes was quite similar to the ones that preceded them. Of particular importance to this study is an understanding of how the relationship among parties, labor, and the state took shape throughout these processes.

In this sense the emergence of the Workers' party represented a singular development not only in Brazil but also in the regime transitions occurring at roughly the same time in other Southern Cone countries. There are a number of reasons for this. The Brazilian military regime dis-organized existing partisan allegiances to a much greater extent than did its counterparts in Chile, Uruguay, and Argentina; unlike the others, the Brazilian military filled the organizational space left by abolition of existing parties with new ones. Its ability to do this may have been due to the relatively shorter duration of those allegiances prior to the takeover and to the nature of the respective party systems prior to the military regimes. There are also crucial differences in the impact of the military regimes on the working classes of the Southern Cone countries: the proportion of industrial workers in the economically active populations of Chile, Argentina, and Uruguay fell substantially under the military, while in Brazil it grew.[34] Unions experienced repression in all four countries, but their relatively greater strength in the first three made union leaders targets of physical repression (that is, torture and assassination) to a greater extent than in Brazil.

Unions adopted political strategies early on in Chile, due to relatively greater opportunities for voicing demands at the political level through parties than through purely trade unionist activities,[35] and the Communist and Socialist parties that had formed early in this century, albeit fragmented, continued to play an important underground role during the Pinochet regime.[36] Prior to the coup, Chilean parties were clearly the backbone of the political system, and the legislature, rather than the bureaucracy, was the central arena for channeling political conflict. The military regime sought to destroy national labor organizations, atomize union representation by restricting it to the workplace level, and promote a new generation of Christian Democratic labor leaders. Nonetheless, preexisting partisan identities remained alive in the unions and continued to structure identities within Chilean civil society; in the transition to democracy, parties *as organizations* were once again the vehicles for negotiation over the parameters of the process.

Parties have also long been central to democratic politics in Uruguay, and the *Blancos* and *Colorados* date back to the nineteenth century. Unlike Chile, however, these were catch-all parties, and channeling of political conflict took place to a significant extent within the parties themselves due to the country's "double simultaneous vote" system, by which parties could run a number of candidates for the same office.[37] Left parties in Uruguay, particularly the Communist party, had substantially more weight in social movements and especially the labor movement than their electoral performance prior to the 1970s indicated. Collective bargaining over wages and working conditions, a sizable welfare state, and substantial income redistribution prior to the 1960s meant that in Uruguay, unlike Chile, working-class parties, while retaining a revolutionary rhetoric, tended to focus on corporative and pressure group activities rather than political strategies.[38] The economic crisis of the 1960s, together with the impact of the Cuban revolution, led to increased union militancy and the formation of a number of new leftist organizations, many of which joined with the Communists in 1971 to create the Frente Amplio as a third electoral force (and some of which joined the Tupamaros in armed struggle).[39] In spite of the repression undergone by left organizations under Uruguay's authoritarian regime, the Frente Amplio reemerged even stronger, albeit with some changes in its internal balance of forces. After the defeat of the military's proposed constitution in 1980, the Uruguayan party system was reconstituted, and parties formally negotiated the transition rules with the military.[40]

In Argentina, partisan identification has historically been both strong and exceedingly polarized, but parties themselves have not been central to political life. The emergence of mass politics produced instead a pattern of direct relationships between the state and corporate bodies, particularly labor unions and the armed forces.[41] Although similar to Brazil in the weakness of parties, Argentina has been characterized by vastly stronger organizations within civil society. Peronism for Argentine workers was (and is) a complex, often paradoxical identity, informed by historical experience and embodied in the unions, but not mediated by a political organization.[42] This unmediated quality of Peronist (and anti-Peronist) political identities has historically meant that parties resist a self-definition as "parts," seeking instead to pass themselves off as the legitimate expression of the nation. They thus personify conflict rather than serve as vehicles for its mediation, and in the past they have exhibited a very low degree of loyalty to democratic institutions.[43] There are some signs that the intensity of this polarization may be waning somewhat in the wake of the last authoritarian regime: collaboration in the *Multipartidaria* formed in 1981 to contest the regime's economic policy and to fortify the impulse toward regime transition, the emergence of the Radical party as a viable electoral alternative, and the struggle over the nature of Peronism post-Perón are all elements that may modify Argentina's tendency toward veto politics. Nonetheless, the historical weight of the Peronist identity continues to frustrate attempts to create new political organizations on the left with meaningful popular bases.

In all three of these cases, preexisting political identities and parties survived military rule, albeit with some changes in the relations among them; in all three, political parties played an active role in negotiating the rules of the transition. The effective abolition of partisan political activity during most periods of Chilean, Argentine, and Uruguayan military regimes had the unintended consequence of freezing party identities. The reconstitution of party organizations and the first elections in these countries had a much clearer "foundational" significance than did elections in Brazil, representing a transfer of power to civilians. The speed of the transition processes, the fact that their stakes were better defined (even though the possibility of reversal remained present), and the survival of preexisting parties meant that discussions among opposition politicians and between these and the military were carried on between fairly well defined organizational actors and focused concretely on the specific institutional arrangements of the transition. In Brazil, the lengthy and relatively unbounded transition and the lack of formal negotiations among institutional actors over its rules produced a very different kind of movement toward democracy—one where the transition itself became a specific political moment, framing a struggle both over the nature and limits of the process itself and over the identities of the actors engaged in the process. The singularity of the Workers' party derives in part from its attempt, within the transition process, to create a political identity that broke both with the pattern of relations characterizing the authoritarian period and with historical traditions. In the other Southern Cone countries, this organizational space was historically occupied by parties that predated the military regime and retained a substantial legitimacy among their constituencies. In Brazil, the problem was not only to occupy that space but also to create it.

OPPOSITION TO

AUTHORITARIANISM

AND THE DEBATE

ABOUT DEMOCRACY

3

Regime transitions of the kind that Brazil has undergone are rare and special historical moments. They are privileged moments for social scientists precisely because, however briefly, the interaction between human agency and structural determinations is rendered visible, and accepted beliefs about limits to what is and is not possible are open to unexpected challenges. They are, therefore, eminently *political* moments. Political struggle is not only a struggle for power within a well-defined arena and according to well-defined rules but also a struggle over the shape of the arena and the nature of the rules themselves. While given actors may possess any number of historical predispositions to accept or reject rules written by others, in a transition they must ratify these predispositions by *choosing,* in a public way, to do so or not.

Transitions are highly interactive moments. The bargaining context is defined, and issues are placed on the agenda concurrently or sequentially, as a result of the relations among the actors involved and the historical experience that informs their evaluation of the situation. Literature on transitions from authoritarian rule has distinguished between a process of liberalization and one of democratization; O'Donnell and Schmitter called the former a process of redefining and extending rights, and the latter an increasing application of the rules and procedures of citizenship. These in turn involve two crucial relationships: the one between the regime incumbents and the groups deemed capable of guaranteeing the least disruptive transfer of power (for liberalization), and the other among groups and individuals within the opposition to the authoritarian regime. The latter is especially important for thinking about democratization.

In this chapter I will be primarily concerned with the second relationship; obviously they are interconnected, as intraopposition relations evolve within the context established by the liberalization process. The state tries to promote some groups and exclude others. Important opposition actors have their own strategies, which can include the empowerment of new political actors or their marginalization, or both at different times in the process. Strategies of state and societal actors change in response to the actions of the other.[1] The way in which this took place in Brazil set the scene both for the emergence of the Workers' party and for the way in which it related to other political and social forces during the transition.

During the liberalization period in Brazil, members of the elite opposition, intellectuals, the press, and the Catholic church encouraged the emergence of a variety of social movements demanding both improvements in their material conditions and (at least by implication, it was claimed) the right to participate in decision making that affected their lives. While urban social movement organizations had existed for decades, in the 1970s they were interpreted as part of a broadly based societal movement for democratization.[2]

The labor movement, which began to undergo major changes in this period as well, was a different kind of phenomenon, with a powerful institutional base of its own. The existence of corporatist structures linking labor to the state meant that changes in labor practices had to take place in an environment where the state was constantly present— for labor, civil society was not a sphere of freedom but rather one which was thoroughly penetrated by hierarchies of state domination in organizational life and capitalist power in the workplace. "Autonomy" for the new union movement was thus not an abstract concept; it had a clear and concrete meaning. This colored its relationship with other groups in the opposition to the regime; the new labor leaders were not out to exchange one form of tutelage for another.

During the late 1970s, opposition intellectuals, political elites, and the press, through their discourse and the events they chose to highlight, wove together a powerful image of opposition consensus on the need for democratization. *A Oposição,* "The Opposition," writ large, included dissident political and economic elites, the Catholic church, social movements, students, and eventually labor; its image was thus the image of a whole society, of society against the state. Differences among these groups were minimized in the name of opposition unity.

While labor leaders participated in this convergence, they never spoke of "the Opposition" with the same reverence as some of the others who participated in this process. After the creation of the Workers' party, some PMDB intellectuals claimed that Lula—Luís Inácio da Silva—was "created" by the press in 1977, that without the publicity given him by opposition leaders and journalists he would have remained an obscure young trade unionist in São Bernardo. Clearly the press helped to make Lula a national figure before he otherwise might have been. But the key to understanding his adoption by the press lies in the interactive process of opposition building.

The rise of the "new unionism" fit with the needs of the political opposition; more than an agglomeration of small and relatively isolated social movement groups, the new unionism signaled the existence of massive, organized popular discontent with the regime, and it constituted powerful evidence that democratization was necessary to resolve the potential for social conflict. There was a convergence between the opposition elites' need for mass momentum and the new labor leaders' need for recognition; they helped each other. Nonetheless, the strength of these labor leaders was not due only to elite recognition but also to their own increasingly solid organizational base, superimposed, paradoxically, on the official union structure that had served so long to suppress them. Their ability to remain in office depended primarily on their ability to retain the loyalty of their memberships. Political action was in large part a means to enlarging the negotiating space for the unions themselves, rather than an end in itself.

In the discussions about democracy that took place at different levels throughout the 1970s, it was increasingly clear that for the majority of political actors, liberal institutions were the point of arrival for a democratic transition; for others they were the point of departure.[3] Beginning with the establishment of minimal institutional rules, new pacts and democratizing processes could be expected to emerge.

Not only the form of the process was at issue, but its content as well. The debate for the progressive opposition—for emerging grass-roots and trade union movements, and for the left—had much more to do with the way in which these two elements of a democratization process, form and content, combined than with the importance and legitimacy of the social demands being raised. This debate, together with growing awareness on the part of segments of the labor and other popular movements of the need to build political institutions with which they could identify, is the background for the creation of the Workers' party. This chapter and the next will trace that debate and some of the actors who participated in it, as the debate about democracy and redemocratization in general came to focus increasingly on the nature of the political parties that would succeed the two-party system created in 1965.

Knitting Together the Strands of Civil Society

President Geisel's decision to promote a gradual liberalization of the authoritarian regime gave opposition activity new legitimacy and vigor, and social and political actors began to look beyond the immediate problems they faced and consider possibilities for the future. During the second half of the 1970s a wide variety of movements arose, some around local demands and others around national political questions. At the same time, the official opposition party, the MDB, began to use the electoral system in a plebiscitary fashion, converting each election from 1974 on into a vote for or against the military regime.

The MDB gains in the 1974 legislative and the 1976 municipal elections convinced the military regime that the existing electoral framework would have to be changed if the liberalization process was to be kept under control. The ban established in 1976 on live radio and television appearances (Article 250 of the Electoral Code as modified by law no. 6339/76, article 1, known as the Lei Falcão),[4] failed to undermine the MDB's appeal, leading regime strategists to the conclusion that the two-party system established in 1965 no longer served its purpose. Building liberalized institutions for a limited democracy required the formation of a broad conservative bloc and the end to the plebiscitary electoral environment.[5] This meant that Geisel had to put an end to the excesses of the military right and win the confidence of MDB liberals. The president finally gained control of the army in the wake of the deaths under torture of journalist Vladimir Herzog and metalworker Manoel Fiel Filho (October 1975 and January 1976, respectively).[6] Winning allies in the opposition proved a more difficult task, even among elites who had profited during the military regime.

Increasing business opposition to government economic policy, especially what business regarded as excessive privileges granted to state enterprises, produced a full-fledged debate on statism beginning in

1974. By 1976 business opposition took on a political cast[7] and through such initiatives as the Gazeta Mercantil Forum began to transform the economic critique of state policy to a political critique of state institutionality.[8] Representatives of the business community thus joined other elite sectors of civil society—the Brazilian Bar Association, for example[9]—in calling for an end to arbitrary rule. Although business's identification with the opposition tended to diminish as working class mobilization increased, in the mid-1970s it was a powerful sign of the breakdown of the regime's base of support and helped to encourage other groups within civil society to speak out.[10]

In 1973, on the eve of Geisel's election to the presidency, Fernando Henrique Cardoso wrote about the need to strengthen the institutions of civil society. It was a strange time to be writing on such a subject: the Médici presidency then drawing to a close had ruled over one of the blackest periods of repression that Brazil had ever seen. One of its objects was precisely to destroy any semblance of autonomous institutions in civil society, leaving instead a widespread depoliticization based on fear. "But even so," wrote Cardoso, "insofar as is possible, important sectors of the Churches—which have begun to behave like a sort of party of the people of God—fall outside of this dark picture of depoliticization, together with parts of the universities, liberal professions (judges, lawyers, journalists, and even some technocrats), and labor militants."[11] The survival of some political initiative on the part of these sectors, Cardoso argued, showed that the potential for democratization from below was greater than many believed:

> Even if the progress of a process like this be relatively slow, it will certainly take even longer if we don't begin now. Not to "ask for" democracy, in the sense of reopening the game of parties controlled by the State and by the dominant classes, but to create a climate of freedom and respect that will allow the reactivation of civil society, making it possible for the professional associations, the trade unions, the churches, the student organizations, the study groups and debaters' circles, the social movements, in other words, to make public their problems, propose solutions, and engage in conflicts that are constructive for the country. In this context, we must not forget that within the State apparatus as well we will have to legitimate constructive disagreements and eliminate the tendencies favorable to pseudo-consensual uniformity. . . . *In brief, it is necessary to knit together the strands of civil society* in such a way that it can express itself in the

political order, and can counterbalance the State, becoming part of the political reality of the Nation.[12] (Emphasis added)

The process that Cardoso foresaw with such prescience in 1973 progressed a remarkable distance over the next half decade. Civil society in Brazil was reactivated and strengthened to an appreciable extent. By the late 1970s, the political debate about the construction of democratic institutions, particularly political parties, reflected a new concern with the need to incorporate popular sectors into politics.

This process took place in a peculiar way, which was to have an important impact on the whole transition process. Rather than developing formal linkages among oppositional forces whose natures and goals were recognizably diverse, the strands of civil society were knit together into a powerful *image* of a united opposition—an image in which each new form of protest contributed to a giant tapestry whose essential message was the demand for change. The lack of institutionalized links among social and political forces, if it was perceived at all by the actors involved, was not considered particularly important; what was important was the growing consensus of society against the authoritarian state.

THE ROLE OF INTELLECTUALS. Intellectuals played a special role in the antiauthoritarian opposition. In São Paulo, for example, based in research institutes like Centro Brasileiro de Análise e Planejamento (CEBRAP) and later Centro de Estudos de Cultura Contemporânia (CEDEC) and Instituto de Estudos Sociais e Políticos (IDESP), intellectuals shouldered the role of curators of political debate in Brazil, in spite of the fact that there was virtually no public space in which such debate could take place. Bit by bit, these intellectuals attempted to reconstruct the verbal and written discourse of society about itself and to mold together the forces opposed to the military regime, sometimes at risk to themselves.[13] They paid particular attention to discussing and preserving the histories of excluded groups—labor and community movements, for example.[14]

Preserving history and a space for debate was particularly important where censorship had for years compressed the boundaries of available information. Opposition newspapers that tried to confront the regime frontally generally folded as a result of the censor's harassment. Nonetheless, new ones continued to spring up in their places, and journalists showed extraordinary creativity and resiliency in attempting to outwit the censors. Censorship was not limited to explicitly oppositional papers like *Opinião* and *Movimento* but extended as well to humor magazines like *Pasquim* and to the mainstream press as well. Censorship on the archdiocesan newspaper *O São Paulo* was not lifted until mid-1978.[15]

THE REVIVAL OF THE STUDENT MOVEMENT. The revival of the student movement in the second half of the 1970s had an important impact because of its visibility. But in spite of a growing wave of protest from students from 1975 on, students were slow to reconstitute the organizations that had been destroyed in 1968—particularly the National Union of Students (UNE), which had functioned precariously underground after the police broke up its 1968 conference at Ibiúna. Military repression and the prohibition on autonomous student organization from the late 1960s on had left students with few avenues for legal political action. Many abandoned the universities to participate in what they romantically saw as an armed struggle for national liberation, while others focused on cultural activities.[16] By the mid-1970s, although leftist groups remained important on campuses, the target of student radicalism had shifted from the bourgeoisie to the dictatorship. The impact of the disastrous defeat of the guerrilla groups, together with a significant expansion of the university student population in the decade following the mid-1960s,[17] brought student sentiment more in line with the mainstream opposition.

In spite of these changes, the military still saw the resurgence of student activism in 1975 as the revival of a dangerous clandestine movement. Efforts to reconstitute student organizations and the first major student strike at the School of Arts and Communications in São Paulo were crushed. In 1976 students managed to hold a national meeting but decided not to revive UNE because of continuing repression. The following year, tensions exploded: violent police repression of a march of 10,000 students, which resulted in major damage to São Paulo's Catholic University, became a cause célèbre. At the University of Brasília, police dragged students who were accused of leading demonstrations out of their classes. An attempt to hold a national student congress in Belo Horizonte led to a major military operation involving roadblocks of all the routes into Belo Horizonte and the arrest of 850 students.[18]

The hysteria of military and police reaction calmed somewhat after the 1977 incidents, although legislation prohibiting any but the government-authorized student organizations remained on the books.

Nonetheless, the troops were withdrawn from the campuses. In 1978 the first State Student Union (União Estadual de Estudantes, UEE) in ten years was formed in São Paulo, and in May 1979 a congress was held in Salvador to a new National Student Union (UNE). In a pattern that was to be typical of the Brazilian opening process, the students had won back their public space, but their right to it was still not legally recognized.

THE CHURCH AND POPULAR MOVEMENTS. It is impossible to overstate the importance of the Catholic church's role in providing space for interaction and organization, a communications network, and human rights advocacy during the most difficult years of the authoritarian period. This is not the place to discuss the theological and historical roots of the Church position in Brazil.[19] The adoption of the defense of human rights and the preferential option for the poor as principles for the *whole* Brazilian Church (obviously with variations in their practical application) meant that the Church qua institution could confront the State. This is not to suggest that the National Conference of Brazilian Bishops declared a holy war against the authoritarian regime. Nonetheless, it took institutional positions against torture, repression, and social and economic oppression that were often stronger than those of its counterparts elsewhere in Latin America.

The Church provided an organizational umbrella for countless organizing initiatives, the best known of which were the *Comunidades Eclesiais de Base* (CEBs), launched in dioceses all over Brazil in the late 1960s, particularly after the 1968 Latin American Bishops' Conference in Medellín, Colombia. Through a reexamination of Christian teachings, many communities, particularly in poor areas, developed a social critique based on immediate experience.[20] There has been enormous variation in the activities of the CEBs, depending in part on the orientation of the priest or religious who advises and may or may not participate in meetings with CEB members and in part on the social context within which they function.[21]

Many CEB members became active in other social movements as well, especially neighborhood movements and the labor movement.[22] The labor pastoral in São Paulo, for example, was composed of union activists who were also CEB members and who headed opposition slates in the São Paulo metalworkers' union elections from 1976 on.[23] Labor and social movement activists in the CEBs collaborated to organize Church support for the metalworkers' strikes in 1978–80. There was a great deal of overlap in personnel among all of these organizations; Church links were a key component of the social movement networks that developed during the 1970s.

While organizations linked to the Catholic church primarily worked at the local level, there were instances of CEBs initiating or participating in broader regional or national movements. One of the best-known movements in the 1970s that grew out of CEB activities was the Cost of Living Movement, which began in 1973 with a struggle against price hikes. By 1977 the cost of living movement had support in more than one hundred neighborhoods in Greater São Paulo; it included Mothers' Clubs, the National Labor Front (Frente Nacional de Trabalho), student leaders from São Paulo universities, regional MDB organizations, the Association of Doctors of Preventive Medicine, the Workers' Pastoral, and the Women's Movement for Amnesty, and others. In March 1977 an assembly with seven hundred CEB delegates elected a coordinating body, and with support from the archdiocese of São Paulo, set out to gather 1,000,000 signatures—a seemingly impossible task. By August 1978 the document had 1,300,000 signatures. When a large rally was held to mark the completion of the petition in São Paulo's Praça da Sé (Cathedral Square), police charged with horses and tear gas, and they were barely prevented from entering the cathedral itself. The following month, a commission presented the petition to Geisel in Brasília. The only government response was an announcement soon after charging that the document contained many false signatures.[24]

The Church thus served simultaneously as arena, promoter, and protector for contestatory movements. Particularly in the urban peripheries, there was no other space in which to participate and develop grass-roots leadership. Where encouragement of lay leadership and initiative was strong, as it was in the area in which the cost of living movement began, the CEBs, mothers' clubs, and church pastorals constituted a center from which flowed a cadre for a host of other grass-roots movements. Holding the movement's rally in the Cathedral Square, more than its logistical centrality, denoted a recognition of the symbolic and practical protection that the Church still offered in the face of a very real threat of repression of popular demands. Indeed, from then on that square became a traditional rallying place for movement groups (and eventually for the PT as well).

We should note, however, that the Catholic church's umbrella role as represented here consciously did not go beyond an aggregating one. There was never an intention of creating a church-based political party, for example—in fact, radical Catholic discourse was often suspicious of political parties and institutions in general. While the CEBs and other church organizations did have delegate assemblies at regional and national levels, these were not intended to centralize the activities of local groups. Rather, there was (and is) a constant emphasis on local initiative and participation, with a prevalent idea that higher-level organizations precluded active participation at the base and permitted the manipulation of popular demands by those whose interests were elsewhere.[25] Grass-roots Catholic organizing promoted an ethos whose key values were autonomy (from state and party) and self-organization, and whose prototypical image was the *caminhada*, or long march of the people of God toward a just society, or the kingdom of heaven. The significance lay in the process itself more than its ends. The resulting ambivalence about the relationship between grass-roots organizing and political action at higher levels has remained characteristic of grass-roots Catholic activists, who carried a belief in the centrality of local initiative with them into the Workers' party.

THE LABOR MOVEMENT. Catholic activists also focused on rank and file organizing in unions whose leaders were considered *pelegos*.[26] In the São Paulo metropolitan area, for example, from the mid-1970s on Catholic labor pastoral promoted opposition movements in the São Paulo metalworkers' union, in Osasco, and to a lesser extent in the ABCD region.[27] They also did shop floor organizing with the goal of establishing factory commissions. As plantwide elections could not be held under existing legislation, these commissions often represented no more than a core group of activist workers, leading other sectors of the labor movement to accuse Catholic union activists of paying more attention to creating parallel structures than winning control of union organizations.[28]

The labor movement was one of the last movements mentioned in Cardoso's 1973 article to emerge into the public sphere. A number of reasons are given for this: the inhibiting effect of corporatist labor legislation; the cautionary effect of severe repression of the last major strikes in 1968; the rapid expansion of the urban working class with emigrants from rural areas, who judged poverty and exploitation in relation to their place of origin and not in relation to urban conditions in general; the growth of the job market in the major metropolitan areas in the late 1960s and early 1970s. Prior to 1978, it was assumed that these factors made it extremely unlikely for a militant labor movement to arise any time soon; lack of leadership with the will to confront the system, weak organization, and relative satisfaction, at least in the advanced industries, would maintain quiescence.[29]

The relative satisfaction hypothesis, however, was dealt a severe blow by the evidence gathered by John Humphrey in his in-plant study of auto workers in the São Bernardo area in the mid-1970s. Humphrey demonstrated that in the advanced industrial sectors, job dissatisfaction was high due to speedup and precarious job security; financial pressure on plant managers from the parent companies forced them to maintain an extraordinarily high rate of turnover in order to keep a low wage floor.[30] While protest did not take an institutional form during this period, it did occur with some regularity in slowdowns, sabotage, and even occasionally with a strike at the level of a single plant. These actions received little publicity, however, and did not necessarily signify ongoing organization.[31]

While there was ample evidence of working-class dissatisfaction in the early and mid-1970s, labor activism differed in fundamental ways from other forms of social movement activism. It took place in a context that was already highly institutionalized, and the form of its institutionalization was regulated by law. Grass-roots labor organizing could either challenge existing union leadership for control of the union or remain at the level of plant discussion groups. It could not, however, create a parallel organization that could compete for legitimacy with the union. A resurgence of the labor movement depended not only on organization at the base but also penetration of or response from the union apparatus that, like it or not, remained the voice of the labor movement. Thus, until the wage recovery campaign in 1977 and the 1978 strikes, discussed in the next chapter, changes in the labor movement were expected to occur very slowly, through consciousness raising from within, in the hope of building a democratic workers' movement that would come to reject the corporatist structures binding it to the state.

Thus, when Luís Inácio da Silva (henceforth Lula) and the São Bernardo Metalworkers' Union, of which he was the president, assumed a leadership position in the new union movement, many observers both within and outside of the labor movement were suspicious. Because they thought that "legitimate" trade union renewal would come from below, from the *oposições sindicais* (union oppositions), they did not expect a leader who already occupied the presidency of his union to encourage rank and file participation and democratization or to press for union autonomy. Lula, on the other hand, believed that the most important task of labor activists was to win institutional control over unions, claiming that the "base organizations" in plants had little representativeness and made no sense in an authoritarian situation. Any recognized shop floor leader ran a serious risk of being fired from his or her job, and attempting to create clandestine organization undermined a call for greater participation and union democracy.[32]

The rebirth of the labor movement therefore surprised most observers—both because it happened when it did and because it happened dramatically enough to gain ascendancy quickly in the social process and claim a leadership role in the broad tissue of movements then appearing. This process will be discussed in more detail in the next chapter. It is important to remember, however, that the leaders of the new labor movement rested their claim to legitimacy on their positions as elected leaders of their unions; it was an institutional claim more than an ideological one.

Civil Society and Political Institutions

This has been a brief and impressionistic introduction to some of the social actors who emerged in the breathing space produced by Geisel's "relaxation." With the exception of linkages among different types of organizations through Catholic activists, there were few organizational connections.[33] Labor leaders established personal networks with other like-minded labor leaders; a number of organizations became involved in issue-oriented movements like the cost of living movement. Attempts to create formal rather than informal networks were rare and often short-lived. In general, articulation among different sectors of the opposition to the regime took place through personal contact among leaders on specific issues. Organization was generally local, and in the rare cases where horizontal connections were built, as in the cost of living movement, a lack of intermediate goals, which would have enriched the day-to-day character of the movement, tended to encourage a situation where the movement itself became the goal; it was thus by nature self-limiting in duration. When the cost of living movement's goal was met, its constituency drifted away in the face of military repression and the regime's refusal to recognize the legitimacy of the movement.

There is nothing unusual about this. The kinds of popular movements and organizations I have been discussing had little in common among themselves except for a general orientation toward establishing the material conditions for a more dignified life, and they had even less in common with elite opposition groups. What, then, of Cardoso's desire to see "knit together the strands of civil society"? To what extent did the emerging grass-roots organizations come together with the elite opposition groups—dissident businessmen, the Brazilian Press Association, the Brazilian Bar Association, and the like?

Two examples will serve to demonstrate the rather contingent and contradictory relationship between elite and popular opposition. The first was a single-issue movement organized around the question of amnesty. The second was the behavior of the opposition political party, the MDB, in the 1978 elections. In both cases members of the elite opposition tried to appeal to popular opposition to the regime as manifested in the labor movement and other social movements. While both were somewhat successful in doing so, the mechanism used for broadening their base was the co-optation of popular leaders into participation in or support for the party or the amnesty movement. It did not involve either the creation of an organized popular base for the organization or the development of ongoing institutional ties among organizations.

THE AMNESTY CAMPAIGN. The campaign for amnesty began in 1975 with the formation of the Women's Movement for Amnesty, which collected 16,000 signatures on an amnesty manifesto. The movement had a built-in army of activists, in the families of exiles or those who had lost congressional mandates or been purged from their jobs after the military came to power. By the end of June 1977, an estimated 4,682 people had been removed from jobs or lost political mandates (including 300 professors, 500 politicians, 50 ex-governors and -mayors, as well as diplomats, union leaders, and public servants); about 10,000 Brazilians were exiled during some period of the military regime.[34]

In February 1978 the movement was broadened with the creation of the Brazilian Committee for Amnesty (Comité Brasileiro pela Anistia, CBA). Even the Bar Association (OAB), which had been afraid to address the question at first, joined the committee. The CBA's organization coincided with revelations about the death under torture of journalist Vladimir Herzog and with hunger strikes by political prisoners. In October 1978, in a path-breaking decision, a federal court judge in São Paulo ruled that Herzog was illegally imprisoned and tortured in the army secret police (DOI-CODI) headquarters in São Paulo and that the government was responsible. By the end of 1978, in spite of some internal divisions, the amnesty campaign had become the main opposition campaign.

It was, however, a campaign whose immediate meaning was most important for the elite opposition, as the great majority of those who had had mandates revoked or who had gone into exile were from elite families. Pressed in an interview with *Pasquim* about the degree of his support for political amnesty, Lula put the matter in a broader perspective:

> I am in favor of it, but let me make my position clear: I am for the amnesty of the working class, which is who really merits pardon. Not pardon, it merits freedom. I am against any citizen being made a prisoner for demonstrating his political ideology, but I also think that the working class is an eternal prisoner. Instead of asking for amnesty for a few I prefer to ask for it for the whole working class, you see. A man who gets up at 4:30 in the morning and sleeps at 10:00 at night to earn Cr$3000 is an eternal prisoner. . . . Resolving only the problem of those who lost their mandates, the workers will stay in the same place, f . . . and badly paid. As they always were. Those who lost their mandates at least were free once.[35]

The sentiments Lula expressed in the *Pasquim* interview reflected an important division between elite opposition to the regime and labor and grass-roots movements. Lula and other social movement leaders supported amnesty; they attended demonstrations and spoke in favor of amnesty. But they wanted to see its focus broadened, arguing that the amnesty movement paid too much attention to the return of exiles and the restoration of rights that workers had never enjoyed, and not enough to social issues. The potential for tension between those stressing political rights and those stressing socioeconomic issues was already evident in the amnesty campaign, and it would only increase as the democratization process continued.

BROADENING THE MDB. The reconstitution of opposition sentiment at both elite and popular levels took place initially outside of the "official" opposition party, which had reached such a low point under Médici that some of its members favored dissolution. But with the beginning of Geisel's liberalization and his relaxation of some of the campaigning restrictions for the 1974 legislative elections, the lack of any other aggregating institution led to a renewal of the party. At first this was exemplified in the steep rise in the MDB vote in the 1974 elections more than by increased party cadre; up to 1974 there were more vacancies than candidates to fill them.[36]

In fielding candidates for the 1978 elections, the MDB sought out people who were not necessarily party members but who had a large popular following and thus vote-getting potential—students, trade unionists, journalists, and other popular leaders. The party also decided to run Fernando Henrique Cardoso, one of the best-known opposition intellectuals, as a second candidate for senator in São Paulo under the sublegenda option.[37] Cardoso's decision to run was motivated by a desire to see the MDB take stronger positions on social questions and promote greater popular participation.[38]

The nomination of grass-roots MDB candidates, many of whom were elected, represented a potential for a stronger relation between the party and social movements than had existed before. Nonetheless, these grass-roots vote-getters had no control over the party machine, and many of the social movements from which these candidates came still viewed the MDB as part of the authoritarian order. In their eyes, parties showed up at election time and made promises, then disappeared; party organizations generally dissolved between elections, without absorbing those they had mobilized.

Cardoso's senatorial campaign attempted to draw upon the resources and participation of groups that the MDB had not hitherto reached, including artists and singers, political leaders purged from office by the military, students and intellectuals, and unions. He chose Maurício Soares de Almeida, a lawyer for the São Bernardo Metalworkers, as his alternate, an important choice from the point of view of the labor movement. He brought combative union leaders into discussions of campaign strategy. Lula publicly called him a "moral resource," and the metalworkers' union in São Bernardo went to the factory gates to campaign for Cardoso. He also attempted to link his campaign to that of other popular candidates with ties to the Catholic church, students, and so on.[39]

The MDB was not transformed into a popular, mass organization, nor did its apparatus maintain a permanent relationship with social movement organizations, yet it was important that some representatives were elected who bridged the space between the two. At the very least, they increased the visibility of grass-roots organizations and campaigns, and gave them more access to public space.[40]

"The Opposition," therefore, was an idea rather than an organization. It was a powerful image of societal convergence, but it was not dependent on any particular form. It was an image of consensus, super-imposed on a society characterized by tremendous social stratification and a multiplicity of visions of the future. Because it attracted the votes of these diverse constituencies, the MDB was perhaps the only inclusive organization; it did so, however, as part of a bipolar system whose days were numbered. In addition, for many Brazilians, it remained suspect because of its origins as the military regime's official opposition party. Voting was compulsory and there were only two effective choices—yes or no, ARENA or MDB, regime or opposition. In thinking about the future, yes or no was not enough.

The Debate about New Political Parties

In 1978, anticipation of a reform in the political party law stimulated a widespread debate among opposition intellectuals about what kinds of new political parties would best contribute to extending and deepening democratization in Brazil. Among the participants in this debate were intellectuals who would eventually help to found the Workers' party. One of those most active in promoting this discussion was Almino Afonso, a former Brazilian Labor party (PTB) congressman and labor minister under João Goulart's presidency. Afonso had spent twelve years in exile under the military regime, returning to Brazil in 1976. He called for a popular, national, and democratic party, with a view of socialism "on the horizon." Such a party would have a truly democratic and participatory structure that would impede the re-emergence of populism. Instead of being manipulated by political leaders who represented other classes, the people and the working class would be inside the party, participating in its leadership and its decisions.[41] In 1978, the first stage of reform of legislation on political parties forced members of the socialist and the nonsocialist left to seek out points of possible unity. In addition to Afonso's proposal for a popular party, options discussed were a revival of the PTB, a popular front, the eventual formation of a workers' party, and the maintenance of the MDB as an alternative that continued to be viable. The debate over what kinds of new parties should be considered included the questions of (1) the regime's intentions in changing the party system and the opportunities available within current or imminent legal structures; and (2) the social and political priorities for a new party or parties.

There were certainly strong reasons for fearing that the regime and traditional elites would tightly control the reform process. The 1977 April package was explicitly designed to slow the seemingly irrevocable advance of the MDB.[42] The "Portella Dialogue," a series of conversations which former justice minister and president of the Senate Petrônio Portella held with opposition leaders (including MDB politicians, leaders of the OAB, the Catholic church, and labor unions), led the government to the conclusion that dividing the opposition was a real possibility.[43]

The long-awaited Reform Package was issued in October 1978 as Constitutional Amendment no. 11, to take effect on January 1, 1979. The package restored a number of political and civil rights, including habeas corpus, and revoked all Institutional and Complementary Acts.[44] However, a number of arbitrary measures remained in effect: the president's right to issue decree laws on financial questions and restrictions on congressional prerogatives on budgetary issues; Decree Law 477, which prohibited political activity in the universities; the antistrike law; and the "ineligibilities" law, which restricted civil liberties, for example, preventing someone whose mandate had been revoked from running for union or political office. In addition, the president retained broad safeguard powers to resort to arbitrary rule by declaring a state of emergency. The other "safeguard" had been passed in August 1978, when the National Security Law was broadened to include under its list of crimes against the nation all strikes by public employees, including banks.[45]

Article 152 of the Reform Package, which dealt with the formation of new political parties, was ambiguous. Geisel was reluctant to dismantle the 1965 party system all at once; instead of taking a definitive step he merely relaxed the rules a bit. According to Article 152, a new party could be provisionally formed by 10 percent of the representatives from each house of Congress. New parties would exist definitively if they won 5 percent of the vote for Congress distributed among at least nine states, with 3 percent of the vote in each of these. It was expected that ARENA would remain as it was and that the MDB would break up into several parties. It was clear, however, from the stipulation that parties be formed by members of Congress, that the intention was to have new parties formed from the top down.

Some participants in the debate believed that fundamentally new forms of political organization were both necessary and possible. Social scientist José Alvaro Moisés, for example, argued that without new kinds of parties capable of political intermediation, the basis of authority could only be coercive. Although the opposition had grown impressively with MDB electoral gains from 1974 on, it still defined itself

primarily by its negation of the military regime or in reference to
abstractions like constituent assembly, democratic liberties, or union
freedom. The MDB lacked a project that had resonance in people's
daily life and experience. Instead of just saying "union freedom,"
Moisés said, it was important to discuss "the roads by which workers
can constitute themselves as political agents, such that this becomes a
guarantee of the democracy we are advocating."[46] For Moisés, this
required an internally democratic, decentralized, popular socialist program capable of seeing the building of socialism as a pedagogy, or a war
of position, and not as a simple assault on power.

Sociologist Francisco Weffort argued that the lack of parties clearly
rooted in society made it hard to clarify differing interpretations of the
relationship between institutional demands (for democracy) and social
and economic demands. Weffort argued for a pluralist view of the
relationship between party and social class, recognizing that more than
one party could exist with reference to a particular social constituency
and that parties exist in relation not only to the state but also to other
forms of expression of social class. These relationships could only be
worked out in practice by the parties that were formed—they could not
be resolved a priori.[47]

Moisés and Weffort supported the creation of a democratic, popular,
and socialist party, and eventually they became founding members of
the PT. Other sectors of the left argued for an explicitly socialist party,
beginning with the organization of a socialist tendency within the
MDB. In the debate on new parties published in *Contraponto,* Júlio
Tavares of Convergência Socialista asserted that although workers
would be the ones to bring about change, more political space had to be
won before a real mass socialist party could be constituted. The Tendência Socialista of the Rio Grande do Sul MDB expected a coalition of
workers, students, and intellectuals to move toward building an independent workers' party. Other left organizations, however, including
the Communist and Maoist parties, considered discussion of a socialist
or workers' party premature and stressed the need to maintain a broad
antiauthoritarian front.[48]

Other participants in the debate were more sanguine about the possibility of using existing political organizations. At the end of 1978,
influenced by the experience of his senatorial campaign, Fernando
Henrique Cardoso began to argue that the MDB *was* that popular party
they had been discussing. However amorphous it might be at the moment, it already had the support of the popular sectors and was a group

around which future parties could organize. To remain outside the
MDB, he claimed, was to facilitate things for the "Party of Order."
Cardoso objected to the idea of a workers' party on the grounds that its
proponents either reduced social relations to workplace relations (ignoring the history of class relations in Brazil, where the working class
and the mass-consumer market were formed essentially at the same
time) or believed that true popular action was possible only "outside
politics," in grass-roots community organizations. Such views, he believed, were a recipe for political marginality.[49] Soon after Cardoso
made his choice, Afonso entered the MDB as well, intending to win
support from members of the *tendência popular* for his proposal.

Another important element in the discussion of new parties was
Leonel Brizola's return from exile in 1979. Brizola had been a close
associate of President Goulart's, a leader of the left of the PTB before
the 1964 coup, a popular governor of Rio Grande do Sul, and a federal
deputy from Rio de Janeiro. During the mid-1970s, he worked among
Brazilians in exile to organize a cadre for a new PTB. Supported by the
German Social Democrats, Brizola and others interested in reestablish-
ing the PTB insisted that "laborism" (*trabalhismo*) had an identity independent from the populism with which the party had long been identified and combined nationalist ideology with an emphasis on social
justice.[50] Claiming that the working class was too poorly organized to
exercise sufficient initiative, Brizola sought to build a multiclass, progressive, nationalist alliance. Expecting the MDB to disintegrate in the
aftermath of the party reform, Brizola thought that the historical
weight of the PTB name would help attract its progressive sectors.

The one thing on which the participants in the debate over appropriate forms of organization agreed was that workers and other popular
sectors, particularly social movement activists, had to be incorporated
as participants in a political party or parties. Although those engaged in
the debate characterized the role and capacity of the popular classes
differently—as agents of democratization because of their special interest in the rights associated with democratic outcomes (Cardoso and, to
a certain extent, Afonso) or agents of socialist transformation (Convergência Socialista and other small left-wing groups) or participants in
large-scale mass mobilizations (Brizola and the laborites)—all attributed a central place to linking socioeconomic demands with political and institutional demands.[51]

At the time that this initial discussion was being held, it was extremely difficult to link socioeconomic with political demands; the

discussion was for the most part about the popular sectors *in the abstract.*
Social movements, though increasingly visible, were weakly organized. The 1977 Wage Recovery Campaign, discussed in the next chapter, had demonstrated that new labor leaders were finding creative
forms of struggle and were beginning to break out of the pelego tradition, but there was not yet any public evidence that they enjoyed a
significant mass following among the working class. Under those circumstances, according to Cardoso, the role of intellectuals was a "mod-
est" one of trying "to formulate in a manner acceptable to these [social
movement] groups, what is already implicit in their action."[52] The
problem, of course, lay in how to interpret what was implicit, and
whether the act of interpretation was to be carried out in isolation from,
or in a process of dialogue with, these groups. "Interpretations" would
vary, colored by differing assessments of the opportunities given the
relative power positions of the military and opposition organizations,
of the political potential of new grass-roots and labor movements, and,
finally, of the meaning and worth of alternative forms of organization.
Antonio Gramsci's formulation of the role of the organic intellectual, to
which Cardoso's statement is very close, was fairly clear on this point,
that an organic relationship existed

> if the intellectuals had been organically the intellectuals of the masses,
> and if they had worked out and made coherent the principles and the
> problems raised by the masses in their practical activity, thus con-
> stituting a cultural and social bloc. The question posed here was the
> one we have already referred to, namely this: is a philosophical move-
> ment properly so called when it is devoted to creating a specialized
> culture among restricted intellectual groups, or rather when, and
> only when, in the process of elaborating a form of thought superior
> to "common sense" and coherent on a scientific plane, it never forgets
> to remain in contact with the "simple" and indeed finds in this contact
> the source of the problems it sets out to study and to resolve? Only by
> this contact does a philosophy become "historical", purify itself of
> intellectualistic elements of an individual character and become
> "life".[53]

The massive strike waves of 1978 and 1979 changed the context of
the debate. They produced new linkages among combative labor
leaders and gave the impression of a massive and mobilized working
class desirous of change. The problem that Cardoso had posed of interpreting what was implicit in the action of social groups ceased to be

only a question to be debated among intellectuals; it became instead a matter for negotiation among increasingly organized constituencies. Many working-class leaders were no longer willing to leave the act of interpretation to others—they wanted to create an organizational opportunity for workers to speak for themselves. The next chapter will discuss the growth of new militancy in the labor movement and the concretization of the project to form a workers' party.

THE NEW UNIONISM

4

AND THE FORMATION OF

THE WORKERS' PARTY

Developments in the Brazilian labor movement in the last two years of the 1970s had a fundamental impact on the debate over the formation of a popularly based party. The strikes of 1978 and 1979, sparked by the metalworkers of São Bernardo and Diadema, and the emergence of publicly recognized working-class leaders like the São Bernardo union's president Luís Inácio da Silva (Lula) brought new elements into the equation. The growth of the new union movement meant that proponents of mass-based parties could no longer refer to workers in the abstract, as components of the base of such a party, but instead had to engage in face-to-face negotiations with them. Both systemic constraints—such as expectations about the content of the party reform and a growing organizational interest in the survival of the MDB—and disagreements over the kind of party to be created contributed to the breakdown of these discussions, with some participants opting to remain with the MDB and others to form a Workers' party. This chapter examines those discussions and looks at the factors that converged to favor the creation of such a party in São Paulo: the existence of nationally known labor leadership interested in the creation of a party, a mass base that was responsive to the idea of the party, the activity of a sector of the organized left in promoting the idea, and the eventual willingness of some MDB legislators to join the effort.

The Rise of the New Unionism

Brazilian labor relations were codified under Vargas in the 1930s and early 1940s, culminating in the Consolidated Labor Laws (Consoliaçao das Leis do Trabalho, CLT) in 1943. One of the keystones of the Brazilian corporatist model, this legislation remained virtually intact up to the end of the military regime. The CLT designated unions as organs of collaboration with the government for the promotion of social peace. State-recognized unions were to have a monopoly of representation in each occupational category. The labor ministry had broad powers to intervene in internal affairs, including the right to replace elected union leaders with government functionaries. Unions were financed through a union tax (*contribuição sindical*), representing one day's pay per year deducted from each worker's paycheck whether or not the worker was a union member and distributed according to criteria determined by the government. Union members paid dues over and above the tax. A system of labor courts was to oversee contracts, with compulsory arbitration in case of disputes. Strikes were only legal in rare instances and after a complex bureaucratic procedure had been followed. Labor contracts were mainly individual contracts between the individual and the employer; collective contracts negotiated directly between unions and employers, while legally allowed, were rare.[1] The law made no provision for union representation at the plant level. Federations and confederations were vertically organized by occupational category, with officers chosen in elections where each union had one vote, regardless of size. There was no provision for legal recognition of central organizations that cut across a broad range of organizational categories, but a specific article outlawing them was not added to the labor code until 1978.[2]

While the labor code gave the government powerful mechanisms with which to control unions, it also included what were at least in principle quite extensive social welfare programs. Together with other incentives for labor leaders to work within the system (such as the prospect of appointments to positions in the social welfare institutes or to labor judgeships in the labor courts), these were important co-optive elements in the labor legislation. Working-class leaders could often use these positions to produce concrete benefits for labor.

Prior to 1964, the application of the more restrictive elements of the labor code varied according to the political conjuncture. Understanding this variation requires an approach to labor relations that takes into account political resources and strategies available to labor movements, in addition to purely corporate forms of regulation.[3] At different moments, political relations between unions and the state provided possibilities for unions and their leaders to win benefits sometimes in spite of and sometimes precisely because of the stipulations of the code. With the second Vargas government, the pattern of what has been called populist unionism began, in which labor supported government policies in exchange for a relaxation of more stringent controls over unions; thus, for example, unions were able to win higher wages in major strike mobilizations in 1953 and 1957. Central labor organizations were formed to stimulate the kinds of intersectoral relations that the corporatist confederations had been designed to thwart.[4] This kind of relationship between labor and the state reached its zenith under Goulart; in the early 1960s, however, cycles of mobilization and scarce government resources led to increasing radicalization on both sides, frightening the middle class and business communities and helping to establish the psychological backdrop for the military coup in 1964.[5]

After the coup in 1964, the military government used the full powers available under existing corporatist labor legislation to tighten control over the labor movement. Between 1964 and 1970, the labor ministry carried out 536 interventions in union organizations, removing the elected leaders from office and appointing replacements; 80.6 percent of these interventions (or a total of 432) took place between 1964 and 1965, of which 383 were in unions, 45 in federations, and 4 in confederations, thus affecting 18.75 percent of the unions in Brazil, 42 percent of the federations, and 82 percent of the confederations. In São Paulo alone, 115 unions and 7 out of 18 federations underwent intervention.[6]

After purging the unions, the new regime handed over to them an increasing amount of social welfare administration, forcing the unions' officers to devote more and more time to running medical and dental programs and the like. At the same time, a wage squeeze policy and the end to job tenure guarantees by the institution of the Time in Service Guarantee Fund (FGTS) brought real hardship to workers. The wage squeeze did not end with the economic recovery and the "miracle" period beginning in 1968; it continued up through 1974.[7]

As if a wage squeeze were not enough, the trade union research organization DIEESE discovered evidence that in 1973 the government had manipulated the cost of living figures. A group of World Bank economists confirmed DIEESE's findings and claimed that in 1973 the correct figure should have been 22.5 percent, and not 14.9 percent as the government had stated.[8] Summaries of large sections of the report were published in *Folha de São Paulo* on July 31, 1977. The Getúlio Vargas Foundation, responsible for calculating such figures, published the same month a "revision in its accounts" for 1973, with the inflation figure it had reported rising from 15.5 to 20.5 percent.[9] Upon learning this, the São Bernardo Metalworkers' Union asked DIEESE for a study of how much more the metalworkers' wages would have increased had the figures not been manipulated. DIEESE returned the figure 34.1 percent.

THE WAGE RECOVERY CAMPAIGN. With the results of the DIEESE study, the São Bernardo Metalworkers, together with other metalworkers' unions from the region (Santo André, Mauá, Ribeirão Pires, and Rio Grande da Serra) launched a campaign for the recovery of the 34.1 percent. Although neither the government nor the labor courts were willing to concede the issue, the wage recovery campaign was nonetheless an important step forward. First, it showed workers that unions could be more than dispensers of social services and pulled together under the demand for wage recovery a number of localized struggles occurring in particular plants. Prior to the wage recovery campaign, union demands tended to be made at the juridical level, requiring good relations with union lawyers more than mobilization and organization of workers in the plants. As a result of the campaign, union leaders came to appreciate the importance of organizing in the factory, and workers in the factories began to see the unions as organizations that supported their demands, as the main instruments they had for making those demands felt.[10]

The São Bernardo union's message during the wage recovery campaign was "get tough." It was time to realize that the state would not resolve workers' problems. The next year, the São Bernardo union decided to boycott the annual wage negotiations in order to show that the results were the same whether they went or not: the annual meeting was a nonevent, where the government handed down that year's wage increase, refused to consider other kinds of demands, and adjourned the meeting. As predicted, São Bernardo received exactly the same wage increase as the others, without having attended the negotiations. The message was that in order to get higher wages, more direct means would have to be used.

THE 1978–79 STRIKES. The union did not officially initiate the strike that began when the workers of Scânia sat down in front of their machines on May 12, 1978, but it responded quickly. Initiated and organized within the plant, the strike began with the 7:00 A.M. shift, and Gilson Menezes, a member of the union leadership working in the plant, called the union at 8:00. Both he and the delegate from General

Motors in Santo André, interviewed later, stressed that it was important that the union not be involved in calling the strike, but that it should do the negotiating. Gilson Menezes preferred to be the only one from the Scania strike committee talking with management, so as not to endanger the jobs of the others.

By lunchtime Devanir Ribeiro from the union was at Scânia, and the company proposed to meet with the union that afternoon. When company representatives asked him to convince the workers to go back to work, Lula refused. At an assembly the following Tuesday, the workers voted to return to work until Friday, by which time a solution was to have been found. Then Ford too went out, followed by other auto firms in the area. By Friday, tension was high, and when Scânia offered 6.5 percent, Lula asked Gilson Menezes to post the offer on the bulletin board and let the workers discuss it. They voted to stay out, but by Monday they were returning to work one by one. Negotiations by the union won an 11 percent raise.[11]

Analyzing the lessons of the strike, Lula commented on his surprise at the workers' confidence in the union and stressed the importance of unity when facing employers, who were themselves going to take a unified position. He departed from his previous refusal to talk about politics:

> I think that we can't separate economic and political factors. . . . The ABC struggle was over wages, but in struggling for wages, the working class won a political victory. Thus the first lesson of the strike is that you can't underestimate the Brazilian worker's capacity for struggle. Second, I think these fourteen years during which strikes were prohibited left not only bosses but also union leaders unprepared to face a movement. I, for example, had never been in a strike, had no experience. And finally, with all this happening, I think the worker realized how much his work is worth."[12]

In 1979, strikes broke out all over Brazil. More than three million workers went out, some in sectors where unions had the capacity to lead them and others not. Lula, Olívio Dutra from the Rio Grande do Sul bank workers, and João Paulo Pires Vasconcelos from the metalworkers in João Monlevade, Minas Gerais, became a sort of consulting squad, helping in some cases to negotiate between union leaders and their rebellious memberships. Commenting on the chaotic nature of the 1979 strikes, labor sociologist Maria Hermínia Tavares de Almeida said that they seemed inspired more by the need to bear witness to the aspirations of workers for freedom, autonomy, and the right to full citizenship than by any short-term demand.[13] By 1979, the question of workers' rights and participation was placed on the agenda of the debate about democracy, no longer abstractly, but explicitly, through the actions and demands of workers themselves.

In 1979, the São Bernardo Metalworkers were much more prepared for a strike than they had been the year before, but so, on the other hand, were the employers. Huge strike assemblies were held in the stadium of São Bernardo, and the major firms in the area were completely stopped. Faced with government intervention in the union and employer resistance, workers decided to return to work and allow a forty-five-day cooling off period before resuming the strike. During this period, while negotiations were going on with the employers, tension was building up to a fever pitch in São Bernardo, with workers prepared to strike at any moment. Finally, after offering a 6 percent increase, the employers refused to go any further. It was clear that they were prepared to resist a strike for longer than the workers were able to maintain one. Lula and the other union officers had to go to the strike assembly with a proposal that they did not support but that they were sure was all they would get. Lula described that assembly as the hardest day of his life. After a May Day rally in the stadium with 150,000 people, the whole city was mobilized. The assembly expected Lula either to bring in a favorable agreement or to lead them out. Instead, after a speech in favor of the agreement by another union officer, he asked for and won a vote of confidence in the union leadership.

The 1979 strikes reached fifteen states and spread far beyond the metalworkers, affecting urban service workers, textile workers, miners, bank workers, construction workers, teachers, and many others. One of the most dramatic strikes involved sugar workers from plantations in Pernambuco, reflecting the rapid growth of rural unionism during the 1970s. While most strikes concentrated on wage demands, some began to go beyond these to challenge aspects of the union legislation, asking for factory-level union representation and job security provisions. While the degree of success of different categories varied, in no case were any concessions made on issues referring to the latter questions. On the other hand, the government's decision to change the wage law—making the wage increase twice yearly rather than annually—was a victory for the labor movement as a whole.

Because of their extent and the attention they and Lula received in the mass media, the 1978 and 1979 strikes showed workers their importance as political actors. But it also convinced some union leaders that industrial action alone was insufficient as long as the labor ministry and repressive apparatus could be counted upon to intervene on the side of the employers. If an industrial strike was to be automatically transformed into a political strike by the government's response, then workers needed a political voice. Particularly for metalworkers, who remained the core of the new union movement, the notion of forming a party of their own was on the table.

Formation of the Workers' Party

During most of 1978 and early 1979, there had been discussion within unions in São Bernardo do Campo, Santo André, Osasco, Santos, Rio de Janeiro, Belo Horizonte, Campinas, and Porto Alegre about the possibility of launching a party. Lula brought up the question at a conference of oil workers in Bahia in late 1978. The idea of a workers' party was first launched officially as a resolution of the São Paulo State Metalworkers' Congress in Lins, São Paulo, in January 1979. The Lins resolution on party politics called for Brazilian workers to overcome their marginalization by uniting to form an internally democratic party, which would recognize the great importance of workers in Brazilian social life and constitute an independent power base. The resolution called upon metalworkers to launch this process nationally.[14]

After the Lins congress, there was considerable disagreement about whether the proposal to launch a workers' party was for the immediate or for the indeterminate future. An informal committee, which included Henos Amorina (Osasco metalworkers), Jacó Bittar (oil workers, Paulinha, São Paulo), Paulo Skromov Matos (leather workers, São Paulo), Robson Camargo (an officer of the São Paulo artists' union), and Wagner Benevides of the Belo Horizonte oil workers, attempted to speed up the process. This group drew up a statement of principles (Carta de Princípios) and distributed two hundred thousand copies during May Day rallies in large cities in São Paulo, Minas Gerais, Rio de Janeiro, Bahia, Rio Grande do Sul, and Ceará. The committee's declared intention was to gather suggestions from union rank and file and then hold state commission meetings in June, which in turn would lead to the formation of a national commission to write the final platform. The group planned to register the party with the electoral tribunal on May 25, 1979.

The committee's preemptive action caused an uproar. Many labor leaders and others sympathetic to the idea of a workers' party argued that the committee was moving too fast and that it was not representative even of the unions to which committee members belonged. João Paulo Pires Vasconcelos said that the document's publication violated an agreement to hold discussions of the party proposal among the unions' rank and file before doing anything about it. He accused the Carta de Princípios group of vanguardism, not only because it took preemptive action but also because several of its members belonged to or were sympathetic to clandestine Trotskyist parties.

The controversy over the Carta de Princípios highlighted the vast differences that still existed over what kind of party should be created and how. Benevides thought that the post-Lins meetings were important because they corrected the impression (or intention) that the new party was to be a party of the metalworkers. Although the committee that drew up the Carta de Princípios was composed exclusively of union leaders, its members were acting as individuals rather than as representatives of their unions. This distinction became an important element in the debate over how the party should be created. Camargo emphasized the functional difference between union and party when defending his participation in the meetings. Agumeron Cavalcanti (doctors' union) and Hugo Perez (president of the electrical workers' federation of São Paulo and president of DIEESE) objected that the decision to launch a party had to be made by the unions as organizations.[15]

Formation of a Workers' party was again on the agenda at the June 1979 national metalworkers' congress in Poços de Caldas, and a resolution similar to the Lins resolution was passed there.[16] Delegates disagreed over whether the time was right to launch a party but agreed that the proposal should be discussed by the rank and file. Lula was one of those who felt that the time was not yet right. He may have been influenced by his assessment of the feeling among union leaders outside of São Paulo; he had apparently raised the question of creating a party two weeks earlier in Porto Alegre and met with strong opposition from the president of the Metalworkers' Union there.

After the Poços de Caldas meeting, however, the tempo of discussions speeded up and their scope broadened. That same month, a meeting was held in São Bernardo between union leaders, intellectuals, and MDB politicians. On June 28 in Belo Horizonte, Lula announced that a draft program would be distributed to workers for discussion the following week, after which the creation of the party would depend on the desire of the workers. In that statement, he was no longer referring only to union rank and file, but also to neighborhood associations. A workers' party, he said, meant a party of all wage earners. This was an important shift in emphasis away from the idea of a party of the unions.

NEGOTIATIONS WITH INTELLECTUALS AND POLITICIANS. A series of meetings took place in mid-1979 between union leaders supporting the formation of a workers' party, intellectuals, and MDB politicians to seek a common ground for a political party that would defend popular interests. The June meeting, promoted by Almino Afonso, Fernando Henrique Cardoso, and Lula, was an attempt by Afonso to convince both labor leaders and members of Congress that the popular party proposal was the best alternative. Even among those who supported the formation of a workers' party, there were very different positions about what it should be. Some argued that a working class organization should break not only with elitist politics but with electoral politics as well, a position which was obviously unacceptable to the politicians present. Some, like Paulo Skromov, argued that dialogue with politicians was a waste of time. Lula maintained that a workers' party had to appeal to wage earners and the poor in general, and not just union members.

The results of the initial discussions were inconclusive. As the government's definitive party reform approached, it became increasingly difficult to shape a common definition. On August 18, 1979, a group of politicians from the left of the MDB organized a large meeting in São Paulo to discuss the idea of the Workers' party. It drew about four hundred people, including MDB politicians, union leaders, students, intellectuals, and representatives of about one hundred diverse movements.[17] At this meeting, Lula came out strongly in favor of the formation of an independent workers' party and said that its doors should be open for progressive politicians from the MDB.[18] "Union leaders who support the formation of the PT," said Lula, "came to the conclusion that they had to participate in politics, because within the current union structure, they already tried everything possible to improve conditions for workers, and failed." At the same time, Lula argued that the PT should not be formed by the unions as institutions, as this might compromise union autonomy; debates on the party should take place *outside* the unions, without requiring that union leaders support the PT.[19]

The discussions that resulted from this meeting were the last attempt to reach a compromise between those calling for the formation of a workers' party and those who supported either the popular party pro-

posal or the renewal of the MDB. A commission composed of seven
members of Congress, seven union leaders, and eight intellectuals was
created to establish a framework of meetings and debates and to draft a
common program. Among the members of Congress on the commission, only Airton Soares would eventually join the PT. While the party
proposals converged in their desire to represent the interests of wage
earners and oppressed people in general, small proprietors, intellectuals, rural and urban workers, and so on, different assessments both of
the political opportunity structure and of group identity and interests
undermined the possibility of agreement.

For Cardoso and Afonso, the objective was to arrive at a formula by
which they could attract a large number of politicians to the proposal,
particularly given the privileges the party reform was to grant to members of Congress in the process of party formation. Roque da Silva
recounted that in the drafting process, Cardoso and Afonso took each
new item and counted the number of politicians who could be counted
upon to support it and those who would be alienated. At the same time,
Afonso was carrying on discussions with politicians from all over the
country and was finding no support for the formation of a popular
party. In a conversation with Francisco Weffort during this period, he
said that MDB members with whom he had spoken had expressed
overwhelming support for continuing within an MDB successor party;
Cardoso then told Weffort that he had finally come to the same decision. Weffort, as well as the great majority of other participants in the
popular party discussions, disagreed.

Different strategic evaluations of the opportunity for new political
parties were largely a response to the imminence of the party reform
and its anticipated contents. The reform was expected to grant so many
privileges to members of Congress in the formation of parties—the
right to form a party with the support of 10 percent of Congress, for
example—that many politicians saw the political game as one that was
theirs alone to control. As it would be difficult to form parties "externally," members of Congress expected to constitute the poles of attraction for those seeking to form new parties, and they did exercise that
attraction for Cardoso and Afonso. This attraction cannot, however, be
explained solely on the basis of an assessment of the probable contents
of the party legislation. The electoral success of the MDB, particularly
in 1978, created an organizational interest, on the part of those who
participated in it, in the party's survival.

While sincere in the desire to create a party with popular participation, some of the participants in the new party debate believed that the MDB's inclusion of popular candidates and Cardoso's senatorial campaign in 1978 demonstrated that the MDB could become that party. For others, and for some of the trade union and popular leaders involved in the discussion, the risk of failure to legalize an externally created party was outweighed by the risk that popular demands would be ignored in an elite-led party. By the time the last meetings were held, everyone knew the discussion was over. Afonso and a few others would remain in the MDB, and the others would support the PT. While the formal break would only come with the founding meeting of the party in October—when Weffort himself finally joined—it was visible long before.[20]

THE DECISION TO CREATE THE WORKERS' PARTY. Meanwhile, as these discussions progressed, ad hoc meetings in different parts of the country were attempting to establish provisional commissions to launch the PT. A group of union leaders in Porto Alegre set up such a commission on May 27, 1979, and proposed to call a regional congress in forty-five days. In Minas Gerais, a statewide meeting was set for July 27 in Contagem to launch the PT. In September meetings to found the PT were reported in Ceará, Paraná, and Rio de Janeiro. Speaking at such a meeting in Salvador, Bahia, Lula defended a nonsectarian PT, which would include everyone who did not own the means of production, as well as rural and urban small property holders.[21] On September 30, a series of debates began to launch the PT in Rio, with a number of trade unionists (from outside—there were none present from Rio itself) and members of Congress. Among Rio unions, only the opposition slate (Chapa 2) of the Rodoviários was willing to participate in the debates; others argued that discussion of the PT was still too restricted and the proposal needed broader debate among workers.[22]

At these meetings, party founders were still concerned with propagating the idea of the PT, not setting up the party as a structured organization (which was in any case not yet permitted by law). At the Rio meeting, Jacó Bittar, just back from a trip to Fortaleza, Belém, and Manaus where nuclei had already formed to discuss the idea of the PT, said that "we are starting from the premise that the movement for the creation of the PT is not a race to form a party right away. The movement wants to be a carrier of information and to stimulate participation in politics by the working class, which will, itself, form the party, winning the space to do so and the legislation that allows it."[23]

The decision to launch the Workers' party in October was most likely due to a combination of the imminence of the party reform and to internal pressures, which will be discussed further in the next section. The proliferation of individuals and groups claiming to speak for the PT, particularly on the organized left, may have convinced the trade unionists involved in the party's organization that to keep the process under control the party would have to begin officially. In any case, October 14 marked a turning point, where the focus shifted to the formal organization of the Partido dos Trabalhadores as a party, and no longer just an idea. At the São Judas Tabeu restaurant in São Bernardo, some one hundred people—intellectuals, members of Congress, and union leaders—decided to structure the PT as a political organization, with the formation of a provisional national commission. The meeting approved a political statement and a document called "Suggestions for an Interim Form of Functioning." The Workers' party was launched.

Factors Contributing to the Formation of the Workers' Party

Aside from the obvious effect of the change in legislation that allowed the creation of new parties, a number of factors came together to make the formation of the Workers' Party possible. That the party began and remained strongest in São Paulo is only partially due to São Paulo's concentration of industrial workers and their experience (albeit not very long) in strike movements. Nor can it be entirely explained by the commonly repeated "there is only one Lula." The PT was established because a combination of factors came together in São Paulo (including the ABC region) at a precise historical moment when alternatives seemed open and the future not determined. Once the party was established, the relative weight of each of these factors changed, and the existence of the party became more important than any one of them for its survival and its influence outside of its initial area of strength. But in 1979 and early 1980, in spite of two years of discussion, the concretization of an autonomous and independent workers' party was far from evident.

First, the core of the nationally known labor leadership associated with the new unionism was in São Paulo, in particular, Luís Inácio Lula da Silva, president of the Metalworkers of São Bernardo and Diadema and leader of the first major strikes in a decade. Second, a mass base had already manifested itself in São Paulo in strikes and a variety of social struggles in the late 1970s. The preceding are the two elements of the PT's formation most often mentioned in attempts to analyze the party's development. But the existence of leaders and of a base is not enough to explain the emergence of such a party in a situation that retained many characteristics of an authoritarian regime. In spite of having flexed their muscle in the strike movements, workers were still very much excluded—and under the military forcibly excluded—from the political system in Brazil. The third factor underlying the emergence of the PT is the preparation of the terrain by the organized left, whose increasing public visibility at the end of the 1970s helped to expand the possibility of occupying space on the left of the political spectrum. Finally, as the Workers' party was being created, a portion of the left of the (P)MDB in São Paulo felt that it was being marginalized from the leadership of the party. The seven members of the São Paulo state congress who left the PMDB and joined the PT in early 1980 provided critical infrastructural and logistical support during the period of party legalization.

NATIONALLY RECOGNIZED LEADERSHIP. Luís Inácio Lula da Silva was born in rural Pernambuco in 1946. His father, a small farmer, left for São Paulo when Lula was still a baby. In 1952, his mother loaded the kids and the family belongings onto a *pau de arara,* a rickety wooden truck that was the cheapest form of intercity travel, only to arrive in São Paulo and discover that her husband was living with another woman.

Lula had a tough childhood, selling peanuts and tapioca pastries on the street with his older brother and living in a two-room apartment with his mother, seven brothers and sisters, and three cousins. Lula went further than his brothers in formal schooling, graduating from primary school. (He later got a high school equivalency diploma, but he was never convinced that it really counted.) In 1960, at the age of fourteen, he got a job in a screw factory and enrolled in the Servicio Nacional de Aprendizagem Industrial, the technical training school. Like most working-class kids in the area, Lula's dream was to work in the automobile industry. "At that time," he said, "the people in the automobile industry got something like ten raises a year. They were the elite—they had houses, they were the first to buy televisions, the first to buy cars. I saw the people at VEMAG pass, because it was close to where I lived, at Christmastime, loaded with boxes of toys for their kids."[24]

Unlike his brother José Ferreira da Silva (known as Frei Chico), who was involved with the Communist party, Lula was not very political as a young man. His first contact with the union came in 1966, when his

brother took him to a union meeting; there was a major dispute between the opposition and the current union leadership, which his
brother supported. Hearing the opposition's attacks on his brother, he
wanted no part of it. Nonetheless, after he began working at Villares
that same year, he began to understand the meaning of exploitation. At
Villares, machines were used on a partner system, with one worker
using a machine on the day shift and another at night; the company
encouraged competition between the two to see who could turn out
more iron rings. Lula realized that workers had increased productivity
about tenfold without receiving a raise. The employers continued to
argue that the plant was not making a profit. He knew that something
was wrong but not yet how to explain what it was.

Asked to run for a union post in 1968 because he was thought to be
easily controllable, Lula accepted, more for the adventure of it than
anything else.[25] In 1969, Lula became an alternate in the union and got
married. Two years later, his first wife died in childbirth. At the next
election Lula became a full-time union official, and union president
Paulo Vidal put him in charge of social security (*previdência*) administration, generally considered the bottom of the barrel as far as union
jobs were concerned. For Lula, however, this was a positive experience, which increased his contact with the rank and file and correspondingly lessened his admiration for the union president, who, Lula realized, knew very little about what the base of the union thought. When
the time for the next election came around, Vidal was tired of the
presidency. He thought that if Lula were president, and he were secretary general, he could continue to run the union through Lula. Thus in
1975, Luís Inácio da Silva became president of the Metalworkers'
Union of São Bernardo and Diadema. Up to this point, there was little
to prevent him from becoming just another career union officer.

Beginning in 1975, however, Lula became more politically conscious. He traveled a great deal for the union; he went to courses and
debates. The imprisonment of his brother Frei Chico shocked him
profoundly, to the point that he lost the fear of speaking in assemblies
and having someone ask him something to which he couldn't respond:
"After my brother went to jail I stopped being afraid. If struggling for
what he was struggling for were a reason to be imprisoned and tortured, then they would have to arrest and torture a lot of people. I know
my brother; he's a solderer, a poor guy who earned 20,000 a month
who's now unemployed going through terrible things—at that time it
was even worse. He was arrested because they said that he was a com-

munist. It was good in that it awoke a very strong class consciousness in me."[26]

While union leaders with connections to leftist political parties were scared by the general climate of repression that continued to hang over working class organizing, Lula's lack of connection with any political group and his political naïveté became assets: he simply plowed ahead and said what he thought. Conscious of the lack of connection between the union and the rank and file, he began to go to the factory gates to discuss the union. He instituted better planning and administrative procedures, and he began to make real use of DIEESE as a research organization.[27]

In 1976, Lula affirmed himself as the real president of the Metalworkers' Union. A first important step was to succeed in separating the union's negotiations from the statewide Metalworkers' Federation. Second, in a confrontation with Ford over its threat to reduce the work day and the wage as well, Lula refused to convoke an assembly of Ford workers, because the company insisted that the assembly take place within the plant, and Lula knew that the workers would be too intimidated to vote independently. Paulo Vidal, in a separate statement to the press, said that Lula would have to convoke an assembly. At that point Lula called a meeting of the union officers and announced that from then on the president spoke for the union to the press; if the president were not available, the vice president would be the spokesperson, and only after that, the secretary general. It was Lula's declaration of independence.[28]

From that point on, Lula and the union redoubled their efforts to develop a new relationship with the union's rank and file. Instead of leaflets with solid text, which few people read, the union invented the cartoon figure of João Ferredor (John Ironworker), an endearing little guy with a cap who became the symbol of the metalworkers. They put out union leaflets in comic book format, mixing humor with mobilization. With the new style, more workers responded to union literature at the factory gates, and the lessons of João Ferredor were that the union was more than a social service organization.

With the 1977 wage recovery campaign, Lula became a national figure. After requesting and receiving the DIEESE study on how much had been lost because of government manipulation of cost of living figures, Lula began to contact other union leaders to discuss the possibility of a campaign around the 34.1 percent. While the response was not enthusiastic, he began to realize that this was something to which the rank and file would react when, after he convoked an assembly to discuss the issue, nine hundred people turned up. He called another assembly for the following week and there were ten thousand—at which point he knew that the campaign would work.

The 1977 campaign definitively transformed Lula into a leader. "I headed it alone," he said. "I talked and I yelled whatever I wanted to. Before I was stuck, because there was always someone beside me who talked more than I did. This was where I managed to take a leap forward, to really be myself."[29] With his brash outspokenness, Lula became a media figure as well. His picture was on the cover of the weekly magazine *Istoé,* and he was interviewed extensively in the popular humor magazine *Pasquim.* Major newspapers reported his statements. Politicians called upon him to speak for the labor movement. In December 1977, for example, he was invited to meet with Senator Petrônio Portella about plans for reforms; Portella promised to bring up ideas Lula had expressed in Congress, but the reform platform he presented mentioned nothing about workers. "In Brazil," commented Lula, "no one talks about workers."[30] Lula's national importance was confirmed the following year by the first major strike in a decade, which spread to other sectors to include a total of some five hundred thousand workers, and the following year by his leadership in a strike wave set off by the metalworkers that eventually involved more than three million workers.[31]

Lula was not the only leader with national credibility involved in the creation of the PT. Developments in the labor movement in the late 1970s had brought to the fore a new generation of leaders, sometimes called *autênticos* (authentics), who had in common both a commitment to stronger shop-floor organization and a willingness to engage in militant action in full cognizance of the risks involved. Although not all these were involved in the creation of the PT, many were. Others besides Lula included Olívio Dutra, president of the bank workers' union in Porto Alegre since 1975. Dutra's work in organizing the rank and file of his union was so effective that by the end of the 1970s he could boast of an 85 percent unionization rate, an astounding figure, even for a small job category. (Of 16,000 bank workers, some 14,500 belonged to the union.) In 1977, the union held a rank-and-file convention to discuss the political aspects of labor struggles, the questions of union autonomy, labor legislation, and the wage squeeze.[32] Together with Lula, Arnaldo Gonçalves (president of the Metalworkers' Union of Santos), João Paulo Pires Vasconcelos (Metalworkers' Union of João

Monlevade), and a few others, Dutra was part of what some have called the *intersindical volante,* the flying interunion organization, which from 1978 on entered into contact with unions all over the country to try to unify demands and struggles. João Paulo Pires Vasconcelos was another who was involved in the discussions of the PT, and although he did not decide to join until 1985, in order to concentrate his energies on union work, he remained sympathetic. Director of the Metalworkers' Union of João Monlevade, Minas Gerais, since 1970, João Paulo was widely respected for the quality of his work with the rank and file. Jacó Bittar, another PT founder and president of the Oil Workers' Union of Paulinha, São Paulo, helped to place his union in the forefront of those demanding an end to restrictions on state sector unions.

Lula, however, was the key figure for the creation of the PT. As the labor leader primarily responsible for sparking the campaigns and strikes that increased the power of the whole Brazilian labor movement, his was the voice needed to give legitimacy to the formation of a party.[33]

MASS BASE. Although the willingness of large numbers of workers to go out on strike did not necessarily prove the propensity of workers to join a party like the PT, the numbers indicate that the *potential* mass base of a party like the PT at the end of the 1970s was quite different from the pre–1964 situation. Between 1960 and 1980 employment in the secondary sector (including manufacturing, construction, and "other industrial activities") went from 2,940,242 to 10,674,977; compared to 1950, the number had almost quintupled.[34] Over the same period, the urban population increased at a rate of about 5.64 percent per year; nonetheless, during the 1970s urban employment grew even faster. The service sector expanded considerably, primarily in the state and social service sectors rather than in the more marginal personal service sector (maids, gardeners, and so forth).[35]

At the same time that employment was increasing, however, wages were falling. Economist Edmar Bacha noted that "in spite of the spectacular increase in per capita GDP after World War II, in terms of purchasing power the mean urban wages today are not higher and probably are lower than they were 30 years ago. As a functional group, in terms of the most basic necessities, it seems that unskilled urban workers did not benefit in the slightest from the fact that the per capita income in the country tripled during the period under consideration."[36] During the 1970s the real minimum wage was 15 percent lower than it had been in 1963—a figure whose significance becomes clear when we realize that according to 1976 data, some 46.5 percent of the Brazilian economically active population, of which somewhat more than half lived in rural areas, earned below one minimum wage. Even in urban areas, and taking family rather than individual income as a reference, in 1976, 12.4 percent of Brazilian families in cities received up to one minimum wage, and 32.2 percent of families brought in up to two minimum wages. In 1974, at the end of the "miracle," 13 percent of the population living in metropolitan areas or the Federal District, 26 percent of those in nonmetropolitan urban areas, and 44 percent of the rural population could be characterized as living in absolute poverty.[37]

The percentage of union members in the economically active population remained fairly stable at just under 25 percent, meaning that in absolute terms, the number of unionized workers increased substantially. In 1960, there were no legal rural unions as yet, and the total number of unionized workers in the country was under 1.5 million. By 1978, almost ten million workers belonged to unions.[38] This was clearly not a reflection of the militancy of the unions involved, nor can we clearly determine what it says about the legitimacy of the union qua institution for those who joined. After the 1964 coup, military intervention in unions had eliminated most left-wing and populist leadership, and the military continued to exercise tight control over labor through a combination of coercive and legal-bureaucratic mechanisms throughout the period in question. In addition to the interventions, unions were hit hard by the government's recessionary economic policy in the mid-1960s, whose central focus was wage control—in effect a wage squeeze. In spite of the growing hardship, until the end of the 1970s labor leaders preferred verbal criticism of the authoritarian government to action; memories of the violent repression of metalworker strikes in Contagem, Minas Gerais, and Osasco, São Paulo, in 1968 were for a long time a warning of what could happen if labor got out of line.[39]

Although the growth of the urban working class was important in itself, other forms of social organization besides the unions could be counted upon to contribute to the PT's potential mass base. The Ecclesial Base Communities (CEBs), of which there were thousands in the São Paulo area alone, whose members played an increasingly active role in other social movements, helped to broaden the party's potential base. The rapidly expanding urban population confronted precarious living conditions in the slums of urban peripheries and city tenements, producing a plethora of local movements around such issues as transport, sewers, housing, and health care. Links between the labor movement and these neighborhood movements, forged largely by the key role of Catholic activists in both, were important in mobilizing local support for strikes in 1978 and 1979, and they proved to be important as well in expanding the base for discussion of the PT project beyond the unions. The ethos of these grass roots movements, stressing autonomy and self-organization, was echoed in PT organizers' insistence that workers and the poor could not rely on elite actors to defend their interests and needed to project their own voice into politics. The student movement, many of whose members sought an alternative to traditional parties, was another source of party recruits.

THE ORGANIZED LEFT. At the time of the Lins congress, the idea of a workers' party seemed to respond to a general need in the working class. But over the next few months, disagreement over what kind of party should be formed produced serious divisions among the trade unionists who had participated in the congress. By mid-1979, the party's union base had begun to narrow to the "autêntico" unions. Union leaders with links to the Brazilian Communist party (PCB) were particularly opposed to the formation of the PT, not only because there could be only one party of the working class, the PCB, but also because the Communists felt that the radicalism of the PT and the unions that supported it could endanger the process of negotiated transition. In their view, the best alternative was to continue to work within the MDB and its successor (PMDB) and eventually to work for the legalization of the PCB itself.

Other parts of the organized left, particularly Trotskyist groups, actively promoted the formation of the party. In the late 1970s, many small leftist organizations, often growing out of the student movement, began to organize more openly. They published newspapers that were sold in public newsstands. Although they remained illegal and a few newsstands that sold their publications were bombed by right-wing terrorists linked to the military, these groups were nonetheless not subject to the kind of repression that had characterized the early 1970s. One of the most active was Convergência Socialista, which had talked since its formation in January 1978 about the need for a socialist party.[40] Convergência was one of the early and ardent supporters of the idea of a workers' party, although, together with other groups on the left, it initially tried to preempt the proposal in order to bring more trade unionists into its orbit. Some of the trade unionists involved in launching the Carta de Princípios were sympathizers of Convêrgencia, and several others were members of other leftist groups.[41]

Several other organized leftist groups that eventually joined the PT held back longer. At the time the PT was formed, Liberty and Struggle (Liberdade e Luta, known as Libelu), a mainly student organization that had developed a presence on campuses around the time of the 1977 student strikes, and the Movement for the Emancipation of the Proletariat (MEP) still considered Lula a pelego, especially because of his role in stopping the 1979 strike.

It is difficult to follow or assess the impact of a single organization on the initial phases of the Workers' party, and except in rare cases, it is not particularly important. It is important, however, that in the late 1970s, these organizations established a public presence, and leftist discourse about socialism and class relations became more visible.

An interesting example of a leftist publication that successfully established a regional presence was the *abcd Jornal* in the Santo André, São Bernardo, São Caetano, and Diadema (ABCD) region. Begun in 1975 by a collective of leftist journalists, the paper came out sporadically at first. Although it was not successful in terms of sales, the paper received a good response when it was handed out at factory gates. By the beginning of 1978, the collective could count on the participation of various local neighborhood organizations, as well as members of organized left groups including MEP, Ala Vermelha, and Convergência Socialista, and the paper was published more regularly. In February 1979 it became a weekly. Excellent coverage of the labor movement in the area won it increasing support from unions and other popular organizations, evident from the steady increase in the number of advertisements taken out by unions in the paper and by the changes in the nature of the ads. While at first these were general or commemorative ads, by 1979 unions were announcing union meetings, workers' assemblies, and other items of interest in *abcd Jornal*. When the paper began to appear weekly, there were congratulatory ads from a large number of the area's unions, demonstrating that it had succeeded in building a loyal labor readership.

Thus the paper's coverage of the origins of the PT is particularly interesting. From the very beginning, with an editorial in the February 1979 issue entitled "Who's Afraid of the Workers' Party" ("Quem tem medo do partído dos trabalhadores"), the paper spoke of the PT as though it had already or was on the brink of coming into being.[42] At the end of July, another editorial on the same subject wrote that the Workers' party rejected the argument that a new MDB had to be created as a large opposition front. Workers needed a political organization in addition to their unions to prevent the government from decreeing laws against the national interest and to help win democracy for the workers and not just the bosses. The editorial went on to say that the rank and file had already discussed and approved the idea.[43] The August 20–28 issue announced that the PT would shortly begin to gather the signatures needed to make it official,[44] and that it would be organized by núcleos in each workplace. The following week an editorial once again condemned those who accused the PT of being divisionist and playing into the hands of the government, or of being workerist.[45] With the next issue, however, the paper no longer wrote as though the party already existed; the editorial entered the fray of the debate frontally—"More Talk Won't Resolve Anything" ("Ficar na bate-boca não resolve")—and called for immediate creation of the party.[46] The following week reports on the return from exile of the historical populist leaders Leonel Brizola (to organize the PTB) and Miguel Arraes (to help make the PMDB an opposition front) were grounds for greater urgency.[47] In response to the passage of the party reform the headline editorial argued, "We can't wait any longer!"[48]

The tendency to rush the formation of the PT cannot be attributed entirely to the left. The enthusiasm of some of its other proponents created confusion as to whether people were organizing pro-PT movements or the party itself. Nonetheless, pressure from the left was significant and probably added to the confusion. This was even more pronounced in northeastern Brazil, where in many cases the PT proposal was carried by the left alone. Attempts to precipitate the formation of the party failed in large part because it was recognized that the party had to include Lula to get off the ground. However much the left might criticize what it called his vacillation, it recognized that Lula was still the authentic working-class leader par excellence, and there would be no Workers' party without him. Although the left's consistent effort to radicalize party discourse sometimes created conflicts with other party founders, the activism of leftist militants contributed significantly to the PT's formation. This was especially true during the legalization process, discussed in the next chapter, when the party had to create large numbers of local organizations quickly.

THE POLITICIANS. The attitude of many PT members toward politicians was ambivalent from the start and remained so over the next several years. The June and August meetings discussed above and the attempt to iron out a compromise between the supporters of the Workers' party and the tendência popular of the MDB did reflect a real interest on the part of many MDB politicians, particularly those legislators elected in 1978 from popular constituencies. Nonetheless, joining the Workers' party was a risky business, which would most likely alienate those who did so from the MDB party leadership were the experiment to fail, and joining would not ensure their reelection were the party to succeed but remain small. The number of members of Congress who took the risk of joining the PT early was thus quite small, and a few of the early supporters, like Edson Khair of Rio de Janeiro, soon fell by the wayside after being unable to carve out a personal sphere of influence by means of the PT. Others found it hard to resist the argument that their constituencies would be better served by maintaining the broadest possible democratic movement and trying to influence its actions. That, after all, was what they had been trying to do since 1978. The only congressman to join the PT in 1979 besides Khair was Antonio Carlos de Oliveira, who was also president of the MDB in the state of Mato Grosso do Sul.

The bulk of congressional affiliations came after mid-January 1980, when a dispute in the MDB over internal party elections in São Paulo made some members of the tendência popular feel they were being marginalized from the party leadership. Over the next month, Lula and other PT leaders met often with members of the tendência popular in the São Paulo state legislature, as those who had already joined tried to recruit others. Deputy Eduardo Suplicy, sympathetic to the PT from the first, went so far as to poll as many of his supporters as possible on their reaction to his joining—an indication of how seriously some legislators took the discussion of the PT option.

In spite of the conflicts that arose over the rights which deputies had in a political party by dint of their position, the benefits they brought with them were enormous. The first PT headquarters had been established in São Bernardo with a commitment on the part of seventy-six members who would contribute between Cr$100–500 (US$3.00–5.00) per month to pay the rent.[49] In Congress, each party was entitled to a staffed office for the party congressional leader, which included meeting rooms, clerical help, and free telephone service to other parts of Brazil. All members of Congress had congressional cars with chauffeurs. There were staff aides for research, mailings, and preparing other printed material. Most of the PT deputies dedicated as much as possible of this resource base to party work. Legal help was available for the process of registering the party and recruiting membership.

The resources that the deputies brought with them were very important, particularly in the early stages of the party. In addition, they helped to broaden the party's constituency. Unlike the party's founders, the deputies did not come primarily from trade union constituencies. In the state of São Paulo, Geraldo Siqueira, for example, had been elected with the support of students; Irma Passoni had been a founder of the cost of living movement and was active among church organizations in the southern zone of São Paulo; Sérgio Santos had won his support in other urban struggles in the Freguesia de O; Marco Aurélio Ribeiro had been active in legal aid work; João Batista Breda, a psychiatrist and an avowed homosexual, had a constituency in new middle-class movements; Airton Soares, who became the PT leader in the Federal Congress, had been active in the amnesty campaign. Finally, in addition to providing resources and contributing to broadening the party's base, their membership obliged the party to take more seriously the relation between grass-roots organizing and political power. Many of the conflicts that took place concerning parliamentary representatives are traceable to the fundamentally unresolved nature of this relation.

The formation of the PT introduced serious tensions into the debate about democratization that had been going on since the mid-1970s. Those who had argued so eloquently (and in fact continued to do so) for the need to insure the participation of workers and popular sectors in the democratization process accused the organizers of the Workers' party of dividing the opposition and playing into the hands of the regime in doing so. To a certain extent, of course, they are right: insofar as the regime's goal in abolishing the two-party system was to divide the MDB, it succeeded. In calling for unity of the opposition, however, there were several assumptions that were fundamentally at odds with the goals and perspectives emerging in the labor movement.

One was to assume that the rights of labor were *subsumed under* democratic rights in general, whereas it is clear from all published interviews and debates in which workers are asked what democracy means to them that labor rights are *identified with* democracy. The difference lies in whether the rights of workers are an equity issue to be

resolved by democratic procedures or whether they are themselves
fundamental democratic procedures.

The second problem was whether party practices during the authoritarian period should be discounted. For most social movement and
labor activists, the period before 1964 was only dimly recollected if at
all. The fact that prior to 1978, and still to a large extent after, the MDB
(to say nothing of ARENA) paid no attention to the popular sectors
outside of election periods did as much to shape the attitudes of PT
founders toward political parties as did a critique of pre-1964 populism.
"It's not enough to have a program that is of interest to workers,"
argued Lula in September 1979. "All the parties have programs like
this, but up to now I have not seen any party defend these interests in
practice. The working class is fed up with these parties, and what we
need is for workers to defend their own interests, they being the most
concerned. In other words, the workers themselves must lead the
party."[50]

Third, in spite of an obvious interest in bringing an end to the
authoritarian regime, most PT leaders harbored a profound distrust of
both elite politicians and the state. The lesson that the São Bernardo
metalworker leadership tried to teach by boycotting the 1978 contract
negotiations was reiterated in Lula's statements in other contexts. In a
visit in 1980 to the *favela* of Maré, in Rio de Janeiro, when Lula was
asked to support the struggle of the occupants there, he agreed, but
responded:

> Are you going to just sit there with your arms folded waiting for the
> government or the politicians at election time to come around here?
> Are you going to wait for the solution to come from outside? No.
> The best solution comes from right here. Politics isn't just something
> for educated people (*doutores*). You have to organize, prepare every
> inhabitant, and don't let the government come here and make trouble
> for you. The least the government can do is to install running water,
> sewers, and light.[51]

In other words, only by relying on their own forces could workers and
the poor expect improve their lot.

Finally, links among the diverse organizations of civil society, while
still rudimentary, were beginning to pose a challenge to the widely
acknowledged "hiatus" between the political and the social. Cardoso's
earlier call for a stronger civil society to counterbalance the authoritarian state (in the short run) and the state in general as a guarantee of

meaningful democratization (in the long run), did not pay enough attention to the very real problems of political mediation—not only between state and society, but also between sharply conflicting visions of both present and future—that would result. His formulation seemed to imply, as was perhaps appropriate at the time, a two-way opposition. Nonetheless, the strengthening of organization in civil society also involved a process of *differentiation* within civil society itself, and the recognition of interests and conflicts that escaped a dualistic image of state and society.

STRUCTURING THE
WORKERS' PARTY:
STATE REGULATION
AND PARTY
ORGANIZATION

5

The legal requirements of the new party law passed in 1979 had a crucial impact on the structure of the Workers' party and on its efforts to become an internally democratic mass membership party. Brazilian law stipulates in minute detail the internal structures and processes of political parties, and it gives the electoral courts power to oversee their internal functioning.[1] For parties interested in establishing more authentic forms of rank and file participation, however, the legislation created impediments to innovation. Many studies exist on party fractionalization, internal party democracy, patterns of leadership selection, policy determination, financing, and membership recruitment, but the impact of state regulation of party structures has received less attention.[2] State regulation of political parties in Brazil was crucial in the development of the Workers' party not only because of the kinds of structures required by the law but also because of its influence on the configuration of power relations within the party.

This chapter begins by examining the legal requirements for party organization and their importance in the initial formative period of PT development, particularly insofar as they facilitated or impeded its proposal to be an internally democratic mass party. This legal context helps to explain the sometimes torturous attempt to superimpose democratic forms of party organization on structures mandated by the law. In spite of the difficulties, however, the party's effort to create the conditions for an actively participating membership differentiated it from other Brazilian parties and helped to make party membership an important political resource for the PT. In so doing, however, it stimulated an ongoing internal struggle over the party's identity. Although this struggle has contributed to a widely held image of the PT as a highly factionalized party, the process of learning to deal with internal differences has been an important part of the PT's institutional development.

The 1979 Party Reform

On October 19, 1979, the government finally sent to Congress the long-awaited draft reform of the political party law. The reform, issued as Law no. 6767 of December 20, 1979, modified important sections of the Organic Law of Political Parties (Law no. 5682 of July 27, 1971), particularly those referring to party formation.[3] It abolished the two existing parties, ARENA and the MDB, which had been established by Institutional Act no. 4 (November 20, 1965) after all previous parties had been rendered extinct the month before by Institutional Act no. 2 (October 27, 1965). The military regime hoped that allowing new parties to form would divide the opposition, thus stemming the rising tide of MDB congressional gains and the likelihood of opposition victories in the next gubernatorial elections, to be held directly for the first time since 1965. Although this was widely recognized as a ploy to divide the MDB, the opposition had long demanded the right to form new political parties and could not very well object when it came. The party reform gave the state a central role in shaping party organization through two mechanisms: detailed legislation on the internal structures of parties and the power to declare them legal or illegal. To my knowledge only the PT protested the extent and content of state regulation; in fact, such regulation was typical of the historical role of the state in Brazil and was not seen as an aberration.[4]

To obtain provisional legal recognition, a new party had to publish a manifesto, program, and statutes, and copies had to be submitted to the Supreme Electoral Tribunal by the party's Provisional National Directive Commission, composed of seven to eleven members elected by the founders of the party (who had to number at least 101). The National Provisional Commission was officially to designate state commissions, which would in turn designate municipal commissions and commissions for the electoral zones in the state capitals (Article 6); notarized copies of the minutes of the meetings held to designate these bodies had to go to the electoral tribunal as well (Article 8). Once initial formalities were completed, a party had twelve months to become organized, which meant holding conventions in at least one-fifth of the municipalities of at least nine states and a convention to elect a national directorate. A party thus registered could immediately begin to function as a party if its founders included at least 10 percent of the representatives in the National Congress (Chamber of Deputies and Senate) or if it received in the most recent elections for the Chamber of Deputies at least 5 percent of the total vote, with a minimum of 3 percent in at least nine states (Article 14,I–II).

The legislation also described permanent party structures and their functions. Here the 1979 reform did not revise the 1971 Organic Law of Political Parties. Deliberative organs were the municipal, regional, and national conventions, and directive organs were the municipal, district, regional, and national diretórios. The parliamentary group was responsible for parliamentary action, and provision was made for the formation of party ethics councils, fiscal and consultive councils, and labor, student, and women's departments. The majority of a parliamentary group could, through the party leadership, require the convocation of any directive organ of the party, at the appropriate level, to deal with specific matters. The cases in which higher party organs could interfere with lower ones were also spelled out (Article 27), along with the terms of elected party leadership, the functioning of party congresses, the right to participate in party congresses, the rules for formation of municipal party organizations, and the procedures for deliberation by different organs.

Enrollment of party members was the responsibility of the Municipal Directorate, using an official membership form approved by the Supreme Electoral Tribunal. The form was to be filled out in triplicate, and after being accepted by the party it was to be sent to the electoral court for authentication. One copy remained with the electoral court, one with the party, and one went back to the party member.

The party law also covered internal party discipline, spelling out conditions for suspension and expulsion of party members and loss of parliamentary mandates for infringement of party positions. It regulated party finances and accounting methods; financial records had to be submitted to the electoral tribunal on a regular basis. Parties were prohibited from receiving financial aid from foreign persons or organizations, organs of the state (including state firms), private corporations, or unions (Article 91).

Title VIII, on the party fund (Special Fund for the Financial Assistance of Political Parties) discussed the constitution, administration, and distribution of state funds for parties. Private donations, whose size was limited, had to be reported at the end of each year in the *Diário Oficial da União,* along with how these funds were used (Article 95,IV,2). As for the party fund administered by the state, 10 percent was to be divided equally among the parties, the remaining 90 percent was to be divided proportionally according to the parties' respective congressional delegations in the Chamber of Deputies (Article 97). Those funds were to be redistributed within the parties by the national diretórios, with at least 80 percent going to regional sections in proportion to the number of representatives each region had in its state legislative assemblies. The proportion of those funds to be redistributed to regional and local party organs was also stipulated by law, with the most going to the areas that were strongest electorally (Article 99).

The monies from the party fund could be used for the maintenance of party headquarters and the payment of personnel (up to 20 percent of the total received), political propaganda, recruitment and elections, and foundation and maintenance of institutes for political education and training party cadre (Article 105). Financial records describing the use of these funds were to be presented annually to the Tribunal de Contas da União.[5]

Such rigorous requirements for the formation of a party clearly favored those parties that could count on inherited local party organizations to fulfill the stipulations on membership and structure. The PDS essentially replicated the ARENA structures. The PMDB and the Partido Popular (PP)[6] before its merger with the PMDB in late 1981 could use the old MDB local organizations to facilitate their legalization; however, they both had to do a significant amount of new organizing, as the MDB did not have enough functioning local structures to make compliance automatic. For the Workers' party, as new in conception as it was in organization, fulfilling the requirements of the law meant starting essentially from scratch.

By creating the Party of the Brazilian Democratic Movement (PMDB) as a successor party, MDB leaders hoped to maintain the momentum and legitimacy the party had developed since the 1974 elections. Although more conservative opposition elites did form their own party, the Partido Popular, they intended to form electoral coalitions with the PMDB in gubernatorial and senatorial races. The package of electoral regulations issued in November 1981, extending the ban on coalitions from congressional and municipal races as stipulated in the 1979 reform to all elected offices, made this impossible, provoking the merger of the PP and PMDB under the name of the latter. Apparently, the military's determination to tighten control over the process backfired with the merger between the two largest opposition parties. The anticoalition rule had sought to ensure that the PDS would profit from a divided opposition; the military seems not to have foreseen the possibility of a merger. The expanded PMDB thus saw its vocation as maintaining a united opposition, of which it was the legitimate representative.

The two parties that deliberately remained outside the framework of an "opposition consensus" were Leonel Brizola's Democratic Labor party (Partido Democrático Trabalhista, PDT) and the Workers' party. Brizola's attempt to revive the charisma of the old PTB after the party reform was foiled when he lost the battle for the PTB name to Ivete Vargas, a great-niece of Getúlio Vargas. He countered by setting up the PDT, intending to fuse traditional Brazilian labor politics and a more modern, social democratic orientation. In fact, during its first years of existence the PDT was mainly organized around the personality of Brizola. (Ivete Vargas's PTB could not really be called an "opposition" party. It served mainly as a vehicle for individual candidates—for example, Sandra Cavalcanti in Rio and Jânio Quadros in São Paulo in 1982, Quadros again in the 1985 mayoral elections, and Antonio Ermírio de Morais in the 1986 São Paulo gubernatorial elections—and frequently voted with the PDS in Congress.)

Structuring the Workers' Party

Several aspects of the party law had particular relevance to the PT's desire to establish a mass party. First, the law specified the number of members a party had to recruit in each locality to obtain recognition and the right to run candidates in elections. The desire of PT organizers to insure that members were making a politically conscious choice by joining was not always feasible during the legalization period. Second, the financing rules that outlawed organizational donors and required that all donors be listed in the official state record, together with the labor law's prohibition of formal relationships between unions and political parties, denied it the kind of financial base typical of many labor-based parties—for example, the British Labour party, which was primarily funded by the unions, and the Swedish Social Democratic party. There are exceptions; faced with a similar regulation, the German Social Democrats managed to institute a viable dues structure.

The political declaration issued at the PT's founding meeting in São Bernardo made it clear that the intent was to create a legally recognized party, which was to be a unifying voice for groups with a common interest: "The movement for the PT demands the democratic right to form a legal party. . . . The idea of the Workers' party arose with the advance and reinforcement of this new and broad-based social movement, which now extends from the factories to the neighborhoods, from the unions to the ecclesial base communities, from the cost of living movements to the dwellers associations, from the student movement to the professional associations, from the movement of black people to the women's movement, as well as others, like those who struggle for the rights of indigenous peoples." It was to be a channel through which these groups could organize politically and participate in politics, transforming the prevalent view of "the political" as an elite sphere of activity into a conception of grass-roots democracy. The party was to be a national organization, creating conditions for real democratization of political institutions and of society over the medium and long term. To place political and economic power in the hands of workers the PT had to build an internally democratic organization, whose decisions and programs should come from the base.[7]

The party did not establish organizing structures immediately after the São Bernardo meeting, and for a while it was unclear either how much support the PT proposal really had or who was entitled to speak in its name. In some states groups were already being formed to convoke party congresses; in others, like Minas Gerais, union leaders issued statements calling the formation of the party precipitous. In mid-November 1979, party organizers in São Paulo finally decided to create secretariats for organization and nucleus[8] formation, finances, and the press, and working commissions were set up to organize meetings. By then pro-PT organizations were reported to exist in fourteen states.

Whether the PT would be judged a "class party" and thus prohibited under Article 5 of the party reform law was a matter of some concern during the party's first months. Faced with this possibility, party leaders considered alternative options.[9] For Lula, whether the party was declared legal mattered less than the educational process of discussion of the party by workers and the organization of base nuclei. Jacó Bittar went so far as to say that if the party was not registered by 1982, it would support candidates of the successor party to the "popular tendency" of the MDB.[10] Nonetheless, all the initial declarations stated that the PT was intended to be a legal party, and its leaders soon began to express more confidence in its future. Although the PT was unlikely to secure its registration by signing up 10 percent of the members of Congress, Lula insisted that the party would run in the 1982 elections on an equal footing with the others.[11]

Creating a new party from the bottom up, without a large parliamentary base to start with, was particularly difficult, so PT organizers decided to publish the manifesto as late as possible in order to gain time for organizing in the municipalities.[12] The first stage in the legalization process took place on January 10, 1980, when the draft manifesto was read in the headquarters of the São Paulo Journalists' Union. A month later, a meeting of approximately one thousand people at the Colégio Sion in São Paulo approved the manifesto, and at least five hundred signed it as charter members of the party. That meeting also decided that the members of the organizing commission would continue to function as the National Provisional Commission until a national meeting of the party could be held.[13] Representatives of local party nuclei were present from seventeen states. Guidelines for a national discussion of the party program were distributed as well. The programmatic discussion was to center around six points: its method of elaboration, its overall conception, a program for democracy, a program for society, a program for the conjuncture, and a plan of action.[14]

The goal was to complete the process of organizing state and municipal provisional commissions by mid-April 1980, at which time a national meeting would be called to discuss the program and elect new national leadership. In fact the process took somewhat longer, in part because of the imprisonment of a number of PT leaders (including Lula) during the forty-one-day metalworkers' strike in April and May. Regional meetings were nonetheless held in nineteen states in May to elect regional commissions, and the national meeting was held at the beginning of June.

The national meeting approved the program but did not succeed in passing the party statutes, due in part to disagreements over the attribution of deliberative or consultive powers to party nuclei.[15] The conference elected a commission of jurists with a mandate to draft a final version of the statutes over the next few days.[16] The national meeting also approved the single slate that was presented for the National Provisional Commission, the composition of which resulted from a compromise between the trade unionists supporting Lula and leftist activists grouped around José Ibrahim.[17]

By late September 1980 the necessary minimum number of municipal commissions had been formed in twelve states (Espirito Santo, Acre, Rio Grande do Sul, Santa Catarina, Mato Grosso do Sul, Maranhão, Piauí, Rio Grande do Norte, Goiás, Amazonas, Ceará, Minas Gerais) and Paraíba and São Paulo were expected to follow shortly.[18] On October 22, the PT requested provisional registration from the Supreme Electoral Tribunal, presenting documentation on the organization of regional commissions in eighteen states, and municipal commissions in 647 municipalities of thirteen of them.[19] The party also named six federal deputies as its delegates to the electoral tribunal.[20] By unanimous decision on December 1, the court recognized that the party had completed the first stage in its request for provisional registration.

The PT was the last of the parties formed at that time to ask for provisional registration. A survey by the newspaper *Movimento* showed that by October 1980 the PDS had registered the most provisional commissions with 3,066, followed by the PMDB with 2,127. The PP was next with 869, followed by the PT with 625, the PDT with 558, and the PTB with 334.[21] The numbers demonstrate the advantage enjoyed by successor parties to previously existing party organizations in the case of the PDS (succeeding ARENA) and the PMDB (succeeding the MDB).

The next step was to create municipal diretórios in one-fifth of the municipalities of each of nine states. This meant that party organizers in each locality had to sign up at least the number of members required by the law and hold conventions in which diretórios were elected and the basic documents of the party were approved by the membership. While the party law did not stipulate the number of party members required to constitute a party congress, the PT statutes required the attendance of at least 10 percent of the membership. This was a measure intended to discourage the formation of local units whose membership existed only on paper.

By June 1981 the PT claimed about 200,000 members, and the party held municipal conventions in eighteen states, succeeding in fulfilling the requirements of the law in ten of them.[22] When sixteen state conventions were held in September, the party had some 212,000 members and had its documentation in order in thirteen states, with decisions pending in the electoral courts on three others.[23] At the national convention in Brasília on September 27, the mood of party members was triumphant; they had overcome seemingly impossible obstacles, and legalization seemed assured. The Workers' party was officially granted its provisional registration on February 11, 1982.

Composition of the Party

To meet the legal requirements in time to participate in the next elections, party founders had to appeal to leaders of already organized constituencies. The spread of grass-roots organizing in the late 1970s had produced a number of new popular leaders who could be expected to sympathize with the goals of the PT.[24] The most important targets of recruitment in the early stages of the PT were members of Congress who identified with the tendência popular of the (P)MDB, leaders of unions and grass-roots movements, members of the Catholic base communities, and members of the organized left.

With the growing determination to legalize the party, discussions between PT organizers and members of the tendência popular of the MDB intensified in January 1980. In mid-January Federal Deputy Airton Soares (São Paulo) announced his adherence and his intention to try to bring like-minded deputies with him. Rio state congressman José Eudes also joined at this time. While courting parliamentary leaders, PT organizers continued to resist the desire of many deputies to see a merger between the PT, the PMDB, and the PTB (of Brizola); Jacó Bittar, meeting with members of Congress, claimed that "our members want to participate in the process of formation of the organization, and won't accept its creation top-down."[25]

Within the São Paulo state assembly there was growing interest in the PT among a small group of those discontented with the PMDB. Announcing his support for the PT on January 16, Geraldo Siqueira cited as reasons the PMDB's authoritarian structure, "which provides little space for participation by social movements in the leadership of the party," and his opinion that the PMDB as a political front of many tendencies was inherently unstable over the long term, likely to respond to the deteriorating economic situation by "co-administering the crisis instead of confronting the regime."[26] Similar discussions occurred in the federal Congress, but although many expressed interest in the party few decided to join. By the end of February 1980, São Paulo state deputies Eduardo Suplicy, Irma Passoni, Marco Aurélio Ribeiro, and Geraldo Siqueira had joined, and they began to organize the party at the congressional level. In the São Paulo state legislature, it was decided that the position of party leader would rotate. In addition, congressmen began to accompany Lula and other PT organizers in visits to other states and were often given prominence in press coverage of such events.

Concentrating on bringing organized constituencies into the party was one way of building a sizable membership quickly. Nonetheless, the attempt to recruit members of Congress, as well as decisions by some organized left groups to enter the PT en masse, made many labor leaders involved in organizing the party uncomfortable. Lula worried that the deputies being recruited might not represent what workers want; he insisted that the only guarantee for a candidate (referring here to the possibility of municipal elections in 1980) was the ability to organize among workers.[27] Nonetheless, initiatives to recruit prominent individuals continued, including a meeting between Lula and popular artists like Chico Buarque, Simone, Gonzaguinha, and the MPB-4. In Goiás, the Santillo brothers were attempting to organize the PT by gaining the support of municipal council members, mayors, and other local political leaders.

The question of how to assimilate leftist organizations within the party was also a serious concern. At a meeting at the São Paulo state assembly in January 1980, Lula made one of the first public references to the problem, saying that "some small groups (*grupelhos*) have tried to restrict entry to the party and create problems for its formation. But these groups will disappear in the normal course of things when serious people take on the leadership of the organization."[28] Lula was convinced that increased working-class participation in the party would eliminate the danger of sectarianism organically, making schisms or expulsions unnecessary.[29]

The variety of leftist organizations that found a home in the PT, as well as their importance for the party's early organizing and recruitment drive, made the problem much more complex than it might have appeared. In addition, because these groups were technically illegal, public discussion of an individual's dual militancy was considered tantamount to denouncing said individual to the police. Frank and open debate about the question of dual militancy, with clear references to those who practiced it, was therefore impossible; instead, it could only be discussed in the abstract.

By early 1980, the largest groups on the organized left—the Brazilian Communist party (PCB), the Communist party of Brazil (PC do B), and the 8th of October Revolutionary Movement (MR-8)—had chosen to work within the PMDB. Many of the smaller groups were favorably inclined toward the PT. A few, like Convergência Socialista, had been involved in the discussion of a Workers' party from the beginning. Attitudes of these groups toward the nature of their involvement in the new party, however, varied widely. Some groups, like the Workers' Faction (Fração Operária, FO), thought that, despite what they considered its initial ideological confusion, the PT could be transformed into a revolutionary party, and thus they chose to dissolve themselves into it. Others, like the Movement for the Emancipation of the Proletariat (MEP), argued that the PT's value was as a political front of workers and that it was useless to struggle to make it into a revolutionary party. Some, like the Revolutionary Brazilian Communist party (Partido Comunista Brasileiro Revolucionário, PCBR) and the Marxist-Leninist Popular Action (Ação Popular Marxista Leninista, APML), viewed the PT as a tactical attempt to create a broad popular front movement to bring down the dictatorship. The extreme fractionalization of these small parties, most of which had originated in the student movement, generally prevented their working together effectively. Initially, at least, the tendency was for each to develop its own arenas of action within the party and argue as much with each other as against the PT's alleged "reformist" tendencies.[30] Their precarious de facto existence made participating in the PT an attractive opportunity to engage in open partisan activity; almost all considered the PT a contingent tactical formation that prefigured the appearance of a truly revolutionary workers' party. The PT was thus an appropriate arena for promoting ideological struggle among workers. While the groups were small, their members maintained an impressive level of militancy, and they seemed exceptionally articulate (although often incomprehensible) to party members coming from the rank and file of unions and grass-roots movements. The ability to speak well was a valued resource, given the high rhetorical content of political discourse in Brazil and the tradition of deference to people who could interact confidently with those in authority.[31]

Members of Congress interested in the PT were especially worried by the organized left. Congressman Airton Soares accused them of making the organization of the party difficult by nitpicking over minor questions. Several meetings were held in February between union leaders and congressmen to discuss the problem of dual militancy and to consider how to increase participation by workers in order to insure that the PT did not become a front. After a meeting of the National Provisional Commission on February 21, Lula issued a statement saying that "it is not the role of the PT to keep an eye on these small groups. We consider that to be police action. But everyone who enters the PT should cease to be members of their small parties and help to form a mass party, abandoning unviable proposals."[32] The National Provisional Commission held a series of meetings with union leaders, congressmen, and intellectuals in Airton Soares's office to discuss ways of insuring that factional problems would not arise at the April convention.

The end of February also marked the beginning of public discussion of the role of Communidades Eclesiais de Base in the organization of the PT. In an interview with the *Folha de São Paulo*, CEB organizer and theologian Frei Betto (Carlos Alberto Libânio Christo) said that although many aspects of the party's structure and its relation to base organizations (such as unions and community groups) were likely to take time to define, the PT's proposal had the closest affinity to the CEB's own philosophy of organizing from the bottom up. He also noted that CEB involvement in politics was nothing new—church *bases* had helped elect a number of popular candidates in 1978.[33]

Survey research done in 1982 by António Flávio de Oliveira Pierucci among parish priests in the São Paulo area confirmed the widespread sympathy among priests and church activists for the PT. In the sample of parish priests surveyed, 49 percent expressed a preference for the PT, followed by 39.3 percent for the PMDB, 3.6 for the PDT, 2.7 for the PDS, and 1.8 for the PTB. Another 3.6 percent expressed a more general preference for the opposition, but did not specify a party.[34] This preference was particularly marked among younger priests, with 83.3 percent of those thirty-five years old and under in favor of the PT.[35] Responses to the question concerning which parties Catholic lay activists in their parishes had supported in the 1982 elections produced the following results: in 1.3 percent of the cases lay activists had worked for the PDS; in 11.2 they had worked for the PMDB; in 21.3 they had worked for the PT; in 28.8 percent of the cases some had worked for the PT and others for the PMDB; in 3.7 percent some had worked for the PT, some for the PMDB, and some for other opposition parties; in 28.7 percent of the cases lay activists had worked for all the parties (including the PDS); and 5 percent of those surveyed responded that they did not know.[36]

Pierucci's research demonstrates that there was clearly a basis for the widespread reports in the press in 1980 and 1981 of sympathy on the part of Catholic activists for the PT. Nonetheless, he also demonstrates that this support was not monolithic, and other opposition parties, particularly the PMDB, enjoyed a great deal of support as well. It was evident in the 1982 elections that the support of a high percentage of priests and lay activists was not generally enough to guarantee that an equally high percentage of the Catholic vote went to the PT. This distinction was not apparent, however, during the period of party organization; the combination of a kind of elective affinity of organizational forms referred to by Frei Betto and the visible support of many priests and lay activists, particularly in parishes in working-class areas, was enough to create a "common sense" assessment that the Church was with the PT.

Thus during the PT's first year recruitment among different constituencies involved a kind of balancing act for party organizers. Some members of Congress who had initially expressed interest desisted, some because they objected to the role of the organized left, some for differences over issues (whether to support a campaign for a Constituent Assembly, for example), and others because they were not given the role they had envisioned for themselves. A few of the leftist factions that had originally supported the party left it as well. It was extremely difficult during this period for party founders to assess the importance of different constituencies; a more accurate appraisal would have to wait until after the elections. As the process of party organization developed, attention turned from targeting well-known leaders to the recruitment of mass membership. Nonetheless, the ability of the party to attract members in different regions of the country was closely related to the identity of its initial sponsors in that region.

Regional Dynamics of Party Formation

The process of party formation took place in a number of different ways, depending on the nature of the group that took responsibility for organizing the party in each state. This in turn mainly depended on the contacts that the core organizing group in the São Paulo area had in the rest of the country (as well as in the interior of the state of São Paulo).

There are many illustrations of this variation; let us examine a few exemplary ones. The attempt by the party founders to convince union leaders in Rio de Janeiro to carry forward the proposal for the PT, for example, was largely a failure. While some union leaders did eventually join, they were not the main instigators of the party in Rio. Devanir

Ribeiro, a São Paulo PT leader who was also an officer of the São Bernardo Metalworkers during this period, admits to having been surprised by the situation there: union leaders who had been allied with the São Paulo group on questions related to the new unionism responded negatively to the proposal for a party. This was in part due to the importance of the Communist party and other smaller groups like the MR-8 within the Rio union movement; these organizations had decided to continue to work within the PMDB, and they were influential in such important Rio unions as the metalworkers' and the bank workers' unions. Thus the initial carrier of the PT proposal in Rio de Janeiro was not the unions but rather a conflictive amalgam of students and intellectuals, community groups based in neighborhood work, and two congressmen who denied each other's sincerity in forwarding the party's organization (Edson Khair and José Eudes). The conflict over who was to control the Workers' party in Rio weakened it significantly from the beginning.

The problems in Rio (which were also to arise elsewhere) grew out of two main factors: the inexperience of the São Paulo core group in evaluating potential allies[37] and the failure to take into account the very salient differences between the party's potential base in Rio and São Paulo. The core group in São Paulo was disappointed by the failure of Rio unions, particularly the industrial unions, to support the PT. But over 70 percent of Rio's economically active population is employed in services. Although unions and associations of service workers did gain significantly more strength in the 1980s, at the time the PT was formed most were quite weak. The most important Rio service workers' union at that time was probably the bank workers' union, whose leadership was close to the Communist party and decidedly unsympathetic to the PT. Although union militancy was an important factor of mobilization in the state at some moments, it did not play the same aggregative role as it did in São Paulo, nor was it conspicuously the leading edge of movement politics in the state. The heterogeneity and fragmentation of movement politics in Rio did in fact come to be reflected within the PT, but still in its fragmented state. Even though the party was legalized in Rio, it was slow to find its identity. Neighborhood movement activists making local demands, leaders of some unions (mainly middle-class unions, such as the engineers'), ideologically oriented intellectuals seeking to produce a "correct" discourse, Catholic grass-roots communities emphasizing microlevel participation, gay rights activists, women's movement leaders, ecologists—all coexisted uneasily within the party. The diversity was such that during its first few years of existence, no one group placed a permanent stamp on the party in Rio in the way the labor movement did in São Paulo, and the party limped along barely surviving on paper. In 1986 an electoral alliance with the nascent Green party around the gubernatorial candidacy of writer and ecological activist Fernando Gabeira reinvigorated the Rio PT, helping to give the party a resonance in the state it had not previously had.[38] (Ironically, although Green party founders saw the alliance as a way of organizing their own party, it probably helped the PT more.) The Rio case highlighted, almost from the beginning, the difficulties involved in the potentially rich coexistence within the PT of a traditional conception of working-class politics and organization, with an emphasis on quantitative goals, and a "new politics" conception emphasizing qualitative concerns.

Acre is an example of a state where PT organizers enjoyed greater initial success from a much more homogeneous base. The primary constituency for organization there was the network of Catholic base communities, on the one hand, and the rural unions on the other (which were in fact highly interconnected with the base communities). The political terrain in Acre was relatively well prepared for the appearance of a party like the PT. In 1978, church and union activists, working with local intellectuals, organized a popular front of progressive forces to influence the elections. Instead of running its own candidates, the front presented a program to be endorsed by MDB candidates who supported its views. Its members then campaigned heavily for those candidates, helping to elect several of them.[39] In addition, two years before the creation of the PT, base communities in Acre had put out a document called the "Decalogue on Party Participation." The decalogue called for the creation of a party which provided an opportunity for grass-roots participation and access to leadership positions, which defended the rights of the oppressed and sought social change, which fought the dictatorship and all oppressive forms of power, which struggled for the economic independence of Brazil, and which had a socialist orientation, that is, aimed to place economic power in the hands of the organized population.[40] When the PT was formed, many saw it as the embodiment of those principles, and it enjoyed widespread sympathy from the beginning.

Several unusual factors about the Acre situation contributed to the favorable reception of the PT in the state. First, the party was supported by the rural union confederation (CONTAG) delegate in the area, João

Maia, who enjoyed considerable prestige because of the rural union's success in forcing concessions from the government on land appropriations. Second, the leaders of church communities in much of Acre seem to have been more ostensibly politicized than they were in most other states, probably because the bishop, Dom Moacyr Grechi, was willing to accept a higher degree of politicization provided that the communities fulfill their religious function. As head of the land pastoral (Comissão Pastoral da Terra), Dom Moacyr had come under heavy attack from the government, which accused the commission of meddling in areas outside the church's jurisdiction, exacerbating land conflicts by supporting peasants being expelled from their land, and "fomenting class struggle."

With this kind of preparation, organization of the PT in Acre proceeded much more smoothly than it did in other parts of the north and northeast of Brazil (where for the most part it did not have the crucial support of the rural unions, and in some places, for example, Pernambuco, it was not well viewed by the Catholic church). Acre is in fact the only state in Brazil where diretórios were organized in all municipalities of the state.

Promoting the organization of the PT all over Brazil was a difficult task for the core group of founders in São Paulo. Travel was expensive, and the party lacked resources to provide seed money for party organizations. It was difficult to identify the appropriate groups in other states capable of carrying the PT message and of structuring the party. Devanir Ribeiro, for example, traveled a great deal, talking with union leaders (primarily metalworkers) and representatives of popular movements all over Brazil. José Ibrahim, who was responsible for the Secretariat of Organization in the national provisional commission, also traveled around Brazil, attempting to rebuild leftist networks from the 1960s, and Lula and other labor leaders in the party sought support among union activists.

Structuring the party in the São Paulo area involved to a large extent the activation of a web of personal contacts. Djalma Bom and Devanir Ribeiro worked to organize the first nucleus, which became the basis for a diretório, in São Bernardo. Activists who worked in São Bernardo but lived elsewhere were encouraged to organize in their neighborhoods: Devanir thus organized the basis for a diretório in Vila Prudente and helped to do so in the neighboring districts of Ipiranga and others.

Recruiting a network of people to do this kind of organizing was a delicate process, in that many of the union leaders involved in founding the party did not want to confuse union and party roles by taking the discussion of the PT to the factory gates themselves. Instead, they held meetings with some of the more active workers from the plants and asked them to carry on from there. Because of the networks already formed in the ABC region, it was evidently easier to organize the party there than in less organized areas. Devanir Ribeiro and Djalma Bom, both from the São Bernardo Metalworkers' Union, took responsibility for organizing the party at the state level in São Paulo, and responsibility for the national party rested primarily with Jacó Bittar and Olívio Dutra; during much of mid-1980, Lula was caught up with the metalworkers' contract negotiation and the strike.

The formation of diretórios in new municipalities normally involved contacting friends or relatives of a PT member or known union leaders in a particular area. A member of the party leadership would then generally go to talk to people in the area about the proposal. In other states this process usually began with the capital, with the exception of a few areas in which important popular leaders from the interior sympathized with the PT project, for example, in Santarém, Pará, where the president of the rural workers' union was an early supporter of the party.[41]

The informality of the process meant that founders of PT organizations in many areas were selected in a rather ad hoc manner. In Itapetininga, for example, a large town in the interior of the state of São Paulo, the proposal to form the PT was pushed forward by two PT members who were natives of Itapetininga but who lived in the capital. One, a journalist, was a former student leader who had been in exile for a number of years, and the other was a student at the University of São Paulo. A provisional commission was formed in the last months of 1980 in Itapetininga, but the party was initially composed mainly of middle-class people with ties to the student movement, which made it difficult for it to grow in poorer neighborhoods. Former progressive leadership in those neighborhoods had been decimated or had left because of police persecution. In 1982 the party founders were hopeful that a veterinarian who had recently arrived in the area and who was sympathetic to the PT, as well as a sympathetic clergyman, would help to broaden the party's work in the rural sector. Nonetheless, the continued weakness of the PT there was in part a function of its lack of implantation on the basis of local issues.

The situation was different where the party was built on the basis of strong movements that already existed. This was true not only for areas with a strong labor movement but also for a city like Cubatão, where party organizers included activists from environmental or transportation movements, or Sumaré, where the party derived strength from the involvement of Catholic activists engaged in a number of community movements.

Internal Organization

The decision to press forward with the attempt to legalize the party, in the face of widespread skepticism, was extremely important. First and most obviously, workers were asserting their right to occupy a public political space and to have an organization of their own making recognized by law. Second, from an organizational standpoint, it forced the party to reach out to the broadest possible constituency from the outset. But the decision to legalize the party in spite of the legal difficulties precluded the kind of organic process envisaged in the initial project— the gradual empowerment of workers and the growth of movements in society, and the constitution of the party on the basis of a *participating* mass membership. Because of the limited time available, it was necessary to identify key constituencies able to contribute to the rapid organization of diretórios and the recruitment of enough members in each municipality to fulfill the legal stipulations. The quality of recruitment was affected by the need for speed: at the beginning, there was a widespread effort to insure that new members, prior to joining, had read and understood the party program and principles, but as the deadline drew closer members were signed up en masse with much less attention to their effective understanding of the party's project and to insuring their participation in a party nucleus.

Two important organizational mechanisms were designed to insure that the Workers' party would be internally democratic and would stimulate participation of party members in decision making on party policy. One was the establishment of a two-stage convention process: prior to holding an official national party meeting, for which the composition was set out in the party law, the PT held "pre-conventions" (*pre-convenções*), which included a broader sample of party membership. These preliminary meetings were held at all levels—municipal, regional, and national—and were the real deliberative meetings. The official national meetings were thus only formal meetings that essentially ratified the decisions that had already been made at the preliminary meetings.

The second mechanism was the institution of the party nucleus.

Although apparently akin to the basic unit of traditional leftist parties, the PT's conception of nucleus also had an affinity with the organizational form of the base communities of the Catholic church, with the profoundly anticentralist bias of much of the latter movement. The nucleus was from the beginning intended to be the basic organizational structure of the party, and all members were encouraged to join one. Organized for the most part on the basis of neighborhood, the number of nuclei varied in each district, in large part depending on the predominant origins of the PT in the area. For example, in Saúde, a district of the city of São Paulo, where Catholic activists (particularly from the labor pastoral) were influential, some fifty nuclei were formed, drawing on the small-group *basista* tradition of the CEBs, which seek to maximize each member's participation. In areas where such basista principles were less influential there might be only one municipal or district nucleus. Confusion over the specific functions of nuclei within the party, coupled with precarious intraparty communications, tended to erode nucleus formation over time, and many of those formed in the initial period were absorbed into electoral committees in 1982 and never reconstituted.

Organization of the party on the basis of nuclei was intended to be the guarantee that decisions in the PT be made democratically on the basis of the informed participation of party members. According to chapter 6, title I of the party statutes, nuclei could be organized by neighborhood, job category, workplace, or social movement. They were to be the primary site of political action by party members, reinforcing the party's links with social movements. They were to express opinions on issues submitted to them by local, regional, or national leadership organs and prod those organs to broaden discussion of questions of interest to the party. They were to promote the political education of party members and activists and to serve as a guarantee of internal party democracy. One third of the nuclei in a municipality could also force the convocation of an extraordinary meeting of the municipal diretório. Title VII of the statutes further elaborated the role of the nuclei, stipulating that they were to be consulted on important decisions of both the diretórios and the parliamentary groups.[42]

The procedural questions involved in the formation of nuclei were further defined in a set of resolutions passed at the national meeting in August 1981. A nucleus was to be registered with the diretório in whose territorial base it functioned, or with the regional diretório if no local one existed, by means of a letter to the local organ containing the names of members, the place and time of its meetings, and the amount of its financial contribution to the party. Within sixty days this information was to be sent to the regional and national diretórios. Each nucleus was to have a minimum of twenty-one members, unless justification for dispensing with this minimum were presented to and approved by the regional diretório. Nuclei were to meet at least once a month and should have a coordinator, a secretary, and a treasurer. They would only be registered if they made a regular monthly financial contribution to the appropriate diretório. No PT member could belong to more than one residentially based nucleus. Nuclei organized in workplaces or within particular social movements would register with the nearest appropriate diretório.

The nuclei would have the right to send delegates to preparatory meetings for conventions in a number to be defined by each diretório, with a minimum criterion for proportional representation to be established by the regional diretórios. At the municipal, zonal, or district level, a representative council of nuclei was to be set up, which would meet with the diretório when convoked by the same in a consulting capacity.

Article 72 of the party statutes stated that representatives of nuclei were to be present in regional and national meetings in a consulting role. The number of representatives from nuclei at the regional meeting would be determined by the regional diretório with advice from local diretórios, taking into account both the number of members and the number present at the meeting held to select delegates. At the national meeting each state would have the right to send, in addition to the official delegates, one delegate for each thousand members in the state, to be chosen in the state preparatory meetings.[43]

The attribution to the nuclei of a purely consultative role in party decision making was hotly debated when the final text of the statutes was approved by the national provisional commission in its meeting of June 23–24, 1980. The mandate from the national meeting at the beginning of June to the group of lawyers selected to write the final draft had been that the nucleus be invested with decision-making power in those instances where the law did not stipulate otherwise. While the lawyers had apparently found a way to get around the fact that the law made no provision for such party organs by subsuming nuclei under Article 22, paragraph 4 of the party law referring to departments, the national provisional commission did not accept that solution, and chose to make the nuclei consulting organs, albeit ones that through their power to convoke meetings of the diretório and to demand consultation on questions of particular interest did have some initiative of their own. According to commentary in the newspaper *Em Tempo,* some members of the national provisional commission feared that nuclei with decision-making power could be too easily instrumentalized by organized groups within the party,[44] a major concern in party discussions in the first half of 1980. The debate about whether to attribute to them decision-making power masked a number of broader questions about the functions of party nuclei, such as whether they were an adequate form to promote effective outreach to social movements. Some, like CEBRAP economist Francisco de Oliveira, an early PT member, feared that a cellular structure might promote a tendency for party members to focus more on internal party disputes than on spreading the party's message.[45]

To some extent, the nucleus policy was the victim of the party's push for legalization. While the initial intention had been to form nuclei and only afterward to create provisional commissions, the need to legalize the party required that emphasis be placed on the commissions.[46] As the party moved toward legalization, the process of nucleus formation did not keep pace with the process of membership recruitment. This was perceived as a problem by party leaders in early 1982, and it led the National Secretariat of Recruitment and Nucleus Formation to circulate a document to state and local diretórios that emphasized the importance of organizing new recruits into nuclei. "The nuclei," stated the document, were "the guarantee that the party would be built democratically from the bottom up, linking the workers to the mass movements. They are what identifies and differentiates the PT's practice from that of other parties, because they are the place for discussion of workers' problems in the neighborhoods, in the factories, on farms, in schools, and in the streets, as the means to the defeat of the dictatorship and the construction of a new society, without exploiters or exploited."[47] According to the document, only about 5 percent of party members were members of nuclei. In addition, many nuclei and diretórios were said to exist only on paper, having been created exclusively in order to send representatives to party conventions. Many nuclei were isolated from party discussions because of the failure of municipal diretórios to distribute documents to the nuclei; in other cases, nuclei had only a precarious relation to the diretório in their area. Some nuclei were faulted for functioning only as discussion groups, without establishing concrete links to popular organizing. The document stressed the importance of nucleus organization and urged the nuclei to become involved in recruiting new members. The nuclei were also encouraged to suggest candidates for the 1982 elections, and they were expected to play a central role in the discussion of the electoral program and platform of the party.

Whether the nuclei should have consultative or deliberative power continued to be a contested issue within the party, and the São Paulo state meeting on August 13–14, 1983, voted to increase their power. Measures intended to implement this goal included stipulations that registered and functioning nuclei would be represented in the deliberations of municipal and district diretórios, and that nuclei organized on the basis of workplaces and job categories could elect delegates with the right to speak and vote at regional pre-conventions. At the same time, the São Paulo party decided to attempt to decentralize leadership structures in order to increase participation in party affairs, creating a subsecretariat for the interior of the state and a regional headquarters for the interior as well as for greater São Paulo. To coordinate the work of the fifty-five district diretórios in the state capital, a political council for the capital was to be created. The conference also voted to pay more attention to the political education of members—a task that had been largely neglected during the legalization and electoral periods.[48]

The national bylaws passed in May 1984 confirmed the opening up of regional meetings to representatives of nuclei, with the right to speak and vote, but did not grant nucleus representatives the right to vote in the local diretórios. The justification given for the latter was the need to reinforce other levels of decision making in the party first.[49] The national newsletter at the same time expressed concern about the diminishing number of functioning nuclei, pointing out that while there once had been some 220 nuclei in the state of São Paulo, dozens had ceased to exist. That this is a concern which has still not been resolved within the party is manifest in the repeated calls, in one party convention after another, for reactivation of nuclei.

Membership Recruitment

In 1982, the Workers' party set itself ambitious goals for membership recruitment. Objectives were to establish diretórios in at least 40 percent of the municipalities of each state by July 1982; to target municipalities whose total electorate would include at least 70 percent of the electorate in each state; to reach one million members by the end of May 1982; to insure that by June 1982 30 percent of those who were not yet members of nuclei had joined nuclei; to have the state diretórios assume responsibility for the task of recruitment and organization of nuclei, organizing campaigns to do so both within the PT and outside of it; and to issue a report on the party's organizational situation in each state.[50]

In the state of São Paulo, the party had more than met its goal of organizing diretórios in municipalities that included 70 percent of the electorate by the time of the 1982 elections. In the interior of the state alone, where the total voting population in 1982 was 7,597,356, the PT had organized diretórios in municipalities that included 5,575,185 voters, or 73.38 percent of the total.[51] The party, however, managed to create diretórios in only 26.6 percent of the state's municipalities (152 out of 572) by the November 1982 elections. The party did succeed in organizing district diretórios in all of the administrative districts of the capital.

The PT's membership during this period was disproportionately concentrated in the largest cities of the state of São Paulo: 64.87 percent of the party's membership in the interior of the state in 1985 was in cities with a population of over 100,000, while only 46.9 percent of the population lived in cities of this size. This was a higher concentration than in other parties: for the PMDB the corresponding figure was 43.30 percent, for the PDT 49.44, for the PTB 52.69, and for the PDS 23.25. It was, however, consistent with the PT's attempt to appeal to industrial workers.[52]

The recruitment effort declined significantly after the 1982 elections and did not pick up again until after the mayoral elections in state capitals in 1985. This was in part due to the widespread disillusionment with the 1982 election results, discussed in detail in the next chapter. It also confirms the importance of the legal requirements for party registration for the PT's initial period of expansion. Repeated statements by party leaders in the early 1980s that the future of the party depended on its continued growth were not translated into an active recruitment policy for the party itself. As we will see in later chapters, the emphasis after the elections shifted to the expansion of the party's influence in other organizing arenas (trade unions and social movements, for example, as well as in the massive campaign for direct elections in 1984). The drop-off in recruitment after 1982 and its subsequent expansion in 1986 and 1988 also correspond to Bartolini's hypothesis that mass party membership tends to expand during an election year or just after.[53] We can see this tendency in PT membership figures for the state of São Paulo for 1982–1988.

Table 5.1 Evolution of PT Membership in São Paulo

	Interior	Capital
1982	52,421	32,849
1985	60,857	37,231
1986	71,540	40,967
1988	107,489	N.A.

Souce: Tribunal Regional Eleitoral, São Paulo.

After the party's relatively strong performance in the mayoral elections in state capitals and former national security zones in 1985, membership growth picked up substantially. While in 1985 the party had no presence in 350 municipalities in São Paulo, by the following election year that number had gone down to 288, and by 1988 it had reached 192. The party's growth was particularly impressive in the 221 municipalities with populations of 10,000–50,000, an important category representing 28.21 percent of the population of the interior, in which the party's presence up to 1985 was quite weak. From 1985 to 1988 the PT more than doubled its membership in this category, with local party organizations counting over a hundred members going from 49 in 1985 to 112 in 1988. At the same time, overall PT membership in the interior of the state went from 60,857 to 107,489.

While the Workers' party did indeed carry out recruitment drives after 1985, it is likely that much of the increase in membership resulted from the party's greater visibility and viability, particularly in the electoral arena, as well as from the declining credibility of other opposition parties. During the second half of the 1980s the party also expanded significantly outside of São Paulo, becoming an increasingly national party. This process merits further study, as it occurred outside of the temporal and geographical scope of this one. From informal conversations with party leaders, it seems clear that an important element in the party's expansion nationally was the growing national influence of the combative labor movement, and especially of the central organization associated with the PT, in rural as well as urban areas. In some parts of the country, the party only began to grow when early local party leaders were displaced by new ones with links to a broader social base. In the absence of new regional or national studies of the party's growth during this period, this must be classified as a hypothesis. Party membership figures are available only from the electoral tribunals in each state; repeated efforts to get them from the national electoral tribunal were unsuccessful. The PT's own figures, taken from reports by state organizations, placed national membership at around 625,000 by June 1989.

Building a Mass Party

Discussing the experience of European social democratic parties, Bartolini argued that "the historical role of party members and activists must be regarded as the basic element in the development and structuring of mass politics."[54] Like the PT, social democratic and labor parties grew up in relatively hostile environments and had to mobilize available resources to overcome ostracism. The major resource was membership, whose activities did much to shape both the societal image and the internal configuration of the party.

A conception of an active and participating membership was basic to the Workers' party's self-definition. The organizational innovations it superimposed on state-mandated structures—the pre-convention and the nucleus—were intended to broaden participation in the party's internal life. Even though the level of membership participation has generally fallen short of the ideal promoted by party rhetoric, it remains far greater than in any other Brazilian party. During the early phases of party development, the requirements of the party law forced PT organizers to pay more attention to the number of members being recruited than to the quality of membership, and the immediate task of all party members was to aid in the legalization of the party itself. Under the circumstances, it was hard for party organizers to be certain just who was joining the party and how strong its different constituencies were. After the 1982 elections, both the party's internal configuration and its initial base of support were much clearer. The diversity of membership and projects led to the concretization of a number of distinct factions and modifications of internal decision rules in such a way as to take these into account.

There are a number of indicators we can choose to discuss the role of membership and the relationship between leaders and members in a party. A detailed discussion of the internal life of the PT is beyond the scope of this study and merits further research. Along some dimensions of participation the party has gone much further than on others. On the weak side are membership financing and the somewhat sporadic nature of the party press; on the strong side are the participatory nature of candidate selection, contested internal elections and leadership turnover, and membership activism.

Financing of the party by the membership has been weak mainly due to lack of organizational effectiveness in dues collection. There have been repeated appeals at national party meetings for regional and local diretórios to collect dues and pay over the percentage of dues that was supposed to go to the national party organization, and in 1985 the national party newspaper began to publish lists of states in arrears (which included most of them). In July 1985, a member of the national executive estimated that two-thirds of the funds of the national organization came from the proportion of their salaries that members of Congress contribute to the party. Another portion of financing came from the government, which divides its party fund in proportion to the number of congressional seats won in the last election. The problem of organizational effectiveness in collecting dues was compounded by a perception of the general poverty level—a factor whose real importance was probably minimal, as monthly dues were set at the equivalent of the price of a cup of coffee, and many party members could afford to contribute a good deal more. Another problem in collecting dues from members was the difficulty in distinguishing the number of meaningful members from those who had signed up to fulfill the legalization requirements or who considered party membership only in terms of voting. Overreliance on contributions by elected officials or the government's party fund has been seen as a problem in the party, which prides itself on its autonomy. Although the prohibition on contributions from unions deprives the PT of a funding source often tapped by labor and socialist parties, there have been cases, like the German Social Democratic party, of parties that have supported themselves substantially through dues collection.

The role of a party press has changed since the development of the early socialist and labor parties; indeed, the growth of mass media has been identified as one of the factors that help to explain changes in the function of these parties. From the beginning, because of the importance of the mass media—particularly television—the informational role of the PT in Brazil was different.[55] Along with the lack of a tradition of looking to political parties for an interpretation of events, the widespread access to modern mass media may have had an inhibiting effect on the development of the party press. Throughout the party's early years, the fragility of intraparty communication reinforced the importance of informal communication networks and placed party members with personal connections in São Paulo in a privileged position. The first national party newspaper came out between the end of March 1982 and the end of November of that year, a period corresponding to the electoral campaign. It was replaced a year later by a newsletter, and a monthly national paper in tabloid format only reappeared in mid-1985. Local party papers in some states, including São Paulo, had somewhat more continuity. During the first few years, the party press concentrated on internal party affairs and to some extent news from the labor movement and social movements, with less attention to debates on national issues. This focus began to change in 1985 and 1986, with the inauguration of the Sarney government and the election of prominent PT leaders to the Constituent Assembly. By 1987, the national newspaper and local papers had become much more professional organs, providing information on a variety of social movements and national issues; they also increasingly served as vehicles for intraparty debate. In 1988, the party began to produce a quarterly theoretical magazine, *Teoria e Debate*. Both the national paper and the magazine, however, remained heavily centered on São Paulo.

Candidate selection in the PT has always been highly participatory. The slate for legislative positions is made up of nominations from nuclei and diretórios; as voting is nominal, no rank order is imposed on the party list. Electoral pre-conventions are held to ratify the slates, with the power to veto particular names deemed inappropriate, generally for ethical reasons; debates over the elimination of names from the party list have occasionally been rather heated. If the number of nominations exceeds the number of slots on the list—something that rarely occurs— the convention has the task of narrowing down the list. Candidates for executive posts are often chosen by consensus; if there is a dispute, the candidates are submitted to an internal primary. An interesting case of a primary that produced an upset was the nomination battle over the PT candidate for mayor of São Paulo in the 1988 elections: the party leadership, including Lula, supported Plínio de Aruda Sampaio, but the membership voted massively for Luiza Erundina (who was in fact elected mayor). The importance of these candidate selection procedures for PT members is demonstrated by the fact that moribund nuclei are often reconstituted in preelectoral periods in order to give their members input into the selection process.

The way in which party leadership organs are selected has had an important impact on the configuration of the PT's internal life. Internal electoral arrangements in the party underwent a significant change in 1983. Prior to that, the internal electoral system was one where the winning slate filled all diretório offices (which in practice meant that a single list was established by negotiations among leaders; there were very few cases in local, state, or national elections where two slates competed). In 1983 that system was changed to a proportional system with an exclusion rule stipulating that a slate had to win a minimum of 10 percent of convention votes to win seats.

This change in internal rules was important for several reasons. First, it resulted from a reassessment by the dominant group of party leadership in the wake of the 1982 election results of the internal balance of forces in the PT and the subsequent formation of a majority coalition— the Articulação dos 113 (Group of 113). Second, it made political alignments and factions within the party more visible. Although this fed a public perception that the PT was a highly factionalized party, arguably this new transparency of existing factional distinctions also made the party more democratic; factional slates in internal elections presented differing positions on issues confronted by the party, to be resolved by a membership vote rather than a leadership compromise that masked these differences. Finally, with the regulation of factional tendencies in the late 1980s, it initiated a process by which the existence of organized factions within the party became institutionalized. While this was most likely an unintended consequence, it is consistent with Sartori's prediction that proportional representation with an exclusion clause in internal party elections would lead to the stabilization of medium-sized factions.[56]

The 1982 elections had an important impact on PT organization. They produced new information about the state of the party in different regions, and they served as a measure against which to test the assertions of regional and factional leaders regarding their strength. In Weffort's words, "the experience of the unified electoral committee was useful in that for the first time within the PT someone was observing at the national level what was going on in the states. As superficial as this was, it was much deeper than what the states said about themselves at national meetings. The great advantage, even if only a very initial step, was that observers from the national executive could determine whether or not their own observations coincided with the reports and analyses they had received before. This opened up the opportunity for more serious debate."[57] Occasionally those observations were quite different from previous reports, and for the first time there were members of the national party leadership who were not from the state in question who felt qualified to say so.

This experience made the PT leadership more concerned with the party's image and development at the national level. As a result, not only did the role of leadership in coordinating the party nationally begin to be taken more seriously, with the designation of members of the national executive to guarantee communications with specific groups of states, but also there began to be a much more active and organized struggle over the national and state leadership of the party, through the creation of the Articulação dos 113 in mid-1983.

According to its founding manifesto, Articulação was formed to combat, on the one hand, sectors of the party that placed primary emphasis on the PT's institutional role and, on the other, those who saw the party as a vanguard acting in the name of the working class. The group sought to promote a serious process of democratic debate within the party. By seeking to mobilize popular forces around social de-mands, the party should combat the regime's effort to promote con-ciliation via a social pact that would isolate the working class. Party members should increase their participation in social, labor, and cul-tural movements, intensify party recruitment and organizational ac-tivities, and pay more attention to the political education of members. This meant that party nuclei should be revitalized around activities carried out in conjunction with social movements, that party leadership should be more carefully chosen and should become more responsive to the base of the party, and that the base in turn should participate more actively in decisions. The organization should be decentralized and communications should be improved—in particular by creating a party press—in order to reinforce internal democracy.[58]

The formation of Articulação was an attempt to consolidate leader-ship of the party. Its proponents were members of the trade unionist wing of the party (including Lula), Catholic activists, and intellectuals. It represented an effort to impose a relatively unified vision of the party's nature and goals, not to the point of eliminating factional differ-ences, but at least as the expression of a clear majority. Four slates were presented in the elections for the São Paulo state diretório in the 1983 convention, and, as expected, the slate presented by Articulação won the overwhelming majority of seats. The constitution of Articulação was duplicated at national and local levels and in other states as well.

The impact of Articulação, which has remained the majority ten-dency in the PT up to the present, can be interpreted in two (not necessarily contradictory) ways. On the one hand, it helped to clarify differing positions within the party and give the membership the opportunity to choose among them, thus contributing to internal democracy in the party. On the other, it constituted a distinct leadership group, corresponding in many ways to Panebianco's thesis that the constitution of a "dominant coalition" is an integral part of a party's organizational development. Panebianco claims that the assets of such a coalition are primarily its control over a series of elements that are key to the party's survival, what he calls "zones of uncertainty": "A party's dominant coalition is composed of those—whether inside or, strictly speaking, outside of the organization itself—organizational actors who control the most vital zones of uncertainty. The control over these resources, in its turn, makes the dominant coalition the principal distribution center of organizational incentives within the party."[59]

He identifies these as competence (organizational expertise); environmental relations (alliances, relations with other organizations, choice of issues); internal communication; formal rules (both their establishment and interpretation); financing; and recruitment. The formation of Articulação represented an attempt to consolidate leadership in most of these areas.

Competence, for Panebianco, involves specialized knowledge regarding the party's internal and external political relations. For the PT leadership group, the possession of this kind of "knowledge" was also a constitutive act: it was an attempt to promote a particular definition of the party's essence as well as to reconfigure internal power relations on the basis of the information about the party's social base provided by the elections. The ability of the leadership group to do this was in turn closely linked to control over the second "zone of uncertainty," environmental relations.

PT leaders interpreted the election results as indicating the need, first and foremost, to stimulate the autonomous organization of civil society. This meant that those PT leaders with the closest links to societal organizations—unions and a variety of grass-roots movements—had a special legitimacy in forming a coalition whose goal was to build alliances with these kinds of movements. The importance of these relations for the party, and particularly relations with the labor movement, is discussed in detail in chapter 7.

The fragility of internal party communications has already been noted. While the Articulação manifesto called for the establishment of a party press and recognized the need to strengthen internal communications, this was slow to develop, and informal communication channels remained crucial. Even slower was the regularization of party finances. Finally, while the manifesto stressed recruitment and the organization of núcleos, this process obeyed a different logic from that of internal party disputes, and it was much more decentralized.

Articulação also played an important role in relation to changes in the formal rules for selection of leadership, discussed above. Certain of its own hegemonic position, the group promoted the rule change. The move from informal composition of a single slate for internal elections to a proportional system had a dual importance: it provided a more democratic form of leadership selection and it allowed greater freedom of action for the leadership group.

In Panebianco's view, "the leadership's legitimacy is a function of its control over the distribution of 'public goods' (collective incentives) [identity, solidarity, and the like] and/or 'private goods' (selective incentives) [paid positions or status, for example]."[60] In the case of a party like the PT, where the level of professionalization during this period was fairly low, very few "selective incentives" were available. The leadership group's legitimacy derived primarily from its ability to shape a credible vision of the party's *identity*. Its centrality reinforced the argument that despite the sectarian divisions with which the party was plagued (and which were often highly publicized in the press), the core or essence of the PT was composed of people who brought to the party a wide range of experiences in popular struggles.

The formation of Articulação and the move to proportional elections for internal party organs began a process that had only two possible outcomes: the dominant coalition could succeed in implanting a unitary vision of the party either through persuasion or through some form of democratic centralism; or procedures would have to be developed for the recognition and regulation of distinct tendencies within the party. Although many of Articulação's members would undoubtedly have preferred to persuade the rest of their positions, most believed that forcibly to exclude dissident positions would undermine the PT's character as a democratic party. Nonetheless, there was clearly a need to establish a conceptual distinction between a faction within the PT and a party organization that was using the PT for its own ends. In 1987, therefore, the party's fifth national meeting produced a resolution on the functioning of tendencies within the party.

The resolution followed an extended debate on the subject, with different positions published in the party press. The open discussion of the "parties within the party" problem reflected the need to consolidate the PT's internal organization, and it was facilitated by changes in the national political context. As the democratic transition progressed, and the two major Communist parties (the PCB and the PC do B) were legalized, leftist parties in general were free to act more visibly. In this new situation, the constraints placed on the discussion by the very real fear of repression, which persisted in the early 1980s, were no longer acceptable. Olívio Dutra noted the response of the organized left to earlier attempts to raise the issue: "Not infrequently, at the slightest criticism of the way in which they were trying to make use of the PT, they reacted in a way that would have made the nineteenth century elders turn over in their graves, unleashing upon their audacious critics and *companheiros* in the party (or their fellow travelers) a barrage of adjectives like 'anticommunist,' 'social democrat,' 'backward,' 'SNI informer,' 'CIA agent,' etcetera. The PT is not a condominium."[61] By 1986–87 this discussion was both necessary and possible. The necessity was dramatized in April 1986 when a group of former members of the Revolutionary Brazilian Communist party,[62] claiming to be members of the PT, were caught robbing a bank in Salvador, Bahia, allegedly to gather funds for the revolution (or, according to some reports, to aid the Nicaraguan revolution). Although the party reacted immediately to the incident by expelling those involved, the national media had a field day.[63] While the contradictory aspects of this incident have never been cleared up, the identification of the perpetrators as *petistas* (PT members) was damaging to the PT despite the party leadership's condemnation of the act. This incident provided an added incentive to resolve the issue of factions. Thus the fourth national meeting of the party, held in São Paulo on May 30 to June 1, 1986, passed a preliminary resolution on factional tendencies within the party and authorized the Diretório Nacional to promote a national discussion of the question and draft new regulatory norms, to be voted at the next national meeting. The resolution emphasized the need to avoid future incidents like the one in Salvador and stressed that factional differences could not be allowed to undermine the party's integrity:

    1. The PT is a democratic, socialist, and mass party. It is therefore not a front of political organizations, nor is it an institutional mass front that can be used as an instrument by any political party.
    2. As a democratic party, the PT defends and exercises the recog-

nition of the will of the majority, assuring, at the same time, the
existence of minorities and their right to be represented and to express themselves in all instances of the party.

3. The national meeting recognizes the right of tendência and
determines that the next national diretório will proceed with their
regulation. But the party understands that this right cannot be extended to groups which do not adopt the program of the PT nor to
those which do not accept its democracy and discipline. In the same
vein, the right of tendência does not authorize militancy in parties
other than the PT.[64]

The ensuing debate brought major advances in the discussion of
tendencies.[65] The discussion was concrete, using names of organizations rather than habitual euphemisms. Furthermore, participants in
the debate focused on the links between the role of factional tendencies,
internal democracy, and the party's view of socialism. Olivio Dutra's
contribution contained pointed criticism of the behavior of Convergência Socialista and the Partido Revolucionário Comunista in particular.
He accused both organizations of treating the PT like a recruiting
ground, supporting its positions only when convenient, and giving
priority to the maintenance of their own party structures, leadership,
cadre formation, and press over corresponding activities within the PT.
He also attacked Convergência for treating party nuclei as if they were
closed cells, which, instead of expanding into the community, behaved
in a quasi-clandestine manner.

Other contributions to the debate stressed the important role that the
organized left had played in the initial organization and consolidation of
the PT and argued that this demonstrated that the revolutionary left
was not solely concerned with its own growth. Seeing the PT as the
organizing pole for all anticapitalist forces in Brazil, proponents of this
position opposed the exclusion of any political force from the PT as
long as it was committed to the radical transformation of Brazilian
society. "The question being discussed involves a definition of the
destiny of the PT: either it advances as an instrument for radical transformation that breaks with the existing order, or it becomes one more
party acting solely within the existing order, thus repeating the international experience of social democracy, which believes in a parliamentary road to the radical transformation of society. Experience has
shown that this position serves as an instrument for administering the
crises of capitalism."[66]

While tendências, in party parlance, generally referred to revolutionary leftist currents and parties acting within the PT, one important contribution to the debate noted that other kinds of organized blocs existed within the party, such as church groups and the majority tendency, Articulação.[67] Raul Pont argued that too many of the party's problems were being attributed to tendencies and that over the course of the PT's history many of the "parties within the party" had been absorbed or had dissolved of their own accord. While he supported the formulation of party rules on factional tendencies, he also favored extending the principle of proportional representation of slates from the party diretórios to the executive commissions, and linking voting rights within the party to dues payment—in other words, seeing the normalization of tendencies as part of a broader process of codifying the relationship between leadership and base in the party.

No one who participated in the debate argued that organized currents of opinion should not be allowed to exist within the PT. The controversy was over the form that these currents should take. The resolution passed at the party's fifth national meeting by a vote of 204–147 recognized the existence of tendencies and established norms for their conduct. It reiterated a commitment to internal democracy, as well as a requirement that decisions, once taken, be accepted. It accepted the formation of groups organized to defend political positions, provided that their actions, meetings, and debates were visible to the party as a whole and were intended to strengthen the party; the party in turn was to commit itself to provide resources for the functioning of such groups.

> It is absolutely incompatible with the character of the PT to have within it, secretly or openly, parties that are competing with the PT. That is, the PT will not allow the existence within it of organizations which have their own policies regarding the PT's general policies; with their own leadership; with their own public presence; with their own discipline, implying inevitably a double allegiance; with parallel and closed structures; with their own organic and institutionalized systems of financing; with regular public news organs.
>
> The recognition of this kind of groups—parties within the PT— would be to accept that the party is a political front, and thus to negate the PT's historical project. And it would put in jeopardy the possibility of consolidating it as a strong working-class party that constitutes a real alternative for popular power for the country.
>
> Nonetheless, taking into consideration that groups which are structured as parties exist within the PT, the PT will carry on a

political debate with these groups with a view toward their dissolution and the complete integration of their militants into PT life, with
the possibility of becoming legitimate tendencies within the party.[68]

The passage of a resolution on tendencies did not resolve the problem, but it did move the debate onto a different plane. The Revolutionary Communist party, for example, decided in 1989 that although it
claimed to be a clandestine revolutionary party, for some time it had
really been acting only as a tendency within the PT; its party congress
therefore voted to dissolve and to reconstitute itself as a PT tendency.
The position of Convergência Socialista, however, perhaps the strongest of the leftist organizations in the PT, was harder to resolve, and its
recognition as a tendency in 1990 made some uneasy. Many had expected that Convergência would eventually leave the PT, which would
have been the first important split within the party.[69] After the 1989
presidential elections, the discussion became still more heated, as the
presence of revolutionary currents within the party was widely seen as
hurting Lula's chances of winning the presidency. In early 1990, an
essay by Apolônio de Carvalho in *Teoria e Debate* explicitly recom-
mended the expulsion of Convêrgencia, Causa Operária, and the
PCBR.[70] Citing numerous instances where the these tendencies had
undermined the PT by acting on their own, he argued that their expulsion would constitute a recognition that these were, in fact, separate
organizations. Nonetheless, in July 1990 the national diretório ruled
that Convergência had met the requirements for recognition, and it was
one of the ten internal groupings recognized at that time. Of the groups
requesting recognition, only Causa Operária was denied.[71]

From the announcement of the formation of the Workers' party in
October 1979 to its legal constitution as a party recognized by the state
as having the right to present candidates in elections there was a considerable distance to travel. The requirements for legalization were
difficult to fulfill, particularly in the case of a party with few experienced politicians among its numbers. The decision to create a legal
party meant that from the end of 1979 through mid-1982 the party's
energies were directed toward fulfilling these requirements. This focus
had a number of consequences.

First, it placed primary emphasis on quantitative rather than qualitative aspects of party organization. Second, the need to organize the
party within the time periods established by the law gave a privileged
position to individuals and groups with the resources, time, and con-

tacts to mount organizational structures in a number of areas. The organized left was particularly active in this process and developed a stronger base in party structures than its numbers would otherwise have led us to expect. Third, the focus on organizational questions left aside until later the development (and resolution) of a clear political and ideological identity for the party.

Not all the consequences were negative. The legislation forced the PT to look beyond its organizational center in the ABC region and consider what it would mean to create a political organization on a national scale. While the effort to do so was not entirely successful, it averted the risk that the party might become a purely local party or that it might sink under an attempt to define a narrow consensus rather than broadening the political base of the party's appeal. Political debate was thus carried out within the context of a constant imperative to broaden the base of the party.

A number of internal organizational questions remain unresolved within the Workers' party. The desire to maintain active grass-roots party organizations outside of election periods has gone largely unfulfilled. Nonetheless, party activists are involved in a variety of other social movement and labor organizations, and arguably this kind of activity expands the social base that is likely to be receptive to a party like the PT. The question of grass-roots party organization is intimately linked to the party's ongoing financial difficulties. Dues collection has never been regularized, and the party coffers depend heavily upon the contributions of its elected officials.

Nonetheless, there is no question that the degree of internal democracy and the level of participation in the PT far outstrips that of any other important Brazilian party, and the PT has initiated into political life thousands of cadre who feel confident about publicly defending party positions. Just how unusual the level of participation by PT members is in Brazilian political life was evident when Brizola charged as part of his 1989 presidential campaign that the PT was paying its activists with money obtained from foreign funding agencies, primarily European church organizations. The charge was false, and widely known to be so. As Brazilian commentators noted, the willingness of so many people to put in time for the PT probably has a great deal to do with the fact that they see themselves as part of a process of deliberation within the party. They may not feel satisfied with it, and often don't, but the differences with other parties are striking.

In spite of widespread dissatisfaction with the inadequacy of internal political education and cadre development, the amount of leadership renewal in the PT has been unusual by Brazilian standards. While the party's original leadership was mainly composed of people who had made a name for themselves in other organizations or as intellectual leaders, an increasing number of new party leaders have come up through the ranks. Although Lula remains the symbolic leader of the PT and became its president again in 1990, the party has had two other presidents, and there has been significant turnover not only in diretórios but in executive bodies as well. Debates in diretório meetings and national party meetings are heated, and the position supported by party leaders (including Lula) is voted down with some frequency; nonetheless, in spite of widely publicized internal disputes, the party has maintained a surprising degree of unity, and defections from the party, up until now, have been by individuals rather than by blocs.

The internal development of the party did not take place in a vacuum; it was influenced in fundamental ways by electoral contests, mobilizational campaigns like the one for direct presidential elections in 1984, the relations between the party and other social and labor movements, as well as by governing municipalities and gaining legislative seats. The euphoria that characterized the early organizational period of the party gave way to a rude shock in the 1982 elections. The PT's approach to those elections and the lessons they drew from them were crucial elements in the party's development.

CAMPAIGNING TO

ORGANIZE: THE

WORKERS' PARTY

AND ELECTIONS

6

Elections in a transitional period are difficult to analyze. The kinds of dynamics involved are quite different from those that characterize normal politics, even when the stakes have been defined rather clearly, as was not the case in Brazil in 1982. Some scholars have suggested that it may be important for the stability of the transition that moderate conservative parties win, in order to convince the right that it is worthwhile to participate in a democratic process.[1] There may be significant public awareness of limits, of the possibility that the process might be derailed if the results are not acceptable to authoritarian incumbents. At the same time, there may be an immense sense of possibility, and aspirations of new political actors may not be bounded by "reasonable" expectations. How to interpret the results of elections early in the transition is a major problem. In an article about the new party system in Spain, for example, Juan Linz attributed greater staying power to the Unión del Centro Democrático than it actually had after the first several elections.[2]

"Foundational" elections are widely seen as important for their contribution to a process of regime transition. In addition to establishing a new balance of political forces, however tentative, they can also tell us a great deal about the political actors involved. Although the Brazilian elections of 1982 did not involve a transfer of power from authoritarian incumbents at a national level, two factors combined to make these sufficiently different from preceding elections that they can be viewed in a foundational sense: the direct election of state governors for the first time since 1965; and the existence of new political parties. Although the military regime continued to try to control the outcome throughout the preelectoral period, the 1982 electoral campaign was waged as if the elections were a major step in Brazilian democratization. For the PT, the elections were an important moment in the definition of the party; for the first time, they posed as a problem the relationship between building a legal electoral party and building a party whose primary sphere of activity was anchored in social movements. Because the party's response to the 1982 elections was such a crucial element in its early development, the 1982 campaign will be examined in considerably more detail in this chapter than will later elections.

The persistence of authoritarian constraints on the 1982 electoral process—restricted access to media, for example, and mid-course alterations in the electoral rules—nonetheless produced competing electoral logics. For the PMDB, it was a case of government versus opposition again. For smaller parties, particularly the PT, it was a horizontal contest among parties, in which the goal was to stake out an electoral territory of its own. The plebiscitary dimension of the elections was both contextually defined, by the fact that the military was still in power and intended to remain there for some time, and interpretively defined. The interpretive element was provided by the PMDB, which both emphasized the importance of the elections for political change and represented itself as the only viable opposition party, the legitimate heir of the MDB and thus the only one which could accomplish that change. An exception was Rio de Janeiro, where the incumbent was a conservative PMDB governor, and Brizola and the PDT were able to don the mantle of the viable opposition for themselves.

In 1982 the PT adopted contradictory postures toward the electoral process, at first claiming that it was running in order to consolidate the party organization, as elections could not be expected to bring about real change for workers, and then later deciding—particularly in São Paulo—that it was running to win. It alternated between a class-centered discourse (representing itself as the party of workers and the PMDB as a party which included bosses) and a broader discourse about participation and citizenship. Its dismal performance at the polls caused many party activists to concentrate on nonparty activities for the next three years, to the point that the survival of the PT was in question. In the 1985 mayoral elections in state capitals, the party changed its tactic significantly, running mainly middle class candidates and making a broader appeal through concentration on local issues; the results were much more successful.

While there were important contextual reasons for this difference, the potential impact of its 1985 electoral success on the PT makes it interesting to consider this development in the light of the electoral dilemma described by Adam Przeworski. Przeworski sees the electoral dilemma of labor-based parties as being that if they remain close to their working-class base of support, continuing to play a role in political class formation, they cannot win majorities in elections; if, on the other hand, they expand their electoral appeal to a multiclass one, they run the risk of becoming just one more party among many and losing the specificity of their relationship to the working class, and possibly its allegiance.[3] This dilemma was posed for the PT very early in its development, and its approach to its first electoral tests should provide some insights on its attempt to come to terms with it. The PT's experience, in turn, may help to cast light on the specific forms that this dilemma takes in countries without entrenched parliamentary traditions.

This chapter will examine the impact of both structural and political constraints on the PT's performance in the 1982 elections. In addition to the constraints that resulted from the nature of the Brazilian transition process, we will look at those whose origins were internal, particularly the party's equivocal attitude toward the electoral process and its difficulty in integrating a vision of political *representation* into a general orientation toward direct action on the part of organized social groups. This difficulty reflects an ongoing and unresolved debate over the nature of political power, on the one hand, and over the nature and role of the Workers' party as a political actor on the other. That the PT's electoral performance continued to improve after 1982 does not mean that this debate has been fully resolved, but rather that the party has managed, through a succession of crises, to maintain conflicting attitudes in a kind of dynamic tension.

The decision to run candidates at all levels in the 1982 elections was fueled by the confidence won in the difficult legalization process, confidence reflected in Lula's speech to the PT's first national convention on September 27, 1981:

> What this national convention proves to all the unbelievers, to all the hopeless and to all the fearful, is that the Workers' party is and was always completely viable. It's worth recalling a few things, com-

panheiros. When we began forming our municipal commissions in June of this year [sic], the skeptics said "the PT will not be able to do it." We did do it, and we formed 627 all over the country. When we began our membership recruitment campaign at the beginning of this year, the skeptics said "The PT is unviable." But we did it and now we're almost 300,000 all over the country. Today, as we hold our national convention, there are those who doubt the next step. There are those who think that the PT will not reach the 5 percent of the vote that the law requires, that the PT will not reach the 3 percent of the vote in nine states. We petistas are certain that the vote will not be our problem, since we are already a mass party. The great challenge before us is to avoid falling into the errors of those who pretend to speak in the name of the working class without at least hearing what it has to say.

The Workers' party is an historical innovation in this country. It is an innovation in political life and an innovation in the Brazilian left as well. It is a party born from the impulse of mass movements, born out of the strikes and popular struggles all over Brazil. It is a party born out of the consciousness that workers won after many decades of serving as a mass to be manipulated by bourgeois politicians and of listening to the ballads of the supposed vanguard parties of the working class. Only the workers can win what they have a right to. No one ever has and no one ever will give us anything for free.[4]

In spite of the confidence expressed in Lula's speech, however, early statements by party leaders about electoral goals generally did not include a reference to winning and using political power. Indeed, many PT leaders claimed that the party did not seek power in the short run. The reasons for running its own candidates in the elections at all levels, therefore, were to disseminate the party's program, to further the organization of the party, and to recruit and involve new members. We can only speculate whether the party might eventually have relaxed its opposition to coalitions had the regime not changed the rules in November 1981 to make this impossible. But once the only alternatives were to merge with another party (as the PP did with the PMDB) or to run candidates of its own, the PT made an unequivocal choice to remain independent.

The Electoral Environment in 1982

The merger between the PP and the PMDB changed the electoral environment from a competition *among* a relatively broad spectrum of parties to a sense of polarization between "government" and "opposition." This context complicated the PT's desire to project itself as a new alternative. Not only did it fall outside the dominant polarization, it also refused to accept that polarization as an accurate definition of the range of alternatives available. In an interview on January 20, 1982, Lula insisted that he was a serious candidate for governor of São Paulo and that the essential divisions in Brazilian society were not between pro- and anti-government forces but between exploiters and exploited.[5] Intent upon differentiating the PT from other parties, party leaders often maintained that there was essentially no difference between the PMDB and the PDS, as both were parties formed by and for political elites without popular participation, and with no reason to pay attention to workers' needs.

This statement was difficult for workers to understand and was alienating to many middle-class voters, because it seemed to ignore recent Brazilian electoral history. The MDB vote from 1974 on had represented a growing antiauthoritarian consensus, which included the working class. Espousing freedom and democratic rights, economic growth coupled with social equity, and a return to the rule of law, the MDB had grown by calling for a change in the context of politics rather than by focusing on political interests. For an antiauthoritarian political movement, functioning within an unusual situation of relatively competitive elections, this was a successful strategy. As Bolivar Lamounier and others have convincingly demonstrated, from 1974 on the MDB turned elections into plebiscites on the authoritarian regime.

Identification of political forces with pro- and anti-regime sentiment continued well beyond the life of the two parties that had embodied these sentiments. "The opposition" encompassed not just party activity but a whole range of movements and campaigns whose implications called the regime into question. Its common denominator was the demand for change; as an essentially negative definition, it could assimilate very sharp differences. As the MDB developed as an opposition movement, workers, especially in the advanced industrial sectors that were to constitute the PT's main target constituency, voted for it en masse. In the municipalities of the ABCD region, the government party had ceased to be a significant force well before 1982.

As long as the competing forces were identified as authoritarian regime versus opposition, it was difficult for the PT to convince masses of people that the dynamics had changed. The argument for a plebiscitary perspective was quite compelling. Many essential elements of authoritarian rule were still in place. The *abertura,* or political opening,

Table 6.1 Evolution of the ARENA Vote as a Percentage of Valid Votes, 1966–1978

Year	Legislative Body	ABC*	Capital	Interior (w/o ABC)	State of São Paulo	Brazil
1966	Senate	52.9	58.9	67.7	63.8	56.6
	Chamber of Deputies	32.6	44.2	60.7	53.5	64.0
	State Legislature	37.5	45.0	61.1	54.2	64.1
1970	Senate	40.6	47.5	52.1	49.9	60.4
	Chamber of Deputies	64.3	70.5	78.0	74.7	69.5
	State Legislature	68.2	71.6	77.9	75.2	69.8
1974	Senate	15.6	21.2	31.9	26.8	41.0
	Chamber of Deputies	24.7	29.3	44.1	37.3	52.0
	State Legislature	24.4	28.2	43.2	36.3	52.1
1978	Senate	10.6	12.3	21.8	17.6	43.0
	Chamber of Deputies	19.4	23.0	41.9	33.1	50.4
	State Legislature	20.7	23.4	42.3	33.7	51.0

Source: Tribunal Superior Eleitoral. Reproduced from Maria Tereza Sadek R. de Sousa, "Concentração Industrial e Estrutura Partidária," p. 76.
* ABC here includes the municipalities of Santo André, São Bernardo do Campo, São Caetano do Sul, Diadema, Mauá, Ribeirão Pires, and Rio Grande da Serra.

held a promise but by no means a guarantee of continued liberalization, and speculation as to what the military would or would not accept was an important element of the electoral environment in 1982. Changes in the electoral rules intended to favor the government party demonstrated the regime's determination to keep the election results within acceptable limits. The *Pacote de Novembro* issued on November 25, 1981, which prohibited electoral coalitions and stipulated that voters must vote for candidates from the same party at all levels, was designed to favor the party with the most extensive network of local organizations, the PDS. The same reasoning lay behind the last-minute change in the form of the ballot, which eliminated the traditional check-off ballot and required that voters write in the names of candidates for each office.

The stakes in the first direct gubernatorial elections in seventeen years did signal a need to go beyond a purely antiregime consensus. The possibility of winning executive power in the states, in spite of the limits imposed by continued centralization of decision making at the level of the federal executive, introduced in principle at least the need for clearer definitions of policy options. The existence of more than one party within the opposition implied that parties had to develop identities of their own.

Within the plebiscitary context, Lula's statement in May 1982 that the PT's main *adversary* in the elections was the PMDB (though the principal *enemy* remained the PDS) had the effect of a bombshell, and it fueled PMDB accusations that the PT was playing the role of a spoiler. In fact, Lula was merely stating the obvious—the votes for which the PT was competing would otherwise go to the PMDB (except in Rio de Janeiro and Rio Grande do Sul, where Brizola's PDT was also an important contender). That such a statement was so widely considered to be divisive and destructive is an indication of the strength of the polarizing definition. Indeed, the PMDB call for a *voto util* ("don't waste your vote"), with its message that an opposition vote for another party was at best wasted and at worst equivalent to a vote for the government party, encouraged this definition and was quite successful in convincing sympathizers of other parties, including and perhaps particularly the PT, that in this election at least, there were only two real choices.

This inherited tendency toward a bipolar dynamic, despite the existence of new parties, imbued the system of parties created after the 1979 party reform with a special transitional character. The political distinctions of a party system were superimposed on the prevailing perception of the opposition as an antiauthoritarian political *movement,* in which the form of regime and the rules of the game were still more at issue than competition for power within the system. Sartori, drawing upon Burke, stressed that party systems involve partitions among sovereigns, rather than between subject and sovereign.[6] He distinguished party systems, requiring a pluralist environment with subsystem autonomy, from party-state systems, lacking subsystem autonomy, and "not, therefore, a system of parties whose systemic properties result from parties (in the plural) interacting among themselves." To move from a hegemonic "party-state" system to a pluralist "party system," points out Sartori, "whatever the intentions, there is a point beyond which we are confronted with alternative mechanisms based on opposite working principles."[7]

Sartori's distinction is pertinent to an understanding of Brazilian parties in the early 1980s. The regime's ability unilaterally to change the electoral rules to favor its party, as it did in November 1981 and again just a few months prior to the elections, meant that the relation among parties certainly did not appear as relations among sovereigns. The objective stakes in the elections were limited by the military's retention of control over a highly centralized federal executive. Indeed, the fact that the state governors elected from the PMDB and PDT continued after the elections to be called "opposition governors" illustrates this point. The primary relation that a political party was called upon to define was still that of its relation to *the government,* and not its potential for governing in relation to that of other parties. It was primarily a vertical definition and only secondarily a horizontal one. Recognizing this does not diminish the importance of either the parties formed or the elections themselves. Brazilian political parties have always been largely "parties of the state": party-state relations were central to party politics in the 1945–64 system as well as in the one established by the military regime.[8] The persistence of this dynamic, however, does help to highlight the anomalous behavior of the Workers' party: while for other parties in the 1982 elections the party-state dimension remained the most salient one, the PT ran its campaign as if it were participating in a *party system,* in which differences were asserted among parties representing different "parts" of the sociopolitical whole, in horizontal rather than vertical terms.

There is one significant exception to this characterization of the electoral environment—the case of Rio Grande do Sul, in which the PMDB and the PDT, both of which had significant bases of support in that state, competed against each other as well as against the PDS. The historical importance of Brizola in Rio Grande do Sul was sufficient to fracture the PMDB's claim to the mantle of legitimate opposition. It is significant that that contest was perceived by opposition elites in other states as having been extremely destructive, and the PDS victory there as having provided an object lesson in the dangers of "dividing the opposition." The case of Rio de Janeiro, in which Brizola won the governorship as a candidate of the PDT, is a less clear example of competition among opposition parties, as the incumbent governor was from the MDB.

Campaign Organization and Objectives

An electoral platform and the electoral charter (Carta Eleitoral) that set forth the PT's general objectives in the 1982 elections were approved in a national pre-convention in São Paulo on March 27–28, 1982, with over four hundred delegates chosen at municipal and state conventions held earlier. The day before the national convention, drafts of the charter and platform were debated in a meeting of the national diretório, which had to reconcile the various drafts prepared at state meetings and produce a compromise proposal.

The electoral charter expressed the PT's objectives in the 1982 campaign as follows:

1. Take the PT program to the workers, using the campaign to carry on social struggles and to increase the organization and political consciousness of the people, tasks which will expand and consolidate the PT.

2. Become the party that brings workers together around a proposal which represents the interests and demands of the workers' and popular movements in the struggle against the dictatorship; in addition, present a political alternative to the bourgeois liberal opposition, raising the question of political power from the point of view of workers.

3. Participate in the electoral campaign alongside workers' and popular organizations (unions, the UNE, dwellers' associations), and to this end espouse the current demands of the masses in struggle.

4. Impose an electoral defeat on the dictatorship and the forces that support it directly or indirectly. During the campaign, denounce the dictatorship's electoral rules, for example, the series of electoral packages issued by the government.[9]

The party aimed to fulfill the legal requirement of winning 5 percent of the votes for the Federal Chamber of Deputies and 3 percent in each of nine states. It hoped to win a significant number of seats in Congress and control of some municipal governments; in addition, it intended to use the electoral campaign as a "period of strengthening its organization, increasing membership, organizing nuclei, and organizing the party in the interior."

In spite of this clear statement of objectives, the party's somewhat equivocal attitude toward the electoral process was also visible in the charter. On the one hand, the document states that "the PT will campaign in order to win" (p. 5). On the other hand, it claims that "The elections represent . . . only an episode, a particular moment in our permanent political activity, oriented toward the final objective of building a socialist society with neither exploited nor exploiters. *Our participation in the electoral process must not therefore cause the party to deviate from its programmatic objectives*" (p. 4; emphasis added).

The intention to campaign to win and the assertion that elections

were only one aspect of the party's activity were not in themselves
contradictory. Nonetheless, the fear that the campaign might cause the
party to deviate from its long-term goals demonstrates that elections
were still viewed with some suspicion. The *relationship* between electoral goals (strong party representation in elective office, etcetera) and
ultimate goals (socialism, or society without exploited or exploiters)
remained unclear.

This uncertainty is also reflected in the document where it addresses
the question of "The Elections and Power":

> Winning places in the executive and legislative branches at different
> levels can help to change the structure of power only if workers can
> maintain the correct linkage between struggles carried on within
> these organisms and the fundamental struggles that take place outside
> of them. The PT's participation in the elections should not cause us to
> confuse winning state and municipal executive positions with win-
> ning power. But they should serve as a front line in the organization
> and mobilization of workers looking toward the construction of pop-
> ular power. (p. 3)

Discussion of the locus and nature of power directly or indirectly
took up a substantial part of the debate over the electoral documents at
both the national diretório meeting and the pre-convention, but it did
not yield conclusive results. Delegates recognized that the reference to
popular power was vague and that the party should relate its discussion
of power more clearly to the question of workers' organization, party
organization, and class, but no consensual formulation arose that succeeded in doing this. Nor was there agreement on whether the electoral
platform should seek to be a plan for government or a propaganda
instrument in a more immediate sense. Most delegates saw it as the
latter, as an outline of the main mobilizing points for a campaign intended to build a political movement.

In addition to discussing campaign objectives, the electoral charter
stipulated how candidates were to be selected ("in democratic municipal, district, and state meetings, guaranteeing substantial participation
by nuclei in the choices," p. 6) and criteria for the choice of candidates
(participation in workers' movements at different levels, social expression in their areas, and participation in building the PT). It was also
stated that in order to make the slate electorally viable, the party should
run as many candidates as possible—preferably the full complement
allowed by the law.

The campaign was to be coordinated by unified electoral committees set up at the municipal, state, and national levels, whose job was to distribute resources, involve party members and sympathizers in the campaign, and try to give it a consistent content. The party would also establish a common electoral fund to try to equalize the financial situations of the different candidates for office.

The charter also addressed the relationship between elected candidates and the party, the accountability of office holders to the party, and their duty to consult with the party when planning activities, presenting bills, and contracting staff, and it mandated that federal and state congressmen and holders of executive offices contribute 40 percent of their salaries to the party. (Other Brazilian parties collect around 3 percent of representatives' salaries.) Elected officials were thus clearly seen more as servants of the party than as its leaders. This was not unusual; leftist parties in Europe as well as in Chile have sometimes had similar policies on the relationship between the party organization and members of parliament, and these have often caused conflict between party officials and office holders. The British Labour party, which discussed this problem for many years, finally resolved its accountability problem in the 1970s by making all incumbents, even those with so-called safe seats, subject to reselection by the local party organization at each election. This is akin to the PT's refusal to accept the idea of the *candidato nato*—a traditional practice among Brazilian parties of guaranteeing that any sitting legislator has the right to a place on the party slate in the next election.

CHOOSING CANDIDATES. Although the party leadership encouraged state and local organs to nominate as many candidates as the law allowed, in most of Brazil party slates were much smaller than they might have been. The electoral committee even called for a second round of nominations to expand the party list, but to little avail. Francisco Weffort, who headed the unified electoral committee, attributed this to weak political understanding of the electoral process and to a failure on the part of PT leadership to prepare party organizations for the nominating process. Sometimes organized groups or individual candidates tried to limit the size of slates, acting on the illusion that this guaranteed them a particular electoral territory. In other instances, local parties were worried that a large list would produce too much competition among PT candidates themselves. In order to elect even one candidate, however, in proportional elections with an open list it is necessary to set up an entire electoral machine. Failure to understand this had predictable results. In Maranhão, for example, where the local party decided that it had the chance of electing only one federal deputy and thus ran a small slate of candidates, not even one was elected. In Piauí, for similar reasons, the party only ran two candidates for federal deputy and elected none. Another explanation often given for the small size of party slates was the lack of candidates with the resources to mount campaigns. Weffort discounted this explanation, as lack of money and/or time was equally a problem for most of those who *were* nominated. Rather, he argues, it was a failure to understand that elections were not just a legal requirement but were also an important way of linking the party with popular struggles.

A similar phenomenon occurred with the party's nominations for governor. In many states, recognizing that its chances in the gubernatorial elections were nil, the PT put up its strongest candidates for state and federal deputy, with weak candidates for governor. As a result, the party was left without candidates able to provide a unifying image for the state campaign as a whole. Where this occurred, it hurt the campaign at all levels. There were notable exceptions—the fact that Lula was the party's gubernatorial candidate in São Paulo, for example. The same kind of problem arose with mayoral nominations. A good example occurred in Osasco, São Paulo, where the two well-known local party leaders (José Ibrahim and José Pedro da Silva) both chose to run for federal deputy. Due to internal divisions the party ran two fairly weak candidates for mayor, using the device of sublegenda. This weakened the party's electoral chances in Osasco, a traditional stronghold of working-class activism. Only one PT member was elected to the municipal council, and neither Zé Ibrahim nor Zé Pedro was elected federal deputy.[10]

These limitations notwithstanding, the PT did present a broad range of candidates in the 1982 elections. The results of a survey of candidates for federal and state deputy by the newsmagazine *Istoé* demonstrated that if a part of the PT's intent in the electoral campaign was to present candidates with diverse social origins and to introduce new faces and new political forces into politics, it was at least somewhat successful.[11] PT candidates were generally younger than those from other parties, included more women at the federal deputy level, and were more widely distributed over different occupational sectors. While the PT's candidates were also somewhat more evenly spread as to educational background than were those of other parties, 59.7 percent of those running for state deputy and 66.6 percent of those running for federal deputy had attended a university. And more of the party's candidates were from the liberal professions than from any other occupational category. One notable difference between PT candidates and others was their political inexperience: only 12.1 percent of the candidates for federal deputy and 8.0 percent of candidates for state deputy had previously held elective office, fewer than in any other party. By contrast, 62.5 percent of the PMDB's candidates for federal deputy and 49.0 percent of its candidates for state deputy had previously held elective office.

COORDINATING THE CAMPAIGN. To coordinate the PT's campaign nationally, a national unified electoral committee was established to monitor the functioning of the state committees. The national committee, composed of Francisco Weffort, Hélio Doyle, and Apolônio de Carvalho, was created at a meeting of the national executive commission in May 1982.[12] The electoral committee was to be responsible to the national executive and would insure the implementation of the electoral charter, the national platform, and the party's resolutions on the campaign. It would also be responsible for campaign literature, organization, campaign finances, and party recruitment during the campaign.

The national committee was to insure that unified electoral committees were formed in each state and municipality by party members who were not candidates in the proportional elections (for federal and state deputy and municipal councils). Candidates in majority elections (for governor, senator, and mayor) could be committee members but could not be coordinators. The state committees were to be formed by the state executive commissions, and they were asked to produce a detailed report by June 20 on the party's electoral situation in the state. A meeting was convoked of all gubernatorial and senatorial candidates and electoral committee coordinators in Brasília for July 3–4. While food, lodging, and local transportation for that meeting were to be provided by the national organization, the costs of getting there were the responsibility of each regional diretório.[13] The fact that only thirteen of the party's twenty-one gubernatorial candidates were able to raise the money to attend the meeting boded ill for the party's ability to finance a campaign.[14]

The discussions at the Brasília meeting illuminated a number of problems that would plague the campaign throughout. Many state organizations were very weak and lacked funds, access to mass media, and legal help in interpreting the election laws. Party leaders in many states also wanted Lula, as PT president, to be involved in the campaign nationwide, not just in São Paulo where he was running for governor. The contradictory demands of his two roles posed serious difficulties for Lula and for the national electoral committee throughout the campaign. Nonetheless, party leaders remained optimistic about using the campaign to consolidate party organization. Another major topic of debate was how to address the PMDB in the campaign; it was decided not to treat the PMDB as a sacred cow but to criticize it as a liberal-bourgeois party (however much individual PMDB candidates might take more "genuinely oppositional" positions). The PMDB's "voto util" campaign implied that the PT was a spoiler, objectively aiding the regime; the PT had to demonstrate its viability, not just as a party of the future but as one with the right to run in these elections. Thus a clear distinction had to be made between the two parties, showing that the PT's roots in labor and popular struggles made it a genuine alternative.

Several conclusions were drawn from the July planning meeting. First, the PT was campaigning to win, even though the elections were not wholly free. Second, the opponent was the military regime and the political forces that sustained it through clientelistic or conciliatory practices, influence peddling, abuse of economic power, and the like. Those who exploited and oppressed the working class could be found in more than one party. Focusing its campaign around the issues of land, labor, and liberty, the PT would bring together and reinforce those groups which had never had a chance either to act or speak for themselves, and the party's victories would be the victories not only of those elected but of the popular movements.[15]

The attempt to unify the party's electoral campaign was largely unsuccessful outside of São Paulo, and to a lesser extent Rio de Janeiro and Rio Grande do Sul. Part of the reason was financial: the national committee had almost no resources to divide among the states, and most of the state committees were no better off. Part of the problem was also political. According to Weffort, the initial discussion of the committees had taken place as if they were to be political organisms capable of unifying the campaign in all its political, propaganda, and organizational aspects, functioning as a kind of electoral and political command center for all candidates in equality of conditions. This was clearly unrealistic, and, claimed Weffort, its idealistic spirit served as a kind of ideological camouflage for unbridled electoralism much of the time. In some states the committees had no funds simply because candidates, all of whom had agreed to contribute a percentage of the funds raised in their campaigns to a common fund, did not do so.[16]

At the end of August 1982, the national electoral committee issued guidelines for the campaign. The electoral committees were to coordinate three areas: finances, campaign literature, and organization. They were to centralize finances based on receipt of a percentage of funds raised by each candidate, stimulate fund-raising activities, and use the common fund to insure equality of resources for those candidates whose personal resources were less. They were to insure that all candidates' campaign literature included the names of the candidates for majority positions. And they were to plan and maintain the calendar of candidates' appearances; arrange caravans throughout the state; organize rallies, meetings, and debates; and generally try to stimulate creative campaign activities. The national committee was worried that most regional and local electoral committees were not focusing on these specific tasks. In some cases they were taking over the direction of virtually all party activity; in others, funds intended for the campaign were being used to bail out diretórios in difficulty, because local infrastructure was in such bad shape. In other areas the electoral committees were practically nonexistent.

The guidelines emphasized the importance of using whatever space was available in the mass media, particularly television and radio, prior to September 15 when the Lei Falcão restrictions would take effect. They encouraged candidates to participate in debates, outlining the PT proposals and discussing what kinds of policies were necessary and possible for state and municipal governments. While candidates were not to avoid conflict with and criticism of other parties, they were advised to emphasize the positive side of the PT position in the process of criticizing others. Although the working-class vote was still considered central, the guidelines suggested that the middle class could be reached through discussion of the high cost of living, lack of job security, urban living conditions, restrictions on the rights of citizens, and the role of multinational corporations in the economy. The guidelines also pointed out the importance of the youth vote: more than 50 percent of voters were voting for governor for the first time.[17]

THE CAMPAIGN IN SÃO PAULO. The PT campaign in São Paulo was launched in an animated rally attended by some 15,000 people in the working-class district of Santo Amaro in the capital on April 21,

1982. Its size surprised even the rally's organizers—particularly as it was being held at the same time that an important soccer match (Flamengo versus Grémio) was being broadcast live on television. The mood was festive, with well-known musicians and other artists sharing the stage with the party's candidates. There was a palpable feeling of anticipation in the crowd, a sense that something new was beginning.[18]

The attempt to unify the electoral campaign was somewhat successful in the state of São Paulo. The campaigns of the majority candidates (Lula for governor, Jacó Bittar for senator, and mayors) were designed to give exposure to candidates in the proportional elections (for state and federal deputies and municipal council members). This was a complicated process in practical terms. Party caravans from the capital to the interior of the state involving as many as eight rallies in a single day had to be carefully timed to reach the events planned in each municipality. For local candidates these caravans provided their only opportunities to appear on the platform with Lula, who continued to be the most important draw for PT events.

The regional committee had to decide who would appear with Lula at the rallies in each municipality. It was hard to balance the claims of the various candidates: one might have come from the region, another might have ties with the area through a popular movement, and yet another might have no links to the area but need (and was seen as having a right to) more exposure in the interior of the state. A few candidates undoubtedly received more exposure in these caravans than did most of the others, in part because of their closer personal ties with Lula.[19]

In addition to organizing the caravans to the interior, the unified electoral committee in São Paulo produced part of the campaign literature for the party as a whole in the state. These materials were distributed to municipal diretórios, which were then to pass them out to candidates for individual use, thus at least potentially benefiting all candidates. (The state electoral committee also produced literature for two specific kinds of candidates: trade unionists running for federal or state legislatures and candidates with serious funding difficulties.) The committee negotiated price breaks with several printers, making production of materials cheaper for individual candidates.

The state committee could not coordinate the campaigns of the candidates for federal and state deputy, apart from scheduling their participation in caravans with the majority candidates and giving them some minimal help with campaign literature. Thus, most had to rely on their own initiative, and most formed their own campaign committees.

Some candidates demonstrated a great deal of initiative; others did not. Here those who had previously either run for election or participated in campaigns were at an advantage, as were those who were closely tied to particular constituencies that were willing to work hard in the campaign. Those who were not well known in a major urban area or with a particular public had little opportunity to spread out from a narrow constituency during the campaign.

The Themes of the 1982 Campaign

The party's campaign had two major themes: empowerment and the working-class majority. Although in many ways complementary, the two differ fundamentally in the kind of discourse they produced, which gave rise to contradictory expectations and images of the party. Over the course of the campaign, while the two continued to coexist as core principles, the second gradually came to predominate over the first. How exactly were these two organizing principles presented and how did the contradictions make themselves felt?

The theme of empowerment was expressed in party discourse on the nature of politics, on questions such as who participates, what is political participation, and what constitutes power. A graphic illustration of this discourse was a cartoon produced by the popular cartoonist Henfil (Henrique Souza Filho),[20] a PT member, which took the form of a conjugation of the verb *poder*. *Poder* in Portuguese, as in most Latin languages, in its noun form (*o poder*) means "power" and in its verb form (*poder*) means "to be able." In the Henfil cartoon, under the heading *Poder* engaging stick figure characters were shown saying *eu posso* (I can), *você pode* (you can), *ele pode* (he can), *ela pode* (she can), and so on. This cartoon and other Henfil cartoons like it were reproduced on T-shirts, which became very popular during the campaign.

The core of the argument about politics and participation was that politics was not merely an elite activity exercised in Congress and in organs of the state, but rather involved all kinds of popular struggles around living and working conditions. Participation in these struggles was political participation, and the special knowledge required for political participation was thus knowledge of one's own situation and that of one's community rather than membership in the political elite. The lack of a university diploma was not an impediment to political participation, PT supporters were told; their diplomas came from life experience, from struggles in the factories, in the neighborhoods, and in the *favelas*. The discourse on participation reflected the PT's general commitment to strengthening popular organizations. The party's approach to power involved the accumulation of forces at the grass roots and the struggle for control over the immediate decisions that affect one's life. It was a discourse very close to that of the popular church.

The discourse on the working-class majority, though related to the theme of empowerment through its stress on the rights of citizens and the need for workers to speak with their own voices in political life, was distinct in its more frontal approach to the question of power relations in the whole society. While the electoral slogan "worker, vote for a worker" expresses the unity of the two themes, another party slogan in São Paulo, "Vote for number 3—the rest is bourgeois" (*Vote em três—o reste é burguês*), expresses their difference. The discourse on empowerment was primarily grounded in the concept of citizenship, while the discourse on the working-class majority had as its key reference the concept of class.

The party's representation of a working-class majority was essentially a traditional one, in which society was seen as divided between those who controlled the product of their labor and those who did not. "Workers" were broadly defined as wage earners. In the process of struggles, workers would become more conscious of both their exploitation and their strength, and they would unite to transform society. For PT leaders, the reference point for this process of becoming conscious was the metalworkers' experience in São Bernardo do Campo. As others have pointed out, this was in many ways a unique experience. The success of metalworker organization gave PT leaders an image of class solidarity and homogeneity that probably did not correspond to the perception that most Brazilian wage earners had of their situation.

The notion of a working-class majority can be viewed either descriptively (as a characterization of an actually existing situation) or prospectively (as part of a process of political class formation).[21] In the latter sense, it is closely tied to the discourse on participation. The expectations generated are long-term ones, and the image of the party which is the carrier of this discourse on class formation is one of a party in formation together with the class. In the former sense—as a descriptive characterization—expectations are generated for short-term success, and the image of the party is either that of the representative of the class or a more vanguardist conception, in which the party appears as carrier of the true consciousness and interpreter of the real interests of the Brazilian working class.

During the 1982 PT campaign in São Paulo, there was a gradual, largely unrecognized, but marked shift in campaign discussions from a primarily prospective to a primarily descriptive conception of the notion of working-class majority. An assumption of social homogeneity began to replace the idea of a political process of knitting together the heterogeneous strands of a highly differentiated society into a perception of common interests and goals as the foundation for party strength. This shift, caused by apparent popular receptivity to the PT campaign, helps to explain the fact that by the end of the campaign, the party had developed extraordinarily high expectations as to electoral outcome.

Thus within the campaign itself we can see a reflection of the problem that recurs constantly in this analysis of the PT's development: the underlying conflict between a vision of the party as the reflection or embodiment of an essentially social process occurring outside of it; and one that sees the party as actively contributing to the shape of this process through political organization. In early stages of the campaign party leaders in São Paulo stressed the importance of the electoral period for organizing workers, yet by the end the emphasis was on winning the election because of the strength of the working class.

Campaign Rallies and False Hopes

What were the elements that contributed to the shift in perception of the party's chances in the 1982 elections in São Paulo? Probably the most important ones were the impact of the televised debates among gubernatorial candidates and the size of party election rallies. There were three major debates among the candidates for governor.[22] The first one, which had the most psychological impact for the PT, took place on August 10 and televised an August 14, 1982; Lula, Franco Montoro (PMDB), Rogê Ferreira (PDT), and Reynaldo de Barros (PDS) took part. Jânio Quadros, the PTB candidate for governor, did not participate in the first two debates because of a long-standing feud with O Estado de São Paulo. The first debate generated a great deal of discussion, primarily due to the surprise of elite commentators that not only could Lula debate the issues on a level of equality with the other participants but that in fact, according to the polls taken afterward, he won the debate.[23]

The size of the crowds at the party's electoral rallies in São Paulo was another factor in the shift in the PT's perception of its strength. It seemed inconceivable to party leaders that the PT could attract larger crowds to its rallies than other parties and still trail by a significant margin in the polls, and some of them began to believe that the major polling organizations (Gallup and IBOPE) were deliberately trying to conceal the party's strength. This conviction persisted even when a poll commissioned by the PT, carried out under the direction of a CEBRAP social scientist who was a party member, came up with virtually the same results. At the huge final PT election rally in the Pacaembu stadium in São Paulo on November 7, 1982, Lula contended that "we will see after this rally that Gallup, *Veja,* Globo, and the *O Estado de São Paulo* will choke on their polls that relegated the PT to last place."[24]

The verdict of the party's own poll seemed less compelling than the presence of 100,000 people at a rally in São Paulo, of 15,000 in Campinas, 20,000 in Sumaré, 10,000 in Catanduva, and the like. The numbers blinded the leadership to the continued fragility of the party organization, and they failed to recognize that for many voters the plebiscitary dynamics characteristic of the last three elections were still central. In his Pacaembu speech, Lula cited the presence of 3,000 people at a rally in Nova Odessa, a town with a voting population of only around 10,000, as conclusive evidence of support for the party; in fact, the party received 948 votes in that city, or 8.97 percent of the total votes cast. He cited the crowd of 20,000 in Sumaré; 8,319 of those showed up as votes. While it is undoubtedly true that attendance at party rallies was an expression of sympathy for and interest in the PT, there was not a direct link between sympathy and the ballot.[25] Before the elections, the PT had 115 members in Nova Odessa and 312 members in Sumaré. While membership figures are not an adequate predictor of votes, the lack of a strong party machine was a serious impediment. In examining these two examples, it is particularly interesting to note that while the party's membership in Nova Odessa barely changed between the fourth quarter of 1982 and the following year, its membership in Sumaré quadrupled, suggesting that a more effective party campaign was carried out in the latter and helping to explain the higher overall party vote in that city.

In addition to the rallies and televised debates, the PT campaign message was carried by individual candidates in legislative and in municipal elections and in campaign literature issued by the candidates and the party, including the radio and television propaganda during the last sixty days of the campaign. The campaigns of individual PT candidates varied significantly, ranging from the countercultural campaign waged by Katerina Koltoi,[26] a candidate for municipal council in the capital, to campaigns aimed principally at industrial workers by some of the trade unionist candidates, to others that emphasized human rights issues or denounced the corruption of previous state governments.

Probably the least effective element in the PT's campaign in São Paulo in 1982 was use of the mass media. The party had a great deal of trouble getting its message across in newspaper coverage of the campaign; news coverage tended to either report party statements flatly or to concentrate on conflict between the PT and the PMDB. The party was not particularly successful in linking electoral positions with topical issues of the kind likely to arouse journalistic interest. Few candidates succeeded in making use of those spaces that might have been available—television talk shows, for example. An exception was state congressman Eduardo Suplicy, running for federal deputy, who, because an important element in his campaign was his exposure of corruption in the Maluf government and in the PDS electoral campaign, often "made" news, and publicized his own and the PT campaign as a result.

The party's own media were also quite weak. The PT launched its first national newspaper (*Jornal dos Trabalhadores*) at the same time as its campaign, and the last issue came out in November 1982. It was often unclear whether the paper was intended as an internal organ or an organ of communication between the party and the population at large, and its potential for communication in the electoral campaign was not realized. More effective were local mimeographed sheets and wall newspapers issued by nuclei and other local party organizations, but these appeared sporadically and usually reached a limited audience.

The party's use of the scheduled free propaganda time on radio and television in the last sixty days of the campaign was particularly ineffective, even within the extremely limited range of possibilities that the format provided. The format was stipulated by the Lei Falcão, first instituted in 1976 to prevent the MDB from duplicating its 1974 success with the media. The law regulated radio and television campaigning in the sixty days before the election by prohibiting live appearances by candidates. Several hours per day of free air time were provided, to be divided equally among the parties; however, during this time parties could only show still photographs of candidates with a voiceover narration giving the curriculum vita of each candidate as his/her photo appeared. The result was extraordinarily dull in the best of circumstances. Nonetheless, this was an important forum in that, while it may not have convinced voters to vote for particular candidates, the impact of a succession of candidates' photos and curricula still affected the image that voters had of the parties in the election.

In attempting to demonstrate in the curricula of its candidates that these were people who had struggled and suffered under the authoritarian regime and thus were truly popular candidates, the party underestimated the image-making aspect of the format.[27] One photo after another appeared with narration saying that this one had been jailed for human rights activities, that one had been purged from a union post for activism, this one had been in exile, that one had been forced to leave school after four years in order to go to work to feed his/her family, this one had been tortured. The result, instead of a positive picture that demonstrated how these people had overcome persecutions and privations to become important popular leaders, was what many PT leaders later described as an essentially negative picture of a group of uneducated jailbirds. The party eventually recognized its mistake and in the last week or so of the campaign substituted a more positive and much more effective filmstrip, but most of the damage had already been done.

Conflict with the PMDB

An aspect of the campaign that generated heated discussion both within and outside of the party was the PT's effort to distinguish itself from the PMDB. The conflict came to a head as early as May 1982. The PMDB accused the PT of divisionism and of "playing the government's game," and PMDB members repeatedly claimed that Lula was not capable of governing.[28] The PT was called "workerist," a party "dressed in a monkey-suit" (*vestido de macacão*, a reference to the popular name for the work clothes worn by metalworkers). The PT in turn called the PMDB a front too broad to have any real political unity and a bourgeois party. The PMDB's voto util ("don't waste your vote") campaign was anathema to the PT, against which it was primarily aimed.[29]

The conflict was exacerbated by an interview that Lula gave to a reporter from *Folha de São Paulo,* published on May 16 under the headline "Our Adversary is the PMDB, affirms Lula." Responding to PMDB insinuations that his candidacy worked in favor of the government party, Lula replied:

> It's our job to show the weakness of Senator Franco Montoro as candidate for governor, that is, the weakness of his proposal, since our adversary is really the PMDB—our adversary at the ballot box. . . . If we are going to support a multiparty system, we need to make up our minds whether we want Mexicanization or a real multiparty system. . . . We do not see the PMDB as our enemy, no. The enemy is the PDS, but we think the PMDB will be the greater political adversary, because it is much stronger than the PDS. The fight

will be between the PT and the PMDB, and those of us who are young enough will see how it comes out.[30]

The following week the same newspaper carried counterattacks from the PMDB. Economist Maria da Conceição Tavares charged that Lula had been catapulted to fame by the mass media. The PT was guilty of being simplistic, sectarian, and electoralist: "'The [PT's] explanation of society is simple and immediate: it is divided between exploiters and exploited. The way to organize society is easy: at the base (or in cells, depending on the tendency involved). How to win electoral space? It's also easy: by attacking the PMDB.[31]'" Editorialist Claudio Abramo criticized the PT for failing to see that if indeed the PMDB was a front composed of very different currents and lacking an ambitious program for change, it was because that was what the situation called for. Abramo recognized, however, that the PT's antagonism toward the PMDB was largely caused by the latter's virulent and "nauseating" offensive against the PT.[32]

It is interesting that most commentaries on the Lula interview did not distinguish between adversary (that is, competitor) and enemy, as Lula himself had done. It is unclear whether the failure to make this distinction was a polemical device on the part of the PT's critics or whether it reflected a deeper difficulty in coming to terms with the existence of nuances in political conflict. The latter interpretation is consistent with historical and anthropological analyses of Brazilian political culture, which highlight the importance of consensus, cordiality, and negotiation, and the refusal to accept the legitimacy of conflict.[33] The recognition of a conflict between the PDS and the PMDB, or of the government versus the opposition, was exempt from this pattern because it had been elevated to a Manichean, quasi-cosmological level: it was a question of good versus evil, and that which was not with the good was necessarily with the evil. The fact that the PT was actively competing for votes was seen, even by sophisticated observers, as endangering the very process of redemocratization. Just how virulent was this critique is illustrated in a column by the PMDB economist Luiz Carlos Bresser Pereira in *Folha de São Paulo.*

> In fact, the PMDB is a complex and contradictory party, which wants the country to follow a democratic, social (but not socialist), and modernizing path. It is the center-left party which, mirroring the contradictions and the diversity of Brazilian society, makes possible the consolidation of a more solid social pact, which will allow us to

face in the 1980s the serious economic crisis in Brazil and in the world within the framework of a democratic regime.

The PT, in turn, is a relatively cohesive party organized around a simplistic analysis of Brazilian society: Brazil is said to be divided between the "good guys" (the workers) and the "bad guys" (the capitalists); for the good to get into power it is necessary to organize workers politically at the base.

Obviously, this kind of classist reasoning cannot lead to power over the medium term in Brazil, a country where bourgeois ideological hegemony is evident. Nonetheless, as Lula's prestige in São Paulo is considerable, PT members contradictorily allow themselves to be caught up in electoral enthusiasm, create the fiction that the candidate for governor is a real trump card, and identify the PMDB as their principal adversary.

By doing this, it is clear that the PT has forgotten its natural alliances and has lost all contact with reality, falling into the most classic forms of electoralism. Since it can't compete with its enemy, the PDS, for votes, it competes with its brother, the PMDB.

Thus while I agree with Cláudio Abramo that it is slanderous to say that the PT is "playing the game of the government," because the PT's goal is exactly the opposite, in practice this is just what is happening. While the PTB deliberately plays the government's game, the PT does it involuntarily. The danger is that the PTB does little harm to the PMDB in São Paulo, while the PT, because of the charismatic appeal of Lula to leftist intellectuals and students, could do a great deal of harm. What Maria Conceição Tavares tried to convey in the political interview that she granted to *Folha* this past Sunday is very simple. . . . The PT's electoralism in São Paulo *is a threat to redemocratization in the country,* in that it only reinforces the government and particularly Mr. Paulo Maluf. The economic crisis in Brazil (and in the world) will persist throughout this decade. The reinforcement of authoritarian and populist politicians on the right in the context of an economic crisis could lead us back to a dictatorship.

PT leaders are unlikely to wake up in time to recognize the mistake they are making. It is more probable that voters will do so. For this to happen, however, it must be clear to everyone that the fundamental priority today in Brazil is the reestablishment and consolidation of democracy in the context of an economy in crisis. This is the challenge that Brazilian society faces in the 1980s. The drama of the PT lies in its failure to understand this, however good its intentions. [Emphasis added.][34]

The PT tried hard to counter the appeal of the voto util argument for potential PT voters, asserting that the class origins of PMDB candidates would prevent their support for policies that benefited workers and the poor. In a campaign speech at Ubatuba, for example, Lula argued that "it's not possible that a party containing *latifundiários* will resolve the land problem in this country. I don't believe that a party supported by big businessmen will resolve the problems of the working class. I don't believe that a party supported by bankers will resolve the problem of interest rates in this country." "Utility" for workers should thus be defined differently: "A lot of people will talk about the voto util. If the PT wins, can it be effective? Wouldn't it make more sense to vote for so and so, who is more powerful? Look, companheiros. We have to be clear about this. Either we'll be judged for having compromised and erred, or we'll be judged for having had the courage to say what we thought in public. And between being judged for having given up and been 'responsible' and being judged for sticking with the working class, I prefer the latter."[35]

Faced with continuing PMDB attacks, the invective became increasingly bitter, culminating in Lula's speech at the final election rally in the Pacaembu stadium in São Paulo.

> There has been a lot of criticism, harassment, slander. All of a sudden, Lula no longer lived in São Bernardo, they said, and had moved to Morumbi. All of a sudden, because Lula belonged to a political party, Lula was no longer the admired worker of the São Bernardo do Campo strikes. . . . All of a sudden Lula could no longer do things any other citizen could do because lying tongues were waiting to denigrate, through the person of Lula, the image of a political organization that is a thousand times more important than Lula personally or than any individual party militant.
>
> We tried to show these people that working-class organization is irreversible. We tried to show them that no one would ever succeed in stopping our movement. We tried to show that conventional politics, the politics of money, the politics of privilege, wouldn't work any more in this state or in Brazil. . . . We tried to show that the PDS and the PMDB are flour out of the same sack and that they won't change the situation of the Brazilian working class. This is even more visible when we go to the interior of São Paulo and see the landowner candidate from the PDS running against the landowner candidate from the PMDB. In both parties, yesterday one was in the PMDB and today he's in ARENA, and yesterday one was in ARENA and

today he's in the PMDB, changing parties with no respect for the people who elected them.

The idea of the voto util was raised all over the country. This confused a lot of people—even some who didn't realize its impact on them. And now the voto util is no longer the issue; what is appearing in some newspaper headlines is the cowardly vote, the vote of fear. . . . When the PMDB says "if Lula wins in São Paulo he won't be allowed to take office, and if Brizola wins in Rio de Janeiro he won't take office," the PMDB is communicating something. It is telling the people that Lula and Brizola, that the PT in São Paulo and the PDT in Rio, are against the regime, and the regime is against the PT and won't want us to take power. When the PMDB says these things, at the same time as it says that if the PMDB wins it will take office, it is affirming nothing more nor less than that the PMDB is the opposition party "of confidence" to the system, and for that reason, if it wins it will take office in this country. And I want the press present here to register that if I'm speaking badly of the PMDB, I'm telling the political truth in this country. And I'm not going to say bad things about the PDS, because there's no use beating a dead horse, and the PDS no longer exists in this country or in the state of São Paulo as a political force.[36]

How much impact did all this have on voters? Critics within the PT claim that the attacks on the PMDB narrowed the party's electoral base and alienated many middle-class voters. There are no survey data of which I am aware that can assess the importance of this question. It seems unlikely that the attacks on the PMDB had a major impact on the election results; those voters who were alienated would probably have responded to the PMDB's campaign for a voto util in any case. Had the party refrained from attacking the PMDB, proving itself a "responsible" ally within a broader opposition, the impact of the voto util campaign might have been even stronger than it was, particularly among working-class voters. Failure to respond would have implied acceptance of the idea that the Workers' party was indeed a "party of the future," whose role in the present was to wait.

This is not to say that the electoral strategy adopted by the party was the only one available; any historical process involves roads not taken as well as the ones that were. Nonetheless, there were powerful incentives operating in its favor. First, the decision to form the party was a decision to *differentiate* working-class political organization from the more general opposition. Second, the electoral legislation mandated that to remain legal, a party had to run in the elections and obtain 5 percent of the vote nationally and at least 3 percent in each of nine states. (This requirement was eventually transferred from the 1982 to the 1986 results). For a new party, this required active organizing and campaigning. Third, attacks by members of the elite opposition against the PT, particularly those which denigrated the intellectual and organizational capacity of workers, had a psychological impact that was almost guaranteed to provoke a response from the party. And finally, the seemingly positive popular response to the campaign convinced many party leaders that the elite opposition was genuinely afraid of a PT victory in São Paulo. While there is no evidence that any of the PMDB leadership ever thought that the PT could win, statements by PMDB members late in the campaign that if Lula were to win in São Paulo or Brizola in Rio de Janeiro the regime would not permit them to take office only reinforced this belief by PT leaders. Early in the campaign treating the PMDB as chief adversary was both electoral realism and a response to the voto util issue; by November some PT leaders had begun to think that the party actually could win in São Paulo, and only the PMDB stood in the way of a PT victory.

The Results of the 1982 Elections

The results of the 1982 elections were a profound shock and disappointment to the PT. It did not meet the law's minimum goal of 5 percent nationally and 3 percent in each of nine states. Indeed, it won over 3 percent of the vote only in São Paulo (9.9) and Acre (5.4). Nationwide, its gubernatorial candidates won only 3.3 percent of the total vote cast.

The party elected eight federal deputies, of whom six were from São Paulo, one from Rio de Janeiro, and one from Minas Gerais. It elected one state deputy in Rio de Janeiro, one in Minas Gerais, one in Acre, and nine in São Paulo. Mayoral candidates from the PT were elected in two municipalities in Brazil, one in the city of Diadema, São Paulo, and one in Santa Quitéria, Maranhão. In the state of São Paulo, the party elected 78 municipal council members in 39 municipalities.[37]

The system for electing members of the Federal Chamber of Deputies and state legislatures combines proportional representation with an open list. All candidates run statewide. Lists are nominal; voters select one candidate for federal deputy, one for state deputy, and one for municipal council. Candidates who are well known in a given region, particularly an urban area, have a significant advantage; in the absence of a focused constituency, a candidate must campaign heavily all over

Table 6.2 Gubernatorial Election Results, 1982

State	PDS	PDT	PT	PTB	PMDB	Blank	Null	Total
Acre	33,879	—	4,637	3,152	36,369	4,214	4,305	86,556
Alagoas	257,898	—	—	—	206,856	75,814	23,494	564,062
Amazonas	164,190	—	5,352	4,203	201,182	14,169	12,029	401,125
Bahia	1,623,422	—	25,113	—	1,030,111	366,923	101,666	3,147,235
Ceará	1,149,468	—	9,961	—	478,853	277,124	41,341	1,956,747
Espírito Santo	282,728	1,236	10,588	—	448,074	63,856	19,449	825,934
Goiás	470,184	845	9,818	—	964,179	82,324	33,070	1,560,420
Maranhão	673,916	12,738	8,643	632	180,287	148,558	32,338	1,057,112
Mato Grosso	203,605	899	887	—	188,878	21,432	14,609	430,310
Mato Grosso do Sul	237,144	5,414	4,541	—	258,192	33,371	14,808	553,470
Minas Gerais	2,424,197	11,160	113,950	—	2,667,595	459,479	147,160	5,823,541
Pará	461,969	—	11,010	7,214	501,605	63,365	42,594	1,087,757
Paraíba	509,855	—	3,918	—	358,146	70,291	22,042	964,252
Paraná	1,127,175	6,679	12,047	30,202	1,708,785	237,748	74,307	3,196,943
Pernambuco	913,774	—	4,027	7,872	816,085	154,406	57,052	1,953,216
Piauí	393,818	—	5,814	—	271,274	85,430	22,087	778,423
Rio de Janeiro	1,530,706	1,709,180	152,614	536,383	1,073,446	243,274	195,063	5,440,666
Rio Grande do Norte	389,677	—	3,207	441	283,266	56,450	15,713	748,854
Rio Grande do Sul	1,294,962	775,546	50,713	—	1,272,319	334,125	71,348	3,799,013
Rondônia	—	—	—	—	—	—	—	—
Santa Catarina	838,150	4,572	6,803	2,281	825,500	121,927	32,578	1,831,811
São Paulo	2,728,732	94,395	1,144,648	1,447,328	5,209,952	664,101	308,829	11,597,985
Sergipe	256,385	1,133	1,354	—	77,965	36,510	10,177	383,524
Amapá	—	—	—	—	—	—	—	—
Roraima	—	—	—	—	—	—	—	—
Total	17,965,834	2,623,797	1,589,645	2,039,708	19,059,019	3,614,059	1,296,059	48,188,956

Source: Reproduced from José Alfredo de Óliveira Baracho, "O Projeto Político Brasileiro e as Eleições Nacionais," *Revista Brasileira de Estudos Políticos* 57 (July 1983): 130.

the state in order to accumulate enough votes in a variety of areas to contest those candidates whose bases are more concentrated. In a state the size of São Paulo, this is an expensive and time-consuming proposition.

The PT in São Paulo ran 38 candidates for federal deputy (out of a possible 60), electing 6, and 68 candidates for state deputy (out of a possible 84), of whom 9 were elected. The urban vote, in the capital and in the ABC region, was decisive for most of the party's successful candidates. Of those elected to the federal congress, four received over 60 percent of their vote in the capital, and one, metalworker leader Djalma Bom, received over 60 percent in the capital and São Bernardo do Campo combined. Only the actress Elizabeth (Bete) Mendes got more than half her vote outside the capital. In the elections for the state legislature, the advantage of a large urban constituency is demonstrated by the fact that the vote for Expedito Soares in São Bernardo alone or for José Cicote in Santo André alone was sufficient to elect them to the state legislature.[38]

The PT candidates elected to Congress from São Paulo in 1982 reflected the diversity of the party's origins. Irma Passoni, elected to the state legislature in 1978, had been an organizer of the cost of living movement and was considered the strongest candidate of the Catholic activist sector of the party. Airton Soares, elected to Congress by the MDB in 1978, was the leading federal deputy to have joined the PT. Eduardo Matarazzo Suplicy, though a member of one of Brazil's wealthiest families, had been one of the earliest politicians to support the PT. Elected to the São Paulo state legislature in 1978, he was known for his well-documented exposés of official corruption, and he had a solid reputation for support of popular struggles. Those three were among those who had been recruited from the MDB's tendência popular. Djalma Bom symbolized the party's trade union base—a founding member of the PT, he had been treasurer of the São Bernardo Metalworkers' Union. Bete Mendes was a well-known television and film actress, as well as a longtime political activist with ties to leftist organizations. José Genoino Neto was a well-known leader on the organized left, with an extensive support network throughout the state.

Although only one PT labor candidate was elected to Congress from São Paulo, the vote for labor candidates was sizeable. Djalma Bom won almost twice the vote of his nearest rival in the party, ranking ninth in votes cast for federal deputy in the state (out of 60). Of the eight state deputies elected, three were labor leaders, as was the first runner-up. In most of the industrial municipalities in the state, labor candidates clearly dominated PT voting. This should not be surprising. Nonetheless, after the 1982 elections a kind of "common sense" appreciation of the PT's poor showing in those elections held that it had demonstrated the falsity of the party's slogan "worker, vote for a worker." Of those who voted for the party, it would seem that a substantial number did indeed vote for workers.[39]

Municipal organization has always been an important element in electoral success in Brazil, a factor which places new parties at a disadvantage. According to Gláucio Soares, this factor has historically favored conservative parties organized around prominent local families, to the detriment of reformist parties.[40] By the time of the 1982 elections, the PT had functioning party organizations in around 149 of the 573 municipalities in the state of São Paulo. The importance of the existence of a party diretório in a municipality was twofold: a party could only run candidates in the municipal elections in those municipalities where it had a diretório; and, evidently, the presence of a local party organization was important for mounting a campaign. The legal requirement to vote a straight ticket meant that PT voters in municipalities where the party had no diretório could not vote for mayor or municipal council members. Parties were thus at a clear disadvantage in municipalities where they were not organized. The advantage that the PDS and PMDB enjoyed as inheritors of preexisting party organizations is evident in the 1982 local election results for the country as a whole: the two parties together won 97.8 percent of municipal council members and 99.2 percent of mayors.[41] The PT's 1982 vote in the 424 São Paulo municipalities where no PT diretório existed surpassed 2 percent in only twelve cases; in the 149 municipalities where the party did have diretórios, it polled under 2 percent in 21 of them, between 2 and 5 percent in 71, and over 5 percent in 57.

The municipalities of São Paulo where the Workers' party did well in the 1982 elections were for the most part predictable: they were, in the main, the largest and most industrialized municipalities in the state, with high concentrations of workers in modern industries. Of the twenty-two municipalities in which the party won over 10 percent of the vote, workers in manufacturing, construction, and transportation made up more than 50 percent of the economically active population in fifteen cases.[42] With a few exceptions, the party's best results came in the industrial districts around São Paulo, especially the ABCD region.

Not surprisingly, the PT experienced the 1982 election results as a severe defeat. Although in public statements party leaders tried to put a good face on it, as in the headline of the party paper in São Paulo saying "We are more than a million," in private there was deep disappointment and a kind of collective depression. Internal evaluations of the PT's electoral performance differed over the cause of the party's poor showing but agreed on two points: that sloganeering had often taken the place of making the party's programmatic goals clear; and that the level of organization—both of the party itself and of the population—was still too weak for electoral success. The solution was to return to the party's origins, promoting popular organization and mobilization and elaborating concrete proposals to solve pressing social problems. [43]

Most internal explanations for the party's poor performance were organizational or attitudinal. A great deal of energy went into trying to distribute blame. The failure to take contextual factors into account was partly due to the intensity with which PT members experienced the electoral campaign, but it also reflects the fact that three years of concentrating on organization building had prevented the development of a political debate within the party that could have more clearly assessed the relationship between the PT and other political forces during the transition period.

The party's disillusionment with the 1982 election results set the context for its subsequent actions. The movement to return to the party's origins and the formation of Articulação, discussed in the preceding chapter, were attempts to consolidate direction of the party in the hands of labor movement leaders and those they considered their allies. The desire to "return to the base" meant that the party would direct its energies toward support for labor and social movement organization, as if the election campaign had represented a *deviation* from the normal goals of party activity.

The rejection of the electoral experience was probably an important factor in the ensuing conflicts between party leaders and elected party officials. It also helps to explain why the party had such difficulty in capitalizing on what successes it did have in the elections. Because the PT could not come to terms with its defeat, it found it difficult to think strategically about its activity in political institutions. The case of the PT mayoral administration in Diadema, discussed in chapter 8, is a dramatic example at a local level of the practical dilemmas that arose from the party's initial lack of a strategy for institutional action.

Although the party did not manage to formulate a clear institutional strategy during this postelection period, it was not entirely moribund.

Party activists established a visible presence in a number of social movements, and the sector of the labor movement associated with the PT grew rapidly. While these did not resolve the organizational problems, they kept the party in the public eye. The PT was also one of the first to call for a popular mobilization in favor of direct elections, and the direct elections campaign was one of the few instances where the party's institutional and mobilizational roles came together. The PT played a major role in the campaign's organization, and Lula's appearance on the platform with PMDB state governors temporarily assuaged some of the bitterness left over from 1982. The failure of that campaign, and the PT's refusal to accept a compromise solution, produced yet another internal crisis.

By mid-1985, the difficulty of coming up with a way of linking institutional and societal action was causing a full-scale crisis of identity in the party. The mayoral elections in 1985 were widely seen as the great test of the party's organizational viability. Unless the results were a vast improvement over the party's performance in 1982, party activists would more than likely opt to concentrate their energies entirely on movement organizations.

The Electoral Turnaround

The PT's strong performance in the mayoral elections in state capitals in 1985 gave it a new lease on life and suddenly projected it onto the national stage as a viable and growing political force. The party ran candidates in all but one state capital and won over 5 percent in twelve of them (and over 3 percent in two others). Its candidate Maria Luiza Fontanelle was elected in Fortaleza, capital of Ceará and fifth largest city in Brazil, and the party lost by a hair in Goiânia. PT candidates also placed second in Vitória (Espirito Santo) and Aracajú (Sergipe). The candidate for mayor of São Paulo, Eduardo Suplicy, won close to 20 percent of the vote.[44]

PT leaders attributed the party's electoral success in part to a change in the tone of the campaign—the party appeared more open, less sectarian, and mixed humor with its programmatic message. In Goiânia, PT candidate Darci Accorci, a university professor, conversed with television spectators from a barber's chair. The PT vote in Goiânia jumped from around 5,000 in 1982 to 97,000 in 1985. In São Paulo, some of the party's television message was in the form of a popular soap opera (*novela*). In Vitória, the party directed its discourse to the middle class and lost its fear of appealing to liberal sectors; PT candidate Vitor Buaiz, a doctor and environmentalist, won 26 percent of the vote. The

PT used the mass media much more effectively than in 1982, and its media style in 1985 became a prototype for future campaigns. Although the elimination of the Lei Falcão restrictions on the format of campaign messages certainly helped, the party had also learned something about how to address voters. Lula commented after the 1985 elections that "we learned that it's one thing to talk at a rally to motivate militants and another to talk on TV to a housewife who you need to convince. You don't convince her unless you get her to keep watching the program."[45]

The other notable aspect of the PT campaign in 1985 was the predominance of middle-class candidates. In the five cities where the party did best, the candidates were from the liberal professions. After the campaign, PT leaders stressed the importance of mixing candidates with middle-class and working-class origins. The idea that a worker should vote for a worker, while still considered important, no longer precluded an appeal to those who were unlikely to vote for a worker.

As with the elections of 1982, the context was important. First, these were exceptional elections, marking the end of authoritarian restrictions that required the indirect election of mayors of state capitals and areas designated "national security zones." Other mayors had been elected in 1982, in conjunction with legislators and governors. Thus the 1985 elections provided the opportunity for more focused campaigns. Secondly, as mid-term elections, they gave voters a chance to express their frustration with the failure of the new government at the national and/or state levels to make the kinds of fundamental changes that were expected to accompany "democracy." This time, with nine state governors and a president who was nominally a member, the PMDB was widely perceived as part of the government. The fact that it was not *the* government (although Sarney had to join the PMDB in order to run as vice president with Tancredo Neves) was a distinction that the PMDB itself had not been prepared to make prior to the elections.

The 1985 mayoral elections in São Paulo were a particularly important illustration that the PMDB could no longer run as "the opposition." In the pre-campaign period, the PMDB attempted to form an alliance with the Liberal Front party (Partido da Frente Liberal, PFL), formed by PDS dissidents at the time of the indirect presidential elections. In São Paulo, the PFL included some of the founders of the old PP, which had merged with the PMDB in 1981. In the PMDB's assessment of the situation, the main danger was on the right; thus an alliance to the right of the party made sense. When the PFL decided instead to form an alliance with the PTB in support of Jânio Quadros, the PMDB candidate, Fernando Henrique Cardoso, attempted to revive the voto util idea to defeat Jânio, representing the latter as a danger to the democratization process. Once again, the voto util argument was directed at potential PT voters, and for running a candidate of its own, this time federal deputy Eduardo Suplicy, the PT was called a spoiler.

In 1985, however, public perceptions of the situation had changed, and Jânio Quadros, however controversial, was not viewed as the equivalent of the military regime. In this election, the PMDB was the party of the incumbents, both in the city and in the governor's office. When Cardoso lost the election to Quadros, with Suplicy a strong third, he expressed his bitterness toward the PT with a good deal of venom. Other PMDB leaders took a different attitude, talking about the possibility of future electoral alliances with the PT and about the need for the PMDB to define itself as a party.

The mayoral elections in 1985 ushered in a new era both for the PT's relationship with other political forces in Brazil and for the party's internal life. In relation to the former, the party demonstrated that it was no longer a marginal actor. While previously the idea of forming coalitions with other parties meant in essence for the PT to stand aside and support another party's candidate, after 1985 it was in a better position to negotiate. As a result, while party leaders continued to state that the PT would present its own candidates in elections, discussion of coalitions was no longer taboo.

The problems of internal definition did not change, but the context in which they were discussed did. The possibility of appealing to a growing mass of voters who were clearly dissatisfied with the alternatives being offered by the leaders of the transition process made the effort to resolve them seem more worthwhile. This implied attributing greater value to electoral politics, as well as to politicians within the party. While this did not preclude continued emphasis on building social movement organizations outside the party, PT leaders began to pay attention to making party organization more effective. The announcement after the mayoral elections of a major recruitment campaign, designed to bring in more of the party's electors, was a sign that the PT's movement-building phase might give way to greater concentration on party building.

That new confidence was reinforced by further electoral advances in subsequent elections. Despite the PMDB's sweep of the 1986 elections in the wake of the highly popular Cruzado plan (an anti-inflation plan involving wage and price freezes), the PT congressional delegation grew from five (after the 1985 departure of Airton Soares, Bete

Mendes, and José Eudes) to sixteen, including for the first time deputies from the states of Rio Grande do Sul and Espirito Santo.[46] Lula was elected to Congress with more votes than any other deputy, his 651,763 votes topping even PMDB president Ulysses Guimarães's 590,873. Other key PT leaders went to Congress as well, including party president Olívio Dutra and prominent PT trade union cadre like João Paulo Pires Vasconcelos of the João Monlevade metalworkers and Paulo Paim of the Canoas metalworkers. From Rio de Janeiro, favela activist Benedita da Silva was elected to the federal congress, after having served a term in the Rio de Janeiro municipal council. Still other popular leaders were elected to state legislatures, where PT deputies went from a total of twelve in four states to thirty-three in thirteen states.[47]

The 1988 mayoral elections were the first clear sign that the electorate was intent upon a massive rejection of the status quo. The PMDB became the status quo party, following in the tracks of ARENA and the PDS before it and losing ground in the more industrialized center and south of the country, while maintaining a position in the northeast, and losing the large cities while winning in the interior.[48] Virtually no state governors succeeded in getting the mayors of their choice elected in state capitals. Even Sarney could not get his candidate elected in São Luís, capital of his home state of Maranhão, which arguably gained a great deal materially from Sarney's presidency; São Luís went to the candidate from the PDT.

For the PT, the 1988 elections were a great leap forward. The party had administered one city hall after 1982 and one in 1985; after 1988 it would administer thirty-one municipalities,[49] among them the state capitals of São Paulo, Espirito Santo (Vitória), and Rio Grande do Sul (Porto Alegre). Also among them were three of the four cities of the ABCD: São Bernardo do Campo, Santo André, and Diadema. While its biggest victory came in São Paulo, where it won thirteen municipalities, the party won mayorships in nine other states as well.[50] A number of the smaller municipalities where the PT won were rural districts where struggles over land tenure during the 1980s had been particularly virulent, and where the PT worked closely with the landless movement and/or rural labor organizations. This was the first time, in fact, that rural struggles had a significant impact on the PT vote. In municipal council elections the numbers were especially startling; an estimated 40 percent of the PT municipal council members elected in 1988 were rural workers or worked with the Catholic land pastoral.[51]

The presidential candidates in 1989 took to heart the message sent the previous year, and all of them attempted to run as opposition candidates. In the first round of the elections, with twenty-two candidates competing for a place on the final runoff ballot, this "oppositional" electoral environment clearly favored those who were seen as the most viable outsiders—primarily Fernando Collor de Melo with 28.52 percent, Leonel Brizola with 15.45, and Luís Inácio Lula da Silva with 16.08.[52] The degree to which the electorate voted against the status quo is evident in the disastrous electoral performance of PMDB candidate Ulysses Guimarães, who came in seventh with only 4.43 percent of the vote.[53]

The three frontrunners had quite different bases for their claims to be outsiders in the transition process. Brizola's appeal was based largely on his personal history in populist politics in Brazil since the 1950s and 1960s. His Democratic Labor party (PDT) maintained its primary base of support in Rio de Janeiro and Rio Grande do Sul, Brizola's states of adoption and of origin, respectively, but made electoral gains in other parts of Brazil as well after 1982. The PDT is still "the party of Brizola" to a greater extent than the PT is the party of Lula, and its appeal is largely personal rather than institutional. Nonetheless, the fact that the party's glue is essentially personalistic does not make it ineffectual; this was evident in Brizola's remarkable success in transferring the overwhelming majority of his voters to Lula on the second round.

Fernando Collor de Melo, running as candidate of the tiny National Reconstruction party (PRN), emerged victorious in both first and second rounds by managing to project himself simultaneously as an establishment and an antiestablishment politician. Collor, scion of one of Alagoas's leading oligarchical families, entered politics as appointed mayor of Maceió under the military regime. He was elected federal congressman in 1982 for the PDS, and in 1986 he won the governorship of Alagoas on the PMDB ticket. Although his political background reflects impeccable establishment credentials, Collor portrayed himself as an implacable opponent of the Sarney government, stressing his highly publicized campaign as governor to clean up corruption in public appointments. With the support of Brazil's largest television network, Rede Globo, Collor transformed his youth, good looks, and political obscurity into assets in the campaign, promising to root out corruption and incompetence at the highest levels of government and proclaiming the bankruptcy of most political parties in Brazil. Collor's appeal was based on an image rather than a program for governing; even after he was elected president in December 1989, many political commentators inside and outside of Brazil continued to refer to him as a black box. Nonetheless, as Jânio Quadros before him had demonstrated both in his rise to national prominence in the 1950s and in his São Paulo mayoral victory in 1985, this kind of direct, populist, anticorruption and anti-institutional appeal is particularly effective among poorer and less educated segments of the population.

Lula's presidential campaign was supported by a coalition of parties including the PT, the PC do B, and the Brazilian Socialist party (PSB), making up the Frente Brasil Popular.[54] While Lula continued to call for a socialist transformation of Brazilian society, he also recognized that socialism could not be implanted by decree. Thus, the campaign stressed the need for national reconciliation and for the formation of a national popular government. His campaign discourse, the party's television spots, and even the PT's catchy and highly popular campaign song all seemed devised to reach a broad constituency.[55]

The problem for the second round was to transform the 16 percent from the first round into an absolute majority. This meant attracting the support of other center-left parties and convincing the Brazilian electorate that Lula could both win the election and put together a viable government. While Brizola's PDT was quick to declare its support for Lula (and in the final vote Brizola was remarkably successful in transferring his vote en masse to the PT candidate), negotiations with the Partido Social Democrático Brasileiro were more difficult. The PSDB, whose candidate Mario Covas placed fourth in the first round with approximately 11 percent of the vote, had split with the PMDB in 1988 at the end of the Constituent Assembly, charging that the latter had abandoned its historical identity. At the national level, the PSDB did eventually endorse Lula, but it was clear from the beginning that the party was divided on the issue and that its electorate was likely to split its vote. A little over a week before the election, it was still unclear whether Covas would appear on the podium with Lula at election rallies. The first of two televised campaign debates, held on December 3 when Collor was ten points ahead in the polls, proved disappointing, and most commentators agreed that it had not contributed anything new to the campaign.[56] Nonetheless, Collor's lead continued to diminish over the next weeks. The second debate, only days before the election, followed upon an intense burst of negative campaign advertising by the Collor campaign.[57] The impact of this advertising on Lula's performance in that debate was dramatic; Collor's victory in the second debate probably helped to consolidate his lead just prior to the election itself.

The results of the 1989 presidential elections, where Collor won

42.75 percent of the valid vote to Lula's 37.86 percent,[58] carried a double message. In what several postelection commentators referred to as a contest between organized Brazil and unorganized Brazil, the elections demonstrated that organized Brazil is not sufficiently strong to carry a national contest, where images projected by the mass media—the political spectacle—outweigh programmatic and institutional considerations. The more surprising message—and one that much of the left, including the PT, was slow to recognize in the midst of disappointment—was that "organized" Brazil was *almost* strong enough to win. In a highly elitist political system, one where politics was considered the purview of the educated and well born, a metalworker with a high school equivalency diploma leading a party dedicated to organizing workers and the poor came within a hair of winning the presidency. The Brazil over which Fernando Collor de Melo would preside beginning March 15, 1990, was not the same as the one that began its transition to democracy fifteen years earlier. The PT both reflected and contributed to that change.

In both the 1988 mayoral elections and the 1989 presidential elections, PT candidates benefited from a massive protest vote. The PT's ability to play that role was due partly to the evolution of the political context in which electoral competition took place and partly to the party's own development. Perhaps ironically, as the PMDB increasingly dropped its oppositional mantle in the second half of the 1980s, the PT was in a position to benefit from the very dynamics that had helped to marginalize it in 1982. By late 1988, national polls on party preference showed that after the PMDB, the PT was the Brazilian party with the most voter identification.

Competition in these later elections can certainly not be called plebiscitary, as we are clearly no longer dealing with bipolar alternatives, and the PT had competition for the mantle of the opposition. The PSDB was one competitor; Brizola's PDT was another. Nonetheless, in 1985, 1988, and 1989, the unexpectedly large PT vote seems to have contained a sizable component of anti–status quo sentiment.

Legislative elections, on the other hand, reflected a more incremental growth in support for the party, as well as the growing nationalization and diversification of that support. A comparison of the PT's federal and state legislative results in 1982, 1986, and 1990 (tables 6.4 and 6.5) demonstrates that a great deal of that incremental growth came from the spread of the party's electoral appeal from its initial base in São Paulo to other parts of Brazil. In addition to more than doubling its

Table 6.3 Party Preferences in State Capitals, November 1988 (In Percentages)

Party	São Paulo	Rio de Janeiro	Belo Horizonte	Porto Alegre	Curitiba	Salvador	Recife	Fortaleza	Goiânia	Belem
PT	15	8	22	19	7	5	5	7	14	8
PMDB	12	5	10	9	16	41	14	19	29	14
PDT	1	26	1	16	13	1	2	4	*	1
PDS	8	1	1	3	2	1	1	2	5	12
PFL	1	1	2	1	2	2	14	4	1	4
PSDB	3	1	8	1	*	*	*	*	*	*
PTB	2	1	1	1	2	1	*	1	*	11
Others	2	5	4	4	2	4	1	2	4	5
None	56	52	51	46	56	45	63	61	47	45
Total	100	100	100	100	100	100	100	100	100	100
N	(1,984)	(1,088)	(786)	(777)	(1,498)	(797)	(800)	(791)	(799)	(798)

Source: DataFolha poll published in *Folha de São Paulo*, November 13, 1988, p. A6.
*Less than 1%.

delegations in the Chamber of Deputies in each successive election, in 1990 the PT also elected its first senator, Eduardo Suplicy from São Paulo. The growing influence of the party (and the Central Unica dos Trabalhadores) in rural areas was reflected both in the vote and in the sharp rise in the number of rural candidates elected from the PT. Beginning in the 1986 elections the party also began to shift its position on electoral alliances. In 1986 this was reflected in the highly successful (though not victorious) coalition with the incipient Rio Green party around the gubernatorial candidacy of Fernando Gabeira. That practice was expanded in the 1988 mayoral elections, and in 1990 the party ran in coalitions in eleven states. Although its most common coalition partners were the small socialist and communist parties, in some states they included the PSDB and PDT as well.

A comparison of the evolution of the PT vote in the state of São Paulo from 1982 to 1986 shows a pattern of incremental growth combined with greater dispersion. In the interior of the state, in 1982 the party won 80.25 percent of its votes in cities with more than 100,000 inhabitants; in 1986 that figure was down to 69.42 percent, even though total PT votes in those cities had grown by 44 percent. (Those thirty-three municipalities represented 48 percent of the total vote in the interior of the state in 1986.) The party increased the number of municipalities in which it polled over 10 percent of the vote from twenty-three in 1982 to thirty-nine in 1986; at the same time, the number in which it polled less than 5 percent went down from 510 to 439. In 1982 49.64 percent of the party's total statewide vote came from the capital city; in 1986 that proportion was down to 38.41 percent. The capital represented 30.28 percent of the total statewide vote in 1982 and 33.70 in 1986. Although the PT did slightly less well overall in the capital in 1986 than in 1982, its improvement in the interior showed the spread of its appeal. Nonetheless, the ABCD region continued to be a core area of support; in 1986 the party came in first only in Santo André (which, interestingly enough, was the center of Communist party voting strength in the 1945–47 period as well).[59]

Elections played a significant role in the evolution of the Workers' party. Both the requirements for legalization and the general attribution of "foundational" importance to the 1982 elections focused the party's attention on that electoral contest. Although there was substantial disagreement within the party on the relationship between electoral competition and the party's societal responsibility for building a grass-

Table 6.4 Number of PT Federal Deputies Elected

State	1982	1986	1990
Acre	—	—	—
Alagoas	—	—	—
Amapá	—	—	1
Amazonas	—	—	1
Bahia	—	—	2
Ceará	—	—	—
Fed. district	N.A.	N.A.	2
Espirito Santo	—	1	—
Goiás	—	—	—
Maranhão	—	—	—
Mato Grosso	—	—	—
Mato Grosso do Sul	—	—	—
Minas Gerais	1	3	6
Pará	—	—	2
Paraíba	—	—	—
Paraná	—	—	3
Pernambuco	—	—	—
Piauí	—	—	—
Rio Grande do Norte	—	—	—
Rio Grande do Sul	—	2	4
Rio de Janeiro	1	2	3
Rondônia	—	—	—
Roraima	—	—	—
Santa Catarina	—	—	1
São Paulo	6	8	10
Sergipe	—	—	—
Tocantins	N.A.	N.A.	—
Total	8	16	35

Source: 1982 and 1986 from congressional lists; 1990 from *Folha de São Paulo* October 29, 1990.

roots political movement, the PT launched itself into the 1982 campaign with verve. The results were correspondingly disappointing.

Nonetheless, participation in these elections and the lessons that the party eventually drew from them had a major impact on the PT's development. Confronted with hard evidence that the working-class majority upon which it had hoped to draw in the elections was far from being a political reality, the party moved in a number of directions at once. First, it implicitly returned to a conception of the party as move-

Table 6.5 Number of PT State Deputies Elected

State	1982	1986	1990
Acre	1	—	3*
Alagoas	—	—	N.A.**
Amapá	—	—	1
Amazonas	—	—	1
Bahia	—	1	3
Ceará	—	2	3*
Fed. district	N.A.	N.A.	5
Espirito Santo	—	3	3
Goiás	—	2	3
Maranhão	—	—	2
Mato Grosso	—	—	3*
Mato Grosso do Sul	—	—	1*
Minas Gerais	1	5	10*
Pará	—	2	9*
Paraíba	—	—	2*
Paraná	—	1	3
Pernambuco	—	—	2
Piauí	—	—	1*
Rio Grande do Norte	—	—	1
Rio Grande do Sul	—	4	5
Rio de Janeiro	1	4	6*
Rondônia	—	2	2
Roraima	—	—	—
Santa Catarina	—	1	6*
São Paulo	9	10	16*
Sergipe	—	2	2
Tocantins	N.A.	N.A.	—
Total	12	33	93*

Source: 1982 and 1986 from PT lists; 1990 from Folha de São Paulo October 29, 1990.
*In coalition with other parties; currently available data do not separate candidates from the PT from those of coalition partners.
**Results in Alagoas were delayed due to fraud; new elections were called.

ment. While this had a number of negative effects on its ability to use effectively the institutional spaces it had won, it deepened the party's roots in societal organizations and reinforced a conception of the PT as a party of civil society, one which was substantially different from other Brazilian parties. Second, the elections provided a mirror in which party leaders could read a more accurate assessment not only of the party's real strength but also of its internal configuration. The formation of a dominant coalition—Articulação—was an attempt by party leaders to consolidate the party's identity in such a way as to promote its survival. The desire to steer a middle course between the revolutionary left, on the one hand, and those seeking a more institutionally and electorally based definition, on the other, led to substantial ambiguity; the members of Articulação were determined to preserve the idea of the party as movement, even as they promoted a higher degree of formal institutionalization within the party. Finally, the failure of a class-based electoral discourse in 1982 produced a willingness to appeal to a broader constituency beginning in 1985. While the notion of building a working-class majority by no means disappeared, what that meant changed. Not only did its meaning shift toward a conception of a class in the process of becoming organized, but also the party's understanding of the concept of working class expanded from a narrow focus on factory workers to one which included new forms of both rural and white-collar organizing. This shift reflected changes taking place in the Brazilian labor movement, which will be discussed in the next chapter. In this broader context, the discourse on citizenship and empowerment that in 1982 had been subsumed under the discourse on class took on a life of its own.

All of these developments were profoundly influenced by the party's experience in 1982. Nonetheless, they emerged piecemeal, rather than as part of a theoretically informed strategic vision. In mid-1985, when the party's very survival seemed highly dubious, the dilemmas the party faced seemed insuperable, and the resources with which to resolve them were all but invisible. As many party leaders seemed to devote much more time to activities in unions or other social movements than they did to the PT's internal life, and as conflicts between the party's elected officials and the party leadership abounded, many predicted the PT's imminent demise.

In retrospect, one can speculate that this ambiguity of self-definition as movement and as political institution may have been a key element in the PT's survival during the Brazilian transition process. In a situation where the rules of the game were often arbitrary or ambiguous, and where the hegemonic view of the political conjuncture posited a very limited set of political options, a purely institutional definition would have rendered the party even more marginal than it was. External legitimation, particularly through the party's relationship with the labor movement, provided political resources that were not forthcoming from the electoral process. At the same time, even the minimal amount of internal consolidation that occurred after 1982 was a crucial element in positioning the party to begin to resolve some of the dilemmas involved in defining its institutional role.

THE WORKERS'

PARTY AND THE

LABOR MOVEMENT

7

In spite of its disappointing performance in the 1982 elections, between 1982 and 1985 the PT retained a much higher degree of sympathy than we would expect had votes been the sole criterion for judging its success. Much of the party's ongoing prestige came from its identification with a combative sector of the labor movement that, throughout this period, continued to evolve new demands, forms of struggle, and organizational sophistication, and to extend its influence over increasingly large numbers of unions and workers.

The relationship between the labor movement and the PT is difficult to analyze because there were no formal institutional links between the two. Thus the party's relations with labor were different from those which characterized the early history of the British Labour party, where unions formed the party *as unions* and maintained control over it through the institution of the bloc vote, or the German Social Democrats, where the parity principle was adopted at the 1906 Mannheim Congress to rule all decisions that affected the interests of both the trade unions and the party.[1] Indeed, for Brazil's PT the establishment of a formal relationship was expressly prohibited by Article 521 of the labor code.[2]

Nonetheless, informally a relationship certainly did exist. The PT was founded largely at the initiative of labor leaders, who continued to dominate its leadership and remained the key spokespersons for the party; the national image of the party was inextricably linked to the figure of Lula. The presence of these labor leaders in the party was the reason it continued to be considered important in spite of its poor

showing in the elections. The party's enumeration of its political demands has always been heavily centered around the question of trade
union rights. And its difficulty in formulating a formal policy on the
union question, illustrated by the fact that it took four years to produce
a party position on the issue, was due to the unwillingness of the PT
leadership to preempt the unions. The party's role was to support
initiatives taken by the unions, not vice versa.

The complex dynamics of the relationship between the party and the
labor movement must be understood in relation to the conjuncture in
which workers' demands were made. The relationship was triangular,
involving the party's relationship to the unions and vice versa, and the
impact of each within the overall political and economic environment.
Of particular importance was the level—whether national or local—at
which workers sought to press their demands.

The Workers' party was formed in the wake of a dramatic upswing
in labor activity. Strikes in 1979 involved over three million workers all
over the country. Nonetheless, the difficulty in winning significant
gains at the local level convinced the union leaders involved in founding
the PT of the need to intervene in national politics in order to *change the
environment* for labor action. They still viewed the unions as the primary
vehicle for winning workers' demands; the party's job was to create a
situation more conducive to their activity, not to take their place. The
period of party organization and legalization and the 1982 campaign
coincided with an essentially defensive period for unions. Between
1981 and 1983 strikes were primarily directed either against layoffs or
against late payment of wages by employers.[3] At the same time, unions
were involved in the formation of national labor organizations, and the
PT was instrumental in reinforcing the tendency that formed the
Central Unica dos Trabalhadores (CUT) in August 1983. The party
also contributed to a national awareness of the growing urgency of
labor's demands.

A new upsurge in union militancy and success in winning demands
at the local level began in 1984, when there was an improvement in both
the economic picture and the political environment in which demands
were being made. It also reinforced the tendency of PT labor leaders to
want to return to the base. This was a somewhat contradictory tendency. On the one hand, the PT's future seemed to depend on strengthening the labor movement and other movements in society. Thus,
concentrating on work in these areas was important for the party as
such. On the other hand, if unions were increasingly capable of win-

ning their demands directly from employers and playing a role in national policy on their own, the party itself became in some respects less relevant, or at least less urgent, for those for whom the improvement of the environment for labor action remained a primary goal.

This chapter will examine developments in the Brazilian labor movement in the early 1980s and the way in which these interacted with developments in the more strictly political sphere. We will look specifically at the relationship between the Workers' party and the labor movement, considering both the institutional relations between the party and union organizations and more diffuse forms of interaction.

With the founding of new political parties in 1979–80 and the appearance of interunion organizations, the idea that the labor upsurge was simply one element in the broad range of oppositional activity within civil society gradually lost much of its power as a political image. The Workers' party's insistence on the *specificity* of workers' demands within the democratic struggle was considered by many leaders of the elite opposition (and by many labor leaders as well) as naively utopian at best and destructively divisive at worst. Differences over opposition strategy in the political sphere had their counterparts in political differences among union leaders as to how best to proceed, how far to push, and to what extent workers and unions *on their own* could expect to win major improvements in their lot.

Labor Action in the 1980s

Strikes in 1980 met with a more determined response from the government than had those of the two preceding years. During the metalworkers' strike that year, São Bernardo was occupied by troops, and the union was placed under intervention. Its leaders were jailed, purged from union office, and charged with violation of the National Security Law. The government's tough stance, together with the economic downturn of the early 1980s, caused the labor movement largely to abandon large-scale strikes. The main trends in the 1980s, however, were in many other ways a continuation of the developments of the 1970s. An important difference was the increased salience of political parties both at the level of union elections and at the level of national organizations.

Labor activity in the first half of the 1980s took place at two organizational levels. First, an increase in plant-level organization fed a growing tendency toward collective bargaining both at the plant and at the industry level, and away from the settlement of disputes by the labor courts. Second, while the number of large-scale, industry-wide strikes decreased between 1979 and 1984, the strengthening of links between union leadership and rank-and-file organization was reflected in the significant increase in 1984 in the number of short strikes in single plants (out of a total of 626 strikes, 500 were in one plant).[4] Large-scale strikes became the rule once again in 1985. Finally, union leadership in the early 1980s paid increasing attention to the creation of national inter-union horizontal organizations.

UNION ORGANIZATION AND DEMANDS. With the difficulty in winning significant wage concessions due to the government's wage legislation and the economic downturn, workers' demands tended to emphasize other issues, such as job security, frequency of wage adjustments, and recognition of shop-floor union representation. All these issues were present in the late 1970s, but they took on added importance with the change in conjuncture, and they were increasingly part of a process of direct bargaining between unions and employers.

Job security, for example, had long been an issue in the metalworking sector, where employers used high turnover to keep wages down. A rise in unemployment in 1981 made it even more important. According to figures from the Instituto Brasileiro de Geografia e Estatística in mid-1981 more than 900,000 people lost jobs in the six major metropolitan areas of Brazil, and by August, unemployment in those cities was estimated at 2,000,000.[5] A DIEESE study completed in June 1981 showed 12.8 percent unemployment in the metropolitan area of São Paulo alone and, still more dramatic, 18.4 percent underemployment among those who had jobs.[6] The Time in Service Guarantee Fund (FGTS) provided little protection in a situation of widespread and protracted unemployment.

The ravages of inflation led to a demand for more frequent wage adjustments. By deciding in 1979 to make wage adjustments biannual, the Figueiredo government hoped to preempt further strike waves; nonetheless, this should be interpreted as a victory for workers who struck in 1979. The measure contributed to the sharp fall in the number of strikes in 1980. Over the next few years the rate of inflation rose from 110.2 percent in 1980 to 211.0 in 1984, and the prices of basic goods, primarily foodstuffs, rose even faster.[7] According to DIEESE figures, the amount of labor time necessary to earn a basic basket of goods at the minimum wage went from 138 hours, 3 minutes in 1978 to 163 hours, 44 minutes in 1981. In 1983, for the first time since the DIEESE study began, the price of a basic basket of goods *exceeded* the monthly mini-mum wage. Thus, in 1984 unions demanded either quarterly wage adjustments or anticipated payment of the biannual adjustment. Many unions won more frequent adjustments in direct bargaining with employers.

The demand for shop-floor union representation took several forms. It was particularly characteristic of the union tendency eventually iden-tified with the PT and the Central Unica dos Trabalhadores (CUT). In some cases, it took the form of factory commissions elected at the plant level and organically associated with the union; in others it meant the designation of shop stewards or sometimes simply the right of union officials to visit the shop floor without being accompanied by an official of the company. Some companies began to recognize the union's right to shop-floor representation de facto, if not de jure in contracts.[8] The advantage of legal recognition, as there was no provision in the labor law for shop-floor representation, was to give shop-floor representa-tives job security during their term in office; the broad prerogatives of companies to dismiss workers at will allowed for considerable arbitrari-ness in the acceptance or not of de facto arrangements. Thus, plant-level questions did become increasingly important for unions, especially in advanced industry. Bargaining over shop-floor issues presupposed a knowledge of local conditions, and union leaders began to cultivate relations with an intermediate level of plant leaders capable of mobiliz-ing the rank and file on the shop floor.

When Almir Pazzianotto was appointed labor minister in the Neves/Sarney government, the trend toward the settlement of disputes by collective bargaining intensified. Pazzianotto, a São Paulo state con-gressman from the PMDB, was an attorney for the São Bernardo metalworkers in the late 1970s, and he had long supported greater union autonomy.[9] Although none of the fundamental tenets of labor legislation were changed during the first years of the "New Republic," Pazzianotto often refrained from intervening, using his influence in-stead to encourage direct negotiation between unions and employers. Employers' associations attempted to adjust to the new situation by sponsoring courses for their members on collective bargaining methods.[10]

NATIONAL ORGANIZATIONS. Unions also began to do some serious organization building at a national level. This process was highly politi-cized. Between 1977, when the idea of holding a National Conference of the Working Class (CONCLAT)[11] was first proposed, and 1981, when it was finally held, the first informal groupings of trade union leaders gave way to increasingly well organized factions with different approaches to union organization and policy.

By the end of 1978, there were three visible tendencies within "combative" unionism. The first, which called itself the *oposições sindicais* (union oppositions), was composed of rank-and-file unionists who favored the organization of factory commissions and action outside of the official union structure. This tendency, important during the periods 1966–68 and 1977–79, lost some of its vitality with the growing activism of union leaders within the official structure. The second tendency stressed organizing to win leadership positions within the labor movement, particularly at the federation and confederation level, and promoted the creation of a Unidade Sindical group to coordinate demands and activities at state and national levels. Union leaders close to the Brazilian Communist party played an important role in this group. The third tendency, called the *autênticos,* worked within the union structure, supported factory-level organization and participation by the rank and file, and emphasized union independence in relation to the state and employers. The autênticos regarded the federations and confederations as too unrepresentative to be worth bothering with.[12] This tendency was led by Lula and the Metalworkers' Union of São Bernardo and Diadema.[13]

The Unidade Sindical thus stressed institutional pressure (from the union hierarchy) as the potential means of winning union demands; for the other tendencies the solution lay in direct action at the union and plant levels. By implication, for Unidade Sindical, labor's demands would be met via direct interaction with state institutions (mediated and supported by political parties) in much the same way as they had been prior to 1964; for the autênticos, the struggle was more directly focused on the firms. While they recognized that the state played an important role, it was not expected to "grant" rights that had not already been won in practice. In October 1979, when many of the autênticos were involved in founding the Workers' party, the major tendencies in the union movement began to be identified with divergent political parties as well.

Tensions increased during 1980 between the autênticos and the Unidade Sindical over the metalworkers' strike in São Bernardo. While the strike was important because of its demands for shop-floor representation, its use of elected rank-and-file strike committees, and the degree of community and Church solidarity which it generated, it failed to win any of the economic demands with which it had set out to challenge the government's new wage policy. Unlike the 1978 and 1979 strikes, this one did not enjoy the support of a broad range of unions; Unidade Sindical saw it as adventurist, potentially weakening the labor movement and closing the space that the government's *abertura* had thus far allowed unions.[14]

The year in which the CONCLAT was finally held, 1981, brought a drastic increase in layoffs and unemployment. The number of strikes declined still more than it had the previous year, and those that did occur were mainly defensive. Strikes against layoffs were common, and a strike at Ford won a landmark agreement in which the company agreed to recognize an elected factory commission whose first task would be to negotiate criteria for readmission of those laid off. The Ford agreement established a precedent for direct bargaining with companies over forms of shop-floor representation.[15] By the time the CONCLAT was to be held, however, the opportunity to win significant economic gains through strikes had been essentially eliminated, both by the display of government repression in 1980, which indicated that the political space for such actions had narrowed, and by the worsening recession. Unions clearly needed to discuss strategy for confronting the new situation.

The CONCLAT was a historic event. Convened on August 21–23, 1981, at Praia Grande, São Paulo, it brought together 5,247 delegates from 1,126 unions and professional associations. Discussion covered a wide range of issues: social security policy, employment and job stability, wage policy, agrarian reform, union unity, freedom, autonomy, and organization. At the insistence of the unions led by Lula, the plenary approved a diluted motion calling for the discussion of a general strike. The major problem at the CONCLAT arose over the composition of the National Pró-CUT Commission, the body which was to continue the work of the CONCLAT on an interim basis, to study the issues involved in the formation of a national organization, and to call the next CONCLAT. The executive commission's attempt to present a unitary slate failed because a majority of the slots were filled by partisans of the Unidade Sindical. Two alternatives were eventually presented, one by Lula and one by Arnaldo Gonçalves, president of the metalworkers of Santos. Both slates contained the names of compromise candidates. When neither slate won a decisive majority, the leaders were forced to hammer out a compromise, conceived mainly by

José Francisco da Silva of CONTAG, in which the rural unions would fill 23 out of 54 seats on the commission, and each of the major blocs present at the conference would fill half of the remainder.[16]

Once established, the pró-CUT was seriously divided: on one side was a group of union leaders led by the São Bernardo Metalworkers, who wanted to promote rank-and-file unionism and who emphasized direct action (particularly strikes); on the other side were those who favored a more moderate approach, that is, the creation of a national organization which would function more from above in the policy arena than from below as a coordinator of new forms of grass-roots initiative. The imminence of the November 1982 elections complicated matters further, and competition for workers' votes between the Workers' party and the PMDB (in which members of the Unidade Sindical participated), sharpened the existing polarization. Some members of the pró-CUT commission argued that it was impossible to imagine holding a unitary trade union conference in the face of the widespread politicization around the elections; they suggested that it be postponed until 1983. José Francisco da Silva of CONTAG defended this postponement, arguing also that in spite of advances by many individual unions since the CONCLAT in 1981, the interunion organizations had not made progress toward unifying the struggle. Better than another CONCLAT that might try to form an unrepresentative central organization before the subject had been debated enough among workers would be to strengthen interunion organizations at the state level and to promote more debate.[17] The São Bernardo tendency countered that the commission's mandate extended only to 1982, and that the conference should be held in any case. The former position carried the day, and the conference was postponed until August 1983.[18]

In spite of the exacerbation of conflict between the Unidade Sindical and the autênticos over the question of CONCLAT, the government's IMF-mandated wage austerity policy in 1983 provided an opportunity for joint action. The wage policy was embodied in a series of decree laws, intended to contain wage increases well under the rate of inflation. The new laws also eliminated the redistributive aspect of wage policy, instituted in 1979, whereby the lowest-paid workers received raises 10 percent over the rise in the official cost of living index (INPC).

Unions responded to the new measures with indignation; the wage squeeze in effect since the military took over had already reduced the real minimum wage to around 50 percent of its pre-1964 level.[19] A series of oil workers' strikes in early July culminated in a one-day general strike on July 21, 1983, to protest the wage austerity bill. São Paulo metalworkers president Joaquim dos Santos Andrade played a major role in coordinating this strike, hoping thus to strengthen his credentials as a combative union leader.[20] Although the Communist party firmly opposed the strike, concerned about its impact on the party's effort to obtain legal status, many PCB union leaders chose to defy their party's position. Although the July 21 strike was far from general,[21] it was important as the first explicitly political strike since 1964, and as a demonstration that divisions in the labor movement did not preclude joint action. The government's response, however, seemed calculated to reinforce divisions. Police repression of strikers in São Paulo was heaviest in the ABC region, provoking protests from state congressmen and the acting president of the PMDB, Teotónio Vilela. The unions that suffered intervention as a result of the strike were those whose leaders were affiliated with the PT,[22] indicating on the one hand that these unions were perceived as more of a threat to the status quo than were those closer to the Unidade Sindical tendency, and on the other that the government still saw repression by removal of the union officers as an effective means of reducing the influence of the autênticos. The São Paulo Metalworkers, whose president was the self-proclaimed leader of the strike, and other unions that had played a leading role, were untouched. Labor leaders did not confine their protest to the strike but went en masse to Brasília to lobby against the laws' passage in Congress; their pressure was important in the defeat of the first two wage bills brought to a vote. After government negotiations with congressional leaders, a somewhat milder version of the bill passed in October 1983.

Joint action in response to the wage squeeze did not prevent the battle that was shaping up over the next CONCLAT. Formally, it was a fight over representation, with the Unidade Sindical arguing for enlarged delegations from federations and confederations and the exclusion of most associations not recognized by the CLT (which included many of the public employees' associations). The autênticos wanted representation on the basis of unions and of rank-and-file delegates elected by workers proportional to the size of their base. They also called for the immediate creation of a central union organization, while the Unidade Sindical still considered such a move precipitous.

Although the battle over organizational questions formally precipitated the split in the pró–CUT, the deeper disputes discussed above had in fact made the prospects for reconciliation more and more difficult to imagine. The opposing tendencies began to devote ever more attention to winning control over unions whose officers were up for election, with the explicit objective no longer being only the defeat of pelego leadership but increasingly an expression of the rivalry between the two activist tendencies. The pró-CUT formally split apart in July 1983, and the autênticos held a convention in São Bernardo in August 1983, with 5,059 delegates from 665 unions and 247 other labor organizations. The convention established a central labor organization—the Central Unica dos Trabalhadores, United Workers' Organization.[23] The opposing tendency met in turn at Praia Grande, São Paulo, in November, with 4,254 delegates from 1,258 unions, federations, and confederations, and formed an organization called CONCLAT—Coordenação Nacional da Classe Trabalhadora (National Coordination of the Working Class), with the word *Coordination* implying a rejection of the immediate creation of a "Central Organization."

The issues that divided the two were not easily resolvable. Different strategic approaches were grounded in different visions of society, which in turn were heavily influenced by the way in which different union leaders experienced the authoritarian period. In an analysis of interviews with leaders of metalworkers' unions from both the CUT and the CONCLAT, Roque Aparecido da Silva found that the fact that the former had as a rule spent most of the authoritarian period as factory workers and the latter as union officers had produced profoundly divergent visions of society. For CONCLAT leaders, the solution to problems of labor relations lay within broader social and political institutions, provided that the rules of the game were changed in such a way as to give workers a fair chance. Leaders of the CUT, on the other hand, who had experienced the difficult conditions on the shop floor during the authoritarian period firsthand, embraced a more syndicalist vision. For them, the problem was structural; the solution could only lie in broad social transformation. Since workers could not rely on allies in other social sectors, workers themselves were the only possible agents of that transformation.[24]

The success of the CUT relative to that of the CONCLAT over the next two years reflects less a conscious choice by workers of one vision of broad social change over another than the fact that the CUT's confrontational strategy, combined with its emphasis on direct bargaining, produced concrete gains for the membership of its affiliates. Emphasis on shop-floor organization and closer relationships between union leaders and rank-and-file workers underlay the success of many of the plant-level strikes in 1984; the greater degree of unity among the CUT leadership facilitated the coordination of strikes in 1985, enabling stronger unions to reinforce the claims of weaker ones. CUT leaders managed to strengthen union identity and solidarity as well as the material well-being of members, thus greatly enhancing its organizational resources. While unions that were members of the CONCLAT won victories during this period as well, the heterogeneity of the CONCLAT, combined with its generally conciliatory approach, made it less effective in consolidating the fruits of those victories.

The role of the labor ministry was also key to the consolidation of the CUT's position. While plant-level victories in the 1984 strikes often occurred in spite of the efforts of the ministry, Pazzianotto's encouragement of direct bargaining and his refusal to intervene in strikes provided a more favorable conjuncture for coordinated action in 1985. In addition, the new labor minister removed the legal restriction on the formation of central organizations. The decrease in the likelihood of repression clearly benefited that sector of the labor movement most able to mobilize its resources.

By late 1985, particularly after the exceptionally well coordinated bank workers' strike in September, the CUT began to be recognized as the predominant organization in the labor movement. Its membership included around 1,250 unions, representing about 15,000,000 workers. In absolute numbers of unions, CONCLAT was still ahead, but those numbers were deceptive; the four bank workers' unions which belonged to the CUT, for example, represented over 70 percent of the bank workers in the country. Of the 6,112,000 workers estimated by the labor ministry to have been on strike during the first eleven months of 1985, some 60 percent were led by CUT unions and most of the other 40 percent received some support from the CUT.[25]

By early 1986, many CONCLAT leaders were sufficiently nervous about the CUT advances that they decided to form a central organization; a loose "coordination" was no longer sufficient. By choosing to call themselves the Confederação Geral dos Trabalhadores (CGT), these leaders were attempting to demonstrate the historical continuity of their movement. The CGT's president, Joaquim dos Santos Andrade, declared his intention to combat the CUT for influence in the unions by contesting union elections with all possible resources and displaying a new militant rhetoric.

Political Parties and Labor Organization
As should be apparent from the above discussion, divergent and finally opposing tendencies in the combative sector of the labor movement

were already implicit prior to the establishment of new political parties. Nonetheless, with the establishment of the parties, union positions became increasingly identified with political party positions. This was especially evident in the case of the autêntico group, particularly as there was a significant overlap between union leadership and the leadership of the Workers' party. Although the CUT included a number of unions whose leaders were not involved in the party, as did its leadership, it was unquestionably dominated by unionists who were also PT members. In 1985, several of the important CUT leaders who had not previously been PT members joined the party, most notably João Paulo Pires Vasconcelos of the João Monlevade Metalworkers and Paulo Renato Paim of the Canoas Metalworkers.

Party identification in the Unidade Sindical and the CONCLAT formed at Praia Grande in November 1983 was initially somewhat more complicated because of the illegality of the Brazilian Communist party (PCB), the Communist party of Brazil (PC do B), and the 8th of October Revolutionary Movement (MR-8), of which the first was by far the most important. Illegal Trotskyist parties similarly included under the umbrellas of the PT and the CUT initially played a smaller, though quite vocal, role. The fact that such organizations were still illegal complicated the debate among different tendencies in the labor movement, as it did in the PT. In an interview in 1982, Olivio Dutra claimed that the illegality of the Communist party, in particular, made honest discussion of party positions within the labor movement impossible; Communist party labor leaders were quick to accuse labor leaders who were members of the PT of promoting party positions within the unions, but when PT members attempted to make the same point in return they were accused of red-baiting.[26]

Although the Unidade Sindical tendency and the CONCLAT coordination formed in 1983 were associated in the public mind with these parties and with the PMDB, there were significant internal differences among components of the organization. Because CONCLAT organizers chose to give a prominent place in the organization to federations and confederations, it included many unionists who were not part of the combative wave in the 1970s. In addition, the first president of CONCLAT was José Francisco da Silva, who prior to the split in the pró-CUT was not entirely identified with either the Unidade Sindical or the autênticos group. Possessing an indisputable power base of his own (rural union membership outnumbered the membership of all urban unions combined), his decision not to attend the São Bernardo conference in August 1983 was of decisive importance for the division between the national organizations along partisan lines. The heterogeneity of the CONCLAT, however, made it difficult for the organization to establish a clear direction; its initial significance derived more from the weight of its individual members than from actions that it proposed. When the Communist party was legalized in 1985, partisan identification of labor leaders became somewhat more visible. Still, particularly within the CONCLAT, a number of defections from the Communist party to other political parties during the legalization process complicated the question of party allegiances.

It is difficult to assess the role of parties in stimulating the growing competition among union tendencies. Partisan competition for leadership of unions and of national organizations did not develop first elsewhere and enter the unions to gain support from labor for goals formed outside the labor movement. There is thus an important difference between partisan struggle *over* the unions and partisan struggle *within* the unions in the Brazilian case. Although struggles over union leadership were referred to (particularly outside the unions) in partisan terms, the players had not changed, and the terrain had not really shifted. Even the excursion of workers into electoral politics in the 1982 elections did not fundamentally change, for the PT, the separation of union activity from the sphere of political institutions.

From the time of the 1978 electoral campaign, the São Paulo PMDB attempted to broaden its base of support by including some union and popular leaders in its slate. Fernando Henrique Cardoso, in his senatorial campaign, consulted regularly with labor leaders and chose Maurício Soares, a lawyer for the São Bernardo Metalworkers' Union, as his alternate. While the PMDB did win widespread support from workers in this election, it did not establish an ongoing relation with unions, and the popular leaders elected in 1978 remained fairly isolated within the party. Opposition politics in the traditional political sphere was still very much a matter for elites.

The Brazilian Communist party approached this situation much as it always had, attempting to approximate itself to power—not to the state, as during the populist period, but to the future state, in the form of the leading opposition party. PCB members ran on MDB and later PMDB tickets for Congress and campaigned actively for the party. As the transition to civilian rule drew near, the party began a campaign for legalization—a situation which it last enjoyed in the mid-1940s. The party's approach to political power, therefore, was to work together with that sector of the opposition that could be expected to occupy the state after the demise of the military regime. The PCB's overall assessment of the Brazilian political situation remained much the same as it was in the 1950s and 1960s: that Brazil needs to experience a liberal democratic period and national economic development before the conditions are ripe for the working class to take power.

Union leaders close to the PCB took a comparable position on union politics. Since the working class was not yet strong enough to impose its will forcefully in society and in the political sphere, the proper strategy was to win hegemony by gaining access to leadership positions within existing class organizations and to win substantial gains through political alliances with the opposition in government. With the growing influence of the CUT and the relative stagnation of the CONCLAT in 1985, however, Communist party labor leaders began to rethink their position. Losses in several key union elections to new leadership affiliated with the CUT—especially the Rio de Janeiro bank workers' union—fueled concern that the party would be left behind if it continued to support the CONCLAT. Ivan Pinheiro, the defeated former president of the Rio bank workers and a member of the Communist party's Central Committee, began to argue that the party's union leaders should shift their allegiance to the CUT; a special party conference to discuss the question was called for March 1986.[27] While Pinheiro's position lost in that encounter, the question remained alive due to the exacerbation of the struggle for leadership in the CGT and its fragmentation in the late 1980s.

The Workers' Party and the Labor Movement

For labor leaders involved in the creation of the Workers' party, the new unionism's focus on shop-floor issues and winning new rights from employers involved a sharp distinction between industrial action and political representation and advocacy. The PT was to be an extension of and at the same time separate from labor organized institutionally in unions, and was—as a party—to respect the autonomy of those unions. At the same time as it was to remain separate, however, its role was seen as complementary: the 1979 strike, according to Lula, had demonstrated the limits of industrial action; to win major gains, workers needed a political organization of their own, founded and headed by and for workers themselves. The party was not so much to *lead* workers as to *express* in the political arena the demands of social movements and unions. The creation of the party was thus a strategic response by a sector of the labor movement for the achievement of goals that had already been articulated elsewhere. It was to be both more than (with regard to what it might achieve) and less than (with regard to its initiative in posing goals and needs) the unions themselves.

With the institutionalization of the party, the PT faced a wide array of challenges. As a party competing in the electoral arena with other parties and laying claim to at least some portion of political power, it had to evolve a broader appeal. This broader appeal was at first largely class-based, making the claim that the rights of workers (and by derivation, the rights of everyone) to participate were central to the process of democratization and that other parties practiced elitist politics which relegated workers' rights to a subordinate plane. The PT's call for participation, organization, and self-determination was an appeal for the creation of an authentic class politics and political strategy. The message was "organize yourselves in your neighborhood associations, in your unions; define your own needs, join the party, and we will be there to help you." But the PT did not formulate a very clear picture of precisely what was involved in this process of working-class self-determination or of the party's specific role in promoting it. After the 1982 elections, conflicts between the party organization and its elected officials, together with statements by party leaders that building grass-roots and union organizations was more important than activity in Congress, further complicated the complex relationship between the party's independent role and its role as the voice of grass-roots demands and goals.

The party's relationship with the labor movement was much more complicated than it appeared. The overlap in leadership personnel in the major unions identified with PT positions, the labor leaders involved in the party, and the heads of the Central Labor Organization (CUT) created in São Bernardo in 1983 was virtually complete. This could be expected to guarantee a harmonious relationship, and it helps to explain why trade unionists associated with the party expressed the most stalwart optimism regarding its potential and progress. To explore the relationship between the two more closely, it is useful to examine (a) the role of labor leaders in the party as a whole; (b) the treatment of labor issues in party documents—both internal discussion documents and party newspapers; and (c) the formation of the programmatic agendas of both labor organizations and the PT. We should also look at how partisan conflict has been expressed in the labor movement itself, and the PT's part in this. We must also consider the formation and practice of the PT in the light of the historical experience of Brazilian working-class politics. Finally, we will consider why its relation to the labor movement was so important in shaping the future of the PT.

Labor leaders were central to the formation of the Workers' party. Other social groups and actors who participated in the party's founding were attracted by the potential social and political force that the strikes of 1978–79 represented in Brazil. Lula was central; until he decided to play a decisive role in founding and promoting the party, others waited. As the leader of the São Bernardo strikes and thus symbolically the hero of the labor upsurge as a whole, he was the key to any viable new political force on the left which claimed to express and build on the dynamism of labor activity and organization.

The weight of labor leaders in PT directive organs was evident from the beginning. The national provisional commission elected in January 1980 had eleven members, of which ten were either union leaders or former trade unionists. That proportion diminished when a new provisional commission was elected in June 1980; the new ten person leadership body included six labor leaders and activists. In the national pre-convention of the party held on August 8–9, 1981, in São Paulo, criteria for the selection of the party's first national diretório included a provision that 40 percent of its members be union leaders. The twelve person national executive commission elected at that meeting included eight members who were or had been union leaders, and two out of the five alternates to the executive commission were union leaders.[28] The formation of the Articulação dos 113, discussed in chapter 5, reaffirmed the centrality of labor leadership in the party.

The formation of the CUT made the meshing of party and labor leadership at the national level even more apparent. The negotiations among different factions of the labor movement involved in forming the CUT demonstrated the continuing importance of Lula, whose personal influence was required for an agreement to be reached on a unitary slate. Nonetheless, the party's desire to maintain a formal separation between CUT and party leadership was evident when Jacó Bittar wanted to run for the CUT's coordinating commission. Bittar was secretary general of the PT at the time, and party policy stipulated that no one could hold an executive position simultaneously in the party and in a national labor organization. Thus his decision at the convention to run for the CUT executive meant that he had to resign from the party executive commission. The policy was subsequently modified to allow him to continue as a member of the executive but not to remain secretary general.

The interpenetration between PT leadership and the leadership of combative trade unions made it difficult for the party to develop a party position on trade union issues, or even to imagine what such a position might be, other than one of support for trade union struggles. This was further complicated by the methodology proposed for elaborating a party position on labor questions. Initial definitions were to be discussed at regional and national meetings of labor activists in the party, with non–trade unionists to be included by invitation only. The results were then to be discussed by the whole party. These regional and national meetings of trade unionists were to consider the relationship between the party and the unions—whether the PT should in fact have a union policy of its own and how, concretely, the PT should act in relation to the union question.

The decision to make the elaboration of a party position on the trade union question the responsibility of trade unionists seems on the surface to have been consistent with the party's attitude toward the autonomy of the labor movement; nonetheless, its effects were problematic, as it failed to attribute an independent role to the party's action on labor issues and added to the party's difficulties in establishing its institutional identity. Over the course of 1981, the struggles around preparations for the CONCLAT were the primary focus of attention for labor leaders in the PT, and their actions constituted de facto the party's position.

After the 1981 CONCLAT, it was decided to create a special party organ to organize discussion of the party-union relationship, and a labor secretariat (Secretaria Sindical) was established at a meeting of the national diretório on October 31–November 2, 1981. The secretariat, coordinated by Olívio Dutra, was to have sixteen members. The first internal party document issued by this secretariat set forth a number of principles for party action vis-à-vis the unions and listed several immediate problems to be faced. First, the document reiterated the principle that unions should be autonomous from both the state and from political parties, saying that PT members could not use the unions as instruments of party purposes. No slate should ever be presented in union elections in the name of the party. On the other hand, it proclaimed that union action was inevitably political. Nonetheless, unions should not be organized along the lines of political divisions, but rather should maintain unity of representation for all workers in a given occupational category. With regard to party members active in unions, the document called for continued participation in the pró-CUT and its secretariat, more effective intervention in joint union assemblies where the Unidade Sindical was also present, and continued pressure for a broad-based National Conference of the Working Class in 1982. The document also proposed that a national meeting of PT union activists be held in São Paulo on July 24–25, 1982, to be preceded by local and state meetings. [29]

The document issued by the party's labor secretariat demonstrated the difficulty in making a clear separation between union questions and party questions. While at the local level such expedients as insuring that union slates not run in the name of the party may have been intended to establish such a distinction, at the national level this was not so easy. The conflict over the control of the pró-CUT commission and organization for the CONCLAT scheduled for August 1982 had its origins in conflicts which predated the formation of the PT, but by 1982 it was identified with party divisions. When the PT as party encouraged its union activists to act more efficiently in areas where the Unidade Sindical was present it was clearly working to reinforce the current of the labor movement with which it was identified. Indeed, it could not have been otherwise, as the leadership of that current and the leadership of the PT contained many of the same people. It was not, however, a case of the party using the unions as instruments of its policy, but rather one of labor leaders attempting to act on two different institutional fronts.

The problem was essentially that these leaders failed to identify a separate institutional arena in which the party could act on its own. The dynamics of the party-union relationship in the early 1980s are extremely difficult to characterize, because the relationship was embodied in the identity of the individuals involved rather than in the evolution of mechanisms of consultation and discussion between organizations acting in different arenas. One cannot even say that a division of labor developed between the party and the autêntico labor current in the process of advancing the union struggle. The primary discussions at the regional and national meetings of PT labor activists in 1982 were centered around how to strengthen the unions *from within* and on the process of building a national labor organization. The party's role was to encourage its members to participate in this process and to devote more space to labor questions in party publications. The party had no autonomous role to play in the political sphere other than to proclaim the importance of union autonomy. Autonomy meant the independence of social organization and of unions from the state, from employers, from religious institutions, and from political parties and groups including the PT, which "was born in the labor movement, but which does not intend to control it, nor does it (unlike other parties) claim to be the sole representative of workers."[30] The party was to carry its proposals to unions and submit itself to the democratic process of union assemblies, from which the process of strengthening the labor movement would have to arise. In none of the reports of discussions at these meetings was there any mention of possible party action in the legislative arena, for example, or of ways to promote the discussion of labor questions in the 1982 electoral campaign then in progress.

An examination of the treatment of labor issues in the party's newspaper reinforces this assessment. There was extensive coverage of strikes and of activities of the CUT, and very little emphasis on specifically political action with regard to labor questions. In an article devoted to the party's campaign against the government's economic policy in September 1983, various forms of action were suggested, including leafletting, vigils, and rallies, but only at the end of the list was there a mention of the need to mobilize the party's deputies to make speeches and present motions in parliament. In a discussion in the same issue of a campaign against unemployment, the goals listed included the repeal of Decree Law 2045 (a wage austerity law passed in 1983), job security, reduction of the work week from 48 to 40 hours, a unified minimum wage which reflected the real cost of living, a mobile wage scale, unemployment compensation, repeal of the IMF agreement, and debt moratorium. The major instrument for attaining these ends was considered to be the general strike, as determined by the Second National Meeting of PT trade unionists on July 21, 1983. Again, there was no mention of a political campaign outside the unions, except as concerned mobilization of support for the demands of a potential general strike.[31]

This is not to say that elected party representatives did not raise labor issues in Congress and present legislation intended to promote union autonomy. Nonetheless, it is clear from the attention that they received (or did not receive) in the party press that legislative activity was not expected to be an important vehicle of change. The June 1985 issue of the São Paulo PT newspaper provides an interesting illustration of this point. It devoted a page and a half to articles on important strikes that had occurred in the preceding month. It also carried a quarter-page article about a presentation by lawyers in the PT to the national diretório critiquing the labor minister's proposal for a new strike law. This article mentioned the fact that PT federal deputy Djalma Bom had presented a bill on April 2 calling for the repeal of existing strike laws, based on the argument that no strike law was needed, as the right to strike was a basic right which required only recognition. There was no extensive discussion of Djalma's bill, nor was the fact that he had presented it tied to an overall party strategy regarding the labor movement. Not until two years later, when labor issues became a significant component in the Constituent Assembly debates, did this essentially syndicalist focus to labor issues begin to change.

Thus the party's role was to encourage and reinforce the independent action of the autêntico labor movement and to act as its publicist. This narrow interpretation of the possibilities for action by a working-class party had a significant impact on the development of the party over the next few years and reinforced the turn away from institutional politics after the 1982 elections. One cannot, however, attribute the narrowness of the interpretation of the party's role simply to a lack of political experience (although this may well have played a part in it) or to a lack of imagination. Its explanation lies mainly in the dynamics of what was happening at the time within the labor movement itself, and in the way that PT members interpreted the historical experience of the Brazilian working class.

The leadership of the Workers' party took the question of trade union autonomy very seriously. The labor leaders who founded the party interpreted the history of the relationship of the labor movement to politics in Brazil as one of subordination—both to the state, in the form of corporatism, and to political parties. Both the PTB and the Communist party were seen as having used labor mobilization instrumentally, to serve ends that were defined elsewhere. The PT's relationship to the labor movement was to be different; if anything, it was the party that should be subordinate to the labor movement, re-presenting in the political arena goals that were identified in the unions.

Autonomy was difficult to define in practice. The PT had many characteristics of a labor party, but it was not only a labor party. It aimed to bring together many excluded groups, not just organized workers, and its performance in the 1985 elections suggested that it could appeal to a substantial protest vote from the middle class as well. But while the party and the labor movement followed separate paths of development, there was a great deal of interdependence between the two.

It is useful to identify three periods in the party's relationship with the labor movement: from the foundation of the party in 1979 to the 1982 elections; from November 1982 to November 1985; and from the November 1985 elections to the present.

During the first period, from the beginning of the party in 1979 to the 1982 elections, union leaders saw the formation of the PT as a way to make the demands of workers heard in a broader public sphere. The party was still mainly a potential, but it was a potential for a national forum and a means to increase workers' participation in political institutions. Although the party denied the legitimacy of the existing system in countless statements, it took extraordinary pains to fulfill the bureaucratic requirements to become and remain legal. In spite of the party's official position that real change could not occur through elections, the possibility of electing working-class leaders to office was clearly taken seriously. In São Paulo at least, the party provided extra support for labor candidates in the 1982 elections. National visibility of PT leaders whose origins were in the unions increased the prestige of the union current that had produced them, and the party served as a voice for the kinds of strategies being advanced within the labor movement, in the struggle over the creation of a central union organization.

The year 1982 was an important turning point. Within the labor movement, it marked the confirmation of a serious split within the movement to establish a central organization; in the political sphere it brought the first elections of the transitional period. Clearly two events were related: partisan differences exacerbated the already major divergences among union leaders, serving as a focus for mistrust and recrimination. Accusations of promoting partisan divisions sometimes took the place of substantive debates, obscuring the underlying strategic differences. The elections served as a convenient excuse for postponing the foundation of a central organization, on the basis of a claim that electoral divisions made trade union unity impossible. The inability of the autênticos to force the convocation of a conference in 1982 seemed to condemn them to a marginal position in the labor movement, reinforcing their confrontational posture.

Several months later the PT did much worse than it had expected at the polls, seemingly confirming its own rhetoric about the hopelessness of expecting major change to come through elections. Discussions of what went wrong abounded but seemed to produce no results. For at least six months after the elections, the party seemed ruled by inertia. Internal disputes, such as the one which quickly emerged in Diadema and the conflicts between party deputies and internal party leaders, seemed insoluble. For union leaders mired in the complications of party politics, the formation of the CUT in August 1983 came like a breath of fresh air. Jacó Bittar's decision at the CUT founding convention to run for its executive body—even if it meant abandoning the executive commission of the party—illustrates the relative importance attributed to the two organizations. Other labor leaders demonstrated a similar attitude later on; when the president of the PT, Luís Inácio Lula da Silva, and its vice president, Olivio Dutra, decided to contest elections in their respective unions in mid-1984 they did not bring their decisions up for discussion in the party executive. Unlike Bittar's decision to participate in the executive of the CUT, participation in leadership bodies of local unions did not require that Lula and Dutra resign from their PT offices. The main impact of their decisions to run for union offices was the decreased amount of time they could devote to party activity. In Dutra's case, this was probably not significant, as he had previously held a full-time job as a bank worker. For Lula, however, who had devoted himself entirely to the presidency of the party, the return to the union had both practical and symbolic importance. These actions represented a clear perception that the labor movement, between 1983 and 1985, was a more dynamic and important arena for action than was the party.

During its period of "return to the base," in which labor and social movement activists who were party members or even leaders attributed relatively less importance to party activity (with the single important exception of the movement for direct elections—notable because there was essentially no distinction between movement and party activity), the party probably benefited from the widespread association of the CUT with the PT. The CUT, unlike the PT, was growing and was winning substantial victories. While in the political arena the party passed from crisis to crisis, with respect to the labor arena its image was substantially reinforced.

Another turning point, from the point of view of both the labor movement and the party, came in 1985. With the coordination of large-scale strikes that year, continued growth, victories in union elections in several unions thought to be strongholds of CONCLAT leaders, and the defection of several important CONCLAT unions to the CUT, the latter began to be recognized as the predominant central union organization. As Ivan Pinheiros put it when he proposed that Communist party labor leaders shift their support to the CUT, the latter was now the axis around which trade union unity had to be organized. During the late 1980s, CUT supporters also won elections in an increasing number of rural unions; they were especially visible in Bahia, Pará, and other parts of Amazonia. While rural delegations to the first CUT congress mainly represented union oppositions, by the third congress in 1988 around half the rural delegates were union officers. The upsurge in white-collar organizing in the late 1980s also primarily benefited the CUT.

At the same time, in the 1985 mayoral elections in state capitals, the PT made a better showing than even its most optimistic supporters had expected. A good bit of its success can be assumed to have come from a protest vote; nonetheless, the party's potential to crystallize discontent with the progress of the "New Republic" gave it national recognition as a political force to be reckoned with for the first time.

The simultaneous strengthening of the PT as a party and of the labor movement as an increasingly autonomous force led to a growing complexity in the relations between the two. Unions led by members of the PMDB (for example, the Osasco Metalworkers led by Antonio Tosci) and the PDT (especially in Rio de Janeiro) joined the CUT and began to play an important role in strengthening the organization. At the organization's third Congress in 1988, the dominant faction (Articulação) pushed through a rule change designed to reinforce the CUT's institutional strength. The changes were intended to make the CUT congresses more accurately reflect the organization's real strength in the labor movement, by limiting participation to delegates from unions affiliated with the CUT, making delegations proportional to the number of union members (instead of the number of workers in a union's jurisdiction), and making delegations from union oppositions proportional to the number of votes they had received in the last union elections. Congresses were made triennial rather than biennial.[32] These changes were also expected to reinforce Articulação's factional position vis-à-vis minority factions, which accused the leadership group of excessive bureaucratization.

PT leaders, in turn, recognized the difficulty they had had in defining the relationship between party and central union organization. As Lula put it, "We didn't know which one should have priority, whether it was the PT or the CUT. . . . We tried to divide our space, our time, between trying to build the central organization and the party."[33] As both the PT and the CUT became more institutionalized, the PT began to have the political confidence to criticize the CUT—even in public—for actions that it considered incorrect, without fearing that the whole edifice of working-class solidarity would fall down. This occurred, for example, in the case of the 1987 general strike call, where party leaders publicly called CUT leadership to task for not paying enough attention to the rank and file's reluctance to go out. The development of a more complex relationship between the Workers' party and the CUT, however, should not be taken to mean that party leaders no longer saw the labor movement as the keystone of the party edifice. This was evident in a comment Lula made when Luís Gushiken, a São Paulo bank workers' leader and federal deputy, was elected as the third president of the party: "The day the PT doesn't have a trade unionist as president its nature will have become distorted."[34]

Beyond São Bernardo: Rethinking the Working Class

Over its first decade, the PT has repeatedly insisted on its identity as a working-class party. During the early discussions of the party, the definition of what that meant expanded from a narrow base among skilled industrial workers—primarily metalworkers—to a broad range of organized workers and a variety of social movements. Nonetheless, from the beginning the party appealed to intellectuals and professionals as well. The Istoé survey of candidates for election in 1982, discussed in chapter 6, noted the number of PT candidates who were liberal professionals. In the 1985 mayoral elections, middle-class candidates predominated, and the party made a greater effort to appeal to the middle-class vote than it had in 1982. An examination of the occupational profile of PT candidates in São Paulo in 1986, of PT deputies, and of the party's national leadership all confirm the predominance of white-collar occupations that, together with metalworkers, make up the great majority of PT slates.[35] The resulting configuration led sociologist Leôncio Martins Rodrigues at the end of the 1980s to make a highly controversial argument that the Workers' Party should be characterized as "a party of the wage-earning middle class, especially liberal professionals and other intellectual professions, with both manual workers and members of the upper classes in a minority, and with proprietors (small, medium, or large) almost nonexistent."[36]

Rodrigues's argument proved extremely troubling to many PT leaders. He also took me to task for my own characterization, in the dissertation in which this research first appeared, of the central role of trade unionists in the party, faulting me for failing to distinguish between industrial unionism and middle-class unionism.[37] His criticism is a valid one, and his studies of the social composition both of PT leadership and of delegates to the congresses of the CUT provide important insights into both. Taken together, the data in Rodrigues's two studies suggest an interesting line of interpretation of the PT's increasing willingness to broaden its appeal in the second half of the 1980s beyond its early focus on industrial workers—an interpretation which confirms, interestingly enough, the importance of the party's relationship with the organized labor movement.

In his analysis of delegations to the first three CUT congresses, Rodrigues notes that the service sector (liberal professionals, bank workers, and transportation workers) and public employees were the sectors that grew most. This reflects the enormous growth in white-collar unionism in Brazil during the 1980s. Even before they were given the right to organize unions by the 1988 constitution, teachers and other professionals and public employees created associations that often won de facto recognition from employers, along with the ability to bargain for their constituents. Strikes by white-collar workers, while less numerous before 1986 than among industrial workers, surpassed the latter in terms of work days lost because of their length and the numbers of strikers involved; teachers' and doctors' strikes tended to be particularly long. In 1987, absolute numbers of white-collar strikes exceeded those of industrial workers.[38] After the new constitution made public-sector unionism possible, organization mushroomed; although solid data is not yet available, a Brazilian labor lawyer recently estimated that since 1988 some three thousand unions have applied for recognition, the great majority of which are white-collar and public-sector unions. The dynamism and militancy of white-collar unionism—particularly teachers, bank workers, and public employees—had an important impact on the development of the CUT, and there has been a consistent expansion of representatives of such unions on the CUT executive.[39]

The expansion of white-collar unionism has had two important, and perhaps contradictory, effects on the labor movement and in a collateral fashion on the PT. One has been to increase the presence in the unions and in the CUT of radical left groups, which Rodrigues argues had been more or less confined to university campuses prior to the formation of associations and unions of well educated employees.[40] Although the radical left did have some weight in industrial unions as well prior to the late 1980s, the rise of white-collar unionism has undoubtedly reinforced its position in the labor movement as a whole. The importance of the radical left in unions, in turn, made it difficult for those opposed to their presence in the PT to argue that these were small and unrepresentative groups. Thus this shift in the composition of the labor movement has been accompanied by increasing factionalism, fueling the ongoing battle within the CUT between those who favor more institutionalization and a greater focus on trade union issues and those who want the organization to play a more politicized role, as a leader of a working-class movement. The latter position would tend to downplay the tendency toward role differentiation between the CUT and the PT.

The second effect is more difficult to measure; it must be cast as a hypothesis whose verification requires both the passage of time and further research. It may be that the rise of white-collar unionism—its militancy, and its increasing importance in the new institutions of the Brazilian labor movement—is wreaking important and largely unperceived changes in the conception that both PT and CUT hold of the working class. If the paradigmatic labor struggles of the late 1970s were the metalworkers' strikes in São Bernardo do Campo, one could argue that the paradigmatic strikes of the 1980s were those of bank workers and teachers. The PT's second president, Olívio Dutra, and its third, Luís Gushiken, were both bank workers. Leaving aside for the moment the issue of possible convergence between wage levels of skilled industrial workers and many white-collar sectors, the conception of working class may have been redefined, and the convergence in forms of organization and struggle made into a more central reference than more traditional indicators of social stratification. A large part of the dismay with which Rodrigues's analysis of the social composition of PT leadership was greeted was probably due to the dissonance between his characterization and this new conception, which corresponds much more closely to Przeworski's notion of political class struggle than it does to more traditional Marxist models.

Przeworski argued that "political class struggle is a struggle about class before it is a struggle among classes."

> Social relations—economic, political, or ideological—are not something that people "act out" in ways reflecting the places that they occupy, but are a struggle of choices given at a particular moment in history.
>
> It is necessary to realize that classes are formed in the course of struggles, that these struggles are structured by economic, political, and ideological conditions under which they take place, and that these objective conditions—simultaneously economic, political, and ideological—mold the practice of movements that seek to organize workers into a class. [41]

In the case of the CUT and the PT, the conjunction between the forms of organization and struggle of the new middle-class unionists and the more traditional urban and rural labor organizations gave primacy to political identity over traditional class distinctions. The implications of this convergence for the PT may have been greater than has previously been recognized. It is likely to have been an important factor in smoothing the transition from a party discourse in the early 1980s that identified its constituency on the basis of the quintessential experiences of its founders and a more inclusive discourse as the decade wore on. When middle-class candidates for elective office were middle-class unionists, they created a bridge between the two.

In summary, during the party's formative years the relationship between the PT and an increasingly autonomous and combative sector of the labor movement was one of mutual reinforcement. Although organizationally independent, at different times in their early development each played an important role in providing the appearance of strength when other, more conventional measures of strength were lacking. The PT's organization and legalization helped to reinforce the capacity of autêntico union leaders at a national level to coordinate their activities and to articulate their differences with more traditional practices in the Brazilian labor movement. In turn, the growing strength of union organization identified with the PT helped to give the party the appearance of possessing important power resources at a societal level, which mitigated to an extent the devastating impact of its electoral defeat in 1982. Finally, changes in the social composition of the labor movement produced a broader conception of working-class identity.

It is interesting to consider these developments in terms of the exchange typology formulated by Lange and Ross in their work on European labor movements. Lange and Ross see unions as "systems of mediation and regularized exchange," whose mediating capacity is a function both of how much workers are willing to let unions mediate for them and how much employers or relevant political actors need or find it useful to accept unions as mediators with workers.[42] Unions thus need coercive support or must win the consent of workers; the latter is achieved through an exchange between unions and their supporters, the resources for which are gained in another set of exchanges between the unions and other actors in the environment. These resources the authors call incentives, which are classified as "material" (wages, working conditions, hours, and the like); "purposive" (political—compromise and bargaining within the rules of the game, which produce political goods in terms of policy and create useful relationships with other actors); "identity" (identification with the values and rights embodied in the organization); and "sociability" (social solidarity, interpersonal bonds, mainly evident during founding periods of trade unions).[43] Consent is generated through one or several of these incentives, depending upon the resources available; the material incentive is always the most basic but is rarely the only one.[44]

Unions offer employers potential regularity and social control of workers; they offer the state the political/economic consent of supporters, in other words, legitimacy. To political parties, unions can offer votes, activism, or behavior that could improve the party's chances in return for incentives. Unions act in both political and market arenas, with their strategic emphasis depending on a number of variables. In the political arena these might include the partisan composition of government, the organization of the state and the degree to which it fulfills functions otherwise carried out by collective bargaining (for example, wage setting), and the competitive dynamic between parties with links to unions or which seek their support. Market variables include the strength and cohesion of unions and their degree of implantation on the shop floor, the role and degree of institutionalization of collective bargaining, and the condition of the economy as a whole.[45]

Unions must be examined with regard to their relations with their rank and file, their level of organization, the extent of centralization and decentralization, and the resources that can be exchanged for support. The relationship between unions and employers, particular political parties, and the state will to a large extent determine the availability and kinds of resources to be used. Finally, the strategic and incentive heritage of each union must be taken into consideration to determine how the history of a union or labor movement conditions its view of the strategic choices available. The authors see "change from below" as possible either when major infusions of "new workers" bring changes in the kinds of demands being made or when a shift in the incentive systems of unions interacts with the effect of other socioeconomic and political changes on workers' desires.[46]

While this approach grew out of a study of the European labor movement, whose history and characteristics are evidently quite different from those of Brazil, its value is more general. When Lange and Ross identify organizational and relational variables, they do not assume a particular type of labor relations system, but only that "performance of labor market mediation, or the attempt at it, is the common characteristic of all institutions which we consider unions."[47] Clearly a different kind of mix of coercion and consent will apply for Brazil than in the European cases the authors studied. Nonetheless, given the existence of a consent relationship, we need to look closely at the mechanisms of union relations both within the unions and between the unions and other actors. If consent is to be generated, a relationship must exist which offers more than control on one side and passivity on the other.

In Brazil, during a period in which labor's ability to act effectively in the market arena was reduced, the formation of a political party strengthened identity and solidarity among workers. When labor's market situation and the *overall* political conjuncture became more favorable in 1984 and 1985, prior gains in identity and solidarity provided important resources for unions as they mobilized workers in strikes to take advantage of this new context. Although the political conjuncture remained important in reducing the probability of repression[48] and eventually in encouraging new methods of resolving conflicts (that is, collective bargaining), the relationship between the unions and the party became less important to the unions; identity and solidarity as sources of leadership legitimacy were promoted by material gains.

The kinds of shifts in the "incentive systems" of unions that this process represents, interacting with the effect of other socioeconomic and political changes, seemed to represent a potential for change from below. The conjunctural shift involved in the kind of conservative transition initiated in Brazil may not have involved intentional action on the part of elites to allow such changes to take place. But the ability of unions to increase their power resources by following strategies designed to take advantage of political ("purposive") and material "incentives" made them significant players in the new political game.

The importance of the political context for labor organization in the 1980s becomes especially evident when we consider that this was a decade marked by economic stagnation for the country as a whole. Literature on labor organization does not lead us to expect a major upsurge in trade union organization during such a period. In this context, however, it is worth reiterating the conclusion that Shorter and Tilly draw from their study of strikes in France: major labor mobilization tends to occur at critical points for workers' interests in national political life, provided that a sufficient degree of organization is present to move from a perception of opportunity to collective action.[49] French sociologist Sabine Erbès-Seguin makes a similar point, arguing that crisis periods, representing a political and social change in the balance of forces, situate union demands in a larger arena of social conflict. Union demands do not by themselves change the balance of forces—it is their political impact that can lead to a change in the dominant discourse about society.[50]

These theoretical contributions help to situate the relationship between the PT and the unions in the context of the Brazilian transition. While the shift between strategies involving material and purposive or political incentives is a common feature of labor relations in any historical period, the fact that a sufficient accumulation of resources took place in the early stages of the transition process made possible forms of labor mobilization in later stages which had important political repercussions. The transition period clearly corresponds to the Shorter and Tilly conception of a critical moment and to Seguin's conception of crisis. In the mid-1980s, labor mobilization—and the problem of distributive justice that it raised—became crucial political issues. The formation of the PT and the CUT provided an institutional basis for the struggle to situate these issues among the core questions of democratic transition.

THE WORKERS'

8

PARTY AND

POLITICAL

INSTITUTIONS

After the 1982 elections, the Workers' party had to relate not only to its social base but also to its own newly elected politicians. Although the party had included members of Congress since the beginning, the relationship had been different; they had been elected on the MDB ticket in 1978, and together with other party leaders were primarily involved in the process of party organization and in preparing for the electoral campaign. The election of members of Congress and mayors on the PT ticket forced the party to face for the first time the form of its participation in institutions of political power.

Two factors made this particularly difficult. First, the party's overall electoral defeat in 1982 decreased its incentive and willingness to think in institutional terms; the primary interest of most party leaders between 1983 and 1985 was in social action. Second, the party had given little thought to this task. In its early growth as both a party organization and a political movement, the PT's focus was societal. In spite of the inflated expectations at the end of the 1982 campaign, the PT still had no clear position on how to act in political institutions; instead it issued general statements about accountability of politicians to the party and its social base and the need to govern together with the organized population. The problem was to remain consistent with the initial proposal to promote grass-roots participation in political life and at the same time to use effectively the institutional spaces made available through participation in electoral politics. This implied learning to live with the tension between often conflicting conceptions of direct and representative democracy.

Part of the difficulty also lay in the still embryonic nature of the party's theorizing on the relations among different kinds of democratic institutions. The PT's focus on democratization from below led to a call for the formation of popular councils and the development of mechanisms of direct democracy. Nonetheless, there was considerable disagreement within the party on the meaning of such instruments: for some, they were to be embryonic organs of dual power; for others, they were a mechanism for increasing popular participation in local decision making.[1] Ideally, such councils would be formed by local movements themselves; in the absence of strong local movements some thought that PT municipal governments should create participatory organs themselves, while others argued that to do so would merely reproduce familiar patterns of corporatist relations. The relation between councils and parliamentary bodies, the subject of a long-standing debate on the left, remains unclear in PT formulations; for some PT members, councils were eventually to replace more traditional organs and for others they were to play a supplementary role.[2] In either case, parliamentary bodies were viewed as insufficient for the kind of democratic politics that the PT wanted to practice—a view which undoubtedly drew sustenance from the weakness of the Brazilian Congress and the historical overrepresentation of traditional oligarchies therein.

This chapter will explore the way in which the institutional challenge was posed initially in three different instances of party activity in the period following the 1982 elections. First, it will examine the first few years of the administration of Gilson Menezes, the PT mayor of Diadema, in the ABCD region of São Paulo. Second, it will examine the dynamics of the party's relation to legislators, both at the federal and São Paulo state levels and in the São Paulo municipal council. Third, it will discuss the PT's participation in the national campaign for direct elections in 1984. As the party grew and matured in the late 1980s, some of the problems posed in these first experiences began to be resolved, while others remained more intractable. The chapter concludes with a look at the evolution of the party's view of the role of elected officials and at the ongoing tensions between its "movement" and electoral identities.

Diadema: The Workers' Party in Power

The case of Diadema, where the Workers' party candidate Gilson Correia de Menezes was elected mayor in 1982, illustrates many of the strengths and weaknesses of the party discussed in previous chapters. The problems and questions, successes and failures, encountered in the process of administering a municipality gave practical content to party debate and stimulated discussion of the party's approach to political power.

Winning the mayoral elections in Diadema gave the PT an opportunity to show that workers could run a government and to put into practice the party's approach to political power and participation. For a number of reasons, both internal and external to the party, the PT was not initially able to create the kind of showcase administration for which many party members had hoped.

First, there were serious political and material impediments to be overcome. The PT won city hall by a very slim margin in a three-way split among the PT, the PMDB, and the PTB candidates, in a municipality where social problems were enormous and the municipal budget largely inadequate to address them. Second, even where the PT administration logged positive achievements, it had trouble projecting these nationally. Unlike the MDB administrations that had experimented with new forms of popular participation in city government in Lajes, Santa Catarina,[3] and Piracicaba, São Paulo, the PT in Diadema did not enjoy a sympathetic national press; there was extensive reporting of intraparty conflict and of the PT's mistakes in Diadema, and very little coverage of successful efforts.

Although these external constraints undoubtedly complicated the situation, internal factors prevented the party from making good use of the opportunity. These internal factors can be divided for analytical purposes into three categories: those which resulted from lack of political preparation for governing; those which stemmed from the nature of the party; and those which reflected the party's overall response to the 1982 elections.

Lack of political preparation for governing was reflected in the lack of prior programmatic consensus within the local party on priorities for municipal policy. The Diadema PT's municipal program was primarily an electoral program, calling for the formation of popular councils and municipal policy benefiting the poor. A program for governing would have required an in-depth appreciation of the city's problems and practical proposals for addressing them. Failure to distinguish between the two kinds of programs contributed to the subsequent tension between the mayor's office and local party leaders.

One justification that was sometimes offered for the lack of a specific program for governing was that once organs of popular participation had been established, the people would decide on priorities for action and would suggest means for policy implementation. This was a false dilemma, as prior analysis of particular policy arenas in no way precluded the possibility of popular input into the process. Indeed, a discussion document published by the São Paulo regional diretório's Secretariat for Political Education explicitly discussed the need to establish priorities and identify means to carry them out, given the generalized paucity of municipal resources.[4] The Workers' party in Diadema had not carried on in-depth research and discussion of the kind suggested in this document prior to the elections. Discussion of appointments to posts in the administration was more of a factional struggle than it might have been had the problem been to match up individuals with programmatic tasks on which there was already substantial agreement. Points in the electoral program—such as the intention to govern through popular councils—became areas of contention between the mayor's office and the diretório far out of proportion to their significance; the problem of rigid or flexible interpretation of the electoral program became a kind of code for the unfolding power struggle between the local party and the administration.

Other factors that made it difficult for the PT to use its position in Diadema effectively came from contradictions inherent in the party. Of particular importance was the party's view of representation and its stress on local decision making. As Diadema was the only significant municipality in which the PT had won the mayoral elections in 1982, what happened there would reflect on the image of the party as a whole.[5] Nonetheless, as conflicts arose in Diadema, state and national party organs were slow to respond, and their statutory ability to intervene was limited.

The political heterogeneity of the PT further complicated the problem, as party factions elsewhere took different sides in the Diadema disputes. It was often difficult to separate substantive issues that required broad and probing debate from factional attempts to score points in an overall power struggle within the party. Personal loyalties among the trade unionist leaders of the party also played an important role. Lula, the national president of the party, Devanir Ribeiro, president of the São Paulo regional diretório, Gilson Menezes, mayor of

Diadema, and Juracy Magalhães, Gilson's controversial chief of staff, had all served together as officers in the São Bernardo and Diadema metalworkers' union in the late 1970s, and they had participated in the founding of the party. This personal relationship reinforced a tendency to ignore the mounting evidence that something was seriously wrong in Gilson's administration.

The party's desire after the 1982 elections to return to the base, and concentrate on reinforcing labor organization and social movements also led to a deemphasis of the importance of PT elected officials in general. The party's future seemed to depend primarily on its action in society; action in political institutions was not the focus of strategic thinking. Conflicts in Diadema were seen as a local problem, and not as an integral part of the party's overall strategic position.

Diadema, part of the industrial belt of Greater São Paulo, only became an autonomous municipality in 1958, before which it was mainly a dormitory suburb for people who worked in neighboring cities, primarily São Bernardo do Campo. In the 1960s, Diadema underwent one of the highest rates of industrial growth in the state. Between 1950 and 1980 the population increased from just over 3,000 to 228,594.[6] By 1980 Diadema was the third most densely populated urban area in Brazil.[7] Population growth was mainly due to migration from northeastern Brazil.[8] Over 70 percent of the population was thirty years old and under, and the majority earned 1–5 minimum wages.

With one-third of the city's population living in *favelas,* lacking even minimal urban infrastructure, precarious health conditions showed up glaringly in the data on infant mortality: the 1980 census placed the mortality rate in Diadema at 82.9 per thousand live births, as opposed to 42.4 in Santo André, 65.1 in São Bernardo do Campo, 29.3 in São Caetano, and an average of 51.2 for the state as a whole.[9] Because children began working very young to contribute to family support, in 1980 only 38.4 percent finished four years of schooling, and only around 8 percent finished eight years.[10] Urban problems in Diadema were visible to the naked eye. When the PT took office in 1982, only a few central roads were paved and public transportation was inadequate. Chronic flooding, mudslides, and lack of sewage and regular garbage collection were only a few of the municipality's glaring problems.[11]

THE 1982 CAMPAIGN IN DIADEMA. The Workers' party victory in Diadema was unexpected, resulting from a complex configuration of local politics and from the prestige of the PT as a whole, rather than from a high level of prior municipal organization. The PT, mainly organized around members of the São Bernardo and Diadema metal-workers and identified with their struggles, had been highly visible in the area since its formation, but both the PTB and the PMDB had good chances of winning. Both the PMDB and the PT benefited from the November 1982 requirement that voters vote a straight ticket, which increased the salience of party identification; Gallup polls from March, July, and September 1982 showed that with the straight ticket require-ment, the combined candidates of the PMDB enjoyed a slight lead over the single PT candidate, with the PT candidate receiving the most individual preferences.[12]

The PT's campaign in Diadema was run on a shoestring budget, and mainly involved canvassing door to door and at local markets on week-ends. The party had 1,025 members in Diadema at the time of the 1982 elections,[13] out of a voting population of 83,838.[14] There were few organized groups and associations in the city; the dwellers' associations (Sociedades de Amigos de Bairro) that did exist generally had clientelis-tic ties to candidates from other parties. PT members had been involved in some initial organizing in the favelas,[15] and in associations of mothers that had begun to organize around demands for day care. The lack of a dense local associational base meant that the party had to rely primarily on personal contact with residents and on its prestige in the region.

Born in Bahia, the PT mayoral candidate, Gilson Luiz Correia de Menezes, was thirty-three years old, married, with three children. He started working at age twelve and became a metalworker at eighteen. He had a high school diploma and had taken professional courses. He became active in the union in 1975. One of the organizers of the strike at Saab-Scania that off the 1978 strike wave, he was elected to the union leadership in 1978 and became director of its strike fund in 1980. Gilson won the mayoral election with 27.80 percent of the vote, against 26.99 for the three PMDB candidates, 26.17 for the three from the PTB, 5.10 for the three from the PDS, and 0.12 for the PDT candidate. He was thus the beneficiary, by a margin of 678 votes, of a three-way split among the PT, the PMDB, and the PTB.[16]

The initial intention of the new Diadema administration had been to govern with the aid of popular councils (Conselhos Populares), to be organized in all neighborhoods of the city as the institutional base of a system of direct democracy. According to a preelectoral document endorsed by all PT candidates, elected officials were to carry out deci-sions made at the base by these councils.[17] Immediately after the elections, Gilson continued to speak of governing through popular councils,[18] but it was soon clear that lack of prior popular organization made the council concept unviable. Too easily manipulated by local political leaders, the councils could not count on a legitimacy derived from real representation of the local population.

The lack of an absolute majority in the elections placed the PT at a disadvantage in the municipal council (Câmara Municipal) as well—a disadvantage intensified by the political inexperience and the factional allegiances of the PT members elected to the council. The municipal council included six members from the PT, five each from the PMDB and PTB, and one from the PDS. Early indications of PMDB willingness to ally with the PT over selection of council officers was viewed with mistrust, as the PMDB was at the time challenging the vote count at two polling places; in addition, the PT delegation's non-negotiable choice for municipal council president, Manuel Boni, was unacceptable to the other parties. The PMDB council members then allied with the PTB, denying the PT any of the executive positions on the council and making it a permanent minority. PT municipal council members were also intransigent in their relations with the mayor's office. Only one of the six PT council members consistently supported measures coming out of city hall, and four of the others condemned any measure which they felt smacked of compromise.

THE ADMINISTRATION AND THE PARTY. The council members' position reflected serious tensions between the mayor and the municipal diretório over different visions of the party and its role in the exercise of power. This conflict grew increasingly bitter as time went on, precluding collaboration between the municipal party organization and the mayor and undermining the PT's ability to use the Diadema experience as its Bologna, as the PMDB had used Lajes and Piracicaba.

Immediately after the elections, Gilson was surrounded by advisers who wanted to contribute to the formation of the Diadema administration. In addition to the local diretório, this included a number of PT politicians and intellectuals from São Paulo, some of whom had contributed to the Diadema campaign. This latter group felt that the governing of Diadema would have an important impact on the PT's national image and was thus a project requiring all the available expertise and experience of party members. Through a network of informal contacts, working groups were constituted to study the situation in Diadema and to give advice on the transition and priorities for the new administration.

Conflict between the administration and the municipal diretório first erupted over who was to head the various departments in the municipal government. The diretório, seeking a decisive role in the selection process, argued that appointees should normally be PT activists in Diadema; where local expertise was genuinely lacking, they should come from the PT in other areas of Greater São Paulo. Nor were all candidates from Diadema acceptable. The Diretório particularly objected to Gilson's choice for chief of staff: his close friend and former union colleague Juracy Magalhães, who had been the candidate from Diadema for the state legislature.[19]

The turning point in the dispute over appointments came on January 4, 1983, when the mayor was voted complete freedom to choose administrative personnel in whom he had confidence; this decision denied the local party a determining or even deliberative role in the matter. The diretório claimed that Gilson had packed the meeting; Gilson accused local party leaders of wanting to keep discussion within a closed group and refusing to work with party members who did not share their position. Cleusa de Oliveira, President of the PT municipal diretório, said that Gilson had been seduced by members of a wing of the party with a "reformist" vision of the party's role, represented in her view by the intellectuals and activists from São Paulo.[20] Gilson maintained that these antagonisms could have been overcome had the diretório been less concerned with its own influence and more willing to respect different positions. "The people from here . . . felt that the election was won here, and that they didn't need outsiders."[21] He claimed to have been shocked by the radicalization of the appointments debate. "The party taught me and other members to go into city hall and implement a PT position. But I can't administer listening only to the party. . . . The party should have an oversight role, but one which fosters debate and discussion."[22]

The São Paulo activists may well have helped to reinforce Gilson's awareness that his was a minority government, and to emphasize his administration's importance for the party as a whole. The administration's early policy initiatives appeared to reflect this broader vision; however, the policymakers also supported the view that associational life should be free not only from state control but from instrumental use by the party as well. The dilemmas inherent in a situation where the PT had won the local government but where autonomous local organization was extremely weak plagued relations between city hall, the local party, the party at the state and national levels, and the local population throughout the Menezes administration. In asserting the autonomy of city hall from imperative deliberations by the local party, the Menezes administration was also leaving itself no organized base in the population to which it was demonstrably responsible and on which it could rely for consistent support.

THE ADMINISTRATION AND PUBLIC POLICY. The general thrust of the early stages of PT administration in Diadema was to try to transform individual demands for assistance into collective demands for urban improvements as social rights, and to develop citizen responsibility in the implementation of policy. When the Popular Councils proved unviable, the attempt to spur popular organization was incorporated into specific policy areas under the leadership of different departments of the municipal government, particularly the departments of health and planning.

Encouraging popular participation—from community work projects to recognition that in a situation where everything seemed urgent, not much was possible—was a financial as well as philosophical imperative. High visibility projects were financially out of reach, yet some visibility was necessary if the population was to perceive the new administration as one working in its interests. The interaction between political commitment to popular organization, the need for visibility to ensure legitimacy of the administration, and the very real limitations of the municipal budget, together with other personal and political conflicts that arose within the administration, created a dynamic that accounts for many of the difficulties encountered in the PT's attempt to inaugurate a popular administration in Diadema.

The Brazilian tax structure, in which only a small percentage of tax revenues returned to the municipalities, left very little flexibility for budgeting for needed programs. One of the only fiscal instruments under municipal control was the tax on industrial property. In its first year, PT administration ran a major audit on the taxes paid by companies installed in the city and found significant discrepancies between land taxed and land actually occupied.[23] Although the resulting reassessment generated some additional revenues, the tax base remained very low in relation to the level of accumulated past debt.[24] After 40 percent of the 1984 budget went to payments on debts of past administrations and 50 percent went to wages of municipal employees, only 10 percent was left for all remaining expenses.

During the first period of the PT administration, the center of initiative was the Planning Department, headed by São Paulo engineer Amir António Khair. Khair became active in the PT in 1981 as a member of the party's team of economists. In Diadema he was seen as one of the outside "technocrats" from São Paulo, and he in fact first met the new mayor in December 1982.[25] Nonetheless, he did maintain relations with the local PT in Diadema, in part through his secretary, Cleusa de Oliveira, president of the municipal diretório, whose job he defended through several crises between the administration and the local party.

The Planning Department put Diadema on the map for innovation in March 1983 when it refused to accept the justifications of the municipality's largest bus company for a fare hike. The department stimulated the creation of a Transit Users' Commission, which carried out an independent study of the number of passengers transported per kilometer, the main datum on which fares were based. The Planning Department then held its negotiations with the company in public hearings and demonstrated that, according to the figures collected, the fare should actually be lowered instead of increased; the bus company had to forgo its fare increase, leaving Diadema with the lowest bus fare in the region. The company also agreed to add new bus lines along the much-traveled São Bernardo–Diadema routes. Continuing the practice of open hearings and negotiations with the transit company, the following year city hall negotiators won, in exchange for the concession of a fare hike, free passes outside of rush hour for senior citizens and the unemployed. These innovations in public transit were imitated elsewhere, and Khair was called in as a consultant to transportation departments in São Paulo and other cities.

The most important and controversial program promoted by the Planning Department was the program to provide urban services to the favelas. When Gilson took office, these 136 shantytown areas housed approximately one-third of the city's population—about 100,000 people—and none had electricity, running water, or sewers. (In fact, only 26 percent of the rest of the city had a regular sewage system.)[26] Lacking both funds and available space to build adequate public housing, the Planning Department embarked on a program of infrastructural improvements to the favelas whose design and implementation depended on the organization of the population in the favela areas. The pedagogical and organizational aspects of the program, for these planners, were considered as important as the actual implantation of infrastructure.

The municipal government made agreements with the state water and sewage company and the state electric company to provide electricity and running water once roads at least four meters wide had been opened up in the favelas.[27] To make the process of urban improvements in the favelas a process of organization and not only of mobilization, the planning office chose a slower method of proceeding than would otherwise have been needed. First, members of the planning group responsible for the project met with activists in a few favelas in meetings involving usually five to ten people. In its first stages, the project centered on five slum areas where the population had been especially active in making urban demands. These activists were to form a committee of the favela dwellers, which would be responsible for discussing the project with and mobilizing their neighbors, discussing the size of streets and lots and the changes necessary in the structure of the area to open up the streets. This involved a considerable amount of work, as opening up streets generally meant tearing down and moving some shacks and making their size and construction more uniform; thus it required the active consent of the inhabitants. Once data had been collected and the community had become involved, with the help of the architects the favela dwellers drew up their own rough plan of what the area should look like. The Planning Department, in consultation with the committee, then drew up a blueprint. The final map had to be approved by an assembly of the community.

Next, surveyors went into the favelas and measured out the new lots. This stage of the process tested the level of community consensus on the plan, as it often involved entering shacks to mark with a peg the corners of new sites. Insufficient prior organization required backtracking on the process until real agreement was reached. Once the new lots had been marked, the community tore down shacks and rebuilt them on new sites, a necessarily slow process, since it had to be done mainly on weekends and shacks had to be rebuilt the same day they were torn down.

The fact that the light and water companies had promised to follow the roads as they were built, rather than wait for the reconstruction of an entire favela, meant that dwellers could see the consequences of their work almost immediately. This did not prevent the inevitable conflicts; for example, the favela committees and the planning department were attacked by the "owners of the light"—local residents, often politically powerful, who had previously siphoned off electricity to the favelas for abusive prices.

"Urbanization" of the favelas led naturally to a discussion of the land question itself, a much more complicated question to resolve. Favelas were constructed on both private and municipal land. Surprisingly, cases involving occupation of private land were often easier to resolve than those involving municipal land. Where land was private, the administration's Legal Department could sometimes intercede with the owner to negotiate an agreement for the gradual purchase of the land by the occupants. With public land, however, cession or sale required legislation by the municipal council and raised a broader discussion of land use in the municipality as a whole.

In addition, many council members, as well as many of Diadema's non-favela dwellers, feared that legalizing land titles would encourage land occupations and the construction of more favelas, which might devalue existing border property and generally downgrade the already precarious physical conditions of the city. Finally, many more traditional political leaders, like the president of the municipal council, José Santos Rocha of the PMDB, feared that the administration's work in the favelas would erode existing power bases in the poorer areas.

Fear that the intention to regularize land titles would lead to new occupations seemed borne out in late 1983 and early 1984 by new land invasions, many with support from PT members linked to the municipal diretório, and there was considerable disagreement within the administration as to how to deal with these cases. The mayor and his chief of staff were inclined to take action to avoid the proliferation of favelas, while the Planning Department wanted to deal with the question through the Municipal Commission of Favela Dwellers. The dispute over the land use question produced tension between the mayor's office and the planners.

The administration had also made provision of day care one of its priorities. As with favela improvements, day care was seen as a policy area where it was possible to encourage popular organization and participation in formulating and executing policy. Other projects included the establishment of a municipal wholesale fruit and vegetable market, a program of community vegetable gardens to combat chronic malnutrition, bureaucratic modernization and simplification of routines in applications for building licenses, production of the first accurate map of the open areas in the city, and provision of technical assistance for self-help construction projects.[28]

The Health Department was also notable for its attempts to devise forms to actively involve the population in the implementation of programs to raise the level of health care and sanitation in the city. The head of the Health Department, José Augusto da Silva Ramos, had worked in the Diadema Health Center (*Pronto-Socorro*) since 1979 and had joined the Workers' party at the time of its formation. The philosophy of health care that Zé Augusto brought to city hall viewed health as a collective rather than an individual problem and advocated a decentralized approach. Instead of merely increasing the centralized capacity of city hospitals, stress had to be placed on primary health care and sanitation at the community level, involving community members as much as possible in policy implementation.

The high mortality rate in Diadema, as well as high rates of pulmonary and other infectious diseases, was largely due to terrible living conditions. Thus the Health Department focused on general health, nutrition, and sanitation levels in poor communities and on combating environmentally caused disease. It promoted educational activities, garbage collection, rat control, cleanups of polluted waterways, and biological methods of lowering the population of disease-carrying insects. It instituted a widespread vaccination program, began a program of mobile health groups, and encouraged the formation of Community Health Commissions, which collaborated with the department in disseminating information and organizing meetings to discuss how the most pressing problems of the community could be solved. It began community programs for prenatal care and education of pregnant mothers, and it directed nutritionists to devise nutrition programs for low-income families.

In spite of his stress on community initiative in health care, Zé Augusto did not see this as a substitute for state responsibility in the area of health. He called for an increase in health professionals—there were only two hundred doctors in Diadema—and for services that more directly targeted existing problems. The population needed to organize to demand the correct policy, and not attempt to replace the state by doing it themselves.[29] By early 1985, the Health Department had made important strides toward broadening access to and information about health care in the city. A new municipal clinic, built in 1983, handled 170,000 cases in 1984, with a high cure rate. Three new community clinics were built, bringing the total to thirteen.

THE CONFLICT OVER DIADEMA. As the only major municipality in Brazil with a PT administration, Diadema received considerable attention from political elites from other parties and from the press, as well as from the Workers' party itself. Within Diadema, relations between city hall and other parties (and a portion of its own) represented in the municipal council were tense from the beginning. The president of the council, PMDB councilman José Rocha, was particularly hostile. In 1983 Rocha initiated a criminal suit charging that Gilson had violated the law in appointing three heads of departments without university degrees—a charge that could have cost the mayor his office and a jail term had the suit not been dismissed. The lawsuit typified the reigning atmosphere, and it was followed by several others charging technical violations. Relations with the PMDB at the state level were a great deal better: at the time of the first lawsuit, for example, São Paulo PMDB president Fernando Henrique Cardoso called Gilson to say that Rocha's action did not represent PMDB policy, and relations with the Montoro government were also relatively cordial, facilitated by personal connections of some members in the Diadema administration.

With the exception of particularly dramatic innovations of the Diadema administration—for example, the agreement with the bus companies to allow free passes to senior citizens and the unemployed outside of rush hour—press coverage, locally and in São Paulo as well as in national magazines, concentrated on the conflicts that arose between the administration and the party and within the administration itself. A survey done in 1983 showed that a majority of Diadema's population did not know about most of the new services and still thought of relations with city hall in individual terms.[30] The mayor's secretary, whose desk was in the main reception area of city hall, confirmed that over half of those individuals who came to the office were seeking work; others came with requests to repair streets, collect garbage, resolve fights with neighbors and between couples, provide food, clothes, or a loan.

While it seems ingenuous to have expected a dramatic change in attitude on the part of the population within so short a period of time, the results of the 1983 survey apparently caused Gilson to wonder whether high visibility projects were not preferable to the kinds of slow participatory processes involved in the Planning Department's initiatives. The ideals of developing forms of popular organization and responsibility seemed to conflict with the need for results that would demonstrate the ability of a PT mayor to run an efficient administration directed toward popular needs. This dilemma would plague all future PT municipal administrations as well. Over the next six months, tensions mounted between the mayor's office and the Planning Department, culminating in the April 1984 decision to transfer the favela improvement program to the Human Services Department and in the resignation of Khair and most of the planning team on May 3, 1984.

The conflicts within city hall had actually started much earlier. They were initially linked to the break between Gilson and the local party organization over the appointment of department heads, discussed above. In May 1983 Juracy's decision to remove control of the municipal theater from the head of the Department of Culture provoked the local party to call a special convention on May 21. Lula and other party leaders who attended the convention considered the party's protest legitimate in this case, as in fact did most members of the administration, and Juracy was forced to retract his decision.[31] The next crisis came in July 1983, when two department heads were dismissed for supposedly having conspired with the diretório to destabilize Gilson's administration. The two directors had been members of the winning slate in diretório elections held June 12; Gilson had supported another slate. The diretório protested the dismissals and asked higher levels of the party to intervene. Lula responded that it was not normal for the party to intervene in another political arena (that is, a municipal administration), but he asked the São Paulo state executive committee to attempt to mediate the situation and give an opinion.[32]

As in the case of the appointment of department heads, the conflict centered on the role of the local party in relation to the administration. Gilson continued to assert that he was "elected by the PT to govern with the whole population." Gentil de Paula, one of the PT members of the municipal council, defended the diretório's position, saying that "legally, he is the mayor of the whole population, but he was elected by the PT, which is a workers' party." The diretório and its allies on the municipal council continued to demand that not only first-line posts but also administrative decisions should first be submitted for approval to the PT delegation to the Council, the diretório, and representatives of the fifteen núcleos of the party. Only two of the PT members of the municipal council supported Gilson on this issue.

Political alignments within the party were made more complex by the dual party identification of some of the participants in these controversies. Some of the opposing members of the municipal council, as well as some of the newly elected officers of the local party, were members of extralegal leftist organizations which functioned within the PT but which had well-defined ideological and political lines of their own. These included Causa Operária, a split-off from Liberdade e Luta (a Trotskyist organization that had become prominent in student politics in the late 1970s), the Movimento de Emancipação do Proletariado, and other groups.

The situation was further complicated by the distinctly authoritarian tendencies on the part of the mayor's chief of staff, Juracy Magalhães. Juracy seemed to be trying to centralize control over administrative departments and projects in his own hands, and many in the administration felt that he was responsible for a growing tendency to define all debate as being for or against the mayor. Apparently jealous of the early fame of Khair and the Planning Department, Juracy wanted to insure that the center of initiative and decision remained in the central office and, as much as possible, under his control. For the local party, Juracy's ouster became the focal point around which demands for changes in administration practices were organized.

For the national and state executives of the party, called upon to mediate the situation, it was an exceptionally difficult problem. First, although the organized tendencies that predominated within the municipal diretório were not a significant force in the party nationally, members of these tendencies were in fact workers from Diadema, legitimate members of the Workers' party, who had been duly elected in a properly convoked convention of the local party. Second, the party's jurisdiction over the actions of party members in governmental positions was unclear because of the lack of an overall PT policy on the question, on the one hand, and because those governmental positions had been conferred by a popular vote ranging far beyond the active membership of the PT, on the other. That Gilson was a minority mayor further complicated the situation. Third, there was no consensus in the party, either within the leadership or through a national discussion of the question, on the nature of political representation and the degree of accountability that elected representatives owed to the party. Finally, the facts of the situation were themselves contested.

Special committees and subcommittees of the PT's ethics commission set up to study the situation in Diadema abounded in 1983 and 1984, but they seemed unable to reach an acceptable compromise: the diretório insisted on Juracy's ouster, and Gilson accused the diretório of refusing to register new members to the party in order to maintain its majority. The latter question, which had been at issue since the time of the January dispute over the composition of the administration, had in fact been a policy decision of the diretório: after the elections, claiming that prior membership drives had resulted in too many "paper members" of the party, the diretório had suspended all new memberships for six months.[33] As a result, new members recruited by Gilson and his allies were unable to have their membership recognized by the party.

The abortive attempts by higher levels of the party to mediate the situation did nothing either to enhance the reputation of the PT administration in Diadema, as reports of internal strife were gleefully reported in the press, or to lessen Gilson's growing isolation behind the increasingly closed doors of the mayor's office. It became more and more difficult even for department heads to reach the mayor's ear, as channels of access were blocked by his secretary and chief of staff. As his isolation increased, so did Gilson's concern about the need to legitimize his administration through visible acts and public works. Not only the party, but also the new forms of association being created in the process of favela improvement, day care organization, and the like seemed insufficient to provide the kind of mass support he sought.

Tensions came to a head in April 1984 when Gilson decided to transfer the favela program from the Planning Department to the Department of Human Services, without consulting either the planning team or the favela organizations. As a result, Khair and most of the key members of his team resigned from the Planning Department and accused the mayor and his supporters of working for their own benefit, ignoring both the PT and the popular movement.[34] The planners' resignation and their scathing indictment of the administration's practice forced the party to take the case of Diadema and the problems that it raised more seriously. On May 12, 1984, the regional diretório in São Paulo decided to open up a column in the party paper for the PT as a whole to debate the Diadema issue. In the July issue of the paper, the former planning team presented its case on one side of the page, and Gilson presented his on the other. The diretório decided that a member of the PT's state organizational commission would go to Diadema once a week to ensure that new party members were properly enrolled.[35] Committees to investigate and resolve the conflicts proliferated over the course of the next year.

The crisis over the PT administration in Diadema diminished significantly in 1985, but not because the political questions it raised were resolved. In the 1985 local diretório elections, a slate favorable to Gilson's administration was elected, thus easing the pressure on city hall from the local party. Second, the issue of clientelistic practices on the part of the administration, which had been personified in the figure of Juracy Magalhães, was administratively resolved when Juracy was fired on May 2, 1985.[36] Rumors of Juracy's corruption had been rampant since 1983. The last straw came when the press reported that Juracy, in collusion with other city employees, had faked an accident between a car he had borrowed and a municipal vehicle, in order that the municipality's insurance would cover damage incurred at another time. Convinced that the Diadema PMDB was preparing to take the question to court, PT leaders insisted upon establishing a commission that would carry out a serious investigation, regardless of any harm that its findings might do the party. As a consequence of the commission's report, which was not made public, Juracy and several other municipal employees were fired.

With the São Paulo mayoral elections coming up in November 1985, the PT leadership decided that with Juracy's dismissal the Diadema question should be considered closed. The party rallied behind Gilson, emphasizing the positive accomplishments of his administration, and chose not to promote a broad debate about the political questions involved, which were not reducible to the corruption issue. The main unresolved question was, as it had been from the beginning in Diadema, that of the relationship among the party, political institutions, and popular organization. The PT administration had promised to open up city hall to the participation of popular organizations in setting priorities and deciding on the allocation of resources, and to promote the growth and autonomy of social movement organizations that would play this participatory role. In the power struggle that took place, however, such organizations were too often seen as power bases for particular factions in the struggle, and their ability to act autonomously was correspondingly less.

This is not to negate a number of positive accomplishments of the PT administration in the city, not only in terms of the provision of social infrastructure but also in terms of participation.[37] It instituted the practice of holding open neighborhood budget hearings, for example, in which delegates were elected to work with the Finance Department on the elaboration of the budget; this was an important step towards increasing the transparency of municipal government and rendering it more susceptible to democratic decision making. Sectoral councils elected in neighborhoods were also established in the areas of health and transportation.[38] Nonetheless, the initiative for popular input continued to come from city hall, and the relationship between city hall and popular organizations tended to reinforce that pattern rather than seek to transform it.

Was anything else possible? The question is difficult to answer. The party's political project of governing on the basis of autonomous popular organizations implicitly assumed that such organizations existed prior to the creation of such a government. This was not the case in Diadema, and the new administration was faced with the problem of governing and of changing the political environment in which it governed at the same time. Unable to do both, it ended up promoting organization by reinforcing vertical rather than horizontal relations. The result was quite consistent with much of the history of Brazilian populism. Attempts to engage in a slower process of participatory planning fell before the political exigencies of factional struggles. Viewed in purely local terms, it is difficult to see how, given the actors involved, the results could have been different.

By insisting on the local character of the problem, the PT leadership was slow to promote a difficult but potentially rich political debate in the party on questions central to the party's future. The importance of this debate became much more evident after 1985, when problems in the PT administration in Fortaleza forced a more general consideration of the relationship between the party and municipal administrations. By 1988, when the number and importance of municipalities with PT mayors had increased substantially, the party's leaders had recognized that municipal administrations could not be seen as tools of the party organization but rather had to respond to a broader constituency. Nonetheless, many of the dilemmas in the Diadema case remain on the agenda in municipalities like São Paulo itself, where the PT candidate was elected to city hall in 1988. In São Paulo, where much higher levels of popular organization predated the PT's assumption of power, their persistence raises much broader questions about the feasibility of creating genuinely participatory spaces in the governance of complex societies, a question that will be discussed further in the final section of this chapter.

Congressional Representatives

Conflicts over the proper roles of party organization and elected officials in the aftermath of the 1982 election characterized the legislative as well as the executive sphere, and the lack of a clear party strategy for using institutional spaces was a problem in both. This section will examine how PT members of Congress elected in 1982 tried to translate party goals into legislative action, and the relationship between the party organization and PT legislators. In the absence of a legislative strategy, discussion of accountability to the party centered around ex post facto judgments of whether a particular action was appropriate, and these judgments were developed in a fairly ad hoc manner. A number of difficulties arose in the first year of the new legislature. Many of those newly elected had no legislative experience, and while they were quite active in making speeches, they lacked focus in other legislative activities. In addition, many were unprepared for the patronage role that representatives are expected to play in legislative bodies in Brazil. Conflicts arose over the financial contribution that all party candidates had agreed prior to the electoral campaign would go to the party. In spite of these limitations, however, PT deputies exhibited both initiative and cohesion during this period.

Conflict between party leaders and elected representatives runs through the history of left parties, whether or not there was statutory accountability, and is particularly difficult to resolve, as each side claims legitimacy based on a different representative base and accountability to a different constituency. Precisely these kinds of conflicts between party organizations and elected representatives led Moisei Ostrogorski[39] to his pessimistic assessment of the impact of mass parties at the turn of the century; in his later work on the Labour party, R. T. McKenzie describes similar conflicts but concludes that the relation between the parliamentary party and the party organization was a great deal more dynamic than Ostrogorski had expected.[40] Party leaders claim that representatives were elected on the basis of party support, and their function is to voice party positions and attempt to implement party policy at the parliamentary level; this gives the party organization the right and the responsibility to dictate, oversee, and judge the actions of representatives. While elected representatives recognize that their function is to advance party goals in parliamentary bodies, they claim a certain freedom of interpretation and action in doing so, on the basis of responsibility to a broader electorate than the party by itself.[41]

Analysis of the actions of deputies at the federal and São Paulo state levels during the first legislative session in 1983 shows that party deputies were particularly active in their expressive role.[42] At each meeting of the legislature, there is a period devoted to first short and then long speeches about whatever subjects a deputy wants to address, generally denunciations, national and international issues, and diverse policy questions. Especially in the state legislature, PT deputies used this open forum proportionally much more than did deputies from other parties.

On the other hand, PT deputies in São Paulo introduced much less legislation than did their colleagues in other parties. This disproportion reflects the party's rejection of the traditional relationship between legislator and constituency in Brazil. The overwhelming majority of all bills and motions presented to the assembly were either specific logrolling or, more often, symbolic questions—for example, changing the name of a street or school to honor someone or granting nonprofit status to an organization. These kinds of measures are intended to increase the visibility of a representative in his or her constituency. In the legislative session studied, PT members of the state congress did not present any bills or motions of this type. Of 222 motions presented, only 20 were presented by PT members, and of 336 bills presented, PT members presented 13. The meaning of this picture changes, however, if we eliminate the logrolling and renaming laws; only about 48 bills of those presented dealt with entitlement or regulative issues.

The content of bills presented by PT state legislators varied according to the particular interests and movement links of the different deputies. Paulo Fratesci presented several bills referring to education and public employees;[43] Geraldo Siqueira presented a bill on ecology issues and a motion on the student movement;[44] Anísio Batista de Oliveira presented a bill granting a daily session on the public television station devoted to trade union issues.[45] Marco Aurélio Ribeiro initiated a bill on regulation of state funds devoted to entertainment.[46] Paulo Diniz sponsored a bill asking that workers be represented on the boards of companies where the state is a major shareholder, with the representative to be elected by workers.[47] Three bills on questions related to unemployment were sponsored by PT deputies; two of these were supported by most PT members and by several deputies from the PMDB. The unemployment initiatives proposed that unemployed workers receive free passes on public transport, that food programs for the unemployed be expanded, and that the unemployed be exempt from taxes.[48]

The legislation proposed by PT deputies did correspond to the party goal of linking parliamentary activity with the needs of social movements. The refusal to deal with patronage issues and traditional forms of symbolic politics was consistent with the orientation of the party but represented a break with popular expectations of a deputy. Although the nature of constituency relations was not a subject of debate in the party as a whole at this time, it did become the subject of extensive discussion among PT deputies and members of the São Paulo municipal council. The majority of people coming to the office of a state deputy or a municipal councillor were seeking individual favors, although some were looking for help in getting various infrastructural improvements for their communities.

While at first PT municipal council members felt that getting someone who had lost his or her job bus fare back to the Northeast was not the appropriate function of an elected official, it soon became clear that the pervasiveness of such requests and needs required a different approach. In the office of Luiza Erundina, elected municipal councillor for the PT in São Paulo in 1982,[49] individual requests were eventually dealt with by intervening with the state bureaucratic agency able to handle the problem, generally involving a phone call from Luiza or one of her aides. When individuals came in to raise community problems, Erundina's staff tried to stimulate local popular organization around the question rather than responding immediately by sponsoring a bill or attempting through bureaucratic channels to get the funding required for the project. Once such organization had taken place, demands could be made directly to the responsible state organ; the staff could help movement activists determine the appropriate organs to address, and if necessary would accompany them.

A collaborative relationship often developed among the members of the PT parliamentary group in state and municipal bodies, which helped them to formulate strategy of their own. The issues they discussed included questions to which the party was devoting a significant amount of attention—unemployment, for example—but were not limited to these. PT federal deputies also collaborated a great deal with progressives from other parties. The question of forming alliances and coalitions, which until 1983 was not an urgent issue for the party as a whole, was much more salient for legislators who were a small minority of a national body, and it was at the root of several conflicts with the party organization. But in most cases, parliamentary representatives enjoyed a substantial amount of freedom of action, in spite of the formal rules subordinating them to the party executive.

The Workers' party statutes called for elected representatives to be accountable to the national executive and mandated that they contribute 40 percent of their salaries to the party. This was substantially higher than the contribution made by deputies from other parties (about 3 percent) and provoked friction in 1983 between the party and federal deputies. The costs of travel to and from Brasília and of living in the capital almost immediately produced a demand for reformulation of the legislative contribution. For the party, on the other hand, the legislative contribution was a major source of party funds, and any reduction was a hardship. Particularly for working class PT leaders, it seemed inconceivable congressional salaries were not more than sufficient for both. This dispute was important primarily because the tensions it raised in the first six or eight months of the new Congress prevented the kind of constructive collaboration between representatives and the party necessary to formulate a clear vision of the parliamentary role.

Although occasional conflicts arose over particular activities and attitudes of federal deputies, by far the most serious involved whether to participate in the electoral college that would elect the new president indirectly. The party opted for nonparticipation; several of its deputies insisted on attending and resigned from the party (under threat of expulsion). This conflict, discussed in the next section, explicitly raised the question of the right of the party organization to dictate the positions to be taken by PT members of Congress as a general principle.

The Campaign for Direct Presidential Elections

The campaign for direct elections of the president of the Republic in 1984 mobilized the PT as it had not been mobilized since the 1982 electoral campaign. It was an opportunity to combine a political campaign with a broad-based movement of societal organizations and unions and to collaborate with other political parties around common goals. For the PT, the direct elections campaign was intended to combine a demand for institutional democratization with demands for social and economic justice; as the campaign developed, the party was caught up in the unitary discourse of the campaign itself.

The PT adopted the idea of a popular campaign for direct presidential elections as one of its three main foci for the next period in its state pre-conventions in August 1983, and by January 1984 the national executive had made it the party's number one priority.[50] For the first time since its formation, the party adopted a policy of working in a front with other parties, as well as with social and labor movements. Campaign coordinators were chosen at the state level in September and at the national level in January, with a mandate to promote the creation of a supraparty coordination for a broad movement.

The first major coordinated effort in 1983 was a demonstration in the Pacaembu stadium in São Paulo on November 27, 1983, convoked by a committee that included the PT, PMDB, PDT, CUT, CONCLAT, the Justice and Peace Commission of the Catholic church, and a large number of unions and associations. The demonstration was not particularly successful, mobilizing only about twenty thousand people, a large portion of whom were PT supporters. Although the PMDB supported the demonstration, and Governor Franco Montoro had cowritten with other governors a manifesto on direct elections, which was broadcast on prime-time television and included a convocation for the demonstration, the PMDB had not yet decided to take the campaign into the streets.[51]

In early January, however, PMDB president Ulysses Guimarães threw his weight behind the idea of a serious popular mobilization. Governor Montoro convoked a meeting of representatives of opposition parties and unions in the governor's palace in São Paulo, and the committee thus formed began to organize a massive demonstration for January 27, 1984. The first large demonstration had been two weeks earlier in Curitiba, convoked by Guimarães with governors Montoro, Tancredo Neves from Minas Gerais, and José Richa from Paraná.[52] In São Paulo, the platform included Brizola and Lula as well, and where the organizers had hoped for 100,000 people, over 250,000 showed up. From then on mobilization built, with demonstrations all over the country. As over a million people filled the streets of Rio de Janeiro, a kind of euphoria took over, a sense that the entire country was in the streets demanding *diretas já*. Polls showed over 80 percent of Brazilians in favor of direct elections (including 75 percent of PDS members).[53]

As far as the PT was concerned, the movement was intended to continue until the government agreed to call elections. For the PMDB, on the other hand, the mobilization was geared toward the congressional vote in mid-April on a constitutional amendment proposed by Deputy Dante de Oliveira. Toward the end of the campaign, it became evident that, behind the scenes, some PMDB leaders were hedging their bets. The nomination of former São Paulo governor Paulo Maluf for the PDS against the fierce opposition of some of his own party raised the possibility that an electoral college majority could be built around conservative PMDB governor Tancredo Neves from Minas Gerais. When the amendment was voted down, PMDB leaders decided that the game was up. If they continued to support the campaign in the streets, the nation risked the possibility of a Maluf presidency. After the failure of the amendment, PMDB energies were focused on building the Democratic Alliance, a coalition between the PMDB and the Liberal Front, constituted by PDS dissidents unwilling to support Maluf.

The PT tried to carry on the campaign on its own, furious at what it saw as PMDB perfidy, but the impetus was gone. Although public sentiments had not changed, the belief that something miraculous might happen had. The enormous sense of possibility created by the campaign died down, and society was confronted once again with a bipolar choice: Maluf or Tancredo. Gradually the energy devoted to the campaign was transferred to Tancredo, who was characterized as the great hope of democracy in Brazil and, upon his death just before taking office, was immediately mythologized as a martyr in the popular mind.

As it had in the 1982 elections, the PT rejected the idea that there were only two choices, and its leadership opposed participation by PT deputies in the electoral college. This intransigent position provoked a crisis among PT deputies, several of whom believed that circumstances obligated the PT to vote for Tancredo, even while continuing to denounce the conservative character of the transition. Airton Soares, furious with the party's stance, resigned as leader of the party's parliamentary group. Other party members also contested the decision. PT leaders, realizing that more debate was needed, called for preconventions at municipal, state, and national levels to discuss the issue. Soares and Deputy José Eudes from Rio de Janeiro polarized the debate further by announcing that they would participate in the electoral college vote no matter what the pre-conventions decided.

From there the situation went from bad to worse. A majority of the parliamentary group, while agreeing with the party's position or at least prepared to go along with the vote of the pre-conventions, refused to accept Soares's resignation on the grounds that the debate was still open. In the official note they issued relating their decision, they stated, "We are prepared to live with disagreements, because our affinities and our ethico-political commitment transcend conjunctural divergences, whatever they might be. Democratically resolved differences only strengthen the higher unity of our action in defense of the workers and the people."[54]

Those in favor of going to the electoral college argued that nonparticipation would lead to yet another elite pact excluding workers from politics, marginalizing the PT at the same time as the party's base was turning out en masse to rallies for Tancredo. Like it or not, they claimed, the choice being offered was between Tancredo and Maluf.[55] Those in favor of boycotting the electoral college argued that the Democratic Alliance had cynically used the popular mobilization to impose their candidate on the regime. They reiterated the position taken by the diretório nacional that the PT should "not allow itself to be blackmailed with the threat of Maluf into accepting the transition project proposed by the dominant classes."[56]

After the pre-conventions had ratified the initial position not to attend, the question became what to do about the deputies who intended to go anyway, which by then included Bete Mendes as well as Eudes and Soares. A heated controversy arose over whether the three should be expelled, and in mid-January a meeting of the diretório nacional voted to ask for their resignations. The decision was bitterly contested by other deputies and might have been reconsidered, but the deputies involved resigned from the party.

With the departure of three of its federal deputies and one of its state deputies over this issue, the PT lost two of its most experienced politicians, who had also been the leaders of its parliamentary group at federal (Airton Soares) and state levels (Marco Aurélio Ribeiro in São Paulo). For refusing to attend the electoral college the party had been denounced as purist; the departure of the deputies made it appear authoritarian as well. The conflict left a residue of tension and bitterness throughout the next year. The wounds only began to heal in 1985 with the mayoral elections, after which Lula declared to the press that anyone who had left the party earlier was welcome to return.

The direct elections campaign was a dramatic moment in PT history, producing contradictory effects and continuing to generate debate for a long time afterward. It was the first time the PT had participated in a front with other parties for popular mobilization around an issue. In spite of reservations when the process began to center around the state governors supporting the campaign, the PT continued to mobilize heavily for it and collaborate in a relatively harmonious manner. Conflicts arose around the PT's desire to introduce socioeconomic issues into the campaign, but in general it participated in creating a unitary discourse. Disillusionment with the waning of the campaign after the defeat of the amendment probably exacerbated the conflict over the boycott of the electoral college. The relatively low attendance at the pre-conventions that made the major decisions on the issues raised increasing concern about the party's future. The PT's success in mobilizing for the campaign could have given the party a needed shot in the arm; its aftermath initially seemed to limit that possibility.

There were, however, positive benefits. The campaign stimulated discussion in the party about the need for a political strategy as well as a program for popular mobilization around major issues in the transition. The success of working in a supraparty front made it possible to think about further activity of this kind; in spite of the PT's condemnation of the PMDB for deserting the direct elections campaign, the two parties collaborated again, together with other groups, in organizing public rallies for a Constituent Assembly in early 1985.

The party's difficulty in combining its focus on societal movements with action in the political-institutional sphere produced serious internal conflicts between 1982 and 1985. Externally, the PT earned respect for its mobilizational capacity in the direct elections campaign, but when popular support turned to Tancredo, the public found its position on the electoral college hard to understand. Neither its actions in institutions nor even its mobilizational capacity explain the party's growing prestige during this period.

One reason for the lack of attention to an institutional strategy was the intense engagement of many PT activists in the labor movement and social movements during this period. These activists believed that the conservative nature of the transition process required a focus on civil society in order to build resistance to the attempt by conservative elites to limit the scope of change. As discussed in the previous chapter, the growth of the CUT helped to feed a public perception that the PT's strength was growing in spite of the widely publicized conflicts that characterized the period. However weak an institutional actor it may have been in the first half of the 1980s, the PT was nonetheless an important organizer of an oppositional political space in civil society. Because of this, as the PMDB increasingly became the "establishment" (or *situação,* in Brazilian parlance), the PT became one of the heirs of the opposition mantle. In the second half of the 1980s, the dichotomy between the party as movement builder and the party as institutional actor began to be bridged.

Movement into Politics

The campaign for direct presidential elections demonstrated the possibility of combining a focus on formal political mechanisms with societal organization. In 1985, the party's success in the mayoral elections in state capitals and participation in discussions of the shape that the upcoming Constituent Assembly should take reinforced, for party leaders, a growing awareness of the need for a political strategy beyond that of strengthening the movements and institutions of civil society.

The conflicts that characterized the relationship between the party organization and its congressional representatives tended to dissipate over time, partly due to the development of more regular forms of consultation but also because of an increasing identity between the two. In 1982, most of the founding leadership of the Workers' party ran for gubernatorial positions, and all of them lost. Those running for federal congress, in many cases, were second-echelon party leaders or party candidates who already had parliamentary experience. Many of them were part of the group of politicians for whom some PT founding members, those more oriented toward social movements or trade unions than toward politics, had always harbored a good deal of mistrust. The struggles over the portion of their salary that members of Congress would contribute to the party, as well as the conflict over the party's refusal to participate in the electoral college election of Tancredo Neves, were both exacerbated by this underlying conflict. The key point was that the party's best-known and most legitimate spokespersons did not hold elective office during this period.

The PT congressional delegation elected in 1986 was quite different from the one elected in 1982. In the forty-seventh legislature (1983–87), from São Paulo, four out of the eight federal deputies elected had joined the party as politicians, one (Bete Mendes) was a well known actress, two were union leaders (Djalma Bom from the São Bernardo metalworkers and Luiz Dulci from the Minas Gerais teachers), and one (José Genoino Neto) was a well known leftist leader. In 1986, Lula was elected to the Chamber of Deputies with more votes than any other candidate in the country and became the leader of the party's parliamentary group; the sixteen PT deputies also included the party's president, Olívio Dutra, and a number of other key party leaders (many of whom were trade unionists). A similar phenomenon took place at the state level; the party's secretary general, José Dirceu, was elected to the São Paulo state legislature.

The tensions between the parliamentary group and the party organization dissipated with this change in the composition of the PT delegation to Congress. If we look at the twenty members and alternates on the party's national executive commission elected in December 1987, five were federal deputies, two were former federal deputies, and two were state deputies.[57] Lula, speaking as the natural leader of the party, and Olívio Dutra, speaking as its president, most often spoke from Brasília.

The decision of so many PT leaders to run for Congress in 1986 was partly due to a perception of the importance of that legislature, which was also to function as a Constituent Assembly. This meant that debates on key social issues were taking place in the legislature. The process of parliamentary negotiation, in which PT deputies became increasingly adept during this period, was seen as part and parcel of societal struggles in which the party was also involved. The PT took the process of constitution writing very seriously. The party was the only one to formulate a complete constitutional project, based on discussions of a draft written at the request of the national executive commission by jurist Fábio Konder Comparato.[58] The party was an important element in the coalition that opened up the constitution writing process to popular initiatives, through passage of an amendment to the internal rules of the Constituent Assembly making possible popular amendments (if these were sponsored by at least three legally constituted entities and signed by at least 30,000 voters). This provoked a broad process of popular mobilization, eventually producing 122 amendments with a total of 12,265,854 signatures,[59] in which a wide array of social movements, unions, and other organizations in civil society participated.

PT deputies were very active during the Constituent Assembly, proposing articles and amendments and negotiating support with deputies from other parties. Although they paid special attention to those parts of the constitution dealing with labor rights and agrarian reform, they were active in other areas as well. The experience of negotiating congressional alliances during the Constituent Assembly was an important source of the PT's increasing openness to coalitional activity. As most parties in the Constituent Assembly did not exercise party discipline in voting, alliances had to be stitched together around each issue with individual deputies. This was true even (and perhaps especially) for the issues that became the central controversies of the process—the length of Sarney's presidential mandate, agrarian reform, and job stability for workers. The consistency of the PT delegation thus stood in sharp contrast to other parties in the Constituent Assembly.

The fluidity of political allegiances in mainstream political parties—further complicated by the existence of "rental parties" whose primary purpose is to provide an electoral vehicle for politicians who were not nominated for desired positions by other parties—means that it is usually quite difficult to predict from a politician's party what kinds of positions he or she will take in Congress. Almost half the PMDB members of the Constituent Congress voted against articles that appeared as platforms in the party's program. Thus, the predominant voting blocs in the Constituent Assembly were not party groupings, but rather groupings of individuals, with the majority bloc—the "Centrão" (big Center)—composed of members drawn from almost all parties. In a comparison of votes of the six major parties[60] on controversial issues in the Constituent Assembly, Mainwaring found that the PT was the only party whose members voted a straight party line, with only the PDT coming close.[61] The PMDB scored the lowest on an index of party cohesion.

The PT's concern with presenting a coherent (and cohesive) position differentiate it starkly from mainstream Brazilian political parties. As Mainwaring has shown, the Brazilian party system grants an unusual amount of autonomy to individual politicians. This is reinforced by the combination of proportional representation and an open list system, which means that candidates compete not only against other parties but against each other, and parties have very little control over their campaigns. The ease of switching parties makes it difficult for party leadership organs to enforce party discipline, although in principle they have the right to do so. The institution of the *candidato nato,* which gives any legislator the right to run for the same office in the next election, increases this autonomy.[62] Frances Hagopian graphically illustrated the impact of the tendency of politicians to aggregate around winners when she described the defection of at least two hundred PDS mayors and diretórios in Minas Gerais to the PMDB in mid-1985.[63]

This fluid and highly permeable party structure, reinforced by the exceptional autonomy of individual politicians in the system, is not conducive to responsible party behavior. Under those circumstances, the PT's consistency and predictability in congressional votes appears more exceptional than it would be if placed in a broader comparative context. It is not only that policies espoused by the party that are important, though the catch-all character of Brazilian parties and the fact that Brazil has never had a significant legal national party on the left (with the possible exception of the PCB between 1945 and 1947) make them noteworthy. The PT's degree of formal institutionalization and the acceptance of party discipline by its elected politicians also highlight the lack of institutional accountability of other parties to either their members or their constituents.

As the party increasingly differentiated itself from other parties in its institutional practice as well as in its relations with social movements, the way in which it framed its mission changed. In the early days of the party, the desire to express the interests of workers and the poor at the political level made the PT suspicious of political alliances; in some ways this reflected a lack of confidence in itself as an institution and thus a presumption that making alliances, even tactically, would dilute the party's program. In its early days the party tended to view itself as the political mouthpiece of the organized labor movement—a view which limited its ability to aggregate diverse sectors of Brazilian society that were dissatisfied with the status quo and limited its ability to take initiatives rather than just follow whatever the unions were doing. This vision, together with the party's electoral weakness, tended to make the

PT dichotomize societal action and political-institutional action, particularly in Congress.

As the party grew and gained experience, these problems began to be resolved. Party discourse evolved from one which constantly emphasized organized labor to one which was much more inclusive. In the second half of the 1980s, the party was much more willing to work with other parties both in particular elections and on particular political campaigns. This position was formalized in the political and organizational plan passed at the party's Fifth National Meeting in December 1987. This meeting, which party leaders called *O Encontro do Crescimento* (the Growth Meeting), reflected the party's growing confidence in its ability to play an important part in national politics. Nowhere was this more evident, in symbolic terms, than in Lula's speech accepting the party's nomination for the presidency, in which he joked about the party's approach to the 1982 elections:

> In 1982, when I was candidate for Governor in São Paulo, I made a big mistake. You remember the PT's propaganda, in which the least dangerous of us had been condemned to ninety years in prison. We created a discourse where I said "Lula, candidate for governor number 13, ex-dye factory assistant, ex-lathe operator, ex-trade unionist, ex-prisoner, ex-I don't know what else, a Brazilian just like you."
>
> I imagined that the working class would understand by this: wow, this guy is all this and is a candidate; we could do this too.
>
> But it seems that workers understood exactly the opposite: nobody wanted to be a Brazilian just like me. They wanted to be Brazilians with a university degree; they wanted to be Brazilians with better living conditions, with better intellectual training, with a better quality of life. Because of this mistake, I began to understand that we couldn't just assume that everyone would understand what we were talking about. In a campaign like the one in 1988 [*sic*], we can't be vanguardistic, we can't speak only to each other.
>
> Sometimes we act as if we were in a Formula One auto race: the vanguard is going 380 kilometers per hour and the mass of the people are in VW beetles going 60 kilometers per hour and getting speeding tickets at every corner. In the campaign, the PT has to use all of the space available to educate the people. To plant a seed, to plant something that will live forever.[64]

The same tone characterized the political and organizational plan passed at the 1987 meeting. The party's new position on alliances recognized the need, given the real balance of political forces in Brazil, to build both strategic and tactical alliances. Strategic alliances should include parties that consider themselves socialist or communist or claim to represent workers, but the PT should also recognize that "a united class front that includes all wage workers is still not sufficient to defeat bourgeois domination in this country. We also need to ally with all those sectors that, because of their differences with the bourgeoisie, are willing to struggle for power together with the workers."[65] In addition to strategic alliances created with a view to winning positions of power, the party would form tactical alliances, both in Congress and in social struggles, around short- and medium-term objectives. The example given was the alliance formed "with progressive and democratic parties" around social policies and against the right wing in the Constituent Assembly.

The PT still claims to represent the interests of workers, the poor, and the excluded. The difference is that it no longer sees itself as only speaking to those sectors of the population; it recognizes that to speak effectively on behalf of those sectors of the population it must broaden its support. Returning to the political and organizational plan for 1988–89:

> The PT's influence in the middle sectors has grown. We need to bring them in to expand the workers' struggle against the transition and for the installation of a democratic and popular government. Together with its presidential campaign, the PT must now call together progressive, democratic, and socialist forces to guarantee the gains won by workers in the Constituent Assembly.
>
> The PT recognizes that neither taking power nor the direct struggle for socialism is currently on the agenda for the working class. Instead, there is a struggle for a democratic and popular alternative, which requires three main activities:
>
> a) holding direct elections in 1988, with presidentialism, occupation of available spaces, and launching as many candidates as possible. Lula's candidacy for the presidency will be backed by a program that will involve more than a simple list of immediate demands;
>
> b) the organization of the PT as a socialist, independent, and mass political force;
>
> c) building the CUT, by means of a class-based and combative trade unionism and the organization of an independent popular movement.[66]

Recurring Dilemmas

In the second half of the 1980s, the PT made substantial progress in reconciling the need to work effectively in Congress with its focus on reinforcing social movements in society. In the process, it retained a strong conception of representation and accountability—the notion that the PT as a programmatic party was broadly representative of a particular constituency and was accountable to its members and to that constituency for the actions of its elected officials. With the development of more consistent patterns of interaction between the party leadership and members of Congress, and the increasing overlap between the two, the conflicts over party discipline characteristic of the early 1980s became increasingly rare.

In instances where PT candidates win executive offices, however, these issues are more difficult to resolve. Up to the present, such instances have been exclusively municipal administrations. The application of comparable notions of representation and accountability to petistas in executive positions is inherently problematic. Mayors must deal with a much broader constituency than the one to whom the PT considers itself primarily responsible; they must negotiate with a broader range of powerful social and political actors, and must often compromise over issues that some party members consider nonnegotiable in order to insure survival and the ability to act on others. Nonetheless, the party's public image is substantially affected by the performance of municipal administrations it controls; therefore, the party has an important stake in how such municipalities are governed, in the policies propsed by PT mayors, and in the mechanisms by which these are formulated and implemented. Thus, the mayors see a need for flexibility and autonomy from the party, and the party—even while recognizing those needs—tends to seek greater control. Tensions appear to be built into the structure of the relationship.

The Workers' party that won important municipal offices in 1988 was a far more mature party than it had been in its first electoral races six years earlier. Though Luiza Erundina's victory in the São Paulo mayoral race produced predictable euphoria among petistas, who celebrated in a huge fiesta on the Avenida Paulista, the deliberations of the party councils were anything but euphoric. Party leaders knew how much of the support they had received was contingent support. They knew that they were taking over city halls suffering from staggering fiscal and financial problems, with depleted urban infrastructure and payrolls bloated by patronage appointments. The deterioration of the national economy had worsened social problems, and popular expectations of the PT administrations were certain to be beyond what PT incumbents could deliver. Everyone recognized that the kinds of sectarian battles that had taken place over Diadema and Fortaleza could not be repeated. It is small wonder that at the national diretório meeting on December 10–11, 1988, held to assess the elections and chart new directions, amid the congratulations the faces of participants were uniformly serious.

The party learned valuable lessons from the Diadema and Fortaleza experiences. The battle between the municipal administration and the local party organization in Diadema forced the party to confront the question of accountability soon after its first electoral victory. The PT eventually emerged with much more positive marks in Diadema than the turbulent first year of the PT administration would have led us to expect, and its candidate again won the mayoral election in 1988. The failure of the first PT administration in a state capital precipitated a crisis that eventually led to the expulsion of Fortaleza mayor Maria Luíza Fontenelle. Aside from factional problems in the Fortaleza case, the Fontenelle administration also served as an object lesson in the dangers of alienating the middle class; rampant problems with such issues as garbage collection and road repair led to a widespread perception that the city administration was out of control. The fact that the PT had *no* representatives on the municipal council in Fortaleza obviously complicated the governing process, as did difficulties in communicating with powerful local business interests. The PT administration there did win credit for "moralizing" the local government's hiring practices.[67]

By 1988, the party's position was that those elected to municipal office were to attempt to carry out the party program but were to represent and be accountable to the needs and interests of the people of the municipality. Accountability to the party meant faithfulness to the general lines of the party's program and policies rather than subordination to the day-to-day dictates of party personnel. Nonetheless, in cases where mayors acted in a manner that was deemed antithetical to PT positions, the party reserved the right, after discussion with the municipal administration involved, to sever the relationship. These distinctions proved easier to make in theory than in practice.

São Paulo was the largest and most visible of the municipalities that PT mayors were to administer after 1988, and the Luiza Erundina administration generated a correspondingly large volume of internal controversy in the party. The party's concern about the administration's early performance was particularly acute because of the 1989 presidential elections; there was widespread belief that an exemplary São Paulo administration would give added impetus to Lula's presidential candidacy. During its first year, however, the Erundina administration was primarily occupied in putting the city's financial house in order—a process that bore fruit over the long run but which brought little or no short-term political accolades to the party. When Erundina took office, the city was bankrupt. It had a debt of approximately one billion dollars and owed more than US$1.5 million in late payments; stocks of basic goods were at zero; public buildings (schools, hospitals, and so forth) and machinery (buses, for example) were in dire need of repair; and the Quadros administration had left the city with scores of high cost unfinished public works of sometimes dubious utility.[68]

Although few of its early accomplishments were highly visible, the Erundina administration achieved a great deal rather quickly. It rationalized debt payments, rescheduled or canceled construction contracts, cut costs in a number of key areas (garbage collection, for example) without cutting services, and began to rationalize the city's enormous administrative machine. It also initiated a process of decentralization in which more authority and resources were given to regional administrations within the city, encouraging at the same time the development of participative mechanisms within these microregions.[69] Although the PT lacked a majority in the municipal council, it won the presidency of that body, and the president, Eduardo Suplicy, proved an adept negotiator. Decentralization was written into the new municipal charter (*lei orgánico*), and other gains were made as well—for the first time the city's property tax was made progressive.[70] Suplicy also demonstrated his well-known flair for muckraking when he succeeded in having several powerful and notoriously corrupt municipal councillors expelled from the council and prosecuted for their activities.

Visible benefits for workers and the poor were longer in coming, with a few exceptions. One accomplishment that had widespread impact was the restoration of meat to school lunches, which had been meatless for four years. (Erundina recounts a story of a parent whose child, upon seeing meat in her school lunch, ran away shrieking, thinking an animal had gotten into her food.)[71] In 1990, the administration was able to turn its attention to social infrastructure, placing a high priority on clinics, day care, and schools. The policy area that proved most intractable was transportation. Bus service in the city remained abysmal, and serious administrative and corruption problems in city hall's management of the municipal bus company raised questions about the adequacy of the PT's stated position on the issue, which called for expropriation of private bus lines.

Conflicts between sectors of the party and the São Paulo municipal administration arose around three issues: public policy and accomplishments; forms of representation; and electoral issues. For PT members who had hoped to see São Paulo revolutionized, the pragmatic approach of the PT administration was both frustrating and unexpected. Of the two party aspirants for the mayoral nomination, Erundina was considered the more radical. Two of her early decisions produced particular ire: the expropriation (with compensation) of one the last remaining mansions on the Avenida Paulista and its designation as a historic landmark, and successful negotiations with Shell for construction of a Formula One auto racing track. These, together with Erundina's concerted efforts to assuage the fears of São Paulo business elites about the possible impact of a PT administration, seemed for some petistas to raise questions about the mayor's commitment to the poor. For business, however, much of which had expected unmitigated hostility to the private sector, Erundina's pragmatism was a welcome surprise; in early 1990, the business magazine *Exame* even ran a two-page article praising the administration for its prowess in balancing the city's books. Leftist factions in the PT accused Erundina of betraying her mandate and led marches on city hall demanding more public housing and social services. In the 1989 presidential elections, Lula—while continuing to defend the administration when it was under attack—nonetheless did not look upon it as a source of strength in his campaign. By the end of 1990 the early pessimistic assessments were beginning to change. The administration hired a public relations firm to broadcast its accomplishments, and polls began to register a shift in public attitudes in Erundina's favor. Critics in the party still abounded, but they tended to focus their attention on other issues.

In its approach to municipal government, the PT has always supported the formation of popular councils as a vehicle for direct popular participation in the policy-making process. The relations between the proposed councils and other vehicles of political representation—municipal councils, for example—have never been clearly defined, nor have such key issues as how and by whom they are to be organized, and what their powers are to be. Immediately after the elections, Erundina declared that popular councils would set the priorities for her administration, pointing to the health councils in the eastern part of the city as an example of this kind of popular organization.[72] The health councils, which grew out of fourteen years of organizing by church-related movements and left groups, are essentially users' groups. They involve 1,500 delegates (representing about 100,000 people) chosen in neighborhood elections by secret ballot for seats on the eighty-odd councils. The health councils have won the right to intervene in the management of local clinics (though not in their budgets).[73] The problem was how to generalize this experience to other issue areas and/or to establish councils based on region rather than on a particular policy question. Church leaders were enthusiastic about the idea of councils; politicians from other parties were highly dubious. Future PT administration members were cautious in discussing the councils after the elections, trying to distinguish between councils organized by the population and deliberative bodies the administration might create, hedging the question of whether councils should be consultative or deliberative, and insisting that councils could not be arms of the PT.[74] As PT leader Celso Daniel put it, "Confusion between power, party, and social movements is dangerous for all concerned. . . . The PT has reached maturity. It is no longer possible to ignore the institutional side."[75]

Paying attention to the institutional side, however, meant confronting head-on a number of questions about the party's attachment to the idea of direct democracy. In a fascinating paper presented at the 1990 meeting of the Brazilian social science association, Ana Maria Doimo examined the contradictory logics of social movement networks and representative institutions in an attempt to situate the council proposal.[76] In her view, the problem lay not in the relative degree of organization of social movements or networks thereof, but rather in the difference in logics between movements whose strength depends on informal social networks, personal loyalties, solidarity, and consensus and institutionalized bodies characterized by permanence and formal relationships. Institutions depend on a set of procedural rules to govern the relation between state and society, balancing different social forces and interests. Social movements, by contrast, seek direct access to decision makers, placing group identity and solidarity above procedural linkages, which are seen as impositions from above. Doimo argues that, in the attempts to create councillor arrangements that she studied, "the strength of the idea that people should organize themselves leads only to the reproduction in the same social space of inter- and intra-group competition, each trying to reaffirm its identity vis-à-vis the others."[77] At a meeting in Campinas designed to bring together social movements as the basis for a popular council, for example, movement representatives limited themselves to enumerating particular demands and showed little interest in discussing how to establish priorities among them. She concludes that, unlike the logic of repre-

sentative institutions, social movements in Brazil have a double logic—
demanding and disruptive on the one hand, in their vigorous struggle
around particular claims, corporativist and integrative on the other, in
their desire for increased access to sectoral decisions. The problems
encountered in trying to organize popular councils are thus written into
the logics of social movements as organizations.

The kind of argument Doimo made does not convince all PT members, and some continue to fault the administration for not paying
enough attention to creating new forms of participation. For the São
Paulo administration, however, the question of popular councils was
gradually transformed from a short-term to a long-term project. In the
process of writing the new municipal charter in 1990, PT representatives abandoned the term *popular councils* and began to discuss the creation of representative councils within the context of the newly decentralized regional administrations. These were to function as regional
congresses. They would draw on such traditional mechanisms of direct
democracy as public hearings, initiative, referendum, and plebiscite.[78]
Luiza Erundina began to speak of councils as a "fundamental political
issue" rather than a methodological one. She argued that councils could
not be an arm of either the administration or the party and that their
creation required a long-term process of building consciousness
through class struggle. Her administration continued to encourage the
formation of sectoral councils and to appear before "popular plenaries,"
but it recognized the limited representativeness of these.[79]

The most serious conflict between the party organization and PT
municipal administrations elected in 1988 arose around the 1990 gubernatorial elections in São Paulo, which for the first time were held in two
rounds, with a runoff between the two candidates who drew the most
votes in the first round. When the runoff produced a choice between
Maluf and Fleury (the candidate favored by incumbent governor
Orestes Quercia), the PT as an organization decided to instruct party
members to nullify their votes. Not all PT leaders agreed: some felt that
faced with a choice between right-winger Maluf and the protégé of a
highly clientelistic Quercia machine they were still better off with
Fleury—in spite of his ambiguous involvement in an effort to discredit
the PT at the end of Lula's presidential campaign.[80] PT mayors in
particular felt that it was to their advantage to support Fleury "crit-
ically," especially if a preelection agreement could be reached guaranteeing that he would end Quercia's alleged boycott of PT-governed
municipalities. After the elections, several PT members of the São

Bernardo municipal council who had actively campaigned for Fleury were expelled from the party, causing São Bernardo's PT mayor Mauricio Soares and other members of the council to resign from the party in protest. Jacó Bittar, mayor of Campinas (which was Quercia's home city), developed strong links with the Quercia machine. After declaring in December 1990 that he was no longer bound by decisions of the Campinas diretório, he was expelled from the party in February 1991.

However much each of these defections had roots much deeper than the particular conflict over which they occurred—the case of Bittar in particular—they still demonstrate that the boundaries of party discipline are not yet fully defined in the PT. This is not surprising, as the exercise of party discipline is foreign to the traditional practice of most Brazilian parties. Nonetheless, the line between consistency (widely considered one of the PT's strengths) and rigidity (generally viewed as a weakness) is very thin, and the price of attempting to present a coherent party position has often been to be judged sectarian. The passage of time sometimes tempers such judgments; after five years of a Sarney government, the PT's boycott of the 1985 indirect elections appeared to many people more reasonable than it had at the time. The definition of the relationship between party and administration, and the autonomous sphere of each, is still evolving. Experiments like São Paulo's political council, which meets weekly with members of Luiza Erundina's administration and plays an advisory role, may contribute to such a definition, even as it attenuates the tensions inherent in the relationship.

The story told in this chapter appears initially as an account of failure. During the early 1980s, it was easy for observers—and even some PT members and activists—to read it in this sense. In my conversations with several PT leaders in mid-1985, many of them expressed serious concerns about whether the party would last out the year. The party seemed to move from one crisis to another. Faced with the problems raised by Diadema, by difficult relations with party legislators, and by the apparent decline in the level of internal party activity, the "return to the base" seemed likely to be permanent. When key party leaders like Lula and Olívio Dutra began to pay more attention to their union jobs than to the party, it was easy to predict that the PT would soon dissolve back into the wide range of movements from which it had initially emerged.

This reading, however understandable, proved to be wrong. When the party reemerged into the public sphere with the 1985 mayoral elections, it began to face the dilemmas posed in the first part of the 1980s with renewed vigor. However difficult they were to resolve, these dilemmas forced the party to confront a number of key political choices early in its development. Reinforcing the organizational capacity of social movements, building a broad political movement to seek fundamental change in social relations, building a membership party with democratic structures, functioning at the electoral level, and participating in political institutions often appeared to be impossible—and irreconcilable—goals. Yet it was precisely the PT's continued effort to balance all of these which constituted its political identity and differentiated it from other political parties in Brazil. The differences that seemed to proclaim its marginality in the early phases of the transition were precisely those that positioned it, in turn, to become the axis of a new opposition at the end of the 1980s.

Conclusions 9

In November 1988 the Workers' party sent shock waves through the Brazilian political elite by winning the mayoral races in three state capitals (São Paulo, Porto Alegre, and Vitória) and twenty-nine other cities in Brazil (including many of the major industrial centers in São Paulo). In 1989, in the first direct presidential elections in three decades, Lula came very close to winning the presidency, losing in the runoff with 47 percent of the valid vote to Fernando Collor de Melo's 53 percent.[1] Nothing in the party's incremental growth in the intervening years had made either of these extraordinary political events inevitable. Once again, the peculiar dynamics of the Brazilian transition itself framed the place the PT was to occupy—that of the last hope for change. Nonetheless, the party's ability to play that role was enhanced by its own maturation process in the intervening years.

To say that the results of the November 1988 mayoral elections represented a sea change in Brazilian politics or voting behavior would be an exaggeration. Nonetheless, many Brazilian voters sent a message to their government (as São Paulo governor Orestes Quercia apparently said, they didn't send a telegram, they set up a billboard on the highway) that they expected greater seriousness and responsiveness from elected politicians. The PT, seen as a serious and responsive party, served as a vehicle for that massive protest. Because it existed, it helped to make that message clearer than it might otherwise have been.

By 1988, the PT's anomalous position during the transition had turned into an advantage. While in 1982 and 1986 the PMDB's claim to be the party of the transition to democracy was a powerful generator of votes, widespread disillusionment with the transition process caused this claim to backfire in 1988. The political bankruptcy of the Sarney government was manifest, and it was coupled with an economic crisis that affected the middle class as well as workers and the poor. The widely reported deliberations of the national Constituent Assembly exposed to national attention the unprincipled behavior of a large proportion of elected politicians, including many from the former party of opposition. Particularly damaging was the willingness of many PMDB politicians to support Sarney's desperate (and highly unpopular) campaign for a fifth year in office in exchange for perquisites for themselves or their constituencies. From a socioeconomic point of view the 1980s were a roller coaster, with a severe downturn at the beginning, a brief improvement in 1986 with the early stages of the government's Cruzado Plan, and the erosion of many of those gains with high inflation at the end of the decade. In aggregate terms, per capita income fell by 6.59 percent during the 1980s,[2] and perversely, income distribution grew even more unequal than at the height of military rule. The National Household Survey published in 1990 showed that between 1981 and 1989, the top decile of the population increased its income share from 46.6 percent to 53.2 percent, while the share of the bottom half fell from 13.4 to 10.4 percent.[3] In 1988 and 1989, Brazilians followed a long tradition of voting against the situação and for the opposition—the PT, and other parties not identified with the status quo.

A number of experiences stimulated the Workers' party to begin to resolve some of the dilemmas that had rent the party during the mid-1980s. The high hopes the party had for exemplary municipal administrations in Diadema and Fortaleza were dashed, but the resulting lessons were valuable. Ongoing difficulties with organized left "parties within the party" were submitted to an extended internal debate and eventually resulted in the formulation of internal rules on the formation and behavior of factional tendencies. The tensions inherent in the desire to be a party of social action and mobilization and the imperative to act effectively in political institutions remained a key element in the party's character, but it was increasingly understood as a tension and not as a contradiction. As the party grew stronger and gained in political experience, the advantages of political alliances around particular issues or candidacies became more relevant than the dangers.

Throughout this study, I have argued that understanding the nature of the Brazilian transition—the context or "political opportunity structure" in which the Workers' party developed—was crucial to understanding the party's actions and evolution. Characteristics of the party that were thought to cause its "failure" in the early stages of the transition became key elements in its political survival and continued evolution. Acts that were initially taken as evidence of rigidity and sectarianism—for example, the decision not to participate in the indirect presidential elections in 1985—eventually came to be seen as evidence of coherence and principled behavior. The PT's continued effort to function democratically and encourage the broadest possible participation of members bore fruit in its growing visibility; by 1988 political commentators counted the party's ability to call upon its activists for social and political campaigns as a political resource that almost made up for its lack of financial resources. As PMDB dissidents struggled to force their party leadership to call a party convention, the PT continued to hold regular meetings at all levels, renew its leadership, and engage in protracted and sometimes impassioned debate on political issues.

I have argued that the Workers' party was a novel development among Brazilian political institutions for several reasons: first, because it set out to be a party that expressed the interests of workers and the poor at a political level; second, because it sought to be an internally democratic party; and finally, because it wanted to represent and be held accountable to its members. All these conceptions have evolved a great deal since the party was founded, but all of them remain central elements in the party's identity and are what make it an innovation.

The very organization of the Workers' party challenged important elements of the dominant conception of politics in Brazil. The notion that workers should represent themselves on the political stage appeared nonsensical in several respects. First, workers did not possess the political *knowledge* to represent themselves; they lacked not only education but also the exposure to public concerns which members of the political elite must have. Second, given the oft-cited importance of personal ties in the politics of conciliation and negotiation considered to be a core characteristic of the Brazilian system, workers clearly did not possess the network of relations that would render them effective actors in the public arena. For most Brazilians, these observations were no more than common sense—an assessment of what was possible and what was simply utopian. The PT, on the other hand, proposed a new common sense for workers, one which recognized the likelihood of betrayal by political elites and argued that "if you want to get something done you have to do it yourself."[4]

Elitism in Brazilian politics did not originate with the authoritarian regime. Various authors have characterized the Brazilian political system as one whose prevailing dynamic was one of elite conciliation and negotiation. Through populist forms of mass mobilization at critical moments (which were nonetheless rarely determinant of political outcomes) and corporatist forms of interest representation a relatively narrow political elite maintained an exceptionally high level of control over the political arena. The instances in which conflicts were translated into widespread social polarization were comparatively rare.

One of the keystones of this model was the co-optability of popular leaders. As long as corporatist control of associations was able to prevent the articulation of an independent power base for class leaders and the perception of a genuine conflict over alternatives, the system was able to offer personal incentives for integrative, "constructive" behavior.[5] An extraordinarily high degree of social stratification and social and economic inequality reinforced popular conviction that very little change was possible, and that personal ties were more reliable than political activity. Brazil lacked a tradition either of citizen responsibility or accountability of politicians. As Schmitter pointed out,

> The System—"o sistema," in the local jargon—is concrete rather than analytic; it is "a complex of experiences which are related in a distinctive and seemingly necessary way to each other." Such a system is not exclusively in the mind of the observer, invisibly conditioning responses and applying homeostatic corrections. Rather, it is real, and is perceived by the enculturated elite actors themselves, who generally seek consciously to preserve it. Its needs consist in a set of structural relationships and value expectations that condition and limit behavior, thereby making it mutually predictable.[6]

Through its form of organization and its insistence on running its own candidates in 1982, the Workers' party attempted to put the principle of self-organization into practice by setting up what was to be a democratic mass party based in the working class. While its form of organization was constrained by the legal requirements of the party law, the PT did attempt to establish structures for grass roots participation and more democratic convention procedures than those contained in the law. The plebiscitary electoral environment in 1982 combined with the party's inexperience and miscalculations to produce disappointing results for the party. In addition, the PT proved largely unable to use the one important municipality in which its mayoral candidate had won in 1982 as a showcase administration through which to extend its influence. By mid-1985, the Workers' party was in the throes of a profound crisis over its future.

In spite of the party's weak electoral performance, it retained a significant amount of prestige in Brazilian society. Of particular importance was its continued identification with the most combative sector of the labor movement, especially in the modern industrial sector but with growing influence in the early 1980s in some more traditional sectors of industry, among newly organizing white-collar workers, and among agricultural workers as well. In the 1985 mayoral elections, the party's electoral discourse became more inclusive, emphasizing both broad questions of citizenship and social justice and local issues. The electorate responded positively, creating at once new problems and new opportunities for the party's process of self-definition.

Did this shift to a multiclass appeal mean that the PT was on the way to becoming a populist party? Several authors have argued that recent developments in Brazilian politics (and in Mexico, Argentina, and Peru as well) show that populism did not disappear with the demise of early import substitution industrialization and the rise of bureaucratic-authoritarian regimes. Perruci and Sanderson attribute the appearance of populist contenders for power to "the state's incapacity to cement a social pact for the purposes of national development."[7] In the tight economic situation of the 1980s, multiclass agreement on the need for political transition could not be translated into agreement on measures to resolve the economic crisis. Perruci and Sanderson stress those aspects of populism associated with political style, involving a direct appeal to the masses (or *povão*), and they include Lula and the PT among resurgent populists.

Their approach, it seems to me, misses some of the key *political* characteristics of the populist resurgence in Latin America. Dominant political actors responded to the dual challenge of political transition and economic crisis with a series of choices about how a political-institutional framework for resolving these would be built. In Brazil these choices almost invariably favored diffuse relational coalitions over representative institution building and the establishment of clear rules and norms of political behavior.[8] This political side of the populist resurgence is captured by Castro-Rea, Ducatenzeiler, and Faucher:

> The attraction of populism is that of short-term consensus obtained through an ambivalent discourse of change and conciliation without the cumbersome responsibilities of representation. . . .
>
> Populism can be understood as a political arrangement characterized by the privileged link between charismatic political leadership of state and the masses, combined with ineffectiveness of social organization and political parties as intermediate channels of mediation. . . .
>
> Beyond specific national cases, populism represents a common denominator of regimes characterized by ineffectual political representation compensated by latent corporatism and flourishing clientelism. The weight of political tradition is reproduced by political actors as a tactic for survival. The populist revival evident in Peru and

Argentina and anticipated in our other cases [Brazil and Mexico] is the manifestation of failure. It is the failure of governments opposing modernizing projects from civil society. It is the refusal to open channels of true democratic competition combined with the inability of governments to respond to reformist expectations confided to them and their inability to deal with the challenges of the present. Populism is an escapist solution. Regardless of concessions, it is more a return to the traditional order than the expression of change towards the building of a democratic society.[9]

The PT's whole project involved a refusal to accept this conception of politics and the massification of civil society that it presumes. Nonetheless, its ability to continue to resist the "populist temptation" will depend largely on its ability to maintain its commitment to institution building, and to devise a conception of representation consistent with its understanding of its social base and institutional development. From the beginning, the Workers' party has been committed to a notion of change from below, of politics from the bottom up—(de baixo para cima). Contained within this conception are two analytically distinct ideas, whose sometimes conflictual integration is integral to the party's identity: one, that "change from below" means primarily the self-activation of the working class; and the other, that it means the development of effective citizenship and democratic participation. I argued that in the 1982 electoral campaign, discourse about class predominated. As the 1980s wore on, the second conception became a much more central part of the party's appeal. A commitment to change from the bottom up came to mean a commitment to change based on initiatives coming from a broad range of societal organizations. While the party has broadened its initial conception of its working-class base to include white-collar workers and small rural landowners, its appeal is still directed to an activated and organized segment of Brazilian civil society.

The PT's origins were deeply influenced by the perception of widespread mobilization around social demands in the late 1970s; in the early 1980s, as it became clear that local organization around specific equity demands did not automatically translate into a societal movement, the party was placed in the ambiguous position of having to help organize what it was claiming to represent. This is entirely consistent with the Przeworskian view of class formation discussed above. Nonetheless, the party's open acceptance of such a role was complicated by the conception of self-organization characteristic of two of the most influential currents in the party: the trade union activists, and Catholic

activists whose view of politics had been influenced by their experience
in the CEBs and other church-linked base organizations. Both of these
groups mistrusted political mediation and conceived the party's role as
one of linking and spreading (but not organizing or transforming) the
demands of unions or movements. At the same time, however, they
felt that party members should participate in and help to fortify unions
and movements (without, however, subordinating them to the party).
Their view of democracy was one of direct democracy, involving delegation rather than representation, reiterating a tradition which goes
back to Rousseau and has recently given rise to intense debate about the
possibility of recombining institutions of representative and direct democracy; it is a strong element in the thinking of the West German
Green party.[10]

Given the importance of this kind of conception in the party, during
the first part of the 1980s it was difficult to formulate an institutional
strategy. The persistent separation between the spheres of social and
political action in Brazil placed the PT in a kind of schizophrenic position between the two. Within civil society, it was dedicated to strengthening social actors whose most potent political resource was their
capacity for disruption;[11] within political institutions, its job was to
expand the political space available for integrating popular participation
and demands in a regularized fashion. It was most effective at moments
when the separation was temporarily dissolved, for example, during
the massive campaign in 1984 for direct presidential elections. Artic-
ulating a demand for democratic citizenship that was supported by the
overwhelming majority of Brazilians, the PT was able to work effectively both in relation to other parties and in relation to movement
organizations. After the defeat of the amendment calling for direct
elections in 1985, the party was once again isolated. It was unable and
unwilling to participate in the negotiations among party elites over the
Tancredo Neves candidacy, and it adopted an intransigent position of
abstention from the indirect elections. As a result the party lost three (or
37.5 percent) of its federal deputies, those who chose to vote for Tancredo in the electoral college contrary to the party's official position.

The PT's position on the direct elections question was consistent
with its commitment to broad democratization in Brazil, and during
the mass mobilizations of 1984 over 80 percent of the Brazilian population held the same position. Nonetheless, after the defeat of the amendment and the PMDB's decision not to press on with the campaign, the
popular mood changed, from one which saw the situation as open,

where real change was possible, to one which accepted very quickly the return to the normal process of elite negotiation. Common sense dictated that there was no point in continuing the struggle. It was no longer an item on the political agenda. The PT's apparently quixotic attempt to promote continued popular mobilization on the question failed.

In spite of the party's anomalous position within the rules governing the context of political action in Brazil, the PT helped to maintain the visibility of social questions at a national level during a period when these could have been expected to take a back seat to political-institutional aspects of the transition. Although the party was unable to change the political agenda, its continued presence testified to that which was left out. Because the PT existed and was not immediately co-opted into the political system, the degree to which politics in Brazil remained an elite phenomenon was more visible than it would otherwise have been during the transitional period.

Underlying much of the PT's approach to the transition was a refusal to accept the limitations of a set of choices that seemed constantly to be structured around two alternatives—government versus opposition, PMDB versus PDS, Tancredo versus Maluf—and that offered little space for the independent expression of the needs of workers and others who sought more creative ways to imagine the future. A pattern of duality, a kind of binary logic, permeated Brazilian politics for the decade following the beginning of the liberalization process. It was a logic of opposition, but it was not yet a logic of democratic politics.

The political context into which the PT was born was one in which political relations took on the appearance of a series of antinomies— authoritarianism and democracy, but also state and society, government and opposition, corporatism and autonomy, integration and resistance (or disruption)—onto which the party superimposed a vision of class polarization as well. During the transition, there was often a tendency to present these concepts as polar opposites on a continuum; in fact, as the history of Brazil's transition to democracy demonstrates, these relationships are complex and dialectical more than they are mutually exclusive. The state plays an important role in structuring civil society, elements of which also penetrate state institutions. The task of the opposition is to become government, and the ambiguity of the process by which this occurred in Brazil led to the characterization of PMDB governors elected in 1982 as "opposition governors." Social movements sought to build autonomous forms of organization, often to negotiate better terms directly with state agencies in what some would characterize as corporatist relations; the "autonomous" labor movement grew up within corporatist state institutions. Resistance and integration, as James points out in the case of Peronist workers in Argentina, are best seen as strategic responses of real historical actors to concrete situations rather than transcendental characterizations of organizational goals with normative significance.[12] Stress on the second half of these antinomies—the association of democracy with society, opposition, autonomy, and resistance—was incorporated into the PT's expanding conception of class, helping to define the party's identity.

Thus the PT did not escape the kind of reasoning that thinks in terms of polarization, but its experience with the translation of polarized logic into political practice helped to nurture a more pluralistic view of alternatives. Its marginalization or autoexclusion from the major polarizations of the early 1980s—the 1982 elections and the anti-Maluf effort—as well as its continued participation in a variety of movements, reinforced the possibility of a more polycentric view of conflict. Within the PT itself, however, as well as in its relations with other groups, tendencies toward homogenization battled with a logic of difference. It would be astonishing if this were not the case.

To a significant extent, the party's early history has to be understood in terms of its need to remain a movement at the same time as it struggled to define what it meant to be a party; the party as institution, for many PT members, was one element in a network of organizations. Insofar as the party felt that its goals and priorities could not find a place on the agenda of the process of conservative transition, it remained part of a broader effort to redefine the agenda of change from outside the political system. Its conception of politics was thus of a process of *claiming rights* in practice, rather than demanding their concession by the state. Through the self-organization of society, the relations of power between state and society would change, and a new agenda based on societal needs would be created. The good society is not theorized in PT discourse, because it will emerge from the democratic practice of autonomous social actors. It includes the idea of a society with neither exploiters nor exploited and some reference to workers' control of the means of production, but it lacks a vision of the state and prescribes no clear mechanism for reaching an end that cannot be clearly described.

To a large extent, the party grew up with less of an ideology than an ethical proposal, within which a number of alternative visions of the good society competed, using different languages. A discourse about class, a discourse about citizenship, and a discourse about autonomy formed an amalgam whose central characteristic was the image of a diffuse "we," currently excluded from the process, who would win in practice rights that were inherently "ours." It is a utopian language, but the PT has no vision of utopia.

It is a logic of movement rather than a logic of ends. In this conception, the party is both catalyst and participant, but it does not yet represent, as that which it wishes to represent is still in formation. This is the main reason that articulation of an institutional strategy was so difficult and that the relation between the party and its elected politicians was initially either so conflictive or so diffuse. In 1986 the election to Congress of PT leaders who had won their spurs in popular struggles mitigated the tension between the party and its elected representatives, but it did not fundamentally resolve the issue. Yet insofar as the PT is a political party, increasingly capable of winning elections, its future depends on its ability to make a place for itself in the political system, to make space in which it can pursue its goals. This process has been very slow. In part this was due to the dynamics of the transition itself, which produced a discourse about democracy more notable for its limits than for its exploration of alternative ways of structuring political relations in Brazil. Nonetheless, as the PT grew more institutionalized and more politically confident in the second half of the 1980s, party leaders became increasingly conscious of the need to craft a more articulated understanding of the relation between movement building in society and political action. This recognition led to an enrichment of political and theoretical debate within the party—in party newspapers, in op ed sections of such papers as *Folha de São Paulo,* and in books intended for a wider audience.[13] A quarterly theoretical journal, *Teoria e Debate,* began to come out in 1988.

The task of clarifying the party's political-ideological definition is complex, not only because of the conditions under which the party was born, but also because of the world-historical moment at which it came to maturity. As Francisco Weffort argued in his contribution to the debate on the nature of the party, "the PT was not born out of a theoretical definition, but a practical intuition that was shown to be theoretically correct about the condition of workers in capitalist society and about the need for a politically independent affirmation of workers as a class."[14] While it has always defined itself as a socialist party, it has resisted efforts by its more doctrinaire factions to classify itself as Marxist-Leninist or even Marxist. At the same time, its leaders have expressed profound misgivings about the dangers of becoming a social-democratic party, which, in their view, represents a legalistic approach to legislating reforms from above without involving the organized masses in a process of political and social change. The latter concern reflects a profoundly antistatist element in the PT's self definition as a democratic socialist mass party, reflecting both its origins and its desire to differentiate itself from available models of socialism:

> The PT is the first Brazilian socialist current that has a real potential to endow the socialist ideal with a mass character. First, because the Workers' party emerged and developed as a party that synthesizes the aspirations and demands of broad sectors of the working population, because it emerged, therefore, as the direct and immediate expression of the masses, which identify it as their party; second, because the PT tries to build the socialist idea and practice on the basis of those aspirations and demands, in place of wanting to shape those aspirations and demands into a preconceived model of socialism.[15]

The PT's vision of socialism is in essence a radical conception of democracy, as Weffort points out: "Fundamentally, our conception of the party is a *radical democratic conception of society and politics in general*: 'The emancipation of the workers will be the work of the workers themselves.' Understanding this means understanding also that *the emancipation of workers is at the root of social emancipation in general*. In other words, the autonomous organization of workers is the road not only to *the construction of political democracy* but also to the *transformation of society*."[16] This kind of radical democratic vision of the empowerment of civil society contains a powerful rejection of the essentially statist view of change that has historically ranged across the political spectrum in Brazil. Power, in this view, is not just something which is "taken," through the state, but also is constructed (in society). The essential tension within PT discourse regarding its role as part of a movement in society and its role as a political institution is also a tension between these two conceptions of power. Yet for a legal party, which competes in elections and expects to hold positions of power in the political system, isn't something more than this needed in terms of a conception of the state?

The ambiguity of political discourse in the Workers' party and its difficulty in coming to terms with its double character as movement and as institution reflect very real contradictions in the political world in which the party emerged. The preceding chapters focused primarily on the ways in which the Brazilian political environment—the legacies of authoritarian domination, the hegemony of a highly conservative definition of the possibility of change during the transition, and the non-institutional and indeed anti-institutional patterns of decision making, as well as the historical weakness of the sectors the party intended to represent—constrained the PT's early development. But there is another dimension essential to an understanding of the party's dilemma, which was partially addressed in the reference made in the introduction to the difference in "world time" between the emergence of the earlier developing socialist parties and the emergence of the Workers' party in Brazil. There were different kinds of opportunities and resources available to earlier movements and parties. More difficult to grasp, but perhaps even more compelling, is the constriction in the repertoire of political discourse available to the left in the late 1980s.

Just before the 1989 presidential elections, I was interviewed by a journalist from *Gazeta Mercantil,* the Brazilian *Wall Street Journal.* The presidential elections coincided with the breathtakingly fast breakdown of Communist regimes in Eastern Europe, and the journalist asked me whether, under the circumstances, I didn't think that the PT represented an anachronistic kind of political force—one that was increasingly irrelevant as socialism seemed to be losing its political base everywhere. I responded that I did not think the situations were comparable. Nonetheless, the question has persisted, not only among journalists and politicians unsympathetic to the Workers' party, but for the party itself and for the left in general, and particularly for the left in the third world.[17] If, as many participants in the PT debate on the subject have argued, what happened in the countries where Communist regimes are breaking down cannot be explained simply on the basis of "historical, material, concrete limitations,"[18] then a radically different conception of socialism is needed, in which democracy is a central characteristic. Yet even as current events daily serve to reinforce this belief, serious dilemmas remain.

As the 1990s begin, the left in Brazil, as in much of the third world, lives in a nation characterized by extremes of poverty and income inequality. There is nothing new about this. Nonetheless, at the same time, the left has been effectively stripped of the repertoire of arguments in which its predecessors could clothe claims that raising the standard of living of the majority of the people was a universal good, a benefit to the whole society. However critical democratic forces on the left may have been of political repression in Eastern Europe and the

Soviet Union, the wholesale collapse of these regimes has left them with only feeble responses. Coupled with the much discussed demise of the Keynesian postwar accommodation[19] under the weight of the stagflation of the 1970s, the changes underway in Eastern Europe and the Soviet Union appear to be ripping away the last vestiges of belief that the state could effectively intervene to bring together the demand for equality with the imperative for economic growth.

In seeking to define what it means to be a democratic socialist party in a country characterized by egregious social problems, therefore, the PT faces a set of enormous dilemmas. How, concretely, can such a party propose to address radical inequality? The party continues to advocate state ownership of key economic sectors as a means to democratize the distribution of wealth. Yet this argument seems inadequate in a country where the state sector of the economy has been substantial for a half-century and has not appreciably benefited the majority of the population, and all the more so in a new political environment where statism in the economy is increasingly identified with political authoritarianism. Even though the PT's notion of state ownership includes a call for democratization of state enterprises, there remains a disjunction between its ongoing vision of the state as panacea for an unequal society and its stress on the autonomy of the latter.

The founding discourse of both the CUT and the PT was characterized by a juxtaposition of a profound antistatism with regard to social relations and the organization of civil society and a fairly traditional left statism regarding the role of the state in the economy and as guarantor of social welfare. As long as statist developmentalism remained relatively unchallenged as the prevailing ideology of mainstream bureaucrats and politicians in Brazil, it was possible to live with the ambiguities implicit in this juxtaposition. The rise of a (still far from consistent) neoliberal agenda coupled with the events in Eastern Europe have led at least to a recognition that these issues have to be discussed. One of the results has been a more serious internal debate in the PT about the accomplishments as well as the contradictions of European social democracy—a debate which previously had tended to focus on the contradictions of "administering capitalist crisis." The fact that Lula came within a hair of winning the presidency in 1989, in a situation where a victory would not have implied the implantation of socialism in Brazil, has further stimulated this debate.

Thinking about what it means to be a socialist at the end of the twentieth century is obviously a problem of international (and monumental) proportions. Nonetheless, there are specifically Latin American dimensions to the problem that are worth stressing. In Latin America the attack on the state is not primarily an attack on the left, but rather on mainstream developmentalist and populist traditions that have, over the past fifty years or so, been foundational elements of the very concept of nationhood in many Latin American countries, Brazil included. Rethinking the state—both from right and left—involves rethinking many of the underpinnings of nationalism as well. Because of recent experience in antiauthoritarian oppositions, the left has begun to shift back and forth between its historic stress on class, or what O'Donnell has called *lo popular* or *pueblo*—the basic component of leftist nationalism in Latin America, and an attempt to redefine the breadth of the notion of citizenship; nonetheless, a shift to the terrain of citizenship is a move onto the historic turf of liberalism.[20] The left's problem, fundamentally, is the need to define simultaneously a political space of its own and potential allies *both* in relation to the neoliberal agenda and to the status-quo ante—that is, to historical forms of statist developmentalism—without conflating the two. Such a definition is complicated by the degree to which the left shares elements of both traditions. It must carry out this task in a context in which, in most cases, the right is neither consistent nor well-identified institutionally and the left is in crisis worldwide.

Although the attempt to resolve this question is likely to be protracted and extremely difficult, the PT begins the process with a number of assets. The fact that it has resisted factional efforts to impose a doctrinaire vision of the "correct" road to socialism—insisting instead on the legitimate coexistence within the party of a variety of conceptions—is likely in the end to prove a strength rather than a weakness. Its vision of the need to strengthen civil society in Brazil, promoting the possibility of democratic change from below in opposition to an authoritarian and elitist political system, provides a basis for rethinking traditional socialist notions of the state as panacea. The party's belief that state institutions must become "transparent" to civil society, an oft-repeated if not always realized goal in its approach to municipal administrations, is the beginning of a vision of a democratic state that is responsive to the population. The party has an intuition, if not a theoretically elaborated argument, that the socialism to which it aspires is also, and essentially, an aspiration for democracy.

Given the centrality of a radical democratic vision of politics to the PT's identity and the distance between this vision and predominant elitist features of the Brazilian political system, it is not surprising that the party's institutionalization has not yet produced a reduction in the degree to which it is seen as a "system of solidarity." The "genetic model" of the PT provides an interesting illustration of Panebianco's hypothesis that environmental factors are likely to be an important intervening variable for understanding a party's institutionalization process.[21] The Workers' party has become increasingly institutionalized along a number of the organizational dimensions Panebianco discusses. It has grown from its initial base in São Paulo to become a national party, at the same time as the party's founders have maintained a high degree of authority in shaping the party's identity. This corresponds to Panebianco's conception of a party that develops primarily (though not exclusively) through territorial penetration. Although external legitimation was critical in early periods of the party's development, the party itself has increasingly become a vehicle for entry into political life; at the same time it continues to encourage its members to participate in a variety of societal organizations, and it continues to integrate leaders of popular organizations into the party at high levels.[22]

Yet in spite of the development of the PT's internal life as a source of opportunity for careers within the party (albeit careers where the selective incentives involved are almost exclusively status rather than material ones), the party has not lost its character as a movement, a "community of fate" whose development remains primarily based on collective incentives. Although in the process of its institutionalization, the organization has indeed become valuable in itself and its survival a central goal, the identification of the organization with its ends has remained exceptionally strong.

The reasons for this, it seems to me, lie in the relation between the PT and the political environment in which it arose. In Brazil's highly conservative transition to democracy, the PT was an anomaly not only because of the kinds of social changes it called for but also because of the kinds of political-institutional changes it represented. In this respect, the development of the Workers' party and of other societal organizations, especially the combative labor movement, highlights important characteristics of the transition from authoritarianism in Brazil. First, the extreme gradualness of the process left open areas of contestation over rules of the game long after the point where the dominant opposition party occupied positions of significant political power, at least in the public perception. There was a great deal of ambiguity, particularly in PMDB discourse, as to whether the situation under the Sarney government was still transitional or whether, in spite of the indirect elections, the democratic transition had been essentially achieved, and the question of presidential elections and other institutional changes was a matter of technical adjustment.

Second, the growth of the PT and the labor movement raised the political costs of postponing for an indeterminate transitional period the questions of redistribution and income inequality. This undercut the ability of the regime to implement authoritative economic policy. Lacking either a substantive or institutional agreement on how long workers would have to wait for their situation to improve, workers had no reason, given their historical experience, to believe a new set of promises. The situation was complicated by the serious economic constraints under which Brazilian democratization took place, which made the kinds of substantive demands raised by the PT and the labor movement difficult to fulfill without radically redistributive measures, which in the eyes of the conservative elites in power would potentially disrupt the transition process.

As long as this impasse existed, the likelihood of the PT's becoming fully integrated into institutional politics in Brazil was very low. The bipolar ordering of choices left little space for invention. The dynamics of the conservative transition were such that its main sphere of opportunity lay outside, rather than within, political institutions. In this respect the dilemmas the PT faced resembled the problems faced by Solidarity in Poland, as it attempted "to institutionalize itself as a trade union and by the same token to provide the foundations of a reconstructed civil society."[23] Ironically, insofar as an important part of the PT's vote in the 1988 and 1989 elections was motivated by a rejection of the political elites who had led the transition to democracy, the party itself ultimately became a beneficiary of the kind of polarized logic it had always rejected. Its ability to go further will depend on its ability to catalyze a movement beyond rejection to the construction, along with a more complex and organized civil society, of a different kind of logic.

Part of imagining democracy should be the comparison and combination of alternatives, accepting conflict as a normal component of creativity. In Brazil, this kind of process often seems far off. If this is indeed the case, it is a problem both for the development of the Workers' party and for the consolidation of democracy. Still largely missing is an important component for the process of imagining democracy in Brazil, the institutional acceptance and mediation of conflict, involving the possibility of comparing and combining many alternatives, rather than a bipolar vision of order or chaos.

Nonetheless, something important has happened in Brazil. In 1987, in an editorial in *Folha de São Paulo*, the political scientist Luciano Martins wrote that the work of the Constituent Assembly resembled nothing so much as a group of politicians sitting in a room surrounded with mirrors, so that everywhere they looked they saw only their own images. The development and survival of the Workers' party sends a powerful signal that important sectors of Brazilian society are seeking to replace those mirrors with glass. The consolidation of Brazilian democracy depends on breaking down the barriers that still exist between change from above and change from below, and the future of the Workers' party will be integrally linked to this process. But whatever its future, its very existence has already helped to redefine the limits of Brazilian politics.

Notes

1 Introduction

1. Guillermo O'Donnell and Philippe C. Schmitter, *Transitions from Authoritarian Rule: Tentative Conclusions about Uncertain Democracies* (Baltimore: Johns Hopkins University Press, 1986), stressed the importance of pact making in the democratization process. Nonetheless, they also recognized potential problems with this formula, noting that "the transitional solution embodied by limited democracy, then, suffers a serious medium- and long-run legitimacy deficit when compared to regimes where citizens seem to be offered real opportunities to throw out incumbents and where leaders seem to be more truly accountable to mass publics" (p. 42).

2. Guillermo O'Donnell, "Challenges to Democratization in Brazil," *World Policy Journal* 5 (Spring 1988): 282.

3. See, e.g., Frances Hagopian, "The Politics of Oligarchy: The Persistence of Traditional Elites in Contemporary Brazil" (Ph.D. diss., Massachusetts Institute of Technology, 1986), and Ben Ross Schneider, "Politics within the State: Elite Bureaucrats and Industrial Policy in Authoritarian Brazil" (Ph.D. diss., University of California, Berkeley, 1987). On the military see Alfred Stepan, *Rethinking Military Politics: Brazil and the Southern Cone* (Princeton: Princeton University Press, 1988).

4. For a discussion of this process, see my "Labor and Transition in Brazil," in *Labor Movements and Transition to Democracy,* ed. Samuel Valenzuela (Notre Dame, Ind.: University of Notre Dame Press, forthcoming 1992).

5. On the Communist party, see Ronald H. Chilcote, *The Brazilian Communist Party: Conflict and Integration, 1922–1972* (New York: Oxford University Press, 1974), and Arnaldo Spindel, *O Partido Comunista na Gênese do Populismo* (São Paulo: Edições Símbolo, 1980). On the main "laborite" (*trabalhista*) populist party in the 1940s, the Partido Trabalhista Brasileiro (Brazilian Labor party, PTB), see Angela de Castro Gomes, *A Invenção do Trabalhismo* (Rio de Janeiro: IUPERJ/Vertice, 1988), and Maria Victoria Benevides, *O PTB e o Trabalhismo* (São Paulo: Editora Brasiliense, 1989).

6. For a review of such approaches, see Sidney Tarrow, "National Politics and Collective Action: Recent Theory and Research in Western Europe and the United States," *Annual Review of Sociology* 14 (1988): 421–40.

7. Rogers M. Smith, "The New Non-Science of Politics: On Turns to History in Political Science," paper prepared for the CSST conference "The Historic Turn in the Human Sciences," Ann Arbor, Mich., October 5–7, 1990.

8. On the electoral dilemma of working-class parties, see Adam Przeworski, *Capitalism and Social Democracy* (Cambridge: Cambridge University Press, 1985), chap. 3.

9. Angelo Panebianco, *Political Parties: Organization and Power* (Cambridge: Cambridge University Press, 1988), p. xiii.

10. Luís Inácio da Silva changed his name legally to Luís Inácio Lula da Silva in 1982 to ensure that votes cast for "Lula" in the 1982 São Paulo gubernatorial elections would be counted.

11. Panebianco, *Political Parties*, p. 51.

12. Seymour Martin Lipset and Stein Rokkan, "Cleavage Structures, Party Systems, and Voter Alignments: An Introduction," in *Party Systems and Voter Alignments*, ed. Seymour Martin Lipset and Stein Rokkan (New York: Free Press, 1967).

13. Examples of such explanations can be found in Otto Kirschheimer's discussion of the decline of class and the appearance of the catch-all party, "The Transformation of the Western European Party Systems," in *Political Parties and Political Development* ed. Joseph LaPalombara and Myron Weiner (Princeton: Princeton University Press, 1966); the convergence or industrial society hypotheses—for example, Ralf Dahrendorf, *Class and Class Conflict in Industrial Society* (Stanford: Stanford University Press, 1959); and William Kornhausser's mass society thesis, *The Politics of Mass Society* (Glencoe: Free Press, 1959).

14. See, as only one example, the two-volume collection by Colin Crouch and Alessandro Pizzorno, eds., *The Resurgence of Class Conflict in Western Europe since 1968* (New York: Holmes & Meier, 1978).

15. Lipset and Rokkan, "Cleavage Structures, Party Systems, and Voter Alignments: An Introduction"; Anthony Downs, *An Economic Theory of Democracy* (New York: Harper & Row, 1957); Giovanni Sartori, "From the Sociology of Politics to Political Sociology," in *Politics and the Social Sciences*, ed. Seymour Martin Lipset (New York: Oxford University Press, 1969).

16. Przeworski, *Capitalism and Social Democracy*, especially chaps. 1–3.

17. Alessandro Pizzorno, "The Individualistic Mobilization of Europe," as cited in Stefano Bartolini, "The Membership of Mass Parties: The Social Democratic Experience, 1889–1978," in *Western European Party Systems*, ed. Hans Daalder and Peter Mair (Beverly Hills: Sage, 1983), p. 213.

18. Robert A. Dahl, "Some Explanations," in *Political Oppositions in Western Democracies*, ed. Robert Dahl (New Haven: Yale University Press, 1966), p. 361.

19. Fernando Henrique Cardoso, "A Democracia na America Latina," *Novos Estudos CEBRAP* 10 (October 1984): 45–56.

20. Prior to 1945, parties were primarily regional; this was reinforced by the importance of state governors during the First Republic. Only with the 1945 party reform were efforts made to ensure the implantation of a national party system. For a discussion of Brazil's successive party systems, see Bolivar Lamounier and Rachel Meneguello, *Partidos Políticos e Consolidação Democrática: O Caso Brasileiro* (São Paulo: Brasiliense, 1986), or a shorter English version that appeared as "Political Parties and Democratic Consolidation" (Washington, D.C.: Wilson Center, Smithsonian Institution, 1985).

21. Guillermo O'Donnell, "Tensions in the Bureaucratic-Authoritarian State and the Question of Democracy," in *The New Authoritarianism in Latin America*, ed. David Collier (Princeton: Princeton University Press, 1980). On class and populism, see Francisco Weffort, *O Populismo na Política Brasileira* (Rio de Janeiro: Paz e Terra, 1978).

22. On the 1945–64 period, see especially Maria do Carmo Campello de Souza, *Estado e Partidos Politicos no Brazil, 1930–1964* (São Paulo: Editora Alfa-Omega, 1976). For a recent and fascinating treatment of the mechanisms of party use of state resources in Minas Gerais, see Hagopian, "Politics of Oligarchy."

23. Douglas A. Chalmers, "Parties and Society in Latin America," in *Friends, Followers and Factions: A Reader in Political Clientelism*, ed. Steffan W. Schmidt, James C. Scott, Carl Lande, and Laura Guasti (Berkeley: University of California Press, 1977).

24. See Souza, *Estado e Partidos Politicos no Brasil*, p. 106, and Robert Packenham, "Functions of the Brazilian National Congress," in *Latin American Legislatures: Their Role and Influence*, ed. Weston Agor (New York: Praeger, 1979), pp. 259–86.

25. Giovanni Sartori, *Partidos e Sistemas Partidários* (Rio de Janeiro: Zahar, 1982).

26. See Panebianco, *Political Parties*, chap. 4.

27. Scott Mainwaring, "Political Parties and Prospects for Democracy in Brazil," paper presented at the 14th World Congress of the International Political Science Association, Washington, D.C., 1988.

28. Huntington measured institutionalization along four dimensions: adaptability-rigidity, complexity-simplicity, autonomy-subordination, and coherence-disunity. See Samuel P. Huntington, *Political Order in Changing Societies* (New Haven: Yale University Press, 1968), especially chap. 1.

29. In their study of party strategy, class organization, and individual voting, Adam Przeworski and John Sprague adopted a definition of workers that included "manual wage earners employed in mining, manufacturing, construction, and agriculture, persons retired from such occupations, and inactive adult members of their households," a more complete definition than the one being used operationally here. See Przeworski, *Capitalism and Social Democracy*, p. 104. For comparative purposes, I am using aggregate figures for the proportion of economically active population employed in mining, manufacturing, construction, and transportation; I recognize that these can only be indicative rather than fully descriptive of class structure.

30. These points are summarized in Bartolini, "Membership of Mass Parties."

31. See Otto Kirchheimer's classic article on the decline of mass parties, in which he discusses his famous notion of the rise of the "catch-all" party; "The Transformation of the Western European Party Systems," in *Political Parties and Political Development*.

32. Cardoso develops this argument in "A Democracia na America Latina." Although Cardoso may place undue emphasis on his claim that Brazil corresponds to a model of a modern mass society, his general point seems valid.

33. On this dilemma and the electoral trade-offs involved, see Przeworski, *Capitalism and Social Democracy*, especially pp. 99–133.

34. For a discussion of "new" social movements in Brazil, see Scott Mainwaring and Eduardo Viola, "New Social Movements, Political Culture, and Democracy," *Telos* 61 (Fall 1984): 17–52.

35. Ronald Inglehart, *The Silent Revolution: Changing Values and Political Styles among Western Publics* (Princeton: Princeton University Press, 1977), chap. 13.

36. See especially Souza, *Estado e Partidos Políticos no Brasil, 1930–1964*; Main-

waring, "Political Parties and Prospects for Democracy in Brazil"; and O'Donnell, "Challenges to Democratization in Brazil."

2 The Brazilian Transition to Democracy

1. Important contributions include the seminal article by Dankwart Rustow, "Transitions to Democracy: Toward a Dynamic Model," *Comparative Politics* 2 (April 1970): 337–63; Douglas Chalmers and Craig Robinson, "Why Power Contenders Choose Liberalization," *International Studies Quarterly* 26 (March 1982): 3–36; and the volumes in the four-volume set *Transitions from Authoritarian Rule: Prospects for Democracy,* ed. Guillermo O'Donnell, Philippe C. Schmitter, and Laurence Whitehead, which include both theoretical and case study materials. These volumes are listed individually in the bibliography.

2. See O'Donnell and Schmitter, *Transitions from Authoritarian Rule: Tentative Conclusions about Uncertain Democracies.*

3. See, e.g., Cándido Procópio Ferreira de Camargo et al., *São Paulo, 1975: Crescimento e Pobreza* (São Paulo: Edições Loyola, 1976); and Paul Singer and Vinícius Caldeira Brant, eds., *São Paulo: O Povo em Movimento* (Petrópolis: Vozes/CEBRAP, 1980).

4. See T. H. Marshall, *Citizenship and Social Class and Other Essays* (Cambridge: Cambridge University Press, 1950). Marshall argues that "the persistence of economic inequalities has been made more difficult by the enrichment of the status of citizenship" (p. 77).

5. The top decile of the EAP earned 39.6 percent of income in 1960, 46.7 in 1970, and 47.7 in 1980. For the bottom 50 percent of the EAP, the corresponding figures were 17.4, 14.9, and 14.2—by 1985 this had fallen even further, to 13.1 percent. Figures from IBGE, census data from 1960, 1970, and 1980, and PNAD (National Household Survey) 1985 are cited in Eduardo Matarazzo Suplicy, *Da Distribuição da Renda e dos Direitos à Cidadania* (São Paulo: Editora Brasiliense, 1988), p. 32.

6. Instituto Brasileiro de Geografia e Estatística, *Tabulações Avançadas do Censo Demogoáfico, IX Recenseamento Geral do Brasil—1980* (Rio de Janeiro: IBGE, 1981), p. 29. For further discussion of the value of the minimum wage, see Margaret E. Keck, "The New Unionism in the Brazilian Transition," in *Democratizing Brazil,* ed. Alfred Stepan (New York: Oxford University Press, 1989), pp. 268–70.

7. O'Donnell, "Tensions in the Bureaucratic-Authoritarian State."

8. Joseph A. Schumpeter, *Capitalism, Socialism, and Democracy* (New York: Harper & Row, 1950), p. 269; Robert A. Dahl, *Polyarchy: Participation and Opposition* (New Haven: Yale University Press, 1971), p. 2.

9. Schumpeter, *Capitalism, Socialism, and Democracy,* especially chap. 23.

10. The publication of John Rawls's *Theory of Justice* (Cambridge: Harvard University Press, 1971), which attempted to provide a rational basis for the derivation of principles of justice, provoked a spate of new work in this area. A different approach, centering on the notion of "complex inequality," is Michael Walzer, *Spheres of Justice* (New York: Basic Books, 1983).

11. See, e.g., Francis G. Castles, ed., *The Impact of Parties: Politics and Policies in Democratic Capitalist States* (London: Sage, 1982).

12. For an overview of current trends in the comparative politics literature reflecting these issues, see Peter Lange and Hudson Meadwell, "Typologies of Democratic Systems: From Political Inputs to Political Economy," in *New Directions in Comparative Politics,* ed. Howard Wiarda (Boulder: Westview Press, 1985), pp. 80–112.

13. See W. B. Gallie, "Essentially Contested Concepts," *Proceedings of the Aristotelian Society* 56 (1955–56): 167–98. William E. Connolly argues that these concepts are not subject to definitive definition through universal criteria of reason and that "this lag between inherited terms of discourse and changing constellations of social life contributes both to the contestability of core concepts and the inherently creative dimension of political conceptualization." See William E. Connolly, *The Terms of Political Discourse* (Princeton: Princeton University Press, 1983), pp. 203–05.

14. Connolly, *Terms of Political Discourse,* p. 220.

15. Relativizing repression is always dangerous; to note that fewer Brazilians than Uruguayans, Chileans, or Argentines were tortured and killed should not downplay the significance of those that were. See Márcio Moreira Alves, *Torturas e Torturados* (Rio de Janeiro: Idade Nova, 1966); Amnesty International, *A Report on Allegations of Torture in Brazil* (London: T. B. Russell, 1972), and subsequent updates; and Joan Dassin, ed., *Torture in Brazil: A Report by the Archdiocese of São Paulo,* tr. Jaime Wright (New York: Vintage Books, 1985).

16. For a summary of Institutional Act no. 5, see Maria Helena Moreira Alves, *State and Opposition in Military Brazil* (Austin: University of Texas Press, 1985), pp. 95–100. The act also gave the executive, for an unspecified amount of time, the power to close or intervene in Congress or the judiciary, to suspend the political rights of citizens, to dismiss public employees and judges, to declare a state of siege, to confiscate private property of "subversives," to rule by decree, and to try political crimes in military courts. Alves discusses the National Security Law of 1969 on pp. 118–19.

17. Juan J. Linz, "The Future of an Authoritarian Situation or the Institutionalization of an Authoritarian Regime: The Case of Brazil," in *Authoritarian Brazil,* ed. Alfred Stepan (New Haven: Yale University Press, 1973).

18. For a comparison of the Brazilian and Spanish cases emphasizing similarities between the two, see Donald Share and Scott Mainwaring, "Transitions through Transaction: Democratization in Brazil and Spain," in *Political Liberalization in Brazil,* ed. Wayne Selcher (Boulder: Westview Press, 1986).

19. Edward Malefakis, "Spain and Its Francoist Heritage," in *From Dictatorship to Democracy,* ed. John H. Herz (Westport, Conn.: Greenwood Press, 1982), pp. 219–20.

20. An exception in the Peruvian case is the rise of a strong, albeit very fragmented, left that, like the Workers' party in Brazil, is highly dependent for its strength on the urban labor movement. See Evelyne Huber Stephens, "The Peruvian Military Government, Labor Mobilization, and the Political Strength of the Left," *Latin American Research Review* 18, no. 2 (1983): 57–94.

21. See Arturo Valenzuela and J. Samuel Valenzuela, "Party Oppositions under the Chilean Authoritarian Regime," in *Military Rule in Chile: Dictatorships and Oppositions,* ed. J. Samuel Valenzuela and Arturo Valenzuela (Baltimore: Johns

Hopkins University Press, 1986), pp. 184–229, and Manuel Antonio Garretón, "Chile: In Search of Lost Democracy," Kellogg Institute Working Paper no. 56, University of Notre Dame, 1986.

22. For a brief description of sequential party systems in Brazilian history, see Lamounier and Meneguello, "Political Parties and Democratic Consolidation."

23. Juan J. Linz, "Opposition in and under an Authoritarian Regime: The Case of Spain," in *Regimes and Oppositions*, ed. Robert A. Dahl (New Haven: Yale University Press, 1973), pp. 191–210.

24. For discussions of parties and elections under the military regime, see Bolivar Lamounier, ed., *Voto de Desconfiança: Eleições e Mudança Política no Brasil, 1970–1979* (Petrópolis: Vozes/CEBRAP, 1980); Bolivar Lamounier and Fernando Henrique Cardoso, eds., *Os Partidos Políticos e as Eleições no Brasil* (Rio de Janeiro: Paz e Terra, 1975); and Fábio Wanderley Reis, ed., *Os Partidos e o Regime* (São Paulo: Edições Símbolo, 1978).

25. See Souza, *Estado e Partidos Políticos no Brasil, 1930–1964*, pp. 114–22, and Phyllis J. Peterson, "Brazilian Political Parties: Formation, Organization, and Leadership, 1945–1959" (Ph.D. diss., University of Michigan, 1962), pp. 48–60.

26. There is a substantial literature on political parties during the 1945–64 period. On the UDN, see especially Maria Victoria de Mesquita Benevides, *A UDN e o Udenismo: Ambiguidades do Liberalismo Brasileiro, 1945–1965* (Rio de Janeiro: Paz e Terra, 1981). On the PSD, see Lucia Hippolito, *De Raposas e Reformistas: O PSD e a Experiência Democrática Brasileira, 1945–1964* (Rio de Janeiro: Paz e Terra, 1985).

27. See Timothy Fox Harding, "The Political History of Organized Labor in Brazil" (Ph.D. diss., Stanford University, 1973), chap. 5.

28. Note the difference between Brazilian labor legislation in the 1930s and 1940s and the Chilean legislation in the 1920s and 1930s. Although both established extensive corporatist controls over the labor movement, in Chile wage setting, social security policy, and reforming the labor code were legislative prerogatives. This gave political parties a much more important role in labor politics in Chile than in Brazil, where such issues were dealt with in the executive bureaucracy. See, e.g., J. Samuel Valenzuela, "The Chilean Labor Movement: The Institutionalization of Conflict," in *Chile: Politics and Society*, ed. Arturo Valenzuela and J. Samuel Valenzuela (New Brunswick, N.J.: Transaction Books, 1976), pp. 135–71, and Alan Angell, *Politics and the Labour Movement in Chile* (London: Oxford University Press, 1972).

29. José Nun, "Elementos para una Teoria de la Democracia: Gramsci y el Sentido Comun," paper presented at the Gramsci Institute, Ferrara, September 11–13, 1985.

30. Liliana de Riz, "Politica y Partidos. Ejercicio de Analisis Comparado: Argentina, Chile, Brasil y Uruguay," *Desarrollo Económico* 25 (January–March 1986): 661.

31. Charles Guy Gillespie, *Negotiating Democracy: Politicians and Generals in Uruguay* (New York: Cambridge University Press, forthcoming), chap. 1.

32. O'Donnell and Schmitter, *Transitions from Authoritarian Rule: Tentative Conclusions about Uncertain Democracies*, pp. 59–61.

33. Scott Mainwaring, "Political Parties and Democratization in Brazil and the Southern Cone," *Comparative Politics* (October 1988): 113–14. Gillespie, *Negotiating Democracy*, attributes fundamental importance to the role of parties in both the breakdown of democracy and the democratic transition in Uruguay.

34. For data on changes in composition of EAP, see Paul W. Drake, "Los Movimientos Urbanos de Trabajadores bajo el Capitalismo Autoritario en el Cono Sur y Brasil, 1964–1983," in *Muerte y Resurreccion: Los Partidos Politicos en el Autoritarismo y las Transiciones del Cono Sur,* ed. Marcelo Cavarozzi and Manuel Antonio Garretón (Santiago: FLACSO, 1989), pp. 102–09.

35. See J. Samuel Valenzuela, "Labor Movement Formation and Politics: The Chilean and French Cases in Comparative Perspective" (Ph.D. diss., Columbia University, 1979).

36. Valenzuela and Valenzuela, "Party Oppositions under the Chilean Authoritarian Regime."

37. The best analysis of Uruguay's double simultaneous vote system and its impact on the party system is found in Luiz Eduardo González, "Political Structures and Prospects for Democracy in Uruguay" (Ph.D. diss., Yale University, 1988). The Brazilian *sublegenda* system functioned similarly under the military regime but, unlike the Uruguayan system, it applied only to offices elected under a majority principle. Uruguayan parties can run several lists in congressional elections (which are proportional) as well.

38. Martin Gargiulo, "El Desafio de la Democracia: La Izquierda Politica y Sindical en el Uruguay Post-Autoritario," paper presented to the Latin American Studies Association Meeting, Boston, October 22–25, 1986, pp. 4–5.

39. Gillespie, *Negotiating Democracy,* chap. 2.

40. This negotiation process is described in detail in Gillespie, *Negotiating Democracy.*

41. Mainwaring, "Political Parties and Democratization in Brazil and the Southern Cone," pp. 100–103.

42. See especially Daniel James, *Resistance and Integration: Peronism and the Argentine Working Class, 1946–1976* (Cambridge: Cambridge University Press, 1988).

43. De Riz, "Politica y Partidos," pp. 672–76.

3 Opposition to Authoritarianism and the Debate about Democracy

1. For a discussion of the dialectical relations between state and society, see Maria Helena Moreira Alves, *State and Opposition in Military Brazil,* and Alfred Stepan, "State Power and the Strength of Civil Society in the Southern Cone of Latin America," in *Bringing the State Back In,* ed. Peter B. Evans, Dietrich Rueschemeyer, and Theda Skocpol (Cambridge: Cambridge University Press, 1985).

2. For a description of tenant organizations in São Paulo in the 1950s and 1960s, see José Alvaro Moisés, "Classes Populares e Protesto Urbano" (Ph.D. diss., Faculdade de Filosofia, Letras e Ciências Humanas, Universidade de São Paulo, 1978).

3. This distinction was made by Marcus Faria Figueiredo and José Antonio Borges Cheibub, "A Abertura Política de 1973 a 1981: Quem Disse o Que, Quando—Inventário de um Debate," *Bib* 14 (1982): 38.

4. *Legislação Eleitoral e Partidária* (Brasília: Senado Federal, Subsecretaria de Edições Técnicas, 1982), p. 88.

5. The best discussion of the evolution of a plebiscitary electoral environment can be found in Bolivar Lamounier, "O Voto em São Paulo, 1970–1978," in *Voto de Desconfiança,* ed. Lamounier, pp. 15–80.

6. Bernardo Kucinski, *Abertura: A História de uma Crise* (São Paulo: Editora Brasil Debates, 1982), pp. 48–50. On the military dimension, see Stepan, *Rethinking Military Politics.* The best bibliographic essay on the liberalization is Figueiredo and Cheibub, "A Abertura Política de 1973 a 1981."

7. See Luiz Carlos Bresser Pereira, *O Colapso de uma Aliança de Classes* (São Paulo: Editora Brasiliense, 1978), pp. 114–35.

8. Fernando Henrique Cardoso, "O Papel dos Empresários no Processo de Transição: O Caso Brasileiro," *Dados* 26, no. 1 (1983): 9–27.

9. See Maria Helena Moreira Alves, *State and Opposition in Military Brazil,* pp. 160–68.

10. Pereira, *O Colapso de uma Aliança de Classe,* p. 127. For an extensive discussion of the alliance supporting the regime, see Peter Evans, *Dependent Development: The Alliance of Multinational, State, and Local Capital in Brazil* (Princeton: Princeton University Press, 1979).

11. Fernando Henrique Cardoso, "A Questão da Democracia," in *Brasil: Do "Milagre" à Abertura,* ed. Paulo Krischke (São Paulo: Cortez Editora, 1982), p. 114.

12. Ibid., pp. 117–18.

13. In September 1976, CEBRAP was the target of a bombing attack by the Aliança Anticomunista Brasileira, which also placed several bombs in the headquarters of the Brazilian Bar Association (OAB) around this time. See chronology in *Almanaque Abril 1983* (São Paulo: Editora Abril, 1983), p. 38.

14. The social focus of this work is encapsulated in the two volumes commissioned by the diocese of São Paulo: Camargo et al., *São Paulo: Crescimento e Pobreza,* and Singer and Brant, eds., *São Paulo: O Povo em Movimento.*

15. On censorship and the response of the Brazilian press, see Joan R. Dassin, "Press Censorship and the Military State in Brazil," in *Press Control around the World,* ed. Jane Leftwich Curry and Joan R. Dassin (New York: Praeger, 1982), pp. 149–86, and Robert N. Pierce, *Keeping the Flame: Media and Government in Latin America* (New York: Hastings House, 1979), pp. 23–54. "O Brasil Proibido," *Coojornal* 4 (November 1980), is a special supplement of the Porto Alegre newspaper on censorship. On the politics of press liberalization see Celina R. Duarte, "The Press and Redemocratization in Brazil," paper presented at the International Political Science Association, Rio de Janeiro, August 9–14, 1982.

16. On the student movement in the 1960s and the move by some students to armed struggle, see João Quartim, *Dictatorship and Armed Struggle in Brazil* (London: New Left Books, 1971), and Antonio Mendes, Jr., *Movimento Estudantil no Brasil* (São Paulo: Brasiliense, 1982), pp. 74–90. A fascinating fictionalized account of this period is Alfredo Syrkis, *Os Carbonários* (São Paulo: Global Editora, 1980).

17. University enrollment in Brazil was 124,214 in 1964; 425,478 in 1970; 937,593 in 1974; 1,377,286 in 1980; and 1,367,609 in 1985 (Instituto Brasileiro de

Geografia e Estatística, *Anuário Estatístico do Brasil 1981*, p. 202; *Anuário Estatístico do Brasil 1987*, p. 233).

18. Kucinski, *Abertura: A História de uma Crise*, p. 106.

19. For a brief introduction to liberation theology, see T. Howland Sanks and Brian Smith, "Liberation Ecclesiology: Praxis, Theory, Praxis," *Theological Studies* 38 (March 1977): 3-38. Documentation on the key Latin American bishops' conferences is in José Marins et al., *De Medellín a Puebla* (São Paulo: Edições Paulinas, 1979). One of the most important documents from the CNBB, "Exigências Cristãs de uma Ordem Política," is in the *Revista de Cultura Contemporânea* 1 (January 1979): 103–06. For the history of the evolution of the "preferential option for the poor" in the Brazilian Catholic church, see Thomas C. Bruneau, *The Political Transformation of the Brazilian Catholic Church* (New York: Cambridge University Press, 1974), and Scott Mainwaring, *The Catholic Church and Politics in Brazil, 1916–1985* (Stanford: Stanford University Press, 1986).

20. See Cándido Procópio Ferreira de Camargo, Beatriz Muniz de Souza, and Antônio Flávio de Oliveira Pierucci, "Comunidades Eclesiais de Base," in *São Paulo: O Povo em Movimento*, ed. Paul Singer and Vinícius Caldeira Brant, pp. 59–82, and Frei Betto, *O Que é Comunidade Eclesial de Base* (São Paulo: Brasiliense, 1981).

21. See the special section of *Novos Estudos CEBRAP* 1 (April 1982): 48–58.

22. See, e.g., Ana Maria Doimo, "Social Movements and the Catholic Church in Vitória, Brazil," in *The Progressive Church in Latin America*, ed. Scott Mainwaring and Alexander Wilde (Notre Dame, Ind.: University of Notre Dame Press, 1989): 193–223, and Mainwaring, *Catholic Church and Politics in Brazil*, pp. 182–206.

23. Interview with Anísio Batista de Oliveira, Pastoral Operária, São Paulo, October 18, 1982.

24. Descriptions of the cost of living movement are drawn from Kucinski, *Abertura*; from *abcd Jornal*, December 1979, p. 13; and from Paul Singer, "Movimentos de Bairro," in *São Paulo: O Povo em Movimento*, ed. Paul Singer and Vinícius Caldeira Brant, pp. 97–101.

25. Scott Mainwaring discusses the possibility that this *basismo* of Catholic organizations could impede the development of political institutions at the same time as it encouraged participation; see *Catholic Church and Politics in Brazil*, chap. 9. For a general critique of "basismo" and opposition politics, see Fernando Henrique Cardoso, "Regime Político e Mudança Social," *Revista de Cultura e Política* 3 (November–January 1981): 7–26, and the discussion which follows by Carlos Estevam Martins, Célia Galvão Quirino, Maurício Tragtemberg, and José Alvaro Moisés, pp. 27–47.

26. *Pelego* is a derogatory term, commonly used to mean "flunky of the labor ministry within the union." Literally, a pelego is a wool pad used between the saddle and the horse to reduce friction.

27. The ABC (or ABCD) region refers to the industrial suburbs of São Paulo where the bulk of large automobile and metalworking plants are located. It includes Santo André, São Bernardo do Campo, and São Caetano do Sul, and usually Diadema as well; broad definitions also include the municipalities of Mauá, Ribeirão Pires, and Rio Grande da Serra.

28. Catholic labor activists related to the Church in different ways during this period. Mainwaring argues that JOC grew increasingly detached from the institutional church and from the sacraments, as its working-class allegiance became stronger than its religious one, in sharp contrast with the CEBs, which maintain strong institutional links. See Scott Mainwaring, "The Catholic Youth Workers' Movement (JOC) and the Emergence of the Popular Church in Brazil," Working Paper no. 6, Kellogg Institute, University of Notre Dame, December 1983.

29. There are a number of excellent historical works on the Brazilian labor movement. See especially Kenneth Paul Erickson, *The Brazilian Corporate State and Working Class Politics* (Berkeley: University of California Press, 1977). For a discussion of the bureaucratization of the trade unions, see Heloisa Helena Teixeira de Souza Martins, *O Estado e a Burocratização do Sindicato no Brasil* (São Paulo: Hucitec, 1979). A classic study of the establishment of state control over trade unions in São Paulo is Azis Simão's *O Sindicato e o Estado* (São Paulo: Dominus, 1966).

30. John Humphrey, *Capitalist Control and Workers' Struggle in the Brazilian Auto Industry* (Princeton: Princeton University Press, 1982).

31. For a retrospective look at forms of plant-level struggle during those years, see *abcd Jornal*, December 1979, pp. 3–4.

32. Many interviews with Lula in 1978 emphasized this point. See, e.g., "São Bernardo: Uma Experiência de Sindicalismo Autêntico," interview with Luís Inácio da Silva, in *Cara a Cara* 1 (July–December 1978): 54–66, especially pp. 58–60.

33. On this point see Vinícius Caldeira Brant, "Da Resistência aos Movimentos Sociais: A Emergência das Classes Populares em São Paulo," in *São Paulo: O Povo em Movimento,* ed. Singer and Brant, pp. 9–28.

34. *Coojornal,* July 1977.

35. Interview with Luís Inácio da Silva, *Pasquim* (March 24–31, 1978), reprinted in Luís Inácio da Silva, *Lula: Entrevistas e Discursos* (Guarulhos, SP: O Repórter de Guarulhos, 1981), p. 35.

36. Fernando Henrique Cardoso, "Partidos Políticos," in *São Paulo: O Povo em Movimento,* ed. Singer and Brant, p. 192.

37. Using *sublegenda* (literally, sub-slate), a party could run up to three candidates for an office. Their votes were then totaled to determine the winning party; within the winning party, the candidate with the most votes took office.

38. Fernando Henrique Cardoso, in "As Opções Políticas dos Empresários," 3d cycle of debates sponsored by the Grupo Casa Grande, Rio de Janeiro, May 8, 1978, published in Alfredo Bosi et al., *Conjuntura Nacional* (Petrópolis: Vozes, 1979), pp. 126–27.

39. On Cardoso's senatorial campaign, see Shiguenoli Miyamoto, "Eleições de 1978 em São Paulo: A Campanha," in *Voto de Desconfiança,* ed. Lamounier, pp. 117–72. Information on the campaign in São Bernardo comes from an interview with Devanir Ribeiro, at the time of the campaign an officer in the São Bernardo metalworkers' union, in São Paulo, November 29, 1982.

40. On the MDB and social movements in the 1978 elections, see Fernando Henrique Cardoso, "Partidos Políticos," in *São Paulo: O Povo em Movimento,* ed.

Singer and Brant, pp. 177–206, and Maria Helena Moreira Alves, *State and Opposition in Military Brazil*, pp. 141–68. The Cardoso article also contains a fascinating description of the internal functioning of the MDB. A collection of articles on the 1978 elections can be found in Lamounier, ed., *Voto de Desconfiança*.

41. See the interview of Almino Afonso by Augusto Nunes and Jorge Escoteguy, "O Diálogo Merece Respeito," *Veja*, March 29, 1978, pp. 3–6. See also Afonso's statements reproduced in Bosi et al., *Conjuntura Nacional*, pp. 46–50, 55–56. This book reproduces a series of debates from April to June 1978 in which prominent social scientists, political leaders, and leaders of important social movements discussed a series of problems of the democratic transition, ranging from party reform to agrarian reform, nuclear policy, and labor legislation.

42. For a good description of the April package, see Maria Helena Moreira Alves, *State and Opposition in Military Brazil*, pp. 148–51.

43. See José Alvaro Moisés, *Lições de Liberdade e de Opressão* (Rio de Janeiro: Paz e Terra, 1982), pp. 51–53.

44. On the Reform Package, see "Emenda Constitucional No. 11," *Constituição da República Federativa do Brasil* (Brasília: Câmara dos Deputados, Centro Gráfico, 1981), pp. 178–85. For a discussion of the package, see Maria Helena Moreira Alves, "The Formation of the National Security State" (Ph.D. diss., Massachusetts Institute of Technology, 1982), pp. 635–41.

45. See Kucinski, *Abertura*, pp. 91–95.

46. See José Alvaro Moisés, in the debate published as "Novos Partidos Políticos: As Tendências das Oposiçoes," *Contraponto* 3 (August 1978): 11–16; the quotation in the text is taken from p. 14.

47. Francisco Weffort, quoted in "A Crise Política e Institucional," *Revista de Cultura Contemporânea* 1 (January 1979): 55, 57–58. This article is a transcript of a debate on the Brazilian political crisis that took place at CEDEC on April 27, 1978. For further reflection in a similar vein, see Francisco Weffort, *Porque Democracia?* (São Paulo: Brasiliense, 1984), or his essay "Why Democracy?" in *Democratizing Brazil*, ed. Alfred Stepan (New York: Oxford University Press, 1989).

48. This point of view was expressed by Raimundo de Oliveira, in "Mesa Redonda: Novos Partidos Políticos," pp. 18–19.

49. Cardoso's comments are also taken from "Mesa Redonda: Novos Partidos Políticos," pp. 25, 26. Cardoso develops his point in a more theoretical vein in "Regime Político e Mudança Social."

50. Cybilis da Rocha, "Mesa Redonda: Novos Partidos Políticos," pp. 40–41.

51. For a theoretical discussion of the gap between the two kinds of demands, see Juan Carlos Torre, "Esquema para a Análise dos Movimentos Sociais na América Latina," *Revista de Cultura Contemporânea* 1 (January 1979): 67–74; see also, in the same issue, the debate "A Crise Política e Institucional," pp. 44–66.

52. Cardoso, in Bosi et al., *Conjuntura Nacional*, p. 116.

53. Antonio Gramsci, *Selections from the Prison Notebook*, ed. and tr. Quintin Hoare and Geoffrey Nowell Smith (New York: International Publishers, 1971), p. 330.

4 The New Unionism and the Formation of the Workers' Party

1. Collective bargaining was possible under the CLT, and where they existed collective contracts took legal precedence over individual ones. There is some evidence that at least in São Paulo, bargaining over wage increases became more common in the early 1960s prior to the military coup. In a survey of twenty-three contract disputes in São Paulo between January and March, 1964, Mericle found that 47.8 percent were resolved by collective bargaining. Nonetheless, the lack of a "duty to bargain" provision in the labor code meant that employers' incentive to bargain was the desire to avoid compulsory arbitration in the labor courts, an incentive which was rarely operative. See Kenneth Scott Mericle, "Conflict Regulation in the Brazilian Industrial Relations System" (Ph.D. diss., University of Wisconsin, 1974), pp. 200–207.

2. The text of the Consolidated Labor Laws of 1943 and amendments is in Adriano Campanhole and Hilton Lobo Campanhole, eds., *Consolidação das Leis do Trabalho e Legislação Complementar*, 62d ed. (São Paulo: Editora Atlas, 1983). The development of this legislation is discussed in José Albertino Rodrigues, *Sindicato e Desenvolvimento no Brasil*, 2d ed. (São Paulo: Edições Símbolo, 1978), chap. 2. Briefer descriptions in English are in Erickson, *Brazilian Corporative State*, pp. 27–49, and in Kenneth S. Mericle, "Corporatist Control of the Working Class: Authoritarian Brazil since 1964," in *Authoritarianism and Corporatism in Latin America*, ed. James M. Malloy (Pittsburgh: University of Pittsburgh Press, 1977).

3. Examples of this kind of approach include Alessandro Pizzorno, "Political Exchange and Collective Identity in Industrial Conflict," in Colin Crouch and Alessandro Pizzorno, eds., *The Resurgence of Class Struggle in Western Europe since 1968*, vol. 2 (New York: Holmes & Meier, 1978); Edward Shorter and Charles Tilly, *Strikes in France, 1830–1968* (London: Cambridge University Press, 1974); and Peter Lange and George Ross, "Conclusions: French and Italian Union Developments in Comparative Perspective," in Peter Lange, George Ross, and Maurizio Vannicelli, *Unions, Change and Crisis: French and Italian Union Strategy and the Political Economy, 1945–1980* (London: George Allen & Unwin, 1982).

4. There is an extensive literature on Brazilian labor from 1930 to 1964. In English, see Erickson, *Brazilian Corporative State*, and Harding, "Political History of Organized Labor." Key works in Portuguese are cited in the bibliography; see especially the work of Moraes Filho, Simão, Rodrigues, Weffort, Moisés, Maranhão, Neves, and Heloisa Martins.

5. For a more extensive discussion of this period, see Margaret E. Keck, "From Movement to Politics: The Formation of the Workers' Party in Brazil" (Ph.D. diss., Columbia University, 1986), pp. 76–101.

6. Angelina Cheibub Figueiredo, "Political Governamental e funções sindicais," 1975, mimeo, cited in Maria Hermínia Tavares de Almeida, "O sindicalismo brasileiro entre a conservação e a mudança," in *Sociedade e Política no Brasil pós-64*, ed. Sorj and Almeida, p. 199.

7. On wage policy and employment, see Fernando Lopes de Almeida, *Política Salarial, Emprego e Sindicalismo, 1964/1981* (Petrópolis: Vozes, 1982).

8. José Alvaro Moisés, "Problemas Atuáis do Movimento Operário no Brasil," *Revista de Cultura Contemporânea* 1 (July 1978): 49.

9. Luís Flávio Rainho and Osvaldo Martines Bargas, *As Lutas Operárias e Sindicais dos Metalúrgicos em São Bernardo, 1977/1979* (São Bernardo do Campo: Associação Benificente e Cultural dos Metalúrgicos de São Bernardo do Campo e Diadema, 1983), p. 39.

10. The importance of factory organization was evident in the fact that the São Bernardo union, which initiated the campaign, had up to seventeen union officers working in plants at any one time, with stability of employment, and that at one of the plants Humphrey studied this had had a significant effect on unionization between 1975 and 1978; Humphrey, *Capitalist Control and Workers' Struggle*, pp. 140–45. See also Rainho and Bargas, *As Lutas Operárias e Sindicais*, pp. 42–43.

11. "A Greve na Voz dos Trabalhadores da Scania a Itu," in *História Imediata*, ed. Oboré (São Paulo: Alfa-Omega, 1979), pp. 8–10.

12. "A Greve na Voz dos Trabalhadores," p. 56.

13. Maria Hermínia Tavares de Almeida, "Novo Sindicalismo e Política (Analise de uma Trajetória)," 1983, mimeo, p. 12.

14. Ninth Congress of Metal, Mechanical, and Electrical Workers of the State of São Paulo, Lins, São Paulo, January 22–26, 1979, *Atos*, Resolution on Party Politics, pp. 5–6.

15. On the *Carta de Princípios* controversy, see "Sindicatos lançam partido," *O Estado do São Paulo*, May 1, 1979; "Lançamento do PT divide sindicalistas," *Folha de São Paulo*, May 1, 1979; "Em seis capitais o PT anuncia seus planos," *Jornal da Tarde*, May 2, 1979; "Responsaveis pelo PT admitem que foram precipitados," *Folha de São Paulo*, May 4, 1979. A copy of the document is included in Mario Pedrosa, *Sobre o PT* (São Paulo: Ched Editorial, 1980), pp. 51–62.

16. Décimo Congresso dos Trabalhadores nas Industrias Metalúrgicas, Mecánicas e de Material Elétrico do Brasil, Poços de Caldas, MG, June 4–9, 1979, *Atos*, especially section from plenary session on national problems.

17. "Forças de oposição visam manter posição unitária," *Folha de São Paulo*, August 19, 1979.

18. "Dirigente Sindical defende um Partido dos Trabalhadores," *Jornal do Brasil*, August 19, 1979.

19. "Lula expõe princípios para o PT," *Folha de São Paulo*, August 19, 1979.

20. For the discussions among the union leaders, politicians, and intellectuals, I have depended in large part on interviews with Francisco Weffort, December 1982 (a meeting at which Lula was also present but rarely intervened); Roque Aparecido da Silva, November 27, 1982; and Maria Helena Moreira Alves, November 28, 1982.

21. "PT não quer ser só dos operários," *Jornal do Brasil*, September 19, 1979.

22. "Sindicalista não vê o PT como opção," *Folha de São Paulo*, September 28, 1979.

23. "Criadores do PT querem debater com estudantes," *Folha de São Paulo*, October 4, 1979.

24. Mario Morel, *Lula o Metalúrgico: Anatomia de uma Liderança* (Rio de Janeiro: Nova Fronteira, 1981), p. 33.

25. Ibid., pp. 41, 66–67.

26. Altino Dantas, Jr., ed., *Lula Sem Censura* (Petrópolis: Vozes, 1981), p. 29.

27. Morel, *Lula o Metalúrgico*, pp. 69–70.

28. Dantas, *Lula Sem Censura*, pp. 31–32.

29. Morel, *Lula o Metalúrgico*, p. 122.

30. Luís Inácio da Silva, *Lula*, p. 32.

31. For data on the number of workers in each sector on strike in 1978 and 1979, see Maria Helena Moreira Alves, "Formation of the National Security State," pp. 743–67.

32. António Hohlfeldt, "Olívio Dutra: Um Líder Sindical" (interview with Olívio Dutra), *Encontros com a Civilização Brasileira* 22 (April 1980): 11–36.

33. On Lula's role, see the interview with José Vilar Sobrinho, president of the Metalworkers' Union of João Monlevade, published as "O Sindicato de João Monlevade," *Cadernos do CEAS* 67 (May–June 1980): 55–67, especially p. 64. Sobrinho recounted that although the level of rank-and-file organization in João Monlevade was quite high by 1978, through the efforts of João Paulo Pires Vasconcelos, only after the ABC strikes was the Monlevade union able to win on a demand for a shorter work day, for which it had been struggling for nine years.

34. Vilmar Faria, "Desenvolvimento, Urbanização e Mudanças na Estrutura de Emprego: A Experiência Brasileira dos Ultimos Trinta Anos," in *Sociedade e Política no Brasil pós-64*, ed. Sorj and Almeida, pp. 146–47, 155.

35. Ibid., pp. 140, 152.

36. Edmar Bacha, "Crescimento Econômico, Salários Urbanos e Rurais: O Caso do Brasil," *Pesquisa e Planejamento Econômico* 5 (December 1979): 585–687, as cited in Faria, "Desenvolvimento, Urbanização e Mudanças," p. 156.

37. Faria, "Desenvolvimento, Urbanização e Mudanças," pp. 156, 158–59.

38. Almeida, "O Sindicalismo Brasileiro entre a Conservação e a Mudança," in *Sociedade e Política no Brasil pós-64*, ed. Sorj and Almeida, pp. 194–96.

39. On the Osasco and Contagem strikes, see Francisco Weffort, "Participação e Conflito Industrial: Contagem e Osasco, 1968," *Cadernos CEBRAP* 5 (1972). For a firsthand account by José Ibrahim, then president of the Metalworkers' Union of Osasco, see José Ibrahim, "A História do Movimento de Osasco," in *Cadernos do Presente* 2, n.d. Differences of approach between the union's left leadership and Catholic activists as to factory commissions, the strike, and other questions are discussed in Fernando Andrade, "Movimento Operário e Sindicatos: A Greve de Osasco vista por José Ibrahim" (interview with José Ibrahim), in *Debate* (Paris) 22 (May 1976): 25–28. For discussion of the strikes in the context of labor-state relations, see Erickson, *Brazilian Corporative State*, pp. 170–71, and Maria Helena Moreira Alves, *State and Opposition in Military Brazil*, pp. 80–91.

40. Maria d'Alva Gil Kinzo, "Novos Partidos: O Início do Debate," in *Voto de Desconfiança*, ed. Lamounier, p. 235.

41. Interview with Roque Aparecido da Silva, São Paulo, November 27, 1982.

42. *abcd Jornal*, February 1979. The editorial marveled at the fact that when

"authentic" unionists discussed the PT they were accused of dividing the opposition.

43. *abcd Jornal*, July 23–29, 1979.

44. This was most likely related to the announcement that Paulo Skromov made on September 2 that a signature campaign was about to begin. See "PT busca apoio com assinaturas," *Jornal do Brasil*, September 3, 1979.

45. *abcd Jornal*, August 27–September 2, 1979.

46. *abcd Jornal*, September 3–10, 1979.

47. *abcd Jornal*, September 10–17, 1979.

48. *abcd Jornal*, October 8–14, 1979.

49. "Dirigentes do PT formam núcleo no ABC," *Jornal do Brasil*, December 1, 1979.

50. "Lula concorde com frente de oposições," *Folha de São Paulo*, September 6, 1979.

51. "Lula visita favela carioca," *Folha de São Paulo*, July 27, 1980.

5 Structuring the Workers' Party

1. The reasons for such extensive regulation, like its effects, are complex and contradictory. According to Phyllis Peterson, the development of party legislation in Brazil from the 1930s to the early 1960s reflected an increasing commitment to making parties genuine vehicles for democratic representation; thus regulation was intended to ensure that parties were not established purely as personal vehicles of their founders and that they possessed some permanent institutional presence. See Peterson, "Brazilian Political Parties."

2. An exception in the Brazilian case is Maria d'Alva Gil Kinzo's study of the MDB, *Oposição e Autoritarismo* (São Paulo: IDESP/Vertice, 1988).

3. The text of the Organic Law of Political Parties, with annotations, is contained in *Legislação Eleitoral e Partidária* (Brasília: Senado Federal, Subsecretaria de Edições Técnicas, 1982).

4. A chartered relationship between organizations and the Brazilian state is by no means a new phenomenon, but it has not generally been examined in relation to the internal dynamics of political party development. For a description of the content of prior party legislation, see Peterson, "Brazilian Political Parties," chap. 2. Peterson interprets legal changes as an attempt "to perfect the workings of democracy through changes in the legal system" (p. 62) rather than as part of a broader tradition of state chartering. For a discussion of the state and interest organization in Brazil, see Philippe Schmitter, *Interest Conflict and Political Change in Brazil* (Stanford: Stanford University Press, 1971).

5. See *Legislação Eleitoral e Partidária*. A more detailed summary of the legislation can be found in Keck, "From Movement to Politics," pp. 228–34.

6. The Partido Popular was a conservative democratic party whose founders included São Paulo businessman Olavo Setubal and Minas Gerais politician Tancredo Neves. The PP merged with the PMDB at the end of 1981.

7. Partido dos Trabalhadores, "Declaração Política," São Bernardo do Campo, October 13, 1979.

8. The PT's use of the term *núcleo* corresponds to Sartori's definition of nuclei as "grass-roots, minimal, and local units. . . . The nucleus level of analysis includes the party militants and participants." Giovanni Sartori, *Parties and Party Systems: A Framework for Analysis* (Cambridge: Cambridge University Press, 1976), pp. 73–74.

9. A meeting to discuss this question was held in São Bernardo on November 21, with the participation of Jacó Bittar, Lula, Henos Amorina, Olivio Dutra, Francisco Weffort, and José Alvaro Moisés.

10. "PT não pretende adiantar-se ao anseio da base," *Folha de São Paulo,* November 25, 1979.

11. "Trabalhadores," *O Estado de São Paulo,* November 30, 1979.

12. On December 4, Lula, Wagner Benevides, Olívio Dutra, Jacó Bittar, and intellectuals involved in the PT met at the home of Vinícius Brant to discuss how it could be done. See "PT quer sair logo depois da sanção da lei," *Folha de São Paulo,* December 5, 1979.

13. These were Jacó Bittar, president of the oil workers' union of Paulinia, SP; Luís Inácio da Silva, president of the metalworkers' union of São Bernardo and Diadema, SP; José Cicote, an officer of the metalworkers' union of Santo André, SP; Paulo Skromov, president of the leather workers' union of São Paulo; Manoel da Conceição, former peasant leader who was imprisoned and exiled under the military regime; Henos Amorina, president of the metalworkers' union of Osasco, SP; José Ibrahim, president of the Osasco metalworkers at the time of the 1968 strike, after which he was imprisoned and exiled; Arnóbio Vieira da Silva, president of the rural workers' union of Itanhaém, SP; Wagner Benevides, president of the oil workers' union of Belo Horizonte, MG; Olívio Dutra, president of the bank workers' union of Porto Alegre, RS; and Edson Khair, federal deputy from Rio de Janeiro.

14. Partido dos Trabalhadores, "Pontos para elaboração do programa," São Paulo, January 1980. For discussions of the meeting at the Colégio Sion, see "PT adia eleição da comissão nacional," *Folha de São Paulo,* February 11, 1980; "PT, um partido que não quer agora o poder," *Jornal da Tarde* (São Paulo), February 11, 1980; *abcd Jornal,* February 12–25, 1980.

15. This issue is discussed in some detail later in this chapter.

16. For newspaper descriptions of the national meeting, see *Movimento,* June 9–15, 1980; "PT fará convenção nacional," *O Estado de São Paulo,* May 31, 1980; "Dirigentes do PT otimistas com seu Encontro Nacional," *Folha de São Paulo,* May 31, 1980; "Encontro Nacional do PT tende para uma chapa única," *Folha de São Paulo,* June 1, 1980; "Moderados devem dirigir PT," *O Estado de São Paulo,* June 1, 1980; and "PT não inclui Constituente em seu programa," "Líder de '68 comanda os radicais," and "Convenção aprova chapa única," all in *Jornal do Brasil,* June 2, 1980.

17. Those elected to the new national provisional commission were Lula, Jacó Bittar, Olívio Dutra, José Ibrahim, Wanderley Farias de Souza (Paraíba), federal deputies António Carlos de Oliveira (MS) and Freitas Deniz (MA), Luís Soares Dulci (former president of the Teachers' Union in Minas Gerais), Joaquim Arnaldo (from Ação Operária Católica, RJ), and Apolônio de Carvalho (long-time left activist who had been a founder of the PCBR).

18. *PT Boletim* 1 (September 1980): 1.

19. Acre, Rio Grande do Norte, Rio de Janeiro, Ceará, Rio Grande do Sul, Minas Gerais, Santa Catarina, Mato Grosso do Sul, Maranhão, Piauí, Espirito Santo, Goiás, and São Paulo.

20. These were Airton Soares, SP; Antônio Carlos de Oliveira, MS; Domingos de Freitas Deniz Neto, MA; Benedito Marcílio, SP; Luís Antônio Cechinel, SC, and João Cunha, SP. See "PT pede registro que deve sair até fim de novembro," *Folha de São Paulo,* October 23, 1980.

21. For a breakdown of party organizations by state in October 1980, see Keck, "From Movement to Politics," table 4.1, p. 245.

22. Acre, Amazonas, Maranhão, Piauí, Ceará, Mato Grosso do Sul, São Paulo, Rio de Janeiro, Goiés, and Espirito Santo. See "PT cumpre primeiras exigências," *Folha de São Paulo,* June 22, 1981; "PT atende à lei só em dez Estados," *Folha de São Paulo,* June 30, 1981.

23. In addition to the ten mentioned above, Paraná, Rio Grande do Sul, and Santa Catarina were legally recognized, and decisions were pending in Minas Gerais, Paraíba, and Pará. See "PT mobiliza 212,000 filiados para convenções em 16 Estados," *Jornal do Brasil,* September 6, 1981.

24. Various authors have noted the tendency of members of such parties to be participants in other kinds of organizations. See, e.g., Samuel H. Barnes, "Party Democracy and the Logic of Collective Action," in *Approaches to the Study of Party Organization,* ed. William J. Crotty (Boston: Allyn and Bacon, 1968), pp. 118–19.

25. "PT procura os discontentes," *O Estado de São Paulo,* January 15, 1980.

26. "PT tem apoio de deputado," *O Estado de São Paulo,* January 16, 1980.

27. "PT deseja disputar a eleição de 80," *O Estado de São Paulo,* January 24, 1980.

28. "Fernando Henrique quer grupo que coordene oposições," *Folha de São Paulo,* January 18, 1980.

29. "Lula não quer 'Clube de Bolinha,'" *Jornal do Brasil,* January 18, 1980.

30. For summary discussions of left positions regarding the PT, see "A crise da esquerda e o PT," *Em Tempo,* January 10–16, 1980, p. 11; "O que a esquerda pensa do PT," *Em Tempo,* June 19–July 2, 1980, p. 2; and Flávio Andrade, "Um partido ou uma frente?" *Em Tempo,* June 19–July 2, 1980, p. 3.

31. On this last point, see Teresa Caldeira, "Electoral Struggles in a Neighborhood on the Periphery of São Paulo," *Politics and Society* 15, no. 1 (1986–87): 43–66.

32. "Ser um partido de massa é a proposta do PT," *Folha de São Paulo,* February 22, 1980.

33. "Comunidade de base julga PT confiável, declara frei Beto," *Folha de São Paulo,* February 23, 1980.

34. António Flávio de Oliveira Pierucci, "Democracia, Igreja e Voto: O Envolvimento dos Padres de Paróquia de São Paulo nas Eleições de 1982" (Ph.D. diss., Departamento de Ciências Sociais, Faculdade de Filosofia, Letras e Ciências Humanas, Universidade de São Paulo, 1984), table 3.25, p. 227.

35. Ibid., p. 237.

36. Ibid., p. 206.

37. This was most notable in the case of Edson Khair, who was immediately accepted as a party leader because he was a congressman, not because he represented

a key constituency; Khair's allegiance to the PT project disappeared as soon as his leadership was challenged.

38. Gabeira has had an interesting history. His decision to join a guerilla group in the late 1960s is recounted in his fictionalized autobiography *O que é isso, companheiro?* (Rio de Janeiro: Editora Nova Fronteira, 1982); in two subsequent books he tells of his experiences in exile, his return to Brazil, and his gradual conversion from a more traditional left politics to ecological politics. For more on the relation between environmentalists and the PT, see Eduardo J. Viola, "The Ecologist Movement in Brazil, 1974–1986: From Environmentalism to Ecopolitics," *International Journal of Urban and Regional Research* 12 (June 1988), especially pp. 218–27.

39. Interview with Nilson Morão, PT candidate for governor in 1982, Rio Branco, Acre, December 19, 1982.

40. Interview with Dom Moacyr Grechi, December 19, 1982.

41. Interview with Devanir Ribeiro, November 29, 1982.

42. The statutes discussed here are reproduced in their entirety in Keck, "From Movement to Politics," pp. 266–69. The party statutes are discussed here as a declaration of intent, and not as a description of the actual functioning of the party. Making members of parliament responsible to the party executive (Art. 73)—and at its discretion to the nuclei (Arts. 72, 77) is a difficult process to carry out in practice. The de facto independence of parliamentary groups in relation to party organs in spite of statutory accountability (for example, to the General Conference in the British Labour party) has been noted in relation to many socialist or social democratic parties. See Klaus von Beyme, "Governments, Parliaments, and the Structure of Power in Political Parties," in *Western European Party Systems,* ed. Daalder and Mair, pp. 341–67, and Lewis Minkin and Patrick Seyd, "The British Labour Party," in *Social Democratic Parties in Western Europe,* ed. William E. Paterson and Alistair Thomas (New York: St. Martin's Press, 1977), pp. 106–07.

43. Partido dos Trabalhadores, "Resoluções Sobre Regimento Interno Aprovadas no Encontro do PT" (August 1981).

44. "Afinal, os Núcleos têm poder ou não?" *Em Tempo,* August 14–27, 1980, p. 5.

45. Flávio Andrade, "O PT é duplamente revolucionário," interview with Chico de Oliveira, *Em Tempo,* February 7–21, 1980, p. 4.

46. Gilberto Negreiros, "PT demonstra força com base em 15 Estados," *Jornal do Brasil,* October 5, 1980.

47. Partido dos Trabalhadores, Secretaria de Filiação e Nucleação, "Circular no. 02/82," São Paulo, March 25, 1982.

48. *PT São Paulo,* special edition, September 1983, p. 5.

49. "Organização: Prioridade para os nuclei" *PT Boletim Nacional* 7 (June 15, 1984), p. 3.

50. Partido dos Trabalhadores, Secretaria de Filiação e Nucleação, "Circular No. 02/82."

51. Information on diretório organization comes from address lists furnished by the PT regional diretório in São Paulo and from dossiers at the Tribunal Regional

Eleitoral of São Paulo. Information on the number of voters in the 1982 elections is from the Tribunal Regional Eleitoral.

52. Membership data for all parties come from the Tribunal Regional Eleitoral, São Paulo (membership reports for the last quarter of 1982 and the first quarter of 1985). These data are discussed in substantially more detail in Keck, "From Movement to Politics," pp. 275–89.

53. Stefano Bartolini, "The Membership of Mass Parties: The Social Democratic Experience, 1889–1978," in *Western European Party Systems*, ed. Hans Daalder and Peter Mair (Beverley Hills: Sage, 1983), pp. 195–96.

54. Ibid., p. 179.

55. For a discussion of the role of television in Brazil, see Joseph D. Straubhaar, "Television and Video in the Transition from Military to Civilian Rule in Brazil," *Latin American Research Review* 24, no. 1 (1989): 140–54.

56. Sartori, *Parties and Party Systems*, pp. 93–104.

57. Interview with Francisco Weffort, January 5, 1983.

58. Manifesto of the Group of 113, São Paulo, June 2, 1983.

59. Panebianco, *Political Parties*, p. 38.

60. Ibid., p. 40.

61. Olívio Dutra, "Um partido para a vida inteira," *PT Boletim Nacional* 25 (February 1987), special supplement: "Caderno das Tendências: O PT Debate o seu Destino."

62. Partido Comunista Brasileiro Revolucionário—Revolutionary Brazilian Communist party; the Fourth International faction of the PCBR was one of the organized tendencies functioning within the PT.

63. Resolution of the Comissão Politica da Comissão Executiva Nacional, April 14, 1986, published in *PT Boletim Nacional* 18 (May 1986), p. 3. See the same issue for extensive commentary on the incident. Some PT commentators believe that the robbery, coming as it did at the beginning of the 1986 electoral campaign, was too convenient to be coincidental. See Apolônio de Carvalho, "Diga não a provocação," in *PT Boletim Nacional* 18 (May 1986).

64. Resolution of Fourth National Meeting: "O Partido e as tendências," *PT Boletim Nacional* 19 (June 1986), p. 9.

65. See *PT Boletim Nacional* nos. 25 and 26, special sections: Caderno das Tendências, with contributions by Olívio Dutra, Raul Pont, Hélio Corbelini and Ruy Guimarães, Adeli Seli, Selvino Heck, and Tarso Genro. The following three numbers (27–29) continued the debate in the letters section. See also Augusto de Franco, "O PT, as tendências e a luta interna," pamphlet distributed by the PT Secretaria Nacional de Organização, 1987. For a summary of the debate, see Moacir Gadotti and Otaviano Pereira, *Pra Que PT* (São Paulo: Cortez Editora, 1989), pp. 143–50.

66. Hélio Corbelini and Ruy Guimarães, "PT: partido da ruptura popular," *PT Boletim Nacional* 25 (February 1987).

67. Raul Pont, "Um partido de massas e militante," *PT Boletim Nacional* 25 (February 1987). See discussion of this point in Moacir Gadotti and Otaviano Pereira, *Pra Que PT*, pp. 145–46.

68. "A Regulamentação das Tendências: PT: Partido estratégico rumo ao socialismo," resolution approved at the Fifth National Meeting, published in *PT Boletim Nacional* 33 (November 1987–January 1988).

69. See "A divergência da Convergência," *PT Boletim Nacional* 47 (October 1989), p. 23.

70. Apolônio de Carvalho, "Aqueles que devem ser excluidos do PT," *Teoria e Debates* 9 (January–March 1990), pp. 64–68.

71. See *PT Boletim Nacional* 52 (September 1990), pp. 6–7.

6 Campaigning to Organize

1. O'Donnell and Schmitter, *Transitions from Authoritarian Rule: Tentative Conclusions about Uncertain Democracies;* Adam Przeworski, "Democracy as a Contingent Outcome of Conflicts," paper presented at the Helen Kellogg Institute for International Affairs, University of Notre Dame, November 14–16, 1983.

2. Juan J. Linz, "The New Spanish Party System," in *Electoral Participation: A Comparative Analysis,* ed. Richard Rose (Beverly Hills: Sage, 1980), pp. 101–90.

3. Przeworski, *Capitalism and Social Democracy,* chaps. 1 and 3. Chapter 1 was originally published as Adam Przeworski, "Social Democracy as a Historical Phenomenon," *New Left Review* 122 (1980). Chapter 3 was co-written with John Sprague.

4. Luís Inácio da Silva, "Discurso pronunciado na I Convenção Nacional do PT," Brasília, September 27, 1981 (Edição da Comissão Executiva Nacional do PT, ND).

5. "Lula pede apoio às oposições," *Jornal do Brasil,* January 21, 1982.

6. Sartori, *Parties and Party Systems,* p. 10.

7. Ibid., p. 282, 281.

8. Scott Mainwaring uses the notion of "parties of the state" to "refer to parties that are to a considerable extent created by the state apparatus, are controlled by the state, and whose continuing existence depends on the use of state resources to secure support in civil society. Parties of the state do have linkages to civil society, but they tend to be constructed through clientelistic mechanisms rather than through representation of organized groups." Scott Mainwaring, "Brazilian Party Underdevelopment in Comparative Perspective," Working Paper no. 134, Kellogg Institute, University of Notre Dame, January 1990, pp. 6–7, 31*n*.

9. Partido dos Trabalhadores, "Carta Eleitoral," in "Carta Eleitoral traz estratégia e tática," *Jornal dos Trabalhadores* 2 (April 1982), special supplement, p. 3. Subsequent page citations are given in the text.

10. Interview with Francisco Weffort, São Paulo, January 5, 1983.

11. Around four thousand questionnaires were sent to candidates from the states of Ceará, Minas Gerais, Paraná, Pernambuco, Rio de Janeiro, Santa Catarina, and São Paulo; the response rate was 12.5 percent, with concentrations in Minas Gerais, Pernambuco, Rio de Janeiro, and São Paulo. See "Perfil do candidato," *Istoé,* November 17, 1982, pp. 46–48. More detailed data from the survey are reproduced in Keck, "From Movement to Politics," pp. 331–34.

12. Partido dos Trabalhadores, Secretaria Geral, "Circular 9/82," May 29–30, 1982.

13. Partido dos Trabalhadores, Comissão Executiva Nacional, "Circular Especial anexo 9/82," July 2, 1982.

14. "O PT distribui a sua renda," *Istoé,* July 14, 1982, p. 19.

15. Partido dos Trabalhadores, Comissão Executiva Nacional, "Informe sobre a reunião dos candidatos majoritários e recomendações da Comissão Eleitoral Unificado Nacional às Comissões Eleitorais Unificadas Estaduais," Brasília, July 3–4, 1982.

16. Interview with Francisco Weffort, São Paulo, January 5, 1983.

17. Partido dos Trabalhadores, Comissão Eleitoral Unificada Nacional, "Circular 02/82," Rio de Janeiro, August 25, 1982.

18. "PT abre sua campanha em São Paulo," *Folha de São Paulo,* April 21, 1982; "Uma festa na praça," *Istoé,* April 28, 1982, pp. 26–27; "O bicho-papão existe?" *Senhor,* May 5, 1982, pp. 14–16.

19. This observation is based on my own impressions from discussions with party members and from personal observation of the campaign rather than from a systematic examination of the composition of party caravans. Without the latter, it is difficult to evaluate conclusively the charges of favoritism that inevitably arose.

20. Henfil was known for both his cartoons and for his columns in the magazine *Istoé,* which took the form of letters to his mother. A hemophiliac, his death from aids in the late 1980s meant the loss of one of the Brazilian opposition's best-loved cultural figures.

21. On political class formation see Przeworski, *Capitalism and Social Democracy,* chap. 2.

22. The first two were cosponsored by TV Globo and the newspaper *O Estado de São Paulo;* the third debate was cosponsored by TV-Bandeirantes and the newspaper *Folha de São Paulo.*

23. See *Istoé,* August 18, 1982, p. 25.

24. Luís Inácio Lula da Silva, election speech, Pacaembu stadium, São Paulo, November 7, 1982. Tape recording.

25. Note also that while illiterates were denied the vote and thus could not be members of parties, they could attend campaign rallies. This was probably less salient in São Paulo than it was in rural states; party leaders in Acre estimated that around half of PT sympathizers were illiterate. Interview with Nilson Morão and Chico Mendes, December 19, 1982.

26. The main slogan of Koltoi's campaign was *Desobedeça* (Disobey), and her style was quite similar to that of a Green party candidate in Germany.

27. The party's use of television was one of the major differences between the 1982 and 1985 campaigns, discusssed below. The problem in 1982 was a combination of inexperience in thinking about political communication together with the rigidity of the *Lei Falcão* format, and fear of experimenting within that format because the party lacked funds to make a new filmstrip if the first one were outlawed (as occurred with the PMDB).

28. The accusation that Lula was incapable of governing was not an official PMDB position, but it was nonetheless widespread in discussion and debate during the campaign.

29. "PMDB e PT, uma profunda rivalidade," *O Estado de São Paulo,* October 8, 1982.

30. Roland M. Serra, "Nosso adversário é o PMDB, afirma Lula," *Folha de São Paulo,* May 16, 1982, p. 5.

31. "Maria Tavares convoca intelectuais à política," *Folha de São Paulo,* May 23, 1982.

32. Claudio Abramo, "O PT, vítima de sua sindrome," *Folha de São Paulo,* May 23, 1982.

33. Schmitter notes this characteristic in his conclusions to *Interest Conflict and Political Change.* See also Roberto da Matta, "Você sabe com quem está falando," *Carnavais, Malandros e Herois: Para uma Sociologia do Dilema Brasileiro* (Rio de Janeiro: Zahar, 1981).

34. Luiz Carlos Bresser Pereira, "O drama do PT," *Folha de São Paulo,* May 25, 1982. It is interesting in the light of Bresser's position in 1982 to note that in late 1989, he was one of those who most strongly advocated that his party (the PSDB) support Lula in the second round of the presidential elections.

35. Luís Inácio Lula da Silva, speech at election rally in Ubatuba, SP, August 28, 1982. Tape recording.

36. Luís Inácio Lula da Silva, election speech, Pacaembu stadium, São Paulo, November 7, 1982. Tape recording.

37. The complete list of municipal council members elected in the state is provided in *PT São Paulo* 2 (December 1982).

38. The data on candidate performance come from the Tribunal Regional Eleitoral, São Paulo. These data appear in table form in Keck, "From Movement to Politics," pp. 364–67.

39. For a more detailed discussion of the legislative elections, see Keck, "From Movement to Politics," pp. 364–69.

40. Gláucio Ary Dillon Soares, *Colégio Eleitoral, Convençoes Partidàrias, e Eleições Diretas* (Petrópolis: Vozes, 1984), pp. 33–35.

41. Ibid., p. 42.

42. See Keck, "From Movement to Politics," p. 371.

43. For a sample of the response of a variety of party leaders to the election results, see *PT São Paulo* 2 (December 1982).

44. *Folha de São Paulo,* November 24, 1985, p. 15; a comparison of 1982 and 1985 PT results is in Keck, "From Movement to Politics," p. 379.

45. "Lula defende candidaturas petistas em todos os Estados," *Folha de São Paulo,* November 24, 1985, p. 15.

46. In 1986 elected PT deputies included the following: from Espirito Santo, Vitor Buaiz, who had placed second in the 1985 mayoral elections in Vitoria; from Minas Gerais, Paulo Delgado, João Paulo Pires Vasconcelos, and Virgílio Guimarães; from Rio de Janeiro, Benedita da Silva and Wladimir Palmeira; from Rio Grande do Sul, Olívio Dutra and Paulo Renato Paim; from São Paulo, Luís Inácio

Lula da Silva, Plínio de Arruda Sampaio, Luiz Gushiken, Florestan Fernandes, Eduardo Jorge, José Genoino Neto, Irma Passoni, and Gumercindo Milhomen. See report on elections in *PT Boletim Nacional* 24 (January 1987), p. 11.

47. A complete list of state deputies elected in 1986 is available in *PT Boletim Nacional* 24 (January 1987), p. 11.

48. Maria Tereza Sadek argues that the PMDB had begun on this trajectory in 1986; see "A Interiorização do PMDB nas Eleições de 1986 em São Paulo," in *Eleições/1986,* ed. Maria Tereza Sadek (São Paulo: IDESP/Vertice, 1989), pp. 67–88.

49. The initial reports that the party had won in thirty-six municipalities, which can be found in much of the news media and even in several books published soon after the elections, were misleading. In fact, the party apparently won in thirty-two, but lost one of those when the mayor changed parties.

50. The complete list is as follows: in São Paulo—the municipalities of Cardoso, Campinas, Cedral, Conchas, Cosmópolis, Diadema, Jaboticabal, Piracicaba, Presidente Bernardes, Santo André, Santos, São Bernardo do Campo, and São Paulo; in Rio Grande do Sul—Porto Alegre, Ronda Alta, and Severiano de Almeira; in Santa Catarina—Campo Erê; in Paraná, Salto do Lontra and São João do Triunfo; in Minas Gerais—Amambai, Ilicinea, Ipatinga, João Monlevade, and Timóteo; Angra dos Reis in Rio de Janeiro; Jaguaré and Vitoria in Espirito Santo; Amelia Rodrigues and Jaguaquara in Bahia; Janduis in Rio Grande do Norte; and Icapuí in Ceará. *PT Boletim Nacional* 47 (October 1989), p. 1.

51. "Pesquisa diz que 40% dos vereadores petistas eleitos são ligados ao campo," *Folha de São Paulo,* December 7, 1988, p. 6.

52. Of the twenty-two candidates, fourteen won less than 1 percent of the vote.

53. Others in the group with more than 1 percent of the vote were Mário Covas, who won 10.78 percent (Covas's PSDB split from the PMDB in 1988, claiming that the latter had abandoned its historic identity in favor of pure opportunism); Paulo Maluf, again the PDS candidate, with 8.28 percent; Afif Domingos of the Liberal party with 4.53; and Roberto Freire of the Communist party with 1.06. Final results from the Tribunal Superior Eleitoral, in *Folha de São Paulo,* November 22, 1989, p. B8.

54. The Green party (PV) was initially part of the coalition but split off after a struggle over the vice presidential slot on the ticket. Initial (though by no means unanimous) PT support for the nomination of Green leader Fernando Gabeira met with implacable opposition from other parties in the coalition (and from important segments of the PT as well) to Gabeira on the basis of the his support for legalizing marijuana and declared bisexuality.

55. The campaign song was called "Sem Medo de Ser Feliz" (Unafraid to be happy). It was reminiscent of the campaign song in the 1988 Chilean plebiscite, with its "joy is on its way" refrain; this may not be coincidental, as Francisco Weffort told me in December 1989 that PT campaign organizers looked at the Chilean campaign as one of the successful examples to be emulated in their campaign style.

56. See "Collor e Lula mostram seus programas e fazem um debate bem-comportado na TV," *Folha de São Paulo,* December 4, 1989, pp. B1.

57. In addition to a series of virulent attacks on PT municipal administrations, which included a number of charges that were patently false (for example, that bus fares in São Paulo were higher than in any other state capital), Collor mounted a personal attack on Lula by paying a woman with whom Lula had had a child fifteen years before, Miriam Cordeiro, to attack him in Collor's television ads. The facts of the case had been widely discussed in the media a year before, and it was generally believed that Lula had behaved responsibly (by acknowledging his daughter and providing support for her). Nonetheless, the ads had a tremendous emotional impact on Lula, largely because of their impact on his daughter.

58. Figures from *Latin American Regional Reports Brazil,* February 15, 1990.

59. See John French, "Workers and the Rise of Adhemarista Populism in São Paulo, Brazil, 1945–47," *Hispanic American Historical Review* 68, no. 1 (1988): 1–43. Percentages for 1982 and 1986 are calculated from election results obtained at the Tribunal Regional Eleitoral, São Paulo.

7 The Workers' Party and the Labor Movement

1. On the early history of the British Labour party, see Ross McKibbon, *The Evolution of the Labour Party, 1910–1924* (Oxford: Clarendon Press, 1974). For Germany see Carl Schorske, *German Social Democracy, 1905–1917* (New York: Harper & Row, 1955), pp. 49–50.

2. Campanhole and Campanhole, eds., *Consolidação das Leis do Trabalho,* p. 119.

3. See *Boletim do DIEESE,* 1981–83.

4. *Brazil Labour Report* (São Paulo), October–December 1984, p. 3.

5. Cited in Luís Roberto Serrano, "Em busca de definições," *Istoé,* August 26, 1981. The IBGE estimates the total Economically Active Population in 1980 at 43,235,712. For an economist's view of unemployment, see Roberto Macedo, "A Dimensão Social da Crise," in *FMI X Brasil: A armadilha da recessão* (São Paulo: Forum Gazeta Mercantil, 1983), pp. 217–49.

6. *Boletim do DIEESE,* vol. 1, no. 1, 1982, p. 13.

7. Inflation figures are drawn from *Almanaque Abril* (São Paulo: Editora Abril, 1983, 1985).

8. On the demands of metalworkers' unions in 1981–82, see Márcia de Paula Leite, "Revindicações Sociais dos Metalúrgicos," *Cadernos Cedec* 3 (1984). Rights to representation won in contract negotiations are listed monthly in the *Boletim do DIEESE.*

9. On Pazzianottto's career, see Renato Faleiros, "Entrevista: Almir Pazzianotto Pinto, um doutor em greves," *Veja,* May 21, 1980, pp. 3–6.

10. "Volta às mesas," *Istoé,* September 25, 1985, pp. 84–86.

11. The acronym CONCLAT has been used on three different occasions, which can lead to a certain amount of confusion. The National Conference of the Working Class (Conferência Nacional da Classe Trabalhadora, CONCLAT) was held in August 1981 in Praia Grande, São Paulo. The National Congress of the Working Class (Congresso Nacional da Classe Trabalhadora, CONCLAT) was held in São Bernardo in August 1983 and founded the United Central Workers' Organization

(Central Unica dos Trabalhadores, CUT). The third CONCLAT, or National Coordination of the Working Class (Coordenação Nacional da Classe Trabalhadora), was founded at a meeting in Praia Grande, SP, in November 1983, by unions that supported a different kind of trade union strategy from that of the CUT.

12. Federation and confederation elections, under the CLT system, take place on the basis of one union, one vote. Thus, the vote of the São Paulo Metalworkers' Union, the largest union in Latin America, which represents over 300,000 workers, carries the same weight as that of a metalworkers' union with only a few hundred members.

13. The combative unions were still a numerical minority; in 1984 pelegos controlled an estimated 70 percent of Brazil's unions. One of the best chronological accounts on the different tendencies in the labor movement during this period is Clarice Melamed Menezes and Ingrid Sarti, *CONCLAT 1981: A Melhor Expressão do Movimento Sindical Brasileiro* (Rio de Janeiro: ILDES, 1982).

14. On the 1980 metalworkers' strike, see Margaret Keck, "Brazil: Metalworkers' Strike," *NACLA Report on the Americas*, July–August 1980, pp. 42–44, and Moisés, *Lições de Liberdade e de Opressão*, pp. 161–96. On criticisms of the strike, see Menezes and Sarti, *CONCLAT 1981*, pp. 29–30.

15. José Carlos Aguiar Brito, *A Tomada da Ford: O Nascimento de um Sindicato Livre* (Petrópolis: Vozes, 1983). The text of the agreement is in *Boletim do DIEESE*, February 1982, pp. 14–24.

16. Menezes and Sarti, *CONCLAT 1981*, pp. 43–57. For good contemporary accounts see Luiz Roberto Serrano, "Em busca de definições," *Istoé*, August 26, 1981, pp. 70–73, and T. Canuto et al., "Falam os Trabalhadores," *Movimento*, August 31–September 6, 1981, pp. 11–14. After the CONCLAT, the National Pró-CUT Commission published a booklet called *Tudo sobre a CONCLAT* (São Paulo: CIDAS, 1981), containing the conference resolutions and short interviews with leading figures.

17. CONTAG, "Porque Decidimos não Participar do Congresso da Classe Trabalhadora e Somos Pelo seu Adiamento para 1983," document signed by the president of CONTAG and presidents of twenty agricultural union federations.

18. For an example of the position of the autêntico tendency, see the pamphlet "CUT Pela Base" produced by ANAMPOS, June 1982. Minutes of the dissident meeting of a section of the pró-CUT Commission held in São Bernardo do Campo on August 28–29, 1982, taken by Maria Helena Moreira Alves, describe the debate that followed the nonattendance of those who favored postponement of the conference. At this meeting it was decided to participate in the September 11–12 meeting of the pró-CUT to be held at CONTAG headquarters in Brasília, at which a final decision would be made about calling the next CONCLAT.

19. "Salário Minimo," *Boletim do Dieese*, Edição Especial, April 1983.

20. Joaquimzão, as he is called, was the military appointee in 1965 to replace the purged president of the São Paulo Metalworkers' Union. He won union elections for the next two decades, despite a growing opposition spearheaded by members of the Catholic church's labor pastoral. In the early 1980s, the strength of the opposi-

tion and the changing political situation forced him to try to shed his pelego image.

21. Labor leaders put the number of strikers at three million nationwide. In São Paulo, there were significant stoppages in the capital and eighteen other cities; in Rio Grande do Sul, the strike reached Porto Alegre, Canoas, and nine other cities. There were also strikes in Pernambuco, Espirito Santo, Rio de Janeiro, Goiás, and Paraná. For more detail, see *Boletim do DIEESE,* July 1983, pp. 17–18. See also Margaret Keck, "Update on the Brazilian Labor Movement," *Latin American Perspectives* 11 (Winter 1984): 27–34.

22. These were the oil workers from Paulinha and São José dos Campos in São Paulo and Mataripe in Bahia, the metalworkers of São Bernardo and Diadema, and the São Paulo bank workers and subway workers.

23. The direct translation of the CUT's name is misleading, as it was not in fact the only central organization created during this period; in the text I use the Portuguese name or the acronym.

24. Roque Aparecido da Silva, "Sindicato e Sociedade na Palavra dos Metalúrgicos," in Comisión de Movimientos Laborales (CLACSO), *El Sindicalismo Latinoamericano en los Ochenta* (Santiago: CLACSO, n. d.). This volume is a collection of papers presented at a seminar in Santiago, Chile, May 20–23, 1985.

25. "O que é que a CUT tem," *Senhor,* February 4, 1986, pp. 30–34.

26. Interview with Olívio Dutra, Porto Alegre, December 14, 1982.

27. See "Jogo aberto no PCB," *Istoé,* January 22, 1986.

28. The national executive was composed of Lula (president), Olívio Dutra (1st vice president), Manoel da Conceição (2d vice president), Apolônio de Carvalho (3d vice president), Jacó Bittar (secretary general), Francisco Weffort (2d secretary), Freitas Deniz (treasurer), Clovis da Silva (2d treasurer), Luís Soares Dulci, José Ibrahim, and Wagner Benevides. Alternates were Helena Greco, Joaquim Arnaldo, Hélio Bicudo, Eleiser, and Luís Eduardo Greenhalg. Six were from São Paulo, five from Minas Gerais, two from Rio Grande do Sul, and one each from Pernambuco, Rio de Janeiro, Maranhão, and Mato Grosso do Sul. See "Lula mantém a presidência nacional do PT," *Folha de São Paulo,* August 10, 1981, and "PT vai reeleger Lula," *Jornal do Brasil,* August 10, 1981.

29. Partido dos Trabalhadores, Diretório Nacional, Secretaria Sindical, "Circular 1/82" (no date).

30. "Manifesto do Encontro Nacional Sindical do PT," July 24–25, 1982.

31. *PT São Paulo,* Special Issue, September 1983, p. 5.

32. See Leôncio Martins Rodrigues, *CUT: Os Militantes e a Ideologia* (São Paulo: Paz e Terra, 1990), p. 21.

33. Interview with Luís Inácio Lula da Silva in Aloísio Mercadante, "A relação partido/sindicato," São Paulo, INCA, *Cadernos de Debates* 1 (1987): 25, cited in Gadotti and Pereira, *Pra Que PT,* p. 160.

34. "Lula faz ataques a Brizola," *Folha de São Paulo,* December 12, 1988, p. A5.

35. For these data see Leôncio Martins Rodrigues, *Partidos e Sindicatos: Escritos de Sociologia Política* (São Paulo: Editora Atica, 1990), pp. 17–24.

36. Ibid., p. 25.

37. Ibid., p. 9.

38. Eduardo Garuti Noronha, "Relações Trabalhistas," *Brasil 1987*, Relatório sobre a Situação Social do Pais (Working Paper, Núcleo de Estudos de Políticas Públicas, UNICAMP, 1987), cited in Rodrigues, *CUT*, p. 52.

39. Rodrigues, *CUT*, p. 64.

40. Ibid., p. 51.

41. Przeworski, *Capitalism and Social Democracy*, pp. 71, 73, 69.

42. Peter Lange and George Ross, "Conclusions: French and Italian Union Developments," in Lange, Ross, and Vannicelli, *Unions, Change and Crisis*, p. 220.

43. Ibid., pp. 221–22.

44. See also in this regard Adam Przeworski, "Material Bases of Consent: Economics and Politics in a Hegemonic System," *Political Power and Social Theory* 1 (1980): 21–66.

45. Lange and Ross, "Conclusions," pp. 273–75.

46. Ibid., p. 277.

47. Ibid., p. 219.

48. For a discussion of repression and opportunity for collective action, see Charles Tilly, *From Mobilization to Revolution* (Reading, Mass.: Addison Wesley, 1978), chap. 4.

49. Shorter and Tilly, *Strikes in France*, p. 345.

50. Sabine Erbès-Seguin, "Les Deux Champs de l'affrontement professionel," *Sociologie du travail* 18 (April–June 1976): 121–38.

8 The Workers' Party and Political Institutions

1. Ricardo de Azevedo, "Conselhos Populares: Uma Varinha de Condão?" *Teoria e Debate* 4 (September 1988): 46–49.

2. For a historical discussion of this debate, see Carmen Sirianni, "Councils and Parliaments: The Problems of Dual Power and Democracy in Comparative Perspective," *Politics and Society* 12, no. 2 (1983): 83–123.

3. For a description of the experiment in popular participation in municipal administration in Lajes, see Márcio Moreira Alves, *A Força do Povo: Democracia Participativa em Lajes* (São Paulo: Editora Brasiliense, 1980).

4. Partido dos Trabalhadores, Secretaria de Educação Política, Diretório Regional de São Paulo, "As Eleições de 82—o PT e a Questão Municipal" (Texto para Discussão, 1982), p. 57.

5. Even most PT members were unaware of the PT administration in Santa Quitéria, a small town in the interior of Maranhão. Members of the Santa Quitéria administration first met the PT's national leadership at the founding meeting of the CUT in São Bernardo in August 1983. In 1985, a member of the PT national executive was unable to tell me what had happened in Santa Quitéria, but he thought that due to local pressures the members of the administration had left the party. The PT's victory there, in a municipality whose voting population is made up of very poor rural workers, was mainly due to support from the local priest and the fact that no other opposition party was represented there. (Information from personal discussions with members of the Santa Quitéria administration, August 1983.)

6. Maria Tereza Sadek R. de Sousa, "Concentração Industrial e Estrutura Partidária: O Processo Eleitoral no ABC, 1966–1982," pp. 34–35.

7. Instituto Brasileiro de Geografia e Estatística, *Anúario Estatístico do Brasil 1983*, pp. 130–31.

8. It is estimated that 90 percent of the population of Diadema comes from the north or northeast of Brazil. See Sousa, "Concentração Industrial e Estrutura Partidária," pp. 188ff.

9. Maria Helena Moreira Alves, "Diadema: An Experience of Popular Government within an Authoritarian Context," paper presented at the 12th International Congress of the Latin American Studies Association, Mexico City, September 28–October 1, 1983, pp. 7–8. As figures for Diadema are not given in isolation in the census summaries, Alves data were obtained directly from the IBGE when she was director of public relations for the municipality of Diadema, 1982–83.

10. Ibid., p. 8.

11. The city did not even have a water and sewage system until 1973. See Sousa, "Concentração Industrial e Estrutura Partidária," p. 188.

12. Ibid., pp. 193–202.

13. Tribunal Regional Eleitoral Estado de São Paulo, "Quadro Demonstrativo de Filiações Partidárias," October-December 1982.

14. Tribunal Regional Eleitoral de São Paulo. This is the number that actually went to the polls in November 1982.

15. *Boletim da Comissão Municipal de Diadema*, March 1981.

16. Tribunal Regional Eleitoral, São Paulo.

17. See "Carta de Compromisso dos Futuros Parlamentares do Partido dos Trabalhadores," approved at Diadema's 1982 electoral preconvention. The candidates also agreed to declare their goods, to refuse bribes, to convoke a yearly assembly of inhabitants in which the mayor would render an accounting of the administration, to dedicate 50 percent of their time to parliamentary activity and 50 percent to grassroots organizing, and to contribute 50 percent of their salaries to the party if their income was more than five times the minimum wage. Noncompliance with this agreement was to lead to expulsion from the party.

18. See, e.g., *Diadema Jornal*, November 24, 1982; on the formation of the first council in the neighborhood of Eldorado, see *Jornal do Planalto*, January 21, 1983.

19. Interview with Cleusa de Oliveira, president of the municipal diretório of the PT of Diadema, SP, September 5, 1983.

20. Ibid.

21. Interview with Mayor Gilson Menezes, Diadema, SP, September 14, 1983.

22. Interview with Gilson Menezes in "Diadema: Lição de Democracia," *Em Tempo*, July 23, 1983, p. 8.

23. Interview with Maria Helena Moreira Alves, director of public relations for the municipality of Diadema, SP, July 20, 1983.

24. *Informativo Municipal*, Diadema, Edição Especial, February 1985.

25. *Diário do Grande ABC*, January 23, 1983.

26. Alves, "Diadema," p. 6.

27. See Alves, "Diadema," p. 10, and *Jornal do Planalto*, April 1, 1983, p. 1.

28. For descriptions of the programs sponsored by the planning department I relied on several informal discussions with Amir António Khair, July–September 1983; discussions with Valeska Peres, internal project coordinator for the planning department, over the same period; numerous discussions and a formal interview on July 20, 1983, with Maria Helena Moreira Alves, director of public relations for the administration, and her paper "Diadema." It is also based on my personal observations in several months of almost weekly visits to Diadema between July and September 1983. A list of the projects initiated by the department is contained in Amir António Khair's letter of resignation as head of the planning department dated May 3, 1984.

29. Interview with José Augusto da Silva Ramos, director of Health Department, Diadema, SP, July 20, 1983.

30. The survey was done by the Department of Public Relations in collaboration with the Young Peoples' Pastoral of the Catholic church.

31. *Em Tempo,* July 23, 1983, p. 8.

32. "Lula admite intervenção do diretório em Diadema," *Diário do Grande ABC,* July 16, 1983, p. 5.

33. Interview with Cleusa de Oliveira, Diadema, SP, September 5, 1983.

34. "Documento elaborado pela equipe do Departamento de Planejamento da Prefeitura de Diadema por ocasião da crise que culminou com a exoneração do seu diretor e respectiva equipe de assessores." Diadema, SP, May 3, 1984. This document and Khair's resignation letter of the same date detail the building tension between the department and the mayor much more fully than can be done here. Khair also explained his position in a page dedicated to debate on the Diadema situation, by decision of the regional diretório of São Paulo on May 12, in "Nosso trabalho sofreu restrições e bloqueios," *PT São Paulo* 4 (July 1984), p. 7, side by side with a reply from Gilson Menezes, "Administração se impõe por suas realizações," which discusses achievements of the administration, mainly in the areas of health, education, and transit, without mention of either the role of the Planning Department or the work in the favelas.

35. *PT São Paulo Boletim,* June 1984.

36. *PT São Paulo Boletim,* May 1985.

37. For a concise assessment of the Diadema administration, see "PT capitaliza governo em Diadema e vence prefeito," *Folha de São Paulo,* November 27, 1988, p. A13. A retrospective analysis in greater depth can be found in Valeska Peres Pinto, "A Vitrine do ABC," *Teoria e Debate* 3 (June 1988): 11–15.

38. Azevedo, "Conselhos Populares," p. 47.

39. M. Ostrogorski, *Democracy and the Organization of Political Parties,* 2 vols. (Chicago: Quadrangle Books, 1964).

40. R. T. McKenzie, *British Political Parties* (London: William Heinemann, 1955).

41. Barnes, "Party Democracy and the Logic of Collective Action"; Minkin and Seyd, "The British Labour Party," in *Social Democratic Parties in Western Europe,* ed. Paterson and Thomas, pp. 106–07.

42. The study involved an analysis of daily transcripts of legislative sessions in

the *Diário do Congresso Nacional* for the federal chamber of deputies and the *Diário Oficial do Estado* for the state legislature in São Paulo.

43. "Projeto de Lei 11/83," *Diário Oficial do Estado*, São Paulo, April 3, 1983; "Projeto de Lei 137/83," *Diário Oficial do Estado*, São Paulo, April 27, 1983; "Projeto de Lei 193/83," *Diário Oficial do Estado*, São Paulo, May 17, 1983.

44. "Projeto de Lei 282/83," *Diário Oficial do Estado*, São Paulo, June 16, 1983; "Moção 51/83," *Diário Oficial do Estado*, São Paulo, June 12, 1983.

45. "Projeto de Lei 221/83," *Diário Oficial do Estado*, São Paulo, May 24, 1983.

46. "Projeto de Lei 232/83," *Diário Oficial do Estado*, São Paulo, May 26, 1983.

47. "Projeto de Lei 246/83," *Diário Oficial do Estado*, São Paulo, May 28, 1983.

48. The two cosponsored with PMDB deputies, on bus passes and food assistance, were "Projeto de Lei 129/83" and "Projeto de Lei 160/83," in *Diário Oficial do Estado*, São Paulo, April 21 and May 5, 1983, respectively. The tax exemption law, sponsored by Eduardo Jorge, was "Projeto de Lei 222/83," *Diário Oficial do Estado*, São Paulo, May 25, 1983.

49. Luiza Erundina was subsequently elected to the state legislature in 1986 and became mayor of São Paulo after the 1988 elections.

50. *PT São Paulo*, Edição Especial, September 1983; *PT Boletim Nacional*, December 20, 1983.

51. *Istoé*, December 7, 1983.

52. *Istoé*, January 18, 1984, pp. 18–20.

53. Results of a Gallup poll noted in *Istoé*, February 1, 1984, pp. 19–20.

54. "Nota da bancada do Partido dos Trabalhadores," Brasília, October 10, 1984.

55. "O Partido dos Trabalhadores, as Diretas, e a Transição," n.d., position paper for party pre-conventions signed by twenty-three prominent PT members, including Soares and São Paulo state deputies Marco Aurélio Ribeiro and Paulo Fratesci.

56. Partido dos Trabalhadores, Diretório Nacional, "O PT e o Momento Político," October 21, 1984, cited in Articulação, "Contra o Continuismo e o Pacto Social Por uma Alternativa Democrática e Popular," São Paulo, December 12, 1984.

57. Federal deputies who were members of the party executive included party president Olívio Dutra, Paulo Delgado (MG), Luiz Gushiken (SP), José Genoino Neto (SP), and Luís Inácio Lula da Silva (SP). Former federal deputies were Djalma de Souza Bom and Luiz Soares Dulci, and state deputies were José Dirceu (SP), the party's secretary general, and Marcelo Deda (SE). See list of members of the new national executive and the national diretório elected at the Fifth National Meeting of the party on December 4–6, 1987, in *PT Boletim Nacional* 33 (November/December 1987–January 1988).

58. Partido dos Trabalhadores, "Constituição da República Federativa Democrática do Brasil: Projeto de Constituição apresentado pela bancada do Partido dos Trabalhadores à Assembléia Nacional Constituinte," Brasília, May 6, 1987. The draft was published as Fábio Konder Comparato, *Muda Brasil* (São Paulo: Editora Brasiliense, 1986).

59. A detailed discussion of the popular amendment process can be found in

Francisco Whitaker et al., *Cidadão Constituinte: A Saga das Emendas Populares* (São Paulo: Paz e Terra, 1989).

60. By 1986, the number of parties registered or seeking registration had gone up significantly. Eleven parties won seats in the 1986 federal congress. The breakdown for the 487 seats in the Chamber of Deputies was as follows: PMDB, 257; PFL, 118; PDS, 33; PDT, 24; PTB, 18; PT, 16; PC do B, 6; PL (Partido Liberal), 6; PDC (Partido Democrata Cristão), 5; PCB, 3; and PSB (Partido Socialista Brasileiro), 1. Figures are taken from Leôncio Martins Rodrigues, *Quem é Quem na Constituinte* (São Paulo: Oesp-Maltese, 1987), p. 17. This breakdown shifted somewhat as deputies left their posts and were replaced by alternates.

61. Mainwaring produced a Rice Index of party cohesion for eleven roll call votes in the Constituent Assembly by taking the percentage of party members voting with the majority of the party, subtracting the percentage of members voting against, and multiplying by 100. He compared the votes only for the six major parties (PMDB, PDS, PFL, PTB, PDT, and PT). The Rice Index for the PT was 100, followed by 86 for the PDT, 58 for the PFL, 47 for the PDS, 41 for the PTB, and 33 for the PMDB. Mainwaring, "Brazilian Party Underdevelopment in Comparative Perspective," p. 13.

62. In the case of the PT, the party's internal bylaws explicitly reject the notion of candidato nato. For an excellent discussion of the autonomy of Brazilian politicians in relation to their parties, see Mainwaring, "Political Parties and Prospects for Democracy in Brazil."

63. Hagopian, "Politics of Oligarchy," pp. 372–74.

64. Speech at the Fifth National Meeting, reproduced in *PT Boletim Nacional* 33 (November/December 1987–January 1988).

65. "Por um PT de Massas, Democrático e Socialista," reproduced in *PT Boletim Nacional* 33.

66. Ibid. The reference to direct elections in 1988 is based on a popular campaign for direct elections and on the struggle in the Constituent Assembly to hold Sarney to a four-year term. Both were unsuccessful, and direct presidential elections were not held until November–December 1989.

67. For a short appraisal of the Fontanelle administration see Mara Bergamaschi, "Guerra de facções determina fracasso do PT em Fortaleza," *Folha de São Paulo,* November 27, 1988, p. A11.

68. Maria Aparecida Damasco and Paola Gentile, "PT recebe São Paulo em crise," *O Estado de São Paulo,* November 20, 1988; Pedro Jacobi, "Gestão Municipal e Conflito: O Municipio de São Paulo," paper presented at 14th annual meeting of ANPOCS, Caxambú, Minas Gerais, October 22–26, 1990, pp. 5–6.

69. Jacobi, "Gestão Municipal e Conflito."

70. Interview with Ladislau Dowbor, Secretário de Negócios Extraordinários, Prefeitura Municipal de São Paulo, October 19, 1990.

71. Alipio Freire and Ricardo Azevedo, "Sem Medo de Ser Governo," interview with Luiza Erundina, *Teoria e Debate* 11 (August 1990): 12.

72. "Erundina diz que conselhos populares definirão prioridades," *Folha de São Paulo,* November 17, 1988, p. A2.

73. William Waack and Marcos Faerman, "A confusão ronda os conselhos populares," *Jornal da Tarde,* November 23, 1988, p. 13; "Estes conselhos vão cobrar o PT," *Jornal da Tarde,* December 5, 1988, p. 18.

74. "PT apóia conselhos populares mas não sabe como trabalhar com eles," *Folha de São Paulo,* December 18, 1988, p. A8.

75. "PT discute fórmula para evitar choque entre prefeitos e conselhos populares," *Folha de São Paulo,* December 14, 1988, p. A4.

76. Ana Maria Doimo, "Movimentos Sociais e Conselhos Populares: Desafios de institucionalidade democrática," paper presented at the 14th annual meeting of ANPOCS, Caxambú, Minas Gerais, October 22–26, 1990.

77. Ibid., p. 29.

78. Ibid., p. 41.

79. Freire and Azevedo, "Sem Medo de Ser Governo," p. 15.

80. When São Paulo businessman Abilio Diniz was kidnapped in the last week of the campaign, PT campaign materials were found (some say planted) in the possession of the kidnappers. This was widely publicized, and some communications media went so far as to say that the PT had been involved in the kidnapping. Fleury later admitted that he (as state secretary of the interior) was under considerable pressure at the time to involve the PT.

9 Conclusions

1. The 1988 constitution stipulates that direct presidential elections in Brazil will take place in two rounds, with the two candidates who receive the most votes in the first round facing off a month later. In the first round on November 15, Lula narrowly beat out Leonel Brizola for second place. The PT formed an electoral alliance, called the Frente Brasil Popular, in the first round with the Brazilian Socialist party (PSB) and the Communist party of Brazil (PC do B); in the second round the Frente garnered endorsements from the Green party, the Communist party, Mario Covas's Brazilian Social Democratic party (PSDB), Brizola's Democratic Labor party, and sectors of the PMDB.

2. Central Bank figures placed per capita income of 147.4 million Brazilians at US$2020 in 1990, compared to US$2400 for 124 million inhabitants in 1981. From *O Globo,* January 29, 1991, reported online in electronic conference ax.crono on the Alternex computer network, "Renda per capita teve queda de 6,59% na década de 80," Topic 25, February 14, 1991. (Ax.crono is an electronic conference, or bulletin board, which summarizes major news stories from major Brazilian newspapers; it is available from many of the computer networks that are part of the Association for Progressive Communication. In the United States these are the networks run by the Institute for Global Communications in San Francisco.)

3. "Trancos e barrancos," *Veja,* November 21, 1990, pp. 42–45.

4. A popular saying in the United States, this is a particularly good illustration of the differential construction of "common sense" in different cultural settings. In Brazil it is non-sense, an absurdity, illustrated by the importance in Brazil of the professional *despachante*—someone who for a fee will take care of the cumbersome legalities of dealing with public agencies, encompassing functions ranging from

renewal of a driver's license on up. To "do it yourself" would be a waste of time and might even be counterproductive, as ordinary citizens lack the requisite knowledge of the inner workings of bureaucracy.

5. Schmitter, *Interest Conflict and Political Change,* part 4.

6. Ibid., p. 377. Schmitter is quoting from Carl J. Friedrich, *Man and His Government* (New York, 1963), p. 24.

7. Gamaliel Perruci, Jr., and Steven E. Sanderson, "Presidential Succession, Economic Crisis, and Populist Resurgence in Brazil," *Studies in Comparative International Development* 24 (Fall 1989): 45.

8. Current research by Alfred Stepan demonstrates that when transitional elites have been confronted with a choice between preserving freedom of action for politicians and establishing rule-based political institutions, they have chosen the former. Conversation with Alfred Stepan, São Paulo, November 17, 1989.

9. Julian Castro-Rea, Graciela Ducatenzeiler, and Philippe Faucher, "Back to Populism: Latin America's Alternative to Democracy," paper prepared for the conference of the American Political Science Association, September 1990.

10. See, e.g., Carole Pateman, *Participation and Democratic Theory* (Cambridge: Cambridge University Press, 1970); Benjamin Barber, *Strong Democracy* (Berkeley: University of California Press, 1983); Carmen Sirianni, "Councils and Parliaments: The Problems of Dual Power and Democracy in Comparative Perspective," *Politics and Society* 12, no. 2 (1983): 83–123. On the German Greens, see Claus Offe, "'Reaching for the Brake': The Greens in Germany," *New Political Science* 11 (Spring 1983): 45–62.

11. On this point see Frances Fox Piven and Richard A. Cloward, *Poor People's Movements: Why They Succeed, How They Fail* (New York: Vintage Books, 1979).

12. In my discussion of these antinomies, I have been influenced by a similar discussion in James, *Resistance and Integration,* p. 3.

13. The first such collection of debates was Emir Sader, ed., *E Agora PT: Caráter e Identidade* (São Paulo: Brasiliense, 1986). See also Francisco Weffort, ed., *PT: Um Projeto para o Brasil* (São Paulo: Editora Brasiliense, 1989), which reproduces the presentations at a seminar organized by the PT in São Paulo on April 15–16, 1989. Gadotti and Pereira, *Pra Que PT,* combine narrative with documentary history of political debates in the party.

14. Francisco Weffort, "Consolidar o Partido, Construir a Democracia," *Teoria e Debate* 4 (September 1988): 33.

15. Wladimir Pomar, "Atos de Hoje Constróem o Amanhã," *Teoria e Debate* 4 (September 1988): 36.

16. Weffort, "Consolidar o Partido, Construir a Democracia," p. 35; emphasis in original.

17. The Workers' party recognized from the beginning that the breakdown of "actually existing" socialist regimes had serious implications for the left in general. See, in this regard, the rich series of debates on the subject in *Teoria e Debate* 8 (October–December 1989) and 9 (January–March 1990).

18. See especially Augusto de Franco, "Muito o que (des)fazer," *Teoria e Debate* 9 (January–March 1990): 49–52.

19. Keynesian doctrines and practices were not by any means adopted equally by all the advanced industrial nations in the postwar period, but they were particularly prevalent under the auspices of social democratic governments. Political as well as economic aspects of receptiveness to Keynesian arguments are discussed in the articles in Peter A. Hall, ed., *The Political Power of Economic Ideas: Keynesianism across Nations* (Princeton: Princeton University Press, 1989).

20. For a theoretically grounded discussion of the limits of the claim of liberalism to a universalistic view of citizenship, see Uday S. Mehta, "Liberal Strategies of Exclusion," *Politics and Society* 18, no. 4 (1990): 427−54.

21. Panebianco, *Political Parties,* p. 67.

22. See ibid., pp. 50, 51−52, 62.

23. Bronislaw Misztal and Barbara A. Misztal, "Democratization Processes as an Objective of New Social Movements," *Research in Social Movements, Conflicts, and Change* 10 (1988): 102.

Selected Bibliography

The list that follows includes books, journal articles, and articles from edited volumes. Newspaper and magazine articles are cited in the notes but are not included here. The following Brazilian periodicals were consulted for this study: *abcd Jornal; Boletim do DIEESE; Coojornal; Diário do Grande ABC; Em Tempo; O Estado de São Paulo; Folha de São Paulo; Gazeta Mercantil; Istoé; Istoé/Senhor; Jornal do Brasil; Jornal do Planalto (Diadema); Movimento; Senhor; Veja; Versus.*

Workers' Party Documentation. References to PT newspapers are confusing because their names change between their various manifestations. *PT São Paulo* came out irregularly between 1980 and 1982 but appeared more or less monthly after July 1983. *Jornal dos Trabalhadores*, the party's first national paper, appeared between April 1982 and November 1982. *PT Boletim* was essentially a national newsletter until mid-1985, when it began to appear in tabloid format as *PT Boletim Nacional. Teoria e Debate*, which began to appear in 1988, is a theoretical journal in magazine format. Workers' party documentation is fully cited in the notes; the material consulted is too extensive to list documents individually.

When I was doing the research, I used archives at the Centro de Estudos de Cultura Contemporânea (CEDEC) and at the Centro Pastoral Vergueiro, both in São Paulo, which included news clippings about the party and some PT documents. Franscisco Weffort, Maria Helena Moreira Alves, and Francisco Salles gave me access to their personal files of party documents. The best documentary source for future researchers on the PT will probably be the archive on the party at the University of Campinas's Arquivo Edgard Leuenroth, whose holdings consolidate a number of previously dispersed collections.

Another important source, as it maintains dossiers containing all correspondence and legal documentation of party *diretórios* in the state of São Paulo, including the minutes of party congresses, is the *Tribunal Regional Eleitoral of São Paulo*. This was also the source for membership figures and election results.

Books and Articles

Almanaque Abril. São Paulo: Editora Abril, annual.

Almeida, Fernando Lopes de. *Política Salarial, Emprego e Sindicalismo, 1964/1981.* Petrópolis: Vozes, 1982.

Almeida, Maria Hermínia Tavares de. "O Sindicato no Brasil: Novos Problemas, Velhas Estruturas." *Debate e Crítica* 6 (July 1975): 49–74.

———. "Tendências Recentes da Negociação Coletiva no Brasil." *Dados* 24, no. 2 (1981): 161–89.

———. "Novo Sindicalismo e Política (Análise de uma Trajetória)." São Paulo, 1983. Mimeo.

Alves, Márcio Moreira. *Torturas e Torturados*. Rio de Janeiro: Idade Nova, 1966.

———. "New Political Parties." *Latin American Perspectives* 23 (Fall 1979): 108–20.

————. *A Força do Povo: Democracia Participativa em Lajes.* São Paulo: Editora Brasiliense, 1980.

Alves, Maria Helena Moreira. "The Formation of the National Security State: The State and the Opposition in Military Brazil." Ph.D. diss., Massachusetts Institute of Technology, 1982.

————. "Diadema: An Experience of Popular Government within an Authoritarian Context." Paper presented at the 12th International Congress of the Latin American Studies Association, Mexico City, September 28–October 1, 1983.

————. *State and Opposition in Military Brazil.* Austin: University of Texas Press, 1985.

Amnesty International. *A Report on Allegations of Torture in Brazil.* London: T. B. Russell, 1972.

Andrade, Fernando. "Movimento Operário e Sindicatos: A Greve de Osasco Visto por José Ibrahim." *Debate* 22 (May 1976): 25–34.

Angell, Alan. *Politics and the Labour Movement in Chile.* London: Oxford University Press, 1972.

Azevedo, Ricardo de. "Conselhos Populares: Uma Varinha de Condão?" *Teoria e Debate* 4 (September 1988): 46–49.

Baracho, José Alfredo de Oliveira. "O Projeto Político Brasileiro e as Eleições Nacionais." *Revista Brasileira de Estudos Políticos* 57 (July 1983).

Barber, Benjamin. *Strong Democracy.* Berkeley: University of California Press, 1983.

Barnes, Samuel H. "Party Democracy and the Logic of Collective Action." In *Approaches to the Study of Party Organization,* pp. 105–38. Edited by William J. Crotty. Boston: Allyn and Bacon, 1968.

Bartolini, Stefano. "The Membership of Mass Parties: The Social Democratic Experience, 1889–1978." In *Western European Party Systems,* pp. 177–220. Edited by Hans Daalder and Peter Mair. Beverly Hills: Sage, 1983.

Benevides, Maria Victora de Mesquita. *A UDN e o Udenismo: Ambiguidades do Liberalismo Brasileiro, 1945–1965.* Rio de Janeiro: Paz e Terra, 1981.

————. *O PTB e o Trabalhismo.* São Paulo: Editora Brasiliense, 1989.

Betto, Frei. *O Que é Comunidade Eclesial de Base.* São Paulo: Editora Brasiliense, 1981.

Boff, Clodovis. "Orientação Partidária para as CEBs." *Tempo e Presença* 166 (March 1981): 20.

Bosi, Alfredo, et al. *Conjuntura Nacional.* Petrópolis: Vozes, 1979.

Brandi, Paulo. *Vargas: Da Vida para a História.* Rio de Janeiro: Zahar Editores, 1983.

Brito, José Carlos Aguiar. *A Tomada da Ford: O Nascimento de um Sindicato Livre.* Petrópolis: Vozes, 1983.

Bruneau, Thomas C. *The Political Transformation of the Brazilian Catholic Church.* New York: Cambridge University Press, 1974.

Caldeira, Teresa. *A Política dos Outros: O Cotidiano dos Moradores da Periferia e o que Pensam do Poder e dos Poderosos.* São Paulo: Editora Brasiliense, 1984.

————. "Electoral Struggles in a Neighborhood on the Periphery of São Paulo." *Politics and Society* 15, no. 1 (1986–87): 43–66.

Camargo, Cándido Procópio Ferreira de, Fernando Henrique Cardoso, Frederico Mazzucchelli, José Alvaro Moisés, Lúcio Kowarick, Maria Hermínia Tavares de Almeida, Paul Israel Singer, and Vinícius Caldeira Brant. *São Paulo, 1975: Crescimento e Pobreza*. São Paulo: Edições Loyola, 1982.

Campanhole, Adriano, and Hilton Lobo Campanhole, eds. *Consolidação das Leis do Trabalho e Legislação Complementar*. 62d ed. São Paulo: Editora Atlas, 1983.

Cardoso, Fernando Henrique. "Regime Político e Mudança Social." *Revista de Cultura e Política* 3 (November–January 1981): 7–26.

———. "A Questão de Democracia." In *Brasil: Do "Milagre" à Abertura*, pp. 103–19. Edited by Paulo Krischke. São Paulo: Cortez Editora, 1982. (Reprinted from *Debate e Crítica* 3, Ed. Hucitec, 1973.)

———. "O Papel dos Empresários no Processo de Transição: O Caso Brasileiro." *Dados* 26, no. 1 (1983): 9–27.

———. "A Democracia na America Latina." *Novos Estudos CEBRAP* 10 (October 1984): 45–56.

Cardoso, Ruth. "Duas Faces de uma Experiência." *Novos Estudos CEBRAP* 1 (April 1982): 53–58.

Carone, Edgard. *Movimento Operário no Brasil, 1945–1964*. São Paulo: Difel, 1981.

———. *Movimento Operário no Brasil, 1964–1984*. São Paulo: Difel, 1984.

Castles, Francis G., ed. *The Impact of Parties: Politics and Policies in Democratic Capitalist States*. London: Sage, 1982.

Castro-Rea, Julian, Graciela Ducatenzeiler, and Philippe Faucher. "Back to Populism: Latin America's Alternative to Democracy." Paper prepared for the conference of the American Political Science Association, San Francisco, September 1990.

Cavarozzi, Marcelo. *Sindicatos y Política en Argentina*. Buenos Aires: CEDES, 1984.

Cavarozzi, Marcelo, and Manuel Antonio Garretón, eds. *Muerte y Resurreccion: Los Partidos Politicos en el Autoritarismo y las Transiciones del Cono Sur*. Santiago: FLACSO, 1989.

CEDEC. *Sindicatos em uma Epoca de Crise*. Petrópolis: Vozes/CEDEC, 1984.

CEDI. "Trabalhadores Urbanos no Brasil/1980." *Aconteceu* 7 (June 1981). Special issue of the magazine of the Centro Ecuménico de Documentação e Informação (CEDI), which presents a summary of press articles on labor struggles in 1980.

Cerqueira Filho, Gisalio. "O Intellectual e os Setores Populares." *Encontros com a Civilização Brasileira* 24 (June 1980): 15–20.

Chalmers, Douglas A. "Parties and Society in Latin America." In *Friends, Followers, and Factions: A Reader in Political Clientelism*, pp. 401–21. Edited by Steffen W. Schmidt, James C. Scott, Carl Lande, and Laura Guasti. Berkeley: University of California Press, 1977.

Chalmers, Douglas, and Craig Robinson. "Why Power Contenders Choose Liberalization." *International Studies Quarterly* 26 (March 1982): 3–36.

Chilcote, Ronald H. *The Brazilian Communist Party: Conflict and Integration, 1922–1972*. New York: Oxford University Press, 1974.

Collier, David, ed. *The New Authoritarianism in Latin America*. Princeton: Princeton University Press, 1980.

Comparato, Fábio Konder. *Muda Brasil*. São Paulo: Editora Brasiliense, 1986.

Connolly, William E. *The Terms of Political Discourse*. Princeton: Princeton University Press, 1983.

Constituição da República Federativa do Brasil. Brasília: Câmara dos Deputados, Centro gráfico, 1981.

Coutinho, Carlos Nelson. "A Democracia como Valor Universal." *Encontros com a Civilização Brasileira* 9 (March 1979): 33–47.

"Crise Política e Institucional, A." *Revista de Cultura Contemporânea* 1 (January 1979): 44–66.

Crotty, William J., ed. *Approaches to the Study of Party Organization*. Boston: Allyn and Bacon, 1968.

Crouch, Colin, and Alessandro Pizzorno, eds. *The Resurgence of Class Conflict in Western Europe since 1968*. 2 vols. New York: Holmes & Meier, 1978.

Dahl, Robert A. *Polyarchy: Participation and Opposition*. New Haven: Yale University Press, 1971.

Dahl, Robert A., ed. *Political Oppositions in Western Democracies*. New Haven: Yale University Press, 1966.

Dahrendorf, Ralf. *Class and Class Conflict in Industrial Society*. Stanford: Stanford University Press, 1959.

Dantas, Altino, Jr., ed. *Lula Sem Censura*. Petrópolis: Vozes, 1981.

D'Araujó, Maria Celina Soares. *O Segundo Governo Vargas, 1951–1954*. Rio de Janeiro: Zahar Editores, 1982.

Dassin, Joan R. "Press Censorship and the Military State in Brazil." In *Press Control around the World*, pp. 149–86. Edited by Jane Leftwich Curry and Joan R. Dassin. New York: Praeger, 1982.

Dassin, Joan R., ed. *Torture in Brazil: A Report by the Archdiocese of São Paulo*. Translated by Jaime Wright. New York: Vintage Books, 1985.

Deldycke, T., H. Gelders, and J.-M. Limbor. *La Population active et sa structure*. Brussels: Université Libre de Bruxelles, Centre d'Economie Politique, Editions de l'Institut de Sociologie, 1968.

de Riz, Liliana. "Politica y Partidos. Ejercicio de Analisis Comparado: Argentina, Chile, Brasil y Uruguay." *Desarrollo Económico* 25 (January–March 1986): 659–82.

Doimo, Ana Maria. "Social Movements and the Catholic Church in Vitória, Brazil." In *The Progressive Church in Latin America*, pp. 193–252. Edited by Scott Mainwaring and Alexander Wilde. Notre Dame, Ind.: University of Notre Dame Press, 1989.

————. "Movimentos Sociais e Conselhos Populares: Desafios de Institucionalidade Democrática." Paper presented at 14th Annual Meeting of ANPOCS, Caxambú, Minas Gerais, October 22–26, 1990.

Downs, Anthony. *An Economic Theory of Democracy*. New York: Harper & Row, 1957.

Duarte, Celina R. "The Press and Redemocratization in Brazil," paper presented at the 12th World Congress of the International Political Science Association, Rio de Janeiro, August 9–14, 1982.

Erbès-Seguin, Sabine. "Les Deux Champs de l'affrontement professionel." *Sociologie du travail* 18 (April–June 1976): 121–38.

Erickson, Kenneth Paul. *The Brazilian Corporative State and Working Class Politics.* Berkeley: University of California Press, 1977.

Esping-Anderson, Gosta. *Politics against Markets: The Social Democratic Road to Power.* Princeton: Princeton University Press, 1985.

Evans, Peter. *Dependent Development: The Alliance of Multinational, State, and Local Capital in Brazil.* Princeton: Princeton University Press, 1979.

Figueiredo, Argelina Cheibub. "Intervenções Sindicais e o 'Novo Sindicalismo.'" *Dados* 17 (1978): 136–45.

Figueiredo, Marcus Faria, and José Antonio Borges Cheibub. "A Abertura Política de 1973 a 1981: Quem Disse o Que, Quando—Inventário de um Debate." *Bib* 14 (1982): 29–61.

Fleischer, David V., ed. *Os Partidos Políticos no Brasil.* 2 vols. Brasília: Editora Universidade de Brasília, 1981.

Foucault, Michel. "A Preface to Transgression." In *Language, Countermemory, Practice,* pp. 29–52. Edited by Donald Bouchard. Ithaca: Cornell University Press, 1977.

———. *Power/Knowledge: Selected Interviews and Other Writings, 1972–1977.* New York: Pantheon Books, 1980.

Franco, Augusto de. "Muito o que (des)fazer." *Teoria e Debate* 9 (January–March 1990): 49–52.

Freire, Alipio, and Ricardo Azevedo. "Sem Medo de Ser Governo." Interview with Luiza Erundina. *Teoria e Debate* 11 (August 1990): 10–15.

French, John. "Workers and the Rise of Adhemarista Populism in São Paulo, Brazil, 1945–47." *Hispanic American Historical Review* 68, no. 1 (1988): 1–43.

Gabeira, Fernando. *O que é isso, companheiro?* Rio de Janeiro: Nova Fronteira, 1982.

Gadotti, Moacir, and Otaviano Pereira. *Pra Que PT.* São Paulo: Cortez Editora, 1989.

Gallie, W. B. "Essentially Contested Concepts." *Proceedings of the Aristotelian Society* 56 (1955–56): 167–98.

Gargiulo, Martin. "El Desafio de la Democracia: La Izquierda Politica y Sindical en el Uruguay Post-Autoritario." Paper presented at the Latin American Studies Association Meeting, Boston, October 22–25, 1986.

Garretón, Manuel Antonio. "Chile: In Search of Lost Democracy." Working Paper no. 56. Kellogg Institute, University of Notre Dame, 1986.

Gillespie, Charles Guy. *Negotiating Democracy: Politicians and Generals in Uruguay.* (New York: Cambridge University Press, forthcoming).

Gomes, Angela de Castro. *A Invenção do Trabalhismo.* Rio de Janeiro: IUPERJ/Vertice, 1988.

González, Luiz Eduardo. "Political Structures and the Prospects for Democracy in Uruguay." Ph.D. diss., Yale University, 1988.

Gramsci, Antonio. *Selections from the Prison Notebooks.* New York: International Publishers, 1971.

"Greve na Voz dos Trabalhadores da Scânia à Itu, A." In *História Imediata*. Edited by Oboré. São Paulo: Alfa-Omega, 1979.

Hagopian, Frances. "The Politics of Oligarchy: The Persistence of Traditional Elites in Contemporary Brazil." Ph.D. diss., Massachusetts Institute of Technology, 1986.

Hall, Peter, ed. *The Political Power of Economic Ideas: Keynesianism across Nations*. Princeton: Princeton University Press, 1989.

Harding, Timothy Fox. "The Political History of Organized Labor in Brazil." Ph.D. diss., Stanford University, 1973.

Hippolito, Lucia. *De Raposas e Reformistas: O PSD e a Experiência Democrática Brasileira, 1945–1964*. Rio de Janeiro: Paz e Terra, 1985.

Hohlfeldt, Antonio. "Olívio Dutra: Um Líder Sindical." *Encontros com a Civilização Brasileira* 22 (April 1980): 11–36.

Humphrey, John. *Capitalist Control and Workers' Struggle in the Brazilian Auto Industry*. Princeton: Princeton University Press, 1982.

Huntington, Samuel P. *Political Order in Changing Societies*. New Haven: Yale University Press, 1968.

Ibrahim, José. "A História do Movimento de Osasco." *Cadernos do Presente* 2 n.d.

Inglehart, Ronald. *The Silent Revolution: Changing Values and Political Styles among Western Publics*. Princeton: Princeton University Press, 1977.

Instituto Brasileiro de Geografia e Estatística. *Tabulações Avançadas do Censo Demográfico, IX Recenseamento Geral do Brasil—1980*. Rio de Janeiro: IBGE, 1981.

———. *Censo Demográfico do Brasil 1980*. Rio de Janeiro: IBGE, 1982.

———. *Anuário Estatístico do Brasil*. Rio de Janeiro: IBGE, various years.

International Labor Office. *Yearbook of Labour Statistics 1979*. Geneva: International Labour Organization, 1979.

Jacobi, Pedro. "Gestão Municipal e Conflito: O Município de São Paulo." Paper presented at 14th Annual Meeting of ANPOCS, Caxambú, Minas Gerais, October 22–26, 1990.

James, Daniel. *Resistance and Integration: Peronism and the Argentine Working Class, 1946–1976*. Cambridge: Cambridge University Press, 1988.

Jelin, Elisabeth. "Spontaneité et organisation dans le mouvement ouvrier: le cas de l'Argentine, du Brésil et du Mexique." *Sociologie du travail* 18 (April-June 1976): 139–68.

Keck, Margaret E. "Brazil: Metalworkers' Strike." *NACLA Report on the Americas* (July-August 1980): 42–44.

———. "Update on the Brazilian Labor Movement." *Latin American Perspectives* 11 (Winter 1984): 27–34.

———. "From Movement to Politics: The Formation of the Workers' Party in Brazil." Ph.D. diss., Columbia University, 1986.

———. "The New Unionism in the Brazilian Transition." In *Democratizing Brazil*, pp. 252–98. Edited by Alfred Stepan. New York: Oxford University Press, 1989.

———. "Labor and Transition in Brazil." In *Labor Movements and Transition to Democracy*. Edited by Samuel Valenzuela. Notre Dame, Ind.: University of Notre Dame Press, forthcoming 1992.

Kinzo, Maria d'Alva Gil. *Oposição e Autoritarismo*. São Paulo: IDESP/Vertice, 1988.

Kirchheimer, Otto. "The Transformation of the Western European Party Systems." In *Political Parties and Political Development*, pp. 177–200. Edited by Joseph LaPalombara and Myron Weiner. Princeton: Princeton University Press, 1966.

Kornhausser, William. *The Politics of Mass Society*. Glencoe: Free Press, 1959.

Kucinski, Bernardo. *Abertura: A História de uma Crise*. São Paulo: Editora Brasil Debates, 1982.

Lamounier, Bolivar, ed. *Voto de Desconfiança: Eleições e Mudança Política no Brasil, 1970–1979*. Petrópolis: Vozes, 1980.

Lamounier, Bolivar, and Fernando Henrique Cardoso, eds. *Os Partidos Políticos e as Eleições no Brasil*. Rio de Janeiro: Paz e Terra, 1975.

Lamounier, Bolivar, and Rachel Meneguello. "Political Parties and Democratic Consolidation: The Brazilian Case." Working Paper no. 165. Washington, D.C.: Wilson Center, Smithsonian Institution, 1985.

———. *Partidos Políticos e Consolidação Democrática: O Caso Brasileiro*. São Paulo: Editora Brasiliense, 1986.

Lange, Peter, and Hudson Meadwell. "Typologies of Democratic Systems: From Political Inputs to Political Economy." In *New Directions in Comparative Politics*, pp. 80–112. Edited by Howard Wiarda. Boulder: Westview Press, 1985.

Lange, Peter, George Ross, and Maurizio Vannicelli. *Unions, Change and Crisis: French and Italian Union Strategy and the Political Economy, 1945–1980*. London: George Allen & Unwin, 1982.

Lechner, Norbert. "Pacto Social nos Processos de Democratização: A Experiência Latino-Americana." *Novos Estudos Cebrap* 13 (October 1985): 29–44.

Lechner, Norbert, ed. *Estado y Política en America Latina*. Mexico: Siglo Veintiuno, 1981.

Legislação Eleitoral e Partidária. Brasília: Senado Federal, Subsecretaria de Edições Técnicas, 1982.

Leite, Márcia de Paula. "Revindicações Sociais dos Metalúrgicos." *Cadernos CEDEC* 3 (1984).

"Liberdade Sindical e Democracia." *Revista de Cultura Contemporânea* 1 (July 1978): 33–48.

Lima Junior, Olavo Brasil de. *Os Partidos Políticos Brasileiros: A Experiência Federal e Regional, 1945–1964*. Rio de Janeiro: Edições Graal, 1983.

Linhares, Herminio. *Contribuição a História das Lutas Operárias no Brasil*. São Paulo: Alfa-Omega, 1977.

Linz, Juan J. "The Future of an Authoritarian Situation or the Institutionalization of an Authoritarian Regime: The Case of Brazil." In *Authoritarian Brazil*, pp. 233–54. Edited by Alfred Stepan. New Haven: Yale University Press, 1973.

———. "Opposition in and under an Authoritarian Regime: The Case of Spain." In *Regimes and Oppositions*, pp. 171–260. Edited by Robert A. Dahl. New Haven: Yale University Press, 1973.

———. "The New Spanish Party System." In *Electoral Participation*, pp. 101–90. Edited by Richard Rose. Beverly Hills: Sage, 1980.

Lipset, Seymour Martin, and Stein Rokkan. "Cleavage Structures, Party Systems,

and Voter Alignments: An Introduction." In *Party Systems and Voter Alignments,*
pp. 1–64. Edited by Seymour Martin Lipset and Stein Rokkan. New York: Free
Press, 1967.

Loyola, Maria Andrea. *Os Sindicatos e o PTB: Estudo de um Caso em Minas Gerais.*
Petrópolis: Vozes/CEBRAP, 1980.

Macedo, Roberto. "A Dimensó Social da Crise." In *FMI x Brasil: A Armadilha da
Recessão,* pp. 217–49. São Paulo: Forum Gazeta Mercantil, 1983.

Mainwaring, Scott. "The Catholic Youth Workers' Movement (JOC) and the
Emergence of the Popular Church in Brazil." Working Paper no. 6. Kellogg
Institute, University of Notre Dame, December 1983.

———. *The Catholic Church and Politics in Brazil, 1916–1985.* Stanford: Stanford
University Press, 1986.

———. "Political Parties and Prospects for Democracy in Brazil." Paper presented
at the 14th World Congress of the International Political Science Association,
Washington, D.C., August 28–September 1, 1988.

———. "Political Parties and Democratization in Brazil and the Southern Cone."
Comparative Politics 21 (October 1988): 91–120.

———. "Brazilian Party Underdevelopment in Comparative Perspective." Working Paper no. 134. Kellogg Institute, University of Notre Dame, January 1990.

Mainwaring, Scott, and Eduardo Viola. "New Social Movements, Political Culture, and Democracy: Brazil and Argentina in the 1980s." *Telos* 61 (Fall 1984): 17–
52.

Malefakis, Edward. "Spain and Its Francoist Heritage." In *From Dictatorship to Democracy,* pp. 215–30. Edited by John H. Herz. Westport, Conn.: Greenwood Press,
1982.

Malloy, James M. *The Politics of Social Security in Brazil.* Pittsburgh: University of
Pittsburgh Press, 1979.

Maranhão, Ricardo. *Sindicatos e Democratização, 1945–1950.* São Paulo: Editora
Brasiliense, 1979.

Marins, José, Teolide Maria Trevisan, and Carolee Chanona. *De Medellín a Puebla.*
São Paulo: Edições Paulinas, 1979.

Marshall, T. H. *Citizenship and Social Class and Other Essays.* Cambridge: Cambridge University Press, 1950.

Martins, Heloisa Helena Teixeira de Souza. *O Estado e a Burocratização do Sindicato no
Brasil.* São Paulo: Hucitec, 1979.

Martins, José de Souza. *Os Camponeses e a Política no Brasil.* Petrópolis: Vozes, 1981.

Matta, Roberto da. *Carnavais, Malandros e Herois: Para uma Sociologia do Dilema
Brasileiro.* Rio de Janeiro: Zahar, 1981.

———. *A Casa e a Rua: Espaco, Cidadania, Mulher e Morte no Brasil.* São Paulo:
Editora Brasiliense, 1985.

McKenzie, R. T. *British Political Parties.* London: William Heinemann, 1955.

McKibbon, Ross. *The Evolution of the Labour Party, 1910–1924.* Oxford: Clarendon
Press, 1974.

Medeiros, Leonilde Servolo de. "CONTAG: Um Balanço." *Reforma Agrária* (Campinas, SP) 11 (November–December 1981): 9–16.

Mehta, Uday S. "Liberal Strategies of Exclusion." *Politics and Society* 18, no. 4 (1990): 427–54.

Mendes, Antonio, Jr. *Movimento Estudantil no Brasil.* São Paulo: Editora Brasiliense (Series Tudo e História), 1982.

Meneguello, Rachel. *PT: A Formação de um Partido, 1979–1982.* São Paulo: Paz e Terra, 1989.

Menezes, Clarice Melamed, and Ingrid Sarti. *CONCLAT 1981: A Melhor Expressão do Movimento Sindical Brasileiro.* Rio de Janeiro: ILDES, 1982.

Mericle, Kenneth Scott. "Conflict Regulation in the Brazilian Industrial Relations System." Ph.D. diss., University of Wisconsin, 1974.

————. "Corporatist Control of the Working Class: Authoritarian Brazil since 1964." In *Authoritarianism and Corporatism in Latin America,* pp. 303–38. Edited by James M. Malloy. Pittsburgh: University of Pittsburgh Press, 1977.

"Mesa Redonda: A Conjuntura e as Alternativas do Movimento Popular." *Contra-ponto* 4 (January–June 1980): 5–52.

"Mesa Redonda: Novos Partídos Políticos—As Tendências das Oposiçoes." *Contra-ponto* 3 (August 1978):11–49.

Minkin, Lewis, and Patrick Seyd. "The British Labour Party." In *Social Democratic Parties in Western Europe,* pp. 101–52. Edited by William E. Patterson and Alistair Thomas. New York: St. Martin's Press, 1977.

Misztal, Bronislaw, and Barbara A. Misztal. "Democratization Processes as an Objective of New Social Movements." *Research in Social Movements, Conflicts, and Change* 10 (1988): 93–106.

Moisés, José Alvaro. "Classes Populares e Protesto Urbano." Ph.D. diss., Faculdade de Filosofia, Letras e Ciências Humanas, Universidade de São Paulo, 1978.

————. *Greve de Massa e Crise Política (Estudo da Greve dos 300 Mil em São Paulo, 1953–1954).* São Paulo: Polis (Teoria e História), 1978.

————. "Problemas Atuais do Movimento Operário no Brasil." *Revista de Cultura Contemporânea* 1 (July 1978): 49–62.

————. "Current Issues in the Labor Movement in Brazil." *Latin American Perspectives* 23 (Fall 1979): 51–70.

————. *Lições de Liberdade e de Opressão.* Rio de Janeiro: Paz e Terra, 1982.

Moraes Filho, Evaristo de. *O Problema do Sindicato Unico no Brasil.* São Paulo: Alfa-Omega, 1952.

Morel, Mario. *Lula o Metalúrgico: Anatomia de uma Liderança.* Rio de Janeiro: Nova Fronteira, 1981.

"Movimento Operário, Hoje." Collective interview. *Cara a Cara* 1 (July–December 1978): 11–53.

Neves, Lucilia de Almeida. *CGT no Brasil, 1961–1964.* Belo Horizonte: Vega, 1981.

Nun, José. "Elementos para una Teoria de la Democracia: Gramsci y el Sentido Commun." Paper prepared for the International Seminar on Gramsci and Latin America, Gramsci Institute, Ferrara, September 11–13, 1985.

O'Donnell, Guillermo. "Corporatism and the Question of the State." In *Authoritarianism and Corporatism in Latin America,* pp. 47–80. Edited by James M. Malloy. Pittsburgh: University of Pittsburgh Press, 1977.

————. "Tensions in the Bureaucratic-Authoritarian State and the Question of Democracy." In *The New Authoritarianism in Latin America*, pp. 285–318. Edited by David Collier. Princeton: Princeton University Press, 1979.

————. "Y a mi, que me Importa? Notas sobre Sociabilidad y Politica en Argentina y Brasil." *Estudios CEDES* (November 1984).

————. "Challenges to Democratization in Brazil." *World Policy Journal* 5 (Spring 1988): 281–300.

O'Donnell, Guillermo, and Philippe C. Schmitter. *Transitions from Authoritarian Rule: Tentative Conclusions about Uncertain Democracies*. Baltimore: Johns Hopkins University Press, 1986.

O'Donnell, Guillermo, Philippe C. Schmitter, and Laurence Whitehead, eds. *Transitions from Authoritarian Rule: Comparative Perspectives*. Baltimore: Johns Hopkins University Press, 1986.

————. *Transitions from Authoritarian Rule: Latin America*. Baltimore: Johns Hopkins University Press, 1986.

————. *Transitions from Authoritarian Rule: Southern Europe*. Baltimore: Johns Hopkins University Press, 1986.

Offe, Claus. "A Democracia Partidária Competitiva e o Welfare State Keynesiano: Fatores de Estabilidade e Desorganização." *Dados* 26, no. 1 (1983): 29–51.

————. "'Reaching for the Brake': The Greens in Germany." *New Political Science* 11 (Spring 1983): 45–62.

Ostrogorski, M. *Democracy and the Organization of Political Parties*. 2 vols. Chicago: Quadrangle Books, 1964.

Packenham, Robert. "Functions of the Brazilian National Congress." In *Latin American Legislatures: Their Role and Influence*, pp. 259–86. Edited by Weston Agor. New York: Praeger, 1971.

Panebianco, Angelo. *Political Parties: Organization and Power*. Cambridge: Cambridge University Press, 1988.

Panich, Leo. "Trade Unions and the State." *New Left Review* 125 (January–February 1981): 21–44.

"Para Onde Vai o Sindicalismo Brasileiro?" *Escrita Ensaio* (São Paulo) 2, no. 4 (1978).

Pateman, Carole. *Participation and Democratic Theory*. Cambridge: Cambridge University Press, 1970.

Paterson, William E., and Alastair H. Thomas. *Social Democratic Parties in Western Europe*. New York: St. Martin's Press, 1977.

Pedrosa, Mario. *Sobre o PT*. São Paulo: Ched Editorial, 1980.

Perani, Claudio. "A Greve dos Boias-Frias em São Paulo." *Cadernos do CEAS* 93 (September–October 1984): 17–23.

Pereira, Luiz Carlos Bresser. *O Colapso de uma Aliança de Classes*. São Paulo: Editora Brasiliense, 1978.

Perruci, Gamaliel, Jr., and Steven E. Sanderson. "Presidential Succession, Economic Crisis, and Populist Resurgence in Brazil." *Studies in Comparative International Development* 24 (Fall 1989): 30–50.

Peterson, Phyllis J. "Brazilian Political Parties: Formation, Organization, and Leadership, 1945–1959." Ph.D. diss., University of Michigan, 1962.

Pierce, Robert N. *Keeping the Flame: Media and Government in Latin America.* New York: Hastings House, 1979.

Pierucci, António Flávio de Oliveira. "Comunidades Eclesiais: Origens e Desenvolvimento." *Novos Estudos CEBRAP* 1 (April 1982): 48–49.

————. "Democracia, Igreja e Voto: O Envolvimento dos Padres de Paróquia de São Paulo nas Eleições de 1982." Ph.D. diss., Departamento de Ciências Sociais, Faculdade de Filosofia, Letras e Ciências Humanas, Universidade de São Paulo, 1984.

Pinto, Valeska Peres. "A Vitrine do ABC." *Teoria e Debate* 3 (June 1988): 11–15.

Piven, Frances Fox, and Richard A. Cloward. *Poor People's Movements: Why They Succeed, How They Fail.* New York: Vintage Books, 1979.

Pizzorno, Alessandro. "Les Sindicats et l'action politique." *Sociologie du travail* 13 (April–June 1971): 115–40.

————. "Entre l'action de classe et le corporatisme." *Sociologie du travail* 20 (April–June 1978): 129–52.

Pomar, Wladimir. "Atos de Hoje Constróem o Amanhã." *Teoria e Debate* 4 (September 1988): 35–38.

Przeworski, Adam. "Material Bases of Consent: Economics and Politics in a Hegemonic System." *Political Power and Social Theory* 1 (1980): 21–66.

————. "Democracy as a Contingent Outcome of Conflicts." Paper presented at the seminar "Issues on Democracy and Democratization: North and South" at the Helen Kellogg Institute for International Affairs, University of Notre Dame, November 14–16, 1983.

————. *Capitalism and Social Democracy.* Cambridge: Cambridge University Press, 1985.

Quartim, João. *Dictatorship and Armed Struggle in Brazil.* London: New Left Books, 1971.

Rainho, Luis Flávio, and Osvaldo Martines Bargas. *As Lutas Operárias e Sindicais dos Metalurgicos em São Bernardo do Campo.* São Bernardo do Campo: Associação Beneficente e Cultural dos Metalúrgicos de São Bernardo e Diadema, 1983.

Rawls, John. *A Theory of Justice.* Cambridge: Harvard University Press, 1971.

Reis, Fábio Wanderley, ed. *Os Partidos e o Regime.* São Paulo: Edições Símbolo, 1978.

Rodrigues, José Albertino. *Sindicato e Desenvolvimento no Brasil.* São Paulo: Edições Símbolo, 1978.

Rodrigues, Leôncio Martins. *Conflito Industrial e Sindicalismo no Brasil.* São Paulo: Difusão Europeia do Livro, 1966.

————. *Quem é Quem na Constituinte.* São Paulo: Oesp-Maltese, 1987.

————. "La Composition sociale des cercles dirigeants du Parti des travailleurs au Brésil." *Problèmes d'Amerique latine* 93 (3ᵉ trimestre 1989): 13–31.

————. *CUT: Os Militantes e a Ideologia.* São Paulo: Paz e Terra, 1990.

————. *Partidos e Sindicatos: Escritos de Sociologia Política.* São Paulo: Editora Atica, 1990.

Rodrigues, Leôncio Martins, ed. *Sindicalismo e Sociedade.* São Paulo: Difusão Europeia do Livro, 1968.

Roxborough, Ian, and Ilan Bizberg. "Union Locals in Mexico: The 'New Unionism' in Steel and Automobiles." *Journal of Latin American Studies* 15, no. 1 (1983): 117–35.

Rustow, Dankwart A. "Transitions to Democracy: Toward a Dynamic Model." *Comparative Politics* 2 (April 1970): 337–63.

Sadek, Maria Tereza, ed. *Eleições/1986.* São Paulo: IDESP/Vertice, 1989.

Sader, Eder. *Quando Novos Personagens Entraram em Cena.* São Paulo: Paz e Terra, 1988.

Sader, Emir, ed. *E Agora PT: Caráter e Identidade.* São Paulo: Editora Brasiliense, 1986.

Sampaio, Regina. *Ademar de Barros e o PSP.* São Paulo: Global Editora, 1982.

Sanks, T. Howland, and Brian Smith. "Liberation Ecclesiology: Praxis, Theory, Praxis." *Theological Studies* 38 (March 1977): 3–38.

Santos, Abidias José dos, and Ercy Rocha Chaves. *Consciência Operária e Luta Sindical: Metalurgicos de Niteroi no Movimento Sindical Brasileiro.* Petrópolis: Vozes, 1980.

Santos, Wanderley Guillerme dos. *Cidadania e Justiça.* Rio de Janeiro: Editora Campus, 1979.

"São Bernardo: Uma Experiência de Sindicalismo 'Autentico'—Entrevista com Luís Inácio da Silva (Lula)." *Cara a Cara* 1 (July–December 1978): 54–66.

Sartori, Giovanni. "From the Sociology of Politics to Political Sociology." In *Politics and the Social Sciences,* pp. 65–100. Edited by Seymour Martin Lipset. New York: Oxford University Press, 1969.

———. *Parties and Party Systems: A Framework for Analysis.* Cambridge: Cambridge University Press, 1976.

———. *Partidos e Sistemas Partidários.* Rio de Janeiro: Zahar, 1982.

Schmitter, Philippe. *Interest Conflict and Political Change in Brazil.* Stanford: Stanford University Press, 1971.

Schneider, Ben Ross. "Politics within the State: Elite Bureaucrats and Industrial Policy in Authoritarian Brazil." Ph.D. diss., University of California, Berkeley, 1987.

Schorske, Carl. *German Social Democracy, 1905–1917.* New York: Harper & Row, 1955.

Schumpeter, Joseph A. *Capitalism, Socialism, and Democracy.* New York: Harper & Row, 1950.

Schwartzman, Simon. *Bases do Autoritarismo Brasileiro.* Rio de Janeiro: Editora Campus, 1982.

Segatto, José Antonio. *Breve História do PCB.* São Paulo: Livraria Editora Ciências Humanas, 1981.

Share, Donald, and Scott Mainwaring. "Transitions through Transaction: Democratization in Brazil and Spain." In *Political Liberalization in Brazil,* pp. 175–216. Edited by Wayne Selcher. Boulder: Westview Press, 1986.

Shorter, Edward, and Charles Tilly. *Strikes in France, 1830–1968.* London: Cambridge University Press, 1974.

Silva, Luís Inácio da. *Lula: Entrevistos e Discursos.* Guarulhos, SP: O Repórter de Guarulhos, 1981.

Silva, Roque Aparecido da. "A Campanha da Reposição de 1977." São Paulo: CEDEC, n.d. Mimeo.

————. "Sindicato e Sociedade na Palavra dos Metalúrgicos." In *El Sindicalismo Latinoamericano en los Ochenta*. Edited by CLACSO. Santiago: CLACSO, n.d.

Simão, Aziz. *O Sindicato e o Estado*. São Paulo: Dominus, 1966.

"Sindicalismo e Política." *Contraponto* 3 (August 1978): 50–58.

"Sindicato de João Monlevade, O." *Cadernos do CEAS* 67 (May–June 1980): 55–67.

Singer, Paul, and Vinícius Caldeira Brant, eds. *São Paulo: O Povo em Movimento*. Petrópolis: Vozes/CEBRAP, 1980.

Sirianni, Carmen. "Councils and Parliaments: The Problems of Dual Power and Democracy in Comparative Perspective." *Politics and Society* 12, no. 2 (1983): 83–123.

Skidmore, Thomas. *Politics in Brazil*. New York: Oxford University Press, 1967.

Smith, Rogers M. "The New Non-Science of Politics: On Turns to History in Political Science." Paper prepared for CSST conference "The Historic Turn in the Human Sciences." Ann Arbor, Mich., October 5–7, 1990.

Soares, Glaucio Ary Dillon. *Colégio Eleitoral, Convençoes Partidárias, e Eleições Diretas*. Petrópolis: Vozes, 1984.

Sodré, Nelson Werneck. "Posiçao e Responsibilidade dos Intellectuais." *Encontros com a Civilização Brasileira* 18 (December 1979): 99–122.

Sorj, Bernardo, and Maria Hermínia Tavares de Almeida, eds. *Sociedade e Política no Brasil pós-64*. São Paulo: Editora Brasiliense, 1983.

Sousa, Maria Tereza Sadek R. de. "Concentração Industrial e Estrutura Partidária: O Processo Eleitoral no ABC, 1966–1982." Ph.D. diss., Universidade de São Paulo, 1984.

Souza, Amaury de, and Bolivar Lamounier. "Governo e Sindicatos no Brasil: A Perspectiva dos Anos '80." *Dados* 24, no. 2 (1981): 139–59.

Souza, Maria do Carmo Campello de. *Estado e Partídos Políticos no Brasil, 1930–1964*. São Paulo: Editora Alfa-Omega, 1976.

Spalding, Hobart A., Jr. *Organized Labor in Latin America*. New York: Harper & Row, 1977.

Spindel, Arnaldo. *O Partido Comunista na Genêse do Populismo*. São Paulo: Edições Símbolo, 1980.

Stepan, Alfred. "State Power and the Strength of Civil Society in the Southern Cone of Latin America." In *Bringing the State Back In*, pp. 317–46. Edited by Peter B. Evans, Dietrich Rueschemeyer, and Theda Skocpol. Cambridge: Cambridge University Press, 1985.

————. *Rethinking Military Politics: Brazil and the Southern Cone*. Princeton: Princeton University Press, 1988.

Stepan, Alfred, ed. *Democratizing Brazil*. New York: Oxford University Press, 1989.

Stephens, Evelyne Huber. "The Peruvian Military Government, Labor Mobilization, and the Political Strength of the Left." *Latin American Research Review* 18, no. 2 (1983): 57–94.

Straubhaar, Joseph D. "Television and Video in the Transition from Military to Civilian Rule in Brazil." *Latin American Research Review* 24, no. 1 (1989): 140–54.

Suplicy, Eduardo Matarazzo. *Da Distribuição da Renda e dos Direitos à Cidadania*. São Paulo: Editora Brasiliense, 1988.

Syrkis, Alfredo. *Os Carbonários*. São Paulo: Global Editora, 1980.

Tarrow, Sidney. "National Politics and Collective Action: Recent Theory and Research in Western Europe and the United States." *Annual Review of Sociology* 14 (1988): 421–40.

Tilly, Charles. *From Mobilization to Revolution.* Reading, Mass.: Addison-Wesley, 1978.

Torre, Juan Carlos. "Esquema para a Análise dos Movimentos Sociais na América Latina." *Revista de Cultura Contemporânea* 1 (January 1979): 67–74.

Valenzuela, Arturo, and J. Samuel Valenzuela. "Party Oppositions under the Chilean Authoritarian Regime." In *Military Rule in Chile: Dictatorships and Oppositions,* pp. 184–229. Edited by J. Samuel Valenzuela and Arturo Valenzuela. Baltimore: Johns Hopkins University Press, 1986.

Valenzuela, J. Samuel. "The Chilean Labor Movement: The Institutionalization of Conflict." In *Chile: Politics and Society,* pp. 135–71. Edited by Arturo Valenzuela and J. Samuel Valenzuela. New Brunswick, N.J.: Transaction Books, 1976.

———. "Labor Movement Formation and Politics: The Chilean and French Cases in Comparative Perspective." Ph.D. diss., Columbia University, 1979.

Viola, Eduardo J. "The Ecologist Movement in Brazil, 1974–1986: From Environmentalism to Ecopolitics." *International Journal of Urban and Regional Research* 12 (June 1988): 211–28.

von Beyme, Klaus. "Governments, Parliaments, and the Structure of Power in Political Parties." In *Western European Party Systems,* pp. 341–67. Edited by Hans Daalder and Peter Mair. Beverly Hills: Sage, 1983.

Walzer, Michael. *Spheres of Justice.* New York: Basic Books, 1983.

Weffort, Francisco. "Sindicatos e Política." Tese de Livre Docência. Faculdade de Filosofia, Letras, e Ciências Humanas, Universidade de São Paulo, 1971.

———. "Participação e Conflito Industrial: Contagem e Osasco, 1968." *Cadernos CEBRAP* 5 (1972).

———. *O Populismo na Política Brasileira.* Rio de Janeiro: Paz e Terra, 1978.

———. "Democracia e Movimento Operário: Algumas Questões para a História do Periodo, 1945–1964 (part 1)." *Revista de Cultura Contemporânea* 1 (July 1978): 7–14.

———. "Democracia e Movimento Operário: Algumas Questões para a História do Periodo, 1945/1964 (part 2)." *Revista de Cultura Contemporânea* 1 (January 1979): 3–12.

———. "A Cidadania dos Trabalhadores." In *Direito, Cidadania e Participação,* pp. 141–52. Edited by Bolivar Lamounier, Francisco Weffort, and Maria Victoria Benevides. São Paulo: T. A. Quieroz, 1981.

———. *Porque Democracia?* São Paulo: Editora Brasiliense, 1984.

———. "Consolidar o Partido, Construir a Democracia." *Teoria e Debate* 4 (September 1988): 32–35.

Weffort, Francisco, ed. *PT: Um Projeto para o Brasil.* São Paulo: Editora Brasiliense, 1989.

Whitaker, Francisco, João Gilberto Lucas Coelho, Carlos Michiles, Emmanuel Gonçalves Vieira Filho, Maria da Glória Moura da Viega, and Regina de Paula Santos Prado. *Cidadão Constituinte: A Saga das Emendas Populares.* São Paulo: Paz e Terra, 1989.

Interviews

Interviewees are identified with information valid at the time of the interview; identifications have not been updated to reflect later offices held or positions taken. Some identified as PT members have since left the PT; some identified with one political office now hold another or none.

Aides in the office of Luiza Erundina, PT vereador São Paulo, including Flávio, Vané, and Adriano, August 1983.

João Carlos Alves (leader of Pastoral Operária and of CEBs in Santo Amaro, elected to the São Paulo municipal council for the PT beginning in 1982), September 1982; September 1, 1983.

Maria Helena Moreira Alves (political scientist, congressional aide to state legislator Eduardo Suplicy and PT activist), São Paulo, November 28, 1982; (in her capacity as director of Public Relations, Diadema municipal government) Diadema, July 20, 1983.

Dom Paulo Evaristo Arns (cardinal, São Paulo), São Paulo, April 3, 1982.

Miguel Arraes (PMDB Pernambuco, governor of Pernambuco, 1962–64), April 7, 1982.

Paulo Azevedo (member of PT national executive and responsible for Union Secretariat, former president of São Paulo subway workers' union), July 27, 1985.

Jorge Bittar (president of the engineers' union in Rio de Janeiro, PT activist), Rio de Janeiro, January 10, 1983.

Jorge Bittar, Isabel Picaluga, and other CUT members from Rio de Janeiro, Rio de Janeiro, September 17, 1983.

Gilmar Carneiro (São Paulo bank workers' union, PT activist, CUT founder, and member of CUT Executive), São Paulo, November 30, 1982.

José Cicote (PT state congressman, former leader of Santo André metalworkers' union), São Paulo, August 9, 1983.

Manoel da Conceição (member of PT national provisional commission and first national diretório, PT founder in Pernambuco), April 8, 1982; December 28, 1982.

Alfonso Delelis (former president of São Paulo metalworkers' union, purged in 1964, active in coordinating labor support for PMDB campaign in São Paulo in 1982), São Paulo, March 30, 1982.

Olívio Dutra (founder and first vice president of PT), Porto Alegre, RS, December 13 and 14, 1982.

Antonio Carlos Fon (aide in the office of PT municipal council member João Carlos Alves), São Paulo, September 1, 1983.

Dom Moacyr Grechi (bishop of Acre, former head of CNBB Pastoral da Terra), Rio Branco, AC, December 18, 1982.

Helena Greco (leader of amnesty movement, elected municipal council member for PT in Belo Horizonte November 1982), Belo Horizonte, MG, April 12, 1982.

Luis Eduardo Greenhalg (human rights lawyer, member PT national executive, head of Foreign Affairs Secretariat, and PT lawyer), São Paulo, March 30, 1982; September 8, 1983.

José Ibrahim (member of the PT national executive until 1983, first director of the Secretariat for Organization), Osasco, SP, March 29, 1982.

Amir Khair (planning director of Diadema municipal government), Diadema, July 20, 1983.

Mauro de Melo Leonel (labor correspondant of Gazeta Mercantil, PT activist), São Paulo, September 2, 1983.

Carlos Lira (director of cultural programs for Diadema municipal government), Diadema, August 31, 1983.

João Maia (CONTAG delegate and a PT founder in Acre), Rio Branco, AC, December 18, 1982.

Chico Mendes (rubber tapper organizer, PT leader, and former MDB municipal council member in Xapuri), Rio Branco, AC, December 19, 1982.

Jair Meneguelli and Oswaldo Bargas (respectively president and secretary general of São Bernardo and Diadema metalworkers' union; Meneguelli became president of the CUT in August 1983), São Bernardo do Campo, April 2, 1982; December 1, 1982; July 1983.

Gilson Menezes (PT mayor of Diadema), Diadema, SP, September 14, 1983.

Nilson Morão (1982 PT candidate for governor, Acre), Rio Branco, AC, December 19, 1982.

Wando Nogueira (Instituto Josué de Castro, Recife, PT member and former secretary of Manuel da Conceição), Recife, PE, December 29, 1983.

Anísio Batista de Oliveira (PT organizer in district of Saúde, SP, active in Pastoral Operária, elected PT state congressman 1982), São Paulo, October 18, 1982; September 1, 1983.

Ari Damasceno de Oliveira (member of the professors' union and PT activist, Natal), Natal, RN, April 9, 1982.

Cleusa de Oliveira (president of PT diretório in Diadema, 1982–83), September 5, 1983.

João Paulo (PT municipal council member, Osasco), Osasco, SP, January 23, 1983.

Almir Pazzianotto Pinto (PMDB state deputy, São Paulo, labor lawyer, minister of labor under Neves/Sarney government), São Paulo, April 1, 1982.

Hugo Perez (president of the Electrical Workers' Federation of São Paulo), São Paulo, April 1, 1982.

Isabel Picaluga (sociologist, president of the Association of Sociologists of Rio de Janeiro, PT activist, and member of the national diretório), Rio de Janeiro, April 1982.

José Augusto da Silva Ramos (director of health, Diadema municipal government), Diadema, July 20, 1983.

Devanir Ribeiro (member of PT state diretório, later its president), São Paulo, November 29, 1982.

Marco Aurélio Ribeiro (leader of the PT in the São Paulo state legislature), December 1982.

José Rodrigues (president of Agricultural Workers' Federation, Pernambuco—FETAPE) and Romeu Fonte (lawyer for FETAPE, Pernambuco), Recife, PE, April 6, 1982.

Luzia Rodrigues (PT activist, former member of collective responsible for *abcd Jornal*), São Paulo, November 25, 1982.

Waldemar Rossi (leader of metalworkers' opposition in São Paulo, active in Pastoral Operária), São Paulo, January 6, 1983.

Miguel Rupp (president of metalworkers' union, Santo André), Santo André April 1982; September 6, 1983.

Luis Inácio Lula da Silva (president of metalworkers' union, São Bernardo do Campo and Diadema, first president of PT), São Paulo, December 10, 1982; September 12, 1983.

José Francisco da Silva (president of Agricultural Workers' Confederation—CONTAG), Brasília, April 5, 1982; December 17, 1982.

José Pedro da Silva (an *oposição sindical* leader and PT leader in Osasco, candidate for federal deputy 1982), Osasco, SP, January 20, 1983.

Roque Aparecido da Silva (sociologist and former labor activist, coordinator of CEDEC labor project, and PT member), São Paulo, November 27, 1982.

Airton Soares (leader of PT in federal Chamber of Deputies, left the party over decision not to attend electoral college), Brasília, September 22, 1983.

Ubirantim (member of PT municipal diretório, Belém, PA), Belém, December 21, 1982.

Umberto (candidate for PT vereador in São Luis, MA), São Luis, December 23, 1982.

João Paulo Pires Vasconcelos (secretary general, João Monlevade metalworkers' union), João Monlevade, MG, April 13, 1982.

Francisco Weffort (sociologist, member of PT national executive and secretary general of the party beginning August 1983, coordinator of PT national electoral commission in 1982, former president of CEDEC), São Paulo, October 1982; November 16, 1982; December 1982; January 1983; August 29, 1983; September 13, 1983; July 25, 1985.

Index

ABCD, 127–28, 152, 157, 162, 175, 198

abcd Jornal, 80–81

Abramo, Claudio, 145

accountability, 133, 218, 229, 230

Acre, organization of PT in, 100–101

Afonso, Almino, and new party debate, 55, 58, 69, 70–71

alliances and coalitions: with PV, 100; discussion of, 156, 226–28; in direct elections campaign, 222; in Constituent Assembly, 225

Almeida, Maurício Soares de. *See* Soares, Maurício

amnesty campaign, 52–53

Andrade, Joaquim dos Santos, 175, 177

ARENA (Aliança de Renovação Nacional): creation of, 26; abolition of, 26, 87; and elections, 55; and party reform, 56, 89; mentioned, 25, 30

Argentina, parties and unions, 37–38

Arraes, Miguel, 81

Articulação (in CUT), 189

Articulação dos *113,* 113–16, 119, 165

autênticos, 172, 174, 175, 186

autonomy, meaning for labor movement, 41, 183, 184, 186, 246

Bacha, Edmar, 77

Barros, Reynaldo de, 141

Bartolini, Stefano, 108, 110

bipolar logic, in Brazilian politics, 55, 124, 126–27, 129, 160, 244–45

Bittar, Jacó: and formation of PT, 67, 71, 77; and party organization, 94, 102; and *1982* elections, 138; and CUT, 182, 187; leaves PT, 235

Bom, Djalma, 101, 102, 151, 185, 224

Brazilian Bar Association (OAB), 44, 52

Breda, João Batista, 83

Brizola, Leonel: and new party debate, 58, 81, 90; and PT, 121; and *1982* elections, 124, 148; and direct elections campaign, 220; and *1989* elections, 158–59

Buaiz, Vitor, 154

Cardoso, Fernando Henrique, 10, 44, 52, 84; and *1978* senatorial campaign, 54, 179; and new party debate, 57–58, 59, 69, 70–71; and *1985* mayoral campaign, 155–56; and PT administration in Diadema, 210

Carta de Princípios, controversy over, 67–68

Carvalho, Apolônio de, 120, 135

Castro-Rea, Julian, 241–42

Catholic church: and labor, 47, 49; and opposition to authoritarian regime, 47–49; and social movements, 47–49; and view of politics, 49; and PT, 97–98, 101; and direct elections campaign, 219. *See also* Comunidades Eclesiais de Base

central labor organizations: illegality of, 62; competition among, 176, 180, 188. *See also* CGT; CONCLAT; CUT

Central Unica dos Trabalhadores (CUT). *See* CUT

Centro Brasileiro de Análise e Planejamento (CEBRAP), 45

Centro de Estudos de Cultura Contemporânea (CEDEC), 45